NONBOOK MEDIA

Collection Management and User Services

John W. Ellison and Patricia Ann Coty, Editors

American Library Association
Chicago and London 1987

Designed by C. J. Petlick

Composed by Pam Frye Typesetting, Inc.
in ITC Garamond on a Compugraphic
8400 Typesetting system

Printed on 50-pound Glatfelter, a
pH-neutral stock, and bound in
10-point Carolina cover stock by
Malloy Lithographing, Inc.
∞

Library of Congress Cataloging-in-Publication Data
Nonbook media.

  Includes bibliographies.
    1. Libraries—Special collections—Non-book materials.
  2. Selection of non-book materials.   3. Acquisition of
  non-book materials.   4. Libraries—Special collections.
  —Audio-visual materials.   5. Audio-visual library
  service.   I. Ellison, John William, 1941–   .
  II. Coty, Patricia Ann.
  Z688.N6N64   1987   025.2'8   87-1340
  ISBN: 0-8389-0479-3

Printed in the United States of America.

Contents

Preface   v

Acknowledgments   vii

Billie Grace Herring
 1 Art Reproductions   1

Gerald R. Barkholz
 2 Audiotapes   20

Paul B. Wiener
 3 Films   32

Diana L. Spirt
 4 Filmstrips   69

J. Gordon Coleman, Jr.
 5 Flat Pictures, Posters, Charts, and Study Prints   85

Clara L. DiFelice
 6 Holographs   94

A. Neil Yerkey
 7 Machine-Readable Data Files   110

Ernest L. Woodson
 8 Maps   128

Marilyn L. Shontz
 9 Microforms   140

Kathleen M. Tessmer
 10 Models   161

Nancy Bren Nuzzo
 11 Music Scores   181

Donald L. Foster
12 Original Art 193

Mildred Knight Laughlin and Patricia Ann Coty
13 Overhead Transparencies 214

Marie Bruce Bruni
14 Pamphlets 227

Lee David Jaffe
15 Phonograph Records 236

Clara L. DiFelice
16 Photographs 262

David H. Jonassen
17 Programmed Materials 274

Esther Green Bierbaum
18 Realia 297

John W. Ellison and Patricia Ann Coty
19 Simulation Materials 324

Leslie J. Walker
20 Slides 338

Daniel R. Schabert
21 Videodiscs 349

Daniel R. Schabert
22 Videotapes 361

*Bibliography of Evaluative and Nonevaluative
Periodicals Cited* 377

Editors and Contributors 387

Preface

The topics of this book were selected and arranged to meet the need for a concise source of nonbook information. Some of the formats in this book have been widely covered in the existing literature, but the information in many cases is either extremely limited, scattered, or treated in comprehensive detail. Other formats tend to receive scant attention in the literature and require the use of varied sources for adequate coverage. NONBOOK MEDIA attempts to gather together information about twenty-two separate nonbook formats and to provide a source for the quick location of facts regarding these formats.

Some nonbook managers are responsible for only one or two specific formats, but the large majority are responsible for many or all of the formats covered in this book. Over the years, practitioners and students have requested a book of this type. Each chapter is arranged for ease of use according to the following outline:

    I. The Medium
       A. Definition
       B. Brief History
       C. Unique Characteristics
       D. Advantages and Disadvantages
   II. Selection
       A. Special Criteria
       B. Evaluative Review Sources
       C. Nonevaluative Sources
 III. Maintenance and Management
       A. Storage and Care
       B. Management Problems and Solutions
       C. Other Concerns
 IV. Additional Resources

Chapters were contributed by practitioners who have had extensive experience with their respective formats. While contributors followed the above outline of coverage, the length and level of detail of each chapter was determined for the most part by the contributor. Persons familiar with the variety in coverage among nonbook formats in the literature will understand and appreciate the lack of precise uniformity among chapters. Future editions will permit expansions and deletions within chapters, and the possible addition of new formats.

Whereas NONBOOK MEDIA does not attempt to be a comprehensive treatise on all aspects of nonbook materials, those who need lengthy and detailed discussions beyond the scope of this work can examine the sources cited in Additional Resources, at the end of each chapter. Hardware (equipment) is discussed only to a limited extent in chapters where the contributors felt some explanation was essential. Descriptive cataloging is not covered. These are areas where widely available sources offer comprehensive coverage.

The chapter sections Evaluative Review Sources and Nonevaluative Sources contain only the titles of periodicals; complete bibliographic information is given in Bibliography of Evaluative and Nonevaluative Sources at the end of this book.

Acknowledgments

Special appreciation is expressed to the many hundreds of students over the past fifteen years in the Selection, Acquisition, and Management of Nonbook Material course for their constant demand for such a book. These same students are credited for their initial examination of the literature for much of the scattered and often limited information on each format. Another special thanks to Elizabeth Smith, a colleague and friend, who also shared in the teaching of this course and the tedious development of its content.

JOHN W. ELLISON
PATRICIA ANN COTY

Billie Grace Herring

Ch. 1

Art Reproductions

THE MEDIUM

Definition

According to the *ALA Glossary of Library and Information Science,* an art reproduction is "a mechanically reproduced copy of a work of art, generally as [a copy] of a commercial edition."[1] This definition is consistent with that of *Anglo-American Cataloguing Rules,* second edition.[2] In *Educational Technology: A Glossary of Terms,*[3] similar definitions are given, but they include the emphasis that the reproduction is issued without instructional text or textual annotation. In each instance, the definition identifies the art reproduction as a two-dimensional work of art, including reproductions of collages, mosaics, textiles, prints, watercolors, or paintings.

The term *art reproduction* often is confused with the term *art print. Art print* refers to an *original* print, such as an engraving, etching, lithograph, woodcut, silk screen, or other multiple original of a work that is printed from a plate, stone, or screen *prepared by the artist.*

1. *The ALA Glossary of Library and Information Science,* ed. Heartsill Young (Chicago: American Library Assn., 1984), 12.
2. *Anglo-American Cataloguing Rules,* 2nd ed. (Chicago: American Library Assn., 1978), 564.
3. *Educational Technology: Definition and Glossary of Terms,* vol. 1 of AECT Task Force on Definition and Terminology (Washington, D.C.: Assn. for Educational Communications and Technology, 1977), 287.

#1, what is the difference between a art reproduction and an art print

Some institutions *do* collect original prints for display and for loan to users. However, since the cost of original prints is rising rapidly, the reproduction is the most widely used means of communicating the messages of artists to the potential user. Thus the emphasis is on providing the aesthetic experience which the user gains from viewing the reproduction of a two-dimensional work of art.

Brief History

While reproductions of decorative art and design have been traced to prehistoric cultures, the reproduction of two-dimensional works of art did not become widespread in the Western world until paper became relatively inexpensive and plentiful. Before the use of paper, art could be reproduced only by the copyist, who often, intentionally or otherwise, distorted the original in the process of copying it onto canvas.

In the 15th century, after paper became readily available, the first mass-produced art reproductions were prints made from wood blocks. Later, copper plate engraving greatly enhanced the attention which could be given to detail; but only if the engraver were skilled could he convey the subtleties of the original work. Both wood block and copper plate engraving allowed reproduction with a single color of ink (usually black).

Engravings continued to be popular, however, and during the 16th and 17th centuries techniques were refined. In attempts to add gradations of light and dark and to suggest gradations of color, mezzotint and aquatint techniques were developed. The printing of art reproductions by such methods continued and became an established trade in the 18th and 19th centuries. Such reproductions often were sold at fairs or by itinerant vendors.

In the late 19th century, however, photomechanical processes began to replace the various engraving techniques that had been used for most art reproductions. In early photography, original colors could not be reproduced. With the development of special cameras, films, developing processes, papers, filters, and printing processes for photographs, it became increasingly possible to reproduce the exact colors and textures of an original work of art. During the 1970s and 1980s, even greater accuracy of color reproduction and texture became possible through the use of electronic scanners or laser scanners.

The method most commonly used to reproduce color in art reproductions is called *process color* or *process printing*. In process printing, the original work is photographed through color filters, producing one plate for each color of ink to be used in printing the final product.

Process inks are transparent, and when all plates are superimposed with the appropriate ink color, the colors of the original are duplicated exactly. Crispness and clarity in a reproduction are controlled by the fineness of the texture of the photographic filter, by the precise "registration" of plates in the printing process, and by appropriate viscosity of the inks.

Today, quality reproduction of works of art has developed to the point that the original can be reproduced without distortion due to interpretation by the person or persons doing the reproduction. High-quality reproduction on high-quality paper is not cheap, but the buyer who is willing to invest in a quality reproduction can be assured of fidelity to the original.

The art reproduction as a circulating item became popular in public libraries in Great Britain and in the United States during the late 1950s and 1960s. School and college libraries also began to lend framed or matted reproductions during the 1960s. Research libraries, special art libraries, and museum libraries have made reproductions available for study by students and researchers for many years, but they have not readily circulated framed reproductions. Outstanding visual research collections were developed in some public libraries as early as 1901, especially at the Newark (N.J.) Public Library, under John Cotton Dana, and at the Westport (Conn.) Public Library under the leadership of Edith Very Sherword.

Unique Characteristics

Statements about the unique characteristics of art reproductions may appear to be redundant, since each reproduction *is* unique. As a class of works represented in collections, however, art reproductions provide experiences to the user that are different from experiences provided by other materials.

An art reproduction differs from some other materials in that viewing it is a *holistic* experience. It reveals its meaning to the viewer all at once rather than in a linear, successive mode in which each part is revealed discretely. The whole of the message is before the user at any time; but fine works of art have complexities that the user may decode only with repeated viewing over a longer time.

From the user's perspective, several other unique characteristics of art reproductions emerge. No special skill is required to use and appreciate an art reproduction. Since the reproduction requires no special equipment for viewing, it can be enjoyed at any location the user chooses. The presence of an art reproduction is nondemanding of the user; the work may be enjoyed casually or studied in depth. Each user experiences the work in an individualized way that is consonant with the ideas and values which the user brings to viewing the work.

Since most agencies circulate art reproductions for the user to keep at home or workplace for several weeks, the user enjoys the opportunity to "live" with the artist's message, embodied in the work, for a period of time. Reproductions bring the world of fine art to users who never would be able to see the originals.

From the perspective of the holding collection, reproductions are one of the few forms of art work that are adaptable to all user groups within an institution's constituency. The same works may serve users of all ages and backgrounds. The availability of reproductions may stimulate the user's interest in composition, techniques, style, and the life of the artist, thus enticing the viewer to use other materials in the collection.

In short, art reproductions help to satisfy the aesthetic needs and tastes of the user:

> Fine art is an expression of the best of the past and the present, of man's hopes and fears, his ambitions and emotions, his religious and political beliefs, his ethics and humanitarianism, his failures and achievements, his philosophy of life and his relationships to other people and to the world around him.[4]

Advantages

The advantages of including art reproductions in institutional collections may be considered in terms of both the user and the holding institution.

FOR THE USER

For the user, art reproductions offer advantages in terms of convenience, aesthetic growth, and pleasurable experience.

Art reproductions provide direct, firsthand, exactly repeatable visual statements that allow the user the freedom to interpret the artist's message. The user's tastes may be accommodated by works in a collection, since almost every style and art movement is represented within the wide variety of reproductions available. When the institution lends art reproductions, the user enjoys them free of charge or at minimal cost.

The presence of the artist's message is not transitory, as are many real-time and projected-media messages. The user chooses the time and

4. *Shorewood Art Programs for Education . . . A Full Scale Collection of the World's Great Masterpieces* (New York: Shorewood Reproductions, 1968), 6.

nature of exposure to the work. Additionally, borrowing reproductions for a period of several weeks enables the user to become accustomed to "living with" art and to overcome reluctance to view art or fear of works designated as "fine art."

Being exposed to art reproductions on a continuing basis provides the user an opportunity to experience a range of emotional responses toward and feelings about the works of art. Exposure to such works adds an extra dimension of beauty and pleasure to life.

The user may experience aesthetic and intellectual growth as his continued exposure to works of art assists in the development of visual vocabulary and visual language. But the user is not forced into such development by an externally directed experience; the user *chooses* to view the work.

Finally, for researchers and students of art and art history, reproductions are more informative than descriptions, and far more convenient than transparencies or slides.

FOR THE LENDING INSTITUTION

Institutions which acquire and lend art reproductions find that the latter are useful in public relations and in programming, and that the internal procedures required to lend art reproductions are manageable.

The availability of reproductions for loan attracts the interest of users, both those who borrow from an institution's other collections regularly and those who may be first-time users when they borrow art reproductions. Good publicity for the institution results. Enticing displays can be created with art reproductions, and the institution usually has other materials which reinforce and complement the visual introduction to art that reproductions provide.

Art reproductions allow versatility in programming with users. They allow the institution to reach out to user groups throughout the community or within the parent institution. Art reproductions may support programming that is educational, informative, aesthetic, or recreational.

While the logistics of administering a collection of art reproductions are not simple, they are workable (selection of items is treated in subsequent sections of this chapter). Acquisition is generally directly from producer or museum, and are relatively small in number. While quality reproductions are not inexpensive, costs are comparable to other nonbook materials that may receive less intense use. With care, framed reproductions are long lasting. By comparison with materials which require special equipment, art reproductions are easy to display, transport, and circulate.

Disadvantages

Because they lack the multisensory stimuli of motion and sound, art reproductions may require somewhat sophisticated viewing skills of the user: translating visual cues that indicate motion, perspective, or the special syntax of the visual composition. Nevertheless, the viewer can enjoy the work without higher-level visual skills.

Art reproductions are not suitable for use with large groups, unless translated into another medium such as slides. Usually, it is better to purchase slides of works of art, rather than try to photograph reproductions (which are often copyrighted).

Some critics insist that since the reproduction is not the same as the original, there is danger that a facsimile, which imitates the original, may become interchangeable with the original in the user's mind. Scholars and critics argue that color reproductions lose some of the depth of perception and texture produced by brush strokes and the play of light on background colors. Some would argue that the viewer may lose a sense of excitement in viewing the work, because the reproduction is not the original piece on which the artist worked. In all likelihood, only a very small percentage of users would be aware of the foregoing objections.

Since there are numerous reproductions of poor quality on the market, selectors must exercise special caution to be sure that size is not distorted, that edges are not cropped, and that the color in the reproduction is true to the original.

Maintaining and circulating a collection of art reproductions requires that the works be framed to prevent ruin, that they be stored in places that protect them from environmental damage, and that personnel be available who have skill in cleaning and in the restoration of small injuries.

A few institutions have had users who wish to save themselves the trouble of purchasing and framing a work by borrowing, then "losing," art reproductions, for which they subsequently pay. Fortunately, such practices are not common.

Altogether, the advantages of stocking and lending art reproductions outweigh the disadvantages.

SELECTION

Special Criteria

Criteria for selection of art reproductions may be summarized as (1) breadth and variety of works in the collection, (2) fidelity to the original, and (3) quality of framing.

BREADTH AND VARIETY IN COLLECTION

Because users vary greatly in their tastes and in their choice of the works they wish to view, the selection should contain a wide range of works which represent all periods and styles of art and as many artists as possible. Sentimental, hackneyed "calendar art" should be avoided. Works of varying levels of complexity should be represented in the collection, as should those of varying degrees of abstractness. The significance of the artist and the importance of the original work are additional considerations. In meeting the criteria of breadth and variety, appeal to users must be considered, but works which "stretch" the users' horizons are highly important.

FIDELITY TO THE ORIGINAL

As for selection of individual reproductions or choice among reproductions of a single work which are available from more than one vendor, fidelity of the reproduction to the original is the *major* criterion. Subsequent paragraphs identify and elaborate on aspects of fidelity to the original.

First-Strike Reproductions. Whenever possible, printing plates should be made from a photograph of the work itself, not from a photograph of a photograph. A first-strike reproduction avoids the loss of resolution and exactness of color, as well as loss of precision in place alignment, as may occur when the reproduction is several generations removed from the original.

Color. The color of the original should be reproduced exactly in terms of hue, value, and intensity. Nuances of tone should be retained. Unless the reproduced work is sepia or black and white, a good-quality reproduction will require more than the usual four-color separations used in color printing. Normally, a minimum of twelve color separations is needed to match the color variations created by the artist,

> for color in painting is not merely added decoration. Color
> and its tones and treatment themselves create space, light, and
> form in a painting and all are important to defining the mood
> and emotional quality of a work of art. . . . It is only recently
> that the perfection of special cameras, film and methods of
> developing have made possible precise reproduction of the
> color and texture of a painting.[5]

Texture. A high-quality reproduction retains the "feel" of texture even when the surface of the reproduction is flat. Attempts at "brush

5. New York Graphic Society, *Fine Art Reproductions of Old and Modern Masters.* (New York: The Society, 1976), ix.

stroke'' texturing often fail to reproduce the texture of the original
and should be avoided, unless the selector is certain that the texture
of the original is reproduced.

Size. A reproduction should approximate the size of the original
insofar as possible. A few extremely large originals (such as contemporary works) may have to be reduced in size in order to make storage and circulation of the reproduction possible. Some producers crop
the size of a work arbitrarily, in order to print on standardized paper
sizes or to meet commonly used frame-size requirements. Whenever
possible, avoid cropped or reduced-size reproductions.

Another consideration concerning size is the attempt by some vendors to sell reproductions in reduced sizes for circulation to children.
Surely children deserve the opportunity to see exact-size reproductions as much as adults!

Depth of Field. The reproduction should preserve shadows, tonal
relationships, and color nuances. Lesser-quality reproductions often
have a flat, lifeless appearance.

Quality of Framing. The aesthetic appeal of a work can be severely
diminished by inappropriate matting and framing. While there is an
element of personal taste in selecting frames, vendors of high-quality
reproductions will provide suggestions for appropriate frames for a
given work. Frames should not be all the same. Just as the style of works
varies, so should the frames. Since reproductions circulate outside the
institution, durability and quality construction are essential.

Evaluative Review Sources

There are no reviews of art reproductions. Some dealers display full-
color reproductions of each work in their catalogs so that the buyer
can see, in miniature, what is being purchased. Other catalogs provide
only lists or black-and-white illustrations, which do not inform the
buyer about the quality of color in the reproduction.

The best guide for selection is to buy from a producer who has
a reputation for providing high-quality reproductions of works of art.
Avoid ''bargains,'' which may crop the size of the original, distort
color, be printed on acidic paper, or be flimsily framed. As a rule, the
reproduction of color will be more accurate when many color separations are used in printing the reproduction.

The selector needs to exercise care to ensure that the collection
of art reproductions is representative of all periods, artists, styles, and
schools of art. The personal taste of the selector must not be the determining factor in deciding which reproductions to purchase.

In the catalogs of some vendors, reproductions are grouped into sets in order to provide the selector with a balanced collection or to focus on a particular theme or subject. In determining whether to purchase such preselected sets, several factors should be considered: the existing collections, user preferences, the expertise and knowledge of the selector, the reputation of the vendor's staff, the cost per item in the set, and the number of titles in the set that may have little appeal. The selector should exercise caution in purchasing sets simply because the cost per reproduction is lower than the cost of purchasing single titles.

Once a collection of art reproductions begins to circulate, it is possible to determine, to some extent, user preferences based on items which are always in circulation or for which there are waiting lists. An institution's collection should not, however, be determined solely by popularity with users. It should provide items which "stretch" the users' imaginations and challenge their preconceptions about art.

Nonevaluative Sources

Some sources index art reproductions by title and artist, and indicate the source from which the work may be purchased. The titles listed below (with one exception) represent publications since 1970.

Bartran, Margaret. *A Guide to Color Reproductions.* 9th ed. Paris: Unesco, 1972.

Catalog of Museum Publications and Media: A Directory and Index of Publications and Audiovisuals Available from United States and Canadian Institutions. 2nd ed. Detroit: Gale, 1980.
> Identifies museums to which one may write for lists of reproductions and provides addresses.

Catalogue of Reproductions of Paintings, 1860–1973. Paris: Unesco, 1974.

Clapp, Jane. *Art Reproductions.* New York: Scarecrow, 1961.
> Lists art reproductions available from 95 museums in the U.S. and Canada; selected by museum personnel for validity of representation.

Other works which may be useful in developing a collection of art reproductions are

Fine Arts Market Place. Edited by Paul Cummings. Archives of American Art and the Smithsonian Institution. New York: Bowker, 1977.

Muehsan, Gerd. *Guide to the Basic Information Sources in the Visual Arts.* Santa Barbara, Calif.: Jeffrey North Publishers/ABC/CLIO, 1978.

Pacey, Phillip, ed. *Art Library Manual: A Guide to Resources and Practice.* London, New York: Bowker, in association with Art Libraries Society, 1977.

Picture Sources 4: Collections of Prints and Photographs in the U.S. and Canada. A Project of the Picture Division, Special Libraries Association and American Society of Picture Professionals. New York: SLA, 1984. Emphasis on pictures as information sources or visual documents rather than as works of art.

MAINTENANCE AND MANAGEMENT

Storage and Care

Storage and care present several dilemmas, since an institution must recognize that it cannot control the conditions under which the users display the work when it is on loan. Care can be exercised within the institution, but care should not overshadow the primary purpose, which is *use*. The assumption is made that all works which circulate are framed or mounted on rigid backing, which preserves the works and enhances their display.

DISPLAY AND STORAGE

Within the institutions, framed works may be hung at eye level, or small framed works may be grouped. If special spotlights are used, they should have incandescent lamps to protect a work from the deteriorating effect of ultraviolet rays. If many reproductions are displayed for browsing, they may be hung on pegboard, metal-mesh, or other hinged panels. They may also be displayed on large, sliding metal-mesh panels which are suspended from the ceiling and which move on tracks, thus allowing display on both sides of the panel—a kind of compact shelving.

An institution which cannot invest in special shelving may display the works throughout its quarters, allowing any item to circulate on user request. Display on easels may provide high visibility and flexibility of location. Works with heavy frames or glass overlay may need to hang on two hooks. Cork bumpers on the lower corners of the frames protect the surface on which works are hung, and aid in keeping them hanging straight.

If works are mounted on a sturdy board but are not framed, they may be housed in large bins for browsing. Such bins should be of baked enameled steel rather than wood, to avoid exposure to acid in the wood.

Small matted, but unframed, works may be stored in metal filing cabinets, and larger, unframed items may be stored in map case-type files. All unframed works should be mounted on acid-free backing to preserve the edges and to prevent damage in removing them from the files. Works also may be stored in acid-free boxes made of paper or fiberboard and kept horizontally on enameled steel shelves. Portfolios of acid-free materials may be used, but for maximum protection of the reproductions, a large space in which to open the portfolio is required.

PRESERVATION

Other than lack of frames, the chief enemies of art reproductions are acidity, air pollution, light, heat, and humidity.

Essentially, the durability of reproductions is highly dependent on the quality of the paper on which they are printed. To reduce acidity, use only acid-free supplies for mounting, paper separators, storage boxes or portfolios, dry-mount tissue, hinges, and glues (rubber cement, traditional dry-mount tissue, and laminating film all contain high concentrations of acids). Housing in filtered, air conditioned quarters helps to reduce air pollution-produced acid.

Light may alter or fade pigments. Display works away from direct sunlight and provide ultraviolet filters for flourescent lights. Unframed reproductions or photographs should be stored in a dark container, if possible.

Heat increases the rate of chemical reactions. Avoid hanging works high on walls, over radiators, or in direct sunlight.

High humidity encourages the growth of fungus or mold, which feeds upon cellulose, sizing, and the binders used in color inks. Low humidity may cause wooden frames to dry out and paper to shrink. Thus it is desirable not to fasten works tightly to a backing material; rather, they should be hinged so as to allow for expansion and contraction. Silica gel or kaken gel may be used in drawers and cases to help control high humidity.

In addition, works should periodically be dusted with a soft silk or cotton cloth, or with a soft natural-fiber brush. Works should be checked and cleaned after each circulation, and inspected annually.

Avoid exposing works to paper clips, pressure-sensitive tape, rubber bands, masking tape, rubber cement, and hand- or fingerprints.

To conserve a work is not to hoard or to hide it, but to value it for its *use* and to take reasonable steps to protect it.

Management Problems and Solutions

The institution which decides to include art reproductions in its collection is deciding, simultaneously, that it will provide certain staff functions and space allocations. It should expect an impact upon its selection, acquisition, cataloging or organization, and circulation processes. Inevitably, adaptations of existing processes must be made in order to accommodate art reproductions. The decision to add art reproductions to an existing collection immediately creates complementing issues: the need to justify a fairly large initial expenditure against the fact that once a collection is in circulation, the cost appears to be justified by the volume of use, the public relations value of the collection, and the enhanced image of the institution which a collection provides.

In fairness to users, a "critical mass" of reproductions must be assembled before circulation begins, perhaps delaying the payoffs of the initial investment for a period of time. Initiating an art reproduction collection may require several years of budgeting and planning, prior to implementation.

SELECTION OF ART REPRODUCTIONS
The institution's selection policy needs to address art reproductions in terms of (1) forms to be purchased (two-dimensional only, or sculpture, ceramics, and textiles as well); (2) disposition of gifts (caution is advised); (3) policy on duplicate copies of popular reproductions; and (4) procedures for dealing with challenged works (art reproductions may invite censorship due to the fact that they may be more graphic than verbal text).

Copyright considerations are best dealt with by purchase from a reputable dealer who will have arranged to provide royalties to the artist or copyright holder. Adherence to copyright may be reflected in higher costs of quality reproductions. Avoid itinerant salespersons or mass appeal sales in hotel rooms; such copies have a greater likelihood of being pirated.

ORGANIZATION AND ARRANGEMENT
In organizing a collection of art reproductions, it must be determined whether works will be classified in the same way as other materials, or by a special scheme, or whether they will be arranged by accession number. Other options for arrangement may be by period, country, school of art, or alphabetically by artist. The most appealing arrangement for users may be a random arrangement that is visually pleasing.

The number of items on display in an institution will seldom be static. As items come and go, fixed arrangements are wasteful of display or storage space. Greater visibility may be gained in displaying reproductions in several areas of the building. Whatever arrangement is chosen, the display space should be easily accessible.

SURROGATION

Art reproductions may receive the same cataloging as other works and be integrated into the public catalog, or they may be accessed through a separate but compatible catalog. Another option may be publication of a widely distributed separate list or brochure to advertise the collection.

Some institutions have had success with a loose-leaf catalog which includes a color photograph of each item, together with catalog data; thus a user, wishing to reserve an item that is in circulation, may be sure that the reserved item is the one desired. Institutions with microform catalogs may wish to use color microform for the art-reproduction part of the catalog, and include an image of the reproduction alongside the catalog data.

One or two vendors have provided small reproductions on the catalog cards that are supplied with reproductions purchased from that vendor.

Aperture cards would seem to be ideal for a catalog of art reproductions, but unless the institution also uses them in some other way, the cost of equipment is not justifiable. A separate art reproduction catalog on videodisc soon may be an alternative.

Indexing the collection may be more useful than cataloging. Access points may be provided by artist, title, conventional title, country of artist, period of art, school of art, themes, topics, curricular relationships, original medium, and even physical size of the reproduction. A data base of such information may be feasible through the institution's automation plan or, for small collections, by using a microcomputer.

STAFFING

There is disagreement over whether staff members who select reproductions should have an extensive art education. While it is advantageous, it does not appear to be essential as long as the selector is careful to choose a variety of styles of work and to avoid personal preference as much as possible.

Support staff requirements are more defined. Usually it is agreed that purchasing framed or mounted works is cheaper than framing in-house, but some institutions have staff members who frame reproductions. A careful examination of the use of staff time for framing may indicate that this time, together with the cost of purchasing quality framing materials, may not be justifiable.

Staff *are* needed for cleaning, inspection after each circulation, minor repairs, and for keeping pictorial catalogs or other access tools up to date.

Circulation staff may be needed if art reproductions are not charged and discharged from the main circulation desk.

CIRCULATION

The guiding principle should be making circulation as easy for the user as possible. Thus, a circulation system similar to that used for other materials should be a goal. Attachment of circulation items (card, bar code, OCR label) to the back of the reproduction saves time and offers convenience.

Determining what individuals, agencies, institutions, and businesses may borrow art reproductions constitutes a major circulation policy decision. If the collection is small, it may be necessary to limit circulation to individuals. Since a number of business and institutional borrowers can deplete a collection rapidly, some institutions may choose to help finance future purchases of reproductions by negotiating a special fee or financial sponsorship from corporate borrowers.

A related circulation decision is the number of reproductions that a person or institution may borrow at one time. Ordinarily, the number of reproductions in the collection and the demand from users are key factors in determining the number of works that are lent at one time.

Related decisions concern loan fees and authorization of users to borrow reproductions. The institution must determine if a separate borrower identification will be necessary or whether the usual borrower identification will suffice. If an annual fee is charged for the privilege of borrowing art reproductions, the borrower identification or borrower record in an automated system must be coded to indicate payment of the fee. If fees are charged, it must be determined whether to charge on a per item or annual basis. Ideally, the standard borrower authorization will be used, and no additional fees will be levied for access to art reproductions.

Additionally, the length of the loan period needs to be determined. A period of one to two months usually is recommended so that the user may "live" with the work of art. Some institutions send a postcard reminder approximately ten days before the work is due. When art reproductions are overdue, an overdue charge usually is made, but the amount per day or per week must be determined.

Because damage may occur, a policy concerning repair and/or replacement costs should be predetermined. A policy similar to that for other materials is preferable, especially with regard to processing fees that are added to replacement costs.

A system with several branches will need to determine whether reproductions may be requested and picked up at branches, or whether they will be available at one central location only.

Upon checkout, packaging for ease of carrying and for protection of a work is necessary. Cloth, or heavy plastic, or portfolios with strong carrying handles are ideal, but costly if purchased commercially. Thus volunteers may construct cloth portfolios. Wrapping in brown paper and sealing with packaging tape is inexpensive (provided brown paper is only left on during transportation). To avoid scratches and punctures, as well as rain, heat, and light damage, the reproduction *must* be packaged in some protective covering when it is transported to and from the institution.

SECURITY

While a collection of art reproductions represents a sizable investment, special security precautions may not be necessary. Provided the institution uses an electronic security system, art reproductions may be tagged with security strips between picture and backing in the same way that book materials are tagged. Given the size of most reproductions, however, it is unlikely that they could be carried out the door without detection, even when a security system is not in use.

If the collections contain only reproductions and no original prints, a special insurance rider probably is not required.

An important aspect of security is the way in which users treat the reproductions when they are in circulation and the means to ensure that they are returned on time. Regulations and instructions to borrowers may be attached to the back of the items.

Whenever measures are taken for security purposes, they should not hinder access for browsing purposes or discourage circulation. Security and conservation do not mean that works should be hidden or used only in the institution.

SERVICES AND PROGRAMMING

A collection of art reproductions may be attractive to users who cannot come to the institution to make their own selections: clients in hospitals, nursing homes, home-bound students, and persons confined to institutions. A service which allows such users to request delivery of reproductions or which takes a mobile exhibit to them is an effective way to reach into the community and to meet aesthetic needs that often are neglected.

Other off-site exhibits are excellent ways in which to promote use of the entire collection, including art reproductions. Among useful exhibit sites are department store windows, shopping centers, utility offices, lobbies of large office buildings, recreation centers, senior citizen centers, and transportation terminals. Security in such sites may be difficult, but if an enclosed space or show window is available, it may be capitalized upon.

Programming either within the institution or at remote sites may be planned around art reproductions. Such programming may allow highlighting of materials in other formats which are related to the reproductions. Cooperative programs with museums and performing arts agencies may be planned around reproductions. Popular in many communities are itinerant docents, who visit both public and private schools with selected reproductions from the collection.

Programming around the collection is easier if there is a staff member who is knowledgeable about art; however, most communities have potential volunteers with such expertise, if it is not available on the institution's staff. Using the collection of reproductions as a way to develop a volunteer program may give entré to the use of volunteers in other programming activities.

For the institution which wishes to reach into its user community in less traditional ways, the collection of art reproductions becomes a superb tool. Even the institution which lacks staff expertise in the visual arts should consider developing such a collection. "What makes a medium artistically important is not any quality of the medium itself but the qualities of mind and heart that its *users* bring to it."[6]

OTHER CONCERNS

Reproductions of two-dimensional works of art are among the most popular items that are lent by libraries and other institutions. Additionally, they are used in displays and in programming for users.

This chapter focuses on photomechanical art reproductions; it excludes reproduction of works of art as slides, sculpture, or realia. Other two-dimensional, nonprojected visual materials are found in many library, learning-resource, and museum collections. Pictures, charts, graphs, study prints, original art prints, and posters are found in the collections of many types of institutions.

Visual materials may be used for several purposes: information, instruction, decoration, and aesthetic experience. Visual material may be used as a source of information about places, particular events, periods of history, social customs, or living conditions. Two-dimensional visuals also provide documentation for the art scholar or re-

6. William Mills Ivins, Jr., *Prints and Visual Communication* (Cambridge, Mass.: Harvard Univ. Pr., 1958), 114.

searcher. Other visual material has a focused instructional purpose, such as recalling experience, correcting or preventing misconceptions, giving meaning to word symbols, stimulating reading, creating a focus for discussion, or developing critical judgment. In recent years, considerable attention has been given to developing visual literacy, the skill of decoding visual images. Many varieties of eye-legible visual materials are appropriate in a collection, depending upon the purpose for which the materials are collected. This chapter, however, focused on the *art reproduction,* usually produced by a photomechanical process, so that unlimited numbers of exact copies can be reproduced. While information or learning may be a by-product, the assumption is that the art reproduction is not expected to provide a deliberate cognitive experience, but to appeal to the imagination and to the spirit of the viewer.

ADDITIONAL RESOURCES

"Art Loan Collections." *Library Journal* 99 (May 1, 1974): 1258–61.

Bartran, Margaret. *A Guide to Color Reproductions.* 2nd ed. Metuchen, N.J.: Scarecrow, 1971.

Brunner, Felix. *A Handbook of Graphic Reproduction Processes.* New York: Hastings House, 1972.

Cabeceiras, James. *The Multimedia Library.* 2nd ed. New York: Academic Pr., 1982. 23–24.

Catalog of Museum Publications and Media: A Directory and Index of Publications and Audiovisuals Available from United States and Canadian Institutions. 2nd ed. Detroit: Gale, 1980.

Catalogue of Reproductions of Paintings prior to 1860. 9th ed. Paris: Unesco, 1972.

Catalogue of Reproductions of Paintings, 1860–1973. Paris: Unesco, 1974.

Clapp, Jane. *Art Reproductions.* New York: Scarecrow, 1961.

Cuhna, George Martin. *Conservation of Library Materials.* Metuchen, N.J.: Scarecrow, 1972.

Current Issues in Fine Arts Collection Development. ARLIS Occasional Papers, no. 3. Tucson: Art Libraries Soc. of North America, 1984.

Debes, John. "Some Foundations for Visual Literacy." *Audiovisual Instruction* (Nov. 1968): 961–64.

Drexel Library Quarterly 19 (Summer 1983).

Ellison, John W., Gloria S. Gerber, and Susan E. Ledders. "Original Paintings/ Prints and Non-Original Prints: Storage and Care Self-Evaluation Form." Washington, D.C.: ERIC Document Reproduction Service, 1980. ED 181 884.

Encyclopedia of Library and Information Science. New York: Dekker, 1968. S.v. "Art Libraries and Collections," 571–621.

The Encyclopedia of Visual Art. Danbury, Conn.: Grolier Educational Corp., 1983. Vol. 10

Encyclopedia of World Art. New York: McGraw-Hill, 1959–68. Supplement, 1983.

Evans, Hilary. *Picture Librarianship.* Outlines of Modern Librarianship. New York: Saur, 1980.

Fawcett, T. C. "On Reproductions." *Art Library Journal* 7 (Spring 1982): 9–16.

Fine Arts Market Place. Ed. Paul Cummings. Archives of American Art and the Smithsonian Institution. New York: Bowker, 1977.

Foster, Donald Leroy. *Prints in the Public Library.* Metuchen, N.J.: Scarecrow, 1973.

Ivins, William M. *Prints and Visual Communication.* New York: Da Capo, 1969.

Keavney, S. S. "Pictures." *Wilson Library Bulletin* 46 (Feb. 1972): 494–95.

Levis, John, and Edwin Smith. *Reproducing Art: The Photography Graphic Reproduction and Printing of Works of Art.* New York: Praeger, 1969.

Levy, Mervyn. *The Pocket Dictionary of Art Terms.* Greenwich, Conn.: New York Graphic Society, 1964.

Library Trends 23 (Jan. 1975). Entire issue devoted to fine-arts collections.

Mayer, Ralph. *A Dictionary of Art Terms and Techniques.* New York: Crowell, 1975.

Muehson, Gerd. *Guide to the Basic Information Sources in the Visual Arts.* Santa Barbara, Calif.: Jeffrey Norton Publishers/ABC-CLIO, 1978.

New York Graphic Society. *Fine Art Reproductions of Old and Modern Masters.* New York: The Society, 1980.

Newmyer, J. "Art Libraries and the Censor." *Library Quarterly* 46 (Jan. 1976): 38–53. Response in vol. 47 (Jan. 1977): 109.

Pacey, Philip, ed. *Art Library Manual: A Guide to Resources and Practice.* London, New York: Bowker, in association with the Art Libraries Society, 1977.

———. *Reader in Art Librarianship.* New York: Saur, 1985.

Petrina, John. *Art Works: How Produced, How Reproduced.* Freeport, N.Y.: Books for Libraries, 1970.

Picture Sources 4: Collections of Prints and Photographs in the U.S. and Canada. A project of the Picture Division, Special Libraries Association and American Society of Picture Professionals. New York: SLA, 1984.

Radel, S. "Circulating Framed Art Collections in Public Libraries: A New Look." *Connecticut Libraries* 19 (1977): 20–24.

Reference Tools for Fine Arts Visual Collections. ARLIS Occasional Papers, no. 4. Tucson: Art Libraries Soc. of North America, 1983.

Smith, Charles Gibbs. *Copyright Law Concerning Works of Art, Photographs, and the Written and Spoken Word.* London: Museums Association, 1974.

Swartzburg, Susan. *Conservation in the Library: A Handbook of Use & Care of Traditional & Nontraditional Materials.* Westport, Conn.: Greenwood Pr., 1983.

Organizations Concerned with Art Reproductions

American Library Association. Association of College and Research Libraries. Art Section. 50 E. Huron St., Chicago, IL 60611.

Art Librarians Society of North America (ARLIS/NA). Executive Secretary, Pamela J. Parry, 3775 Bear Creek Circle, Tucson, AZ 85749.

American Society of Picture Professionals. P.O. Box 5283, Grand Central Station, New York, N.Y. 10069.

International Visual Literacy Association. Association for Educational Communications and Technology. 1126 16th St. N.W., Washington, D.C. 20036.

Special Libraries Association. Picture Division. Museum Arts and Humanities Division. 235 Park Ave. S., New York, N.Y. 10003.

Gerald R. Barkholz

Audiotapes

THE MEDIUM

Definition

Audiotape is a ribbon of acetate or polyester which has a metallic oxide coating on one side. When this coating is exposed to the magnetic field of a recording head, the metallic particles are arranged in a pattern corresponding to the sound being recorded. Audiotapes generally come in two widths, ¼ in. and ⅛ in., and are available in open reels (¼ in.), cartridges (¼ in.), and cassettes (⅛ in.).

Brief History

The first magnetic recorded sound was accomplished by a Danish engineer, Valdemar Paulsen, in 1898. His "telegraphone" consisted of a steel wire which was run between the poles of an electromagnet. Although the telegraphone appeared on European and American markets, the wire recorders failed to attract a wide market because of the difficulties of tangled and broken wires, and editing was nearly impossible.

In 1928, Fritz Pfleumer, a German, came out with a flexible strip coated with iron oxide. This was the prototype for tape recording as still used today. As sound waves were picked up by a microphone, the waves were converted to electrical impulses which were amplified and sent to the recording head of the recording machine. The

20

recording head was an electromagnet, the strength of which was determined by the electrical impulses. This electromagnet, then, rearranged the iron oxide particles according to the pattern of the original sound.

With this system, sounds could be easily recorded, stored, and erased. And because the base material of the tapes was a kind of paper, editing could be accomplished simply by cutting and splicing. The major drawback of these early tapes was that they lacked the strength for extended usage. Also, the rough paper surface caused the lack of uniformity of the iron oxide coating, resulting in a high noise level.

Plastic tapes soon replaced paper as the base material on which the coating of resin, containing particles of iron oxide, was spread evenly, dried, and smoothed.

In 1963, the Philips Company of the Netherlands invented the cassette, which consisted of $\frac{1}{8}$ in.-wide tape mounted on two hubs within a small plastic case. The cassette was to be played on a small machine called the Carry-Corder at a speed of $1\frac{7}{8}$ inches per second (ips). Through an unusual agreement, the Philips Company gave other manufacturers the right to make cassettes and cassette recorder/players if they met the same specifications for cassette size and speed. Thus the first industry standard was established and still exists today.

Ray Dolby, in 1967, invented a noise reduction system, known as the Dolby system, which greatly improved the response of cassette recorders to overcoming background hiss.

Recently, tapes have changed only in coating materials, to bring about truer reproduction of sound. In addition to ferric oxide tapes, there are tapes with chromium dioxide and professional-type tapes which have a layer of ferric oxide and a layer of chromium dioxide.

In terms of a library collection of audiotapes, some institutions began acquiring recordings of musical pieces in the late 1920s with the help of Carnegie grants. By the mid- to late fifties, taped oral histories became popular. At this time, as a result of the National Defense Education Act, school libraries also began to acquire tapes for their collections. In 1960, books on tape began to appear, and service to blind readers was proposed using this medium. The early sixties saw language courses on tape appearing in institutions; and with the advent of cassettes, by the late sixties audiotapes were in extensive use.

Unique Characteristics

Tapes can store sound on more than one track. Depending on the recording system being used, information can be stored on the entire coated side of the tape as it passes through the machine. This is *single-track monaural*. If only half the tape is used in each of two passes through the machine, it is either *two-track monaural* or *four-track stereo*. (Stereo recordings require two tracks recorded or played at the same time.) And if one-fourth of the tape is recorded in each pass, it is *eight-track stereo*.

Recorded sound can also be compressed or expanded for listening convenience. An electronic device can break up recorded speech and eliminate bits of sound and pauses to increase the listening speed from 150 words per minute (normal listening speed) to 400 or 500 words per minute. Some electronic speech compressors can also expand speech patterns to slow down listening speeds. This is useful for, say, the mentally handicapped, who have difficulty understanding speech at a normal speed.

Tapes can be easily erased and re-recorded.

Tapes can be programmed to operate both slide and filmstrip projections.

Due to the size of audiotapes, they are extremely portable. The largest open reel of tape measures 7 inches in diameter, while the audio cassette is only 2½ by 4 by ½ inches.

Cartridges provide continuous play, since the tape is wound in a continuous loop on one reel.

Advantages and Disadvantages

Audiotapes have some distinct advantages over other sound media:

Tapes require less storage space than records.

Tapes provide an alternative medium for people with low reading skills or visual impairment.

Equipment for playing tapes is generally compact, portable, and easy to use.

Quality of reproduction remains constant through repeated and extended use.

Original programs are easily made by the amateur.

There is the capability for instant playback.

Tapes are easy to edit.

Tapes may be erased and reused.

Duplication is easy and economical.

Auditory portions of events may be preserved for future analysis, interpretation, and transcription.

Tapes can be used in conjunction with several media.

This medium can be easily circulated.

With special equipment, programs can be adjusted to the user's listening speed.

Tapes, as a whole, also have *dis*advantages:

They lack visual or tactile experiencing of the material being presented.
They can be accidentally erased.
Scanning for information is difficult because of the linearity of the
    medium.

Since audiotapes come in different formats, there are advantages
and disadvantages specific to the formats:

There is better fidelity because of faster speed and wider (¼ in.) tape
    in the open reel format.
Open reel tape is more versatile because of the selection of speeds.
    Most open reel machines will operate at 7½, 3¾, or 1⅞ ips.
Because the tape is ¼ in. wide and not enclosed, it is easy to edit and
    splice.

The disadvantages of the open reel format are as follows:

The tape must be manually threaded and handled.
Because of handling, it is more easily erased and broken.
Playing equipment is more bulky.
Stereo and monaural formats are not interchangeable, because of track
    pattern.
Tape must be rewound or run off one reel before removing it from
    the player.
Using different reel sizes could be awkward if the corresponding takeup
    reel is not available.

Advantages of cassette format:

The tape is enclosed in a plastic housing (100mm by 64mm by 9mm).
The cassette can be inserted or removed without regard to how much
    tape is used.
This is the most portable of the tape formats.
The equipment is easy to operate.
Playing times range from 15 minutes to 120 minutes (both sides).
Cassettes have a standardized speed of 1⅞ ips.
Pushout tabs may be knocked out to prevent erasure.
Monaural and stereo tape recordings may be interchanged on the same
    players.

Disadvantages of cassette format:

The tape width and the fact that it is encased make it difficult to edit
    and splice.
There is poorer fidelity, due to the slow speed (1⅞ ips) and ⅛ in. width
    of the tape.

Ninety- and 120-minute tapes (C-90 and C-120, respectively) are thinner and may get caught and wound around the inner components of the machine.

The glue-sealed housing used by most manufacturers makes repair difficult.

Discount-priced tapes may jam easily and cause head damage because of their poor quality.

Advantages of cartridge format:

The tape is encased in a plastic housing (100mm by 138mm by 23mm), making it easy to handle.

There is continuous play, due to the tape's being mounted in a continuous loop on a single hub.

No threading is necessary.

There is better fidelity than cassettes, because of faster speed ($3\frac{3}{4}$ ips) and wider tape ($\frac{1}{4}$ in.).

Disadvantages of cartridge format:

It is a playback medium; one cannot make his or her own recordings.

The design of the cartridge does not allow for fast forward or rewind.

Indexing and locating material is virtually impossible.

The narrow tracks cause difficulty with head alignment.

This format is gradually being phased out in favor of cassettes.

SELECTION

Special Criteria

When audiotapes are selected, most criteria pertain to their physical qualities.

LENGTH AND THICKNESS

Longer tapes are thinner, which can cause problems in the mechanical system being used. The tape is more easily caught in the mechanism, which will always ruin the tape and not be good for the recorder/player. The thinner tapes are also more susceptible to stretching, which distorts the sound and leads to breaking. Print-through is also a problem for thinner tapes. The layering of the tape on itself may cause the magnetic arrangement on one layer to be transferred to an adjacent layer.

Even though there are problems inherent to these thin tapes, it is sometimes necessary to have longer tapes for programs that should not or could not be interrupted while the tape is changed.

Cassette tapes, which are commonplace today, should be C-60

(60 minutes) or shorter. Longer (C-90 or C-120) cassettes have all of the problems just discussed.

It is further recommended that whatever format is selected, the minimum thickness should be 1 mil (.001 in.).

FORMAT OF TAPES

The most obvious point, when talking about format, is whether the tape is open reel, cartridge, or cassette. But in addition to selecting one of these, one must also take into consideration the number of tracks. Blank tapes do not have tracks, since it is the type of recorder that determines this. Therefore, if one is to purchase prerecorded tapes, care must be given as to whether the tape uses 1, 2, 4, or 8 tracks, so that the proper playback equipment is available. A similar concern is whether the tape is monaural or stereo, since they are not always interchangeable. And a final format consideration is the use of the Dolby system for noise reduction. If a tape has been recorded using this system, it should be played on equipment with the noise-reduction feature.

TAPE SPEED

There are primarily three speeds at which tapes are recorded and played. Open reel tapes are recorded and played back at all three speeds: 7½ inches per second (ips), 3¾ ips, and 1⅞ ips. The faster speed, 7½ ips, has excellent fidelity; the medium speed, 3¾ ips, gives good fidelity; the slow speed, 1⅞ ips, results in fair to good fidelity. Cartridge tapes all operate at 3¾ ips, and cassettes operate at 1⅞ ips.

There are machines available today that run tapes at $^{15}/_{16}$ ips, but these have poor fidelity and are in very limited use.

TECHNICAL QUALITY

When judging a prerecorded tape, one should listen for clarity of the program, making sure that the sound levels are adequate and that the recording is free from background noises.

TAPE CONSTRUCTION

How the tape is constructed is very important for determining the overall quality of the tape. The tape should have a backing material of polyester if it is to be used in an institution where it will receive repeated use. Tensilized or prestretched polyester is best, but more expensive.

The polyester is then layered with a metallic oxide. Ferric oxide (Fe_2O_3) is the most common in both normal and high bias tapes. Chromium dioxide (CrO_2) is found on high bias tapes. Ferrichrome (FeCr), a third tape of layering, is also known as "metal" tape.

Cassettes and cartridges should be examined for the quality and durability of their parts. The shells and rollers should be able to withstand hard use. Cassette shells, sealed with screws, are preferable to cassettes sealed with glue.

It is generally a good practice to buy blank tapes that are first-line quality, brand names.

Evaluative Review Sources

The following are some of the evaluative selection sources for prerecorded audio tapes:

PERIODICALS

Absolute Sound   *Instructional Innovator*
American Record Guide   *Library Journal*
Billboard   *Notes*
Booklist   *Previews*
Creem   *Rockingchair*
Down Beat   *Rolling Stone*
Ear for Children   *School Library Journal*
High Fidelity   *Stereo Review*

MONOGRAPHS

Record and Tape Reviews Index. Metuchen, N.J.: Scarecrow, 1972– (annual).
Records in Review. Great Barrington, Mass.: Wyeth Pr., 1955– (annual).

Nonevaluative Sources

Titles listed below represent publications since 1970.

PERIODICALS
Listening Post   *Schwann-1 Record and Tape Guide*
List-O-Tapes   *Schwann-2 Supplementary Record*
                                                        and Tape Guide

BOOKS

Audio-Cassette Directory. Glendale, Calif.: Cassette Information Services, 1972– (biennial).
Billboard Audio/Video/Tape Sourcebook. Cincinnati: Billboard Directories (annual).
Educators' Guide to Free Audio and Video Materials. Randolph, Wis.: Educators' Progress Service, 1977– (annual).

Index to Educational Audiotapes. 5th ed. Los Angeles: National Information Center for Educational Media (NICEM), University of Southern California, 1980.

National Center for Audio Tapes Catalog. Boulder, Colo.: National Center for Audio Tapes, University of Colorado, 1966– (triennial).

Records and Cassettes for Young Adults: A Selected List. New York: New York Library Assn., 1972.

Stereo Review's Tape Recording and Buyers' Guide. New York: Ziff-Davis, 1965– (annual).

Words on Tape. Westport, Conn.: Meckler, 1984– (biennial).

MAINTENANCE AND MANAGEMENT

Storage and Care

Tapes should be stored on their edges in dust-proof containers. Open reel tapes are generally stored in cardboard containers and plastic containers, or circulation binders are used for cassettes.

The storage area should be maintained at room temperature (67°F ± 3°), with a relative humidity of 50 percent (± 10%).

Most important of all, the tapes must not be placed near magnetic fields (permanent magnets, electric motors, and high-power lines), which may erase the tapes. Since metal shelving can conduct magnetic fields, wooden shelves are a better choice. Tapes may be intershelved with print materials or kept separately.

To ensure long life to tapes, certain procedures can be followed:

Don't touch tapes unnecessarily with fingers; use lint-free gloves when splicing.

Keep tapes dust and dirt free.

Wind tapes loosely and evenly.

Play tapes at least twice a year. This improves their condition because it helps remove tension and helps release adhesions. Lack of use could cause print-through, a magnetic printing effect between layers of the tape.

Clean the heads, capstan, and tape guides on the machine after every 8–10 hours of play. Use swabs and isopropyl alcohol for this purpose.

Discard takeup reels when imperfections are found.

Remove wrinkled or damaged tape ends, which may damage the recorder heads and cause uneven winding.

Remove breakout tabs to protect cassettes from erasure.

Protective circulation containers, such as manila envelopes, should be used when tapes are checked out.

Always use appropriate equipment that has been properly maintained.

Management Problems and Solutions

Many questions arise in terms of the management of audiotapes in any institution. Many of these problems cannot be answered for all institutions, since each institution will be unique in its program, its users, and its budget.

The selection and acquisition of audiotapes should probably be limited to one particular format. Since the institution is likely to provide players as well as tapes for its users, it would be more economical to try to stick to a single format. This would also help in terms of storage space and maintenance.

Even though it is tempting (and even logical) for an institution to acquire the longest tapes available, the thinness of long tapes will cause more problems than they are worth. This will also increase the cost in the long run, because of the expense involved with the replacement and repair of the equipment, as well as the replacement of the tapes.

It is also reasonable for an institution to wish to have as large a collection of tapes as possible. But this should never be done at the expense of quality. The quality of the tapes not only affects the sound quality of the program reproduction, it can also affect the record and playback heads on the machines.

In terms of developing the collection, an institution may safely use disc reviews as a guide in the selection of audiotapes. If the audiotapes are produced by the same company that produces the record, chances are they're both made from the same "master" and should therefore be of equal quality.

The collection can also be examined for duplication. Since print holdings are often duplicated, it is reasonable to duplicate certain audiotape holdings because of popularity of circulation, etc. The policy of the institution toward duplicating holdings would be the best determinant as to what practice to follow for audiotapes.

The preservation and storage of this medium presents only minor problems that can be handled without difficulty. The institution must decide, for instance, whether the use of tapes and equipment should be entirely supervised by the staff, or whether they should be checked out to the users with the hope that they will be cared for.

Whatever the decision in this matter, tapes become broken and will need repair. The facilities for repair would consist of a splicing block and a roll of splicing tape or splicing tabs. The cost would be less than $20 and take up less space than a cigar box. Therefore, it would certainly be to the institution's advantage to have these materials for easy repair. However, if tapes should become damaged, incomplete, or worn to the extent that they no longer can be considered quality reproductions, they should be discarded. Poor-quality tapes can harm equipment, and tapes in this condition are of no value to the user. The same care and maintenance should be given to any nonprint collection that would be given to any quality print collection.

Organization and cataloging of audiotapes should suit the needs of the institution and its patrons. Since the staff of any institution is striving for maximum utilization of its collection, convenience for the user is a primary consideration. Tapes may be shelved right along with the print collection, if space permits, or they may be stored in a separate location with other nonprint materials, or even in a designated area for that medium alone. Similarly, the method of cataloging should be any method that will best serve the users. Some suggest that the playing equipment should be located near the tapes themselves. If this would maximize utilization, it certainly should be considered.

Even though audiotapes come in different formats, it would not be logical to store them according to their format. Just as an institution would not organize books by the color or style of binding, we would not organize tapes according to their reel size or packaging.

Whatever method of cataloging and storage is used, the tapes should be identified with a collation statement in several places on the package. It should appear on the tape itself, its container, and its place of storage. All of these statements would help keep track of the material and aid in preventing mixups.

The philosophy and policies of the specific institution will dictate how tapes will be circulated. It is possible that tapes would be used only within the institution and not be circulated at all. On the other hand, audiotapes *and* equipment to play them may be circulated like any other material. This latter procedure is sometimes accompanied by a program in the use of tapes and equipment before a user can check them out. Again, the institution should be looking at maximum utilization.

There are general considerations that need attention in the establishment of a tape collection. The first is whether an institution should even have audiotapes. The role and scope and philosophy of the institution must be the guiding factors in the establishment of a tape collection and the extent to which staff and users will play a role in the selection and use of facilities.

Even though a tape collection may be considered a part of the institution, how it is used is another consideration. If headsets are provided, tapes can be used in carrels, at tables, or in a lounge chair, without disturbing other users. Some institutions may even provide small rooms where a person can go to listen without disturbing others.

If tapes are checked out, the staff has no control over what the user does with them. The users may choose to duplicate the tapes for their personal collections. On this point, it would behoove the institution to provide users with a notice of copyright restrictions, as well as having these restrictions prominently posted.

Other Concerns

In this section, a more detailed explanation of terms and ideas used throughout the text on audiotapes will be given. For instance, to determine which side of the tape has the oxide coating (it is only on one side), look for the "dull" side. This is where the recording and playback take place. "Side A" or "side B" of a tape refers to turning a tape over so that recording or playback takes place on the same dull surface, but in the opposite direction on different tracks.

The number of tracks used and the pattern in which they are used determines the audio format. Monaural may use a full track, where the full width of the tape is used as the tape passes through the equipment. More common is the half-track or dual track system; in this, two tracks are on one tape; half the width of the tape passes through the equipment in one direction, and then the other half, when the tape is turned over and passed through the equipment a second time.

Stereophonic sound is such that two tracks are needed to carry material originally obtained through separate microphones. A stereo player reproduces two sounds from the two tracks simultaneously, using two playback heads and sending the sound through two separate speakers. These sounds can be recorded, using two, four, or eight tracks on the tape. The two-track or half-track consists of two parallel tracks recorded in the same direction. Four-track or quarter-track is accomplished by using two tracks recorded simultaneously in one direction, and then the tape is turned over and two new tracks are recorded. The placement of these tracks differs between open reel tapes and cassettes. On open reel tapes, the first and third tracks are recorded on side A, and the second and fourth tracks on side B. Cassettes utilize the first and second tracks on side A and the third and fourth tracks on side B.

The eight-track cartridge is much more complicated. The tracks are paired one and five, two and six, three and seven, four and eight. Since these tapes do not have "sides," the playback heads on the equipment must adjust to align with the proper pair of tracks. Proper alignment has been a recurring problem with eight-track equipment, which is the major cause for its decline in popularity.

A new format, the microcassette, has recently come on the scene, but has too many drawbacks to be considered for institutional use. These tapes are only ⅛ in. wide and run at ¹⁵⁄₁₆ ips. Their tiny size and slow speed make them satisfactory for dictation, but result in poor fidelity for any other use.

ADDITIONAL RESOURCES

Association for Educational Communications and Technology. *Standards for Cataloging of Non-Print Materials.* Washington, D.C.: Association for Educational Communications and Technology, 1971.

Banerjee, Sumanta. *Audio Cassettes: The User Medium.* Paris: U.N. Educational, Scientific and Cultural Organization, 1977.

Boucher, Brian G., Merril J. Gottlieb, and Martin L. Morganlander. *Handbook and Catalog for Instructional Media Selection.* Englewood Cliffs, N.J.: Educational Technology Publications, 1973.

Cabaceiras, James. *The Multimedia Library.* New York: Academic Pr., 1982.

Colburn, Dave. "Building a Cassette Tape Bank: Everything You Wanted to Know." *Educational Screen and Audiovisual Guide* 50 (Apr. 1971): 6–17.

Colorado, University of. *Guidelines for Audio Tape Libraries.* Boulder: National Center for Audio Tapes, 1971.

Doak, W. A. *How to Start an AV Collection.* Metuchen, N.J.: Scarecrow, 1978.

Egan, C. M. "Establishing a Cassette Program for a Public Library." *Illinois Librarian* 56 (Mar. 1974): 239–43.

Higgins, Judith. "Coping with Cassettes." *School Library Journal* 18 (Apr. 1972): 41–44.

Hopkinson, Shirley L. *The Descriptive Cataloging of Library Materials.* 4th ed. San Jose, Calif.: Claremont House, 1974.

Laybourne, Kit, and Pauline Cianciolo, eds. *Doing the Media.* New York: McGraw-Hill, 1978.

Lewis, Philip, and Linda Thomas Iglewski. *Educator's Guide to Creative Audio Tape Techniques.* Gardena, Calif.: Audio Magnetic Corp., 1973.

Lowman, Charles E. *Magnetic Recording.* New York: McGraw-Hill, 1972.

McGraw-Hill Encyclopedia of Science and Technology. 5th ed. New York: McGraw-Hill. Vol. 8, 46–52.

Rosenberg, Kenyon C. "Look Before You Leap: Tape Recorders: Open Reel vs. Cassettes." *Library Journal/School Library Journal Reviews* 1 (Oct. 1972): 5–11.

———. "Direct and Digital Sound Recordings: Basics for Librarians." *Library Journal* 108 (May 1, 1983): 879–80.

Rusvold, Margaret I., and Carolyn Guss. *Guide to Educational Media.* 3rd ed. Chicago: American Library Assn., 1971.

Saddington, G. H., and E. Cooper. *Audiocassettes as Library Materials. Audiovisual Librarian* (London) (1976).

Paul B. Wiener

ch 3

Films

THE MEDIUM

Definition

Motion picture film is a thin, flexible, side-perforated strip of transparent base material coated with a light-sensitive emulsion on which photographic images are recorded sequentially as transparencies.[1] These images are transmitted through a mechanical projector, which gives them the appearance of motion by pulling them along their perforations, or sprocket holes, between a strong light and a lens at a quick, fixed rate. Each image, or frame, is held in front of the lens for a fraction of a second. Projection of these images on a screen or clear surface, many times a second, makes them seem to be in continuous motion. It is thought by many that the biological phenomenon of persistence of vision, whereby the image lingers on the retina for a fraction of a second longer than it takes for it to cross the projector lens, is responsible for the success and appeal of motion pictures. Motion seen on the screen may be either the speed of real time, or may be slowed, accelerated, or distorted by special photographic techniques.

---

1. Some experimental films don't depend on using sequences of photographic images. Instead, images are put directly onto the clear, blank—or exposed black—film by the filmmaker, usually by hand.

Brief History

The history of motion pictures began with innovations in technology and perception: the development of a camera that could record a series of live-action photographs, and a projector that could display this series in a way that action would be simulated; the development of film stock that would permit photography and processing under a variety of conditions of light and motion; and an increasing desire to analyze behavior and activity by "stopping" it photographically and re-creating it in a medium, mechanically. The reduction in a photograph's exposure time from 15 minutes to 1/1000 of a second was achieved when collodion wet plates were replaced by gelatine dry plates in the late 1870s. Marey, in 1882, invented the chronophotographic gun, which recorded sequential action photographs in a single camera, improving on Muybridge's famous efforts to stop action by sequencing 12 electronically coordinated cameras.

In 1887 the first celluloid roll film was used as a base for light-sensitive emulsions. Dickson's Kinetograph of 1889, meant to illustrate the sound from a phonograph, was the first application of sound to movies. In 1893 Edison began to market the Kinetoscope, into which a single viewer looked to watch a short film loop. With this entertainment device, the public's insatiable craving for moving pictures began. In the early 1890s Messter perfected the Maltese Cross mechanism that enabled projectors to standardize projection speed and the rate of film frame movement. And in 1895 the Lumiére brothers of France invented the Cinematograph, which, rather like some VCRs, served as camera, printer, and projector in one, and had a standard speed of 16 fps. By 1896, according to David Cook, all basic technological principles of film recording and projection had been discovered and incorporated into existing machines . . . which have essentially remained unchanged to this day.[2] In 1899, 35mm cellulose nitrate stock became the commercial standard, projected at 16 fps (later, at 18 fps).

Until the turn of the century, almost all films were simple documentaries, records of a photographed "reality." Cameras were always stationary and action unfolded before the lens. Georges Meliés is usually credited with discovering the narrative, or fictional, potential of movies. His best-known effort, *A Trip to the Moon* (1902), almost surrealistically manipulates the imagery chosen to represent the story. Edwin Porter, and especially D. W. Griffith, developed the "language of the cinema" by inventing many techniques of editing, cinematog-

---

2. David A. Cook, *A History of Narrative Film* (New York: Norton, 1981), 12–13.

raphy, lighting, and composition. Griffith pioneered the "tracking shot" around 1908, giving much greater dynamism to film storytelling.

Further advances in storytelling techniques were made in Germany by Robert Wiene (*Das Kabinett des Dr. Caligari,* 1919) and Fritz Lang (*Metropolis,* 1926), in Russia by Eisenstein (*Battleship Potemkin,* 1925) and Pudovkin (*Mother,* 1926), and in America by Charlie Chaplin (*The Tramp,* 1925) and Buster Keaton (*The General,* 1927), who also were the first great actor-producers. The first animated film, *The Humpty Dumpty Circus* (ca. 1898), manipulated objects; the first cartoon animation was *The Enchanted Drawing* (1900).

By the 1920s, 80 percent of American features were tinted. *Toll of the Sea* (1922), using a two-color subtractive system, was the first all-color film, and by the early 1930s there were many others. But since the color registration was so poor, audiences didn't flock to them until the three-color Technicolor system, using negatives, was perfected in 1932, when it was used for Disney animations. By the late 1930s, major color films began to appear (*Gone with the Wind,* 1939) and to do well commercially.

Hollywood began to convert to color in 1952, with the coming of the inexpensive Eastmancolor process. Unfortunately, Eastmancolor film fades much more rapidly than Technicolor, and the older color films are actually better preserved. By 1979, 96 percent of American feature films were in color.

Although sound accompaniment had nearly always been a part of film viewing, either with live piano or orchestral music, or on discs synchronized to the picture and action (which Vitaphone pioneered), the invention of a sound track, laid onto the film itself, came in 1919 with the Tri-Ergon system. A photoelectric cell converted sound to electric and then to light impulses; to hear sound, the process was reversed.

The first "talkie," *The Jazz Singer* (1927), used the synchronized disc sound system, but Fox Movietone News, also around 1927, used the newer light conversion system. Some historians have claimed that the movies stopped moving when they started talking, an effect of the primitive recording equipment and techniques that immobilized actors. But by the end of 1929 most American films had sound.

Projection speed for sound film was standardized at 24 fps in 1929. This meant that movies couldn't be under- or overcranked by hand to achieve special effects. Although a cellulose acetate base was invented in 1912 by Kodak, and was used in 16mm film production, the tough, highly flammable cellulose nitrate base was used until about 1951. Some of these early nitrate films have been converted to acetate, but 80 percent of the nitrate films made before 1930 have been lost.

16mm film was introduced for amateurs in 1923 by Kodak, and was much less costly to produce, but it wasn't until World War II that it became popular, since using it conformed to the tight wartime budgeting. After the war, 16mm film became the major gauge for educational, training, and industrial purposes, and its editing and camera equipment now rival 35mm film in sophistication.

8mm film was introduced in 1935, when photo emulsion technology evolved and permitted recording an image on an area one-fourth that of 16mm film. Thus 16mm film could be used to make 8mm film, by exposing two rows of photographs on its width. 8mm production costs were one-third those of 16mm production, and cameras were lighter and cheaper, as was film. 8mm was always intended for amateur, nontheatrical use. In 1965 Kodak brought out the super-8mm film, which had a photographic image 50 percent larger than that on regular 8mm. There was also room for a magnetic or optical soundtrack.

Film was sold in cartridges and didn't need to be threaded. Because of its better recording, sound, and projection capabilities, super-8 began to replace much of the market for 8mm film. However, incompatibilities between 8mm and super-8 films and projectors have hindered the expansion of the super-8 market. In the 1960s, improved technology caused a revival of 8mm film use, but this was soon offset, as was super-8 use, by the development of home video technology and inexpensive video recording in the late 1970s.

Developments in video have affected the use, production, and collection of film in general—many films and film uses are now routinely replaced by video—and evidence has begun to mount that film circulation, collection size, and library, educational, and industrial services are falling off as video takes over. The preservation of motion pictures, recorded on their original film medium, especially older and rare films, is thus becoming increasingly urgent and problematic.

Following close behind the development of film and its instant popularity came the film libraries, services, organizations, and reference tools. A St. Louis, Missouri, school system started a visual education department in 1905; the Madison, Wisconsin, Public Library in 1910 began using films to dramatize children's stories; in 1912 the Department of Agriculture began depositing films at land grant colleges. Having no formal procedures for acquiring this new format, the Library of Congress didn't collect the early movies, but kept motion picture images on paper strips instead. In 1934 the National Archives started preserving films, but the Library of Congress didn't form its Motion Picture Division until 1943, almost ten years after the Museum of Modern Art had begun a film collection. To a great extent, the Museum of Modern Art was responsible for inspiring and helping to organize the Library of Congress film collection.

The Educational Film Library Association was also founded in 1943. As early as 1923, the National Education Association established its Department of Visual Instruction, which in 1946 became the Department of Audio-Visual Instruction. In 1924 the American Library Association formed its Visual Methods Committee. By 1951, 100 of the large public libraries circulated over 36,000 films. The first instructional film catalog, the *Catalogue of Educational Motion Pictures,* was published in 1910. National Information Center for Educational Media (NICEM) began publishing its 16mm film index in 1969, and the *Educational Film Locator* was first published in 1978.

Film distribution is no longer dominated by conglomerates, though some, like Films Inc. and Time-Life Video, are still going strong. Now much distribution is managed by hundreds of small, independent distributors, some of them filmmakers, many of whom also distribute their materials on video cassettes as well. Despite the threat from the video culture, film history continues to be made as more and more old, rare films are discovered, restored, and released, and as filmmakers and film managers concentrate on using the unique characteristics of the medium to bring us unique visions.

Unique Characteristics

The listed characteristics are not primarily physical; rather, they apply to the *use* of film in motion picture format, as opposed to film used in still photography, slide presentations, filmstrips, or video recording. Characteristics shared by other media are not discussed.

Film can reach large audiences (of over 2,000) with a clear image and sound, and can do this with one screen.

It is the only medium that is projected at a rate of 24 (or 18) frames per second, that can animate the stationary imagery of other media (photos, maps, slides, drawings), that can incorporate all other media in a single presentation, and that records motion on celluloid.

It created, and is the major outlet for, the art of animation, which has created, in turn, new forms of education and entertainment.

It encourages multiple viewing (of works that need or deserve it) without leaving the viewers feeling they have wasted their time.

When projected, it is very rarely interrupted by commercials or news reports.

Film is the only nonbroadcast medium that is usually a group creation, sometimes of hundreds of individuals and organizations. (Indivi-

duals, of course, can and do create entire films too.) As group crea-
tions, films are often an expression of group mentality and their
messages may be hard to decipher. Individual artists are often given
too much credit for the accomplishments of particular films.

It is the only medium that has a history, a "literature" and "language,"
and an impact to rival that of print.

It provides the only way to study or observe the behavior of people,
historical figures, or events that came before the television era.
It has thus created a sense of a "living" past.

It can pull a community together, in a room or building, solely to experience mediated imagery. In this way it creates social bonds. It
is the only nonbroadcast medium that can give the same message
to millions of people, virtually at the same time. This creates a
group response to the exact same phenomenon, a commonality,
that is often measurable and has obvious consequences. Unlike
theatre, its performers are tireless and its stages countless.

It is the medium that, currently at least, dominates television imagery
and production.

It is primarily a medium that records behavior, expression, and events
that have already happened, as opposed to television's emphasis
on immediacy and currency.

It is the only nonbroadcast medium that, through electrical and chemical processing of light and sound, can convince audiences they're
seeing or participating in an actual event when, in fact, they're
sitting in the dark, watching a story with strangers. This has special
consequences for young viewers and can be applied very successfully to a child's sense of wonder and fantasy.

Advantages

While the use of film offers many advantages over other styles of
presentation, many of them, such as its ability to overcome language
barriers or literacy level, are shared by other audiovisual and electronic
media. This section will deal with advantages that films alone offer.

16MM FILM AND FILM IN GENERAL

Film can be used for large audiences without sacrificing clarity or
sound. It creates real or imagined events with great attention to detail,
and is a mode of communication that stimulates the intellect with
multisensory appeals. It gains attention easily, influences attitudes,
especially when its images are larger than life, and has enormous power
over children.

Film has developed highly sophisticated special effects and animation technology that permit the visualization of otherwise unseeable

material. Before film, there were no time-lapse photography, slow motion, closeups, flashbacks, pixillation, talking clay figures, sound effects, pinboard animation—no Donald Duck or E. T., no journeys through the aorta, no kung-fu movies, and many fewer public devils, monsters, creatures, killers, ghouls, aliens, and vigilantes.

Film offers visual historical and news documentation of dynamic events unavailable elsewhere between about 1893 and 1948. It has evolved into a variety of genres analogous to literary styles: westerns, musicals, documentary, promotional, cartoon, film noir, thriller, etc. Film draws on its own history and traditions for appeal and power. A film today is almost always seen within the context of film history and production (and often unconsciously compared to television), which causes it to be trusted and accepted as a natural part of a culture's group identity and artifacts. It provides the largest number of non-theatrical titles of all visual media, as well as the largest number of libraries and distributors of audiovisual media. Film comes in a great variety of raw stock for shooting in all kinds of situations. With a "film chain," it can be projected via television.

Compared to 8mm and super-8mm film, 16mm film has a higher-quality picture and sound, a much larger picture, and is better suited to long running.

8MM AND SUPER-8MM FILM

The projectors and cameras for this format are lighter, simpler to operate, much cheaper, and more portable than those for 16mm film. The film is also much cheaper. Both film and equipment require less storage space. Projection cartridges facilitate easy operation, and the film user can usually work the projector alone. This is a personalized format, designed for individual and small-group use and production, ideally used in beginning courses in film production, as well as for quick, simple documentation (local history), home movies, and experimentation. Inexpensive home video outfits have begun to replace it.

On 8mm and super-8mm film, magnetic soundtracks can be added later and easily erased, if necessary. Sound can be directly recorded onto the film, while shooting. Laboratories can easily reduce 16mm film to super-8mm film gauge. This medium is best suited to single-concept presentations: short, repeatable films on one topic or procedure.

FILM LOOPS

Film loops are used easily and quickly, the user often operating the projector alone and independently. Rewinding, threading, and film handling are unnecessary and the projector can't be loaded improperly. The viewer, of course, can repeat the program as often as desired.

Loops can be easily stopped and continued another time, and can be used hundreds of times with little wear (if properly lubricated). Single-concept presentations can be repeated as many times as necessary to get the message or lesson across. Silent loops encourage audience involvement. Some projectors permit advancement of single frames.

Film loops can be used in public places without human monitoring, or as self-instructional tools in private carrels.

Disadvantages

16MM FILM AND FILM IN GENERAL

The many disadvantages of using film are a reflection of its ubiquitousness. Many films are simply too long to accommodate the optimal attention span (20 minutes for nonfeature films). The imagery or data in even a recently released film is usually at least one or two years old. Many titles are unavailable or very difficult to access or borrow; others are very expensive to rent.

Color dyes fade with time and heat, particularly in films made after 1951. Special viewing conditions are usually necessary: a well-darkened room, a good sound system, enough seats, a projectionist.

The film's message must be experienced (except in rare cases) in one, continuous sitting. Rarely do viewers or students get a second or third screening, even when it would be advantageous. Many film programmers, also, don't preview their films.

It's hard to take notes during screening, and hard to stop films on a frame, to rewind, or to fast-forward films. Often films are substituted for teaching or speaking, in an effort to keep and please a captive audience. In this way, resentment is sometimes built up against a film.

Films easily lend themselves to stereotyped usage ("for education"), description ("a nature film"), and evaluation ("it's offensive"). They're often seen as panaceas for boredom. Many still use "talking heads," which bore many viewers.

Rarely can only one or two persons view a film; screening areas aren't set up for it. Film presenters sometimes simply project films without regard for group dynamics.

Many nonfiction films over ten years old look dated and lose their appeal, even when they deserve attention. The camera ages the image, but purchasing fresh film can become hard to justify.

Special effects may be confusing to naive viewers and can distort information or the purpose of the film. Other viewers are satisfied *only* by special effects.

Many people are usually required to produce a 16mm film, calling for great coordination and scheduling. Film is very perishable and damageable; so are projectors, which are often hard for a neophyte to operate. 16mm hardware, film, and production are much more expensive than in any other audiovisual format.

In addition, expensive storage, care, and delivery charges are required. Film collection and services are especially sensitive to economic/budgeting factors, as well as to trends in education, politics, and cultural priorities (e.g., for video).

Finally, the use, advantages, and disadvantages of film are easily confused with video programming.

8MM AND SUPER-8MM FILM

This format is not suited to large audiences generally, and offers limited image definition and sound clarity. The film content has limited scope and style (unless it's merely converted from larger formats or feature films). Magnetic soundtracks can be unintentionally erased. Much 8mm hardware is for silent film, which may restricte the type of film you use or purchase.

There are many incompatibilities between films, cartridges/loops, and projectors. There is now a diminishing interest in these formats by the public and by schools, due mostly to the limits of 8mm production and the growth of easily operated video equipment and narrow-gauge videotape.

FILM LOOPS

Loops are difficult to repair and subject to very high wear, requiring frequent lubrication. Many projectors can't stop or reverse the film, or go to slow motion. It's hard to edit material out of closed cartridges. Loops offer a limited range of subjects, concepts, and titles. Viewers must often watch the loop to the end before they can see a desired section repeated. If the film is removed from the projector before it's over, the next user will first have to see it to the end, before it begins.

SELECTION

Special Criteria

The basic criteria for deciding what films to use, rent, or purchase are similar to those applied to any medium. There are probably as many sets of selection guidelines as there are film managers or critics, and most basic texts on film use cover the issue in some detail. Like most evaluative processes, film selection has objective and subjective components. Issues of content and technical quality are usually objective;

issues of film utilization and ambience are more subjective. Many judgments, of course, combine taste, experience, pragmatism, and various formal guidelines.

An overriding issue in film selection is suitability to the intended audience. Factors of sex, age, special interests, and political, religious, and educational background must usually be considered, and considered before other factors. And you must know *why* you are using the film: to entertain, stimulate, provoke, instruct, divert, soothe, mobilize, etc. If you don't know why, don't be surprised if your audience is confused.

The technical aspects of the film's production must be known and evaluated, including:

Script or concept, quality of writing, narrative style.

Organization or continuity of ideas: the story.

Direction. You should be able to recognize strong and weak direction, the "talking heads" style, a film's impersonality, bias, honesty.

Cinematography, including special effects, animation, graphics, subtitles, use of color, suitability to size of the screen.

Sound, whether music, speech, effects, multitracks—or the absence of sound.

Performance, including narration, voice quality, clarity, hidden effect, authority.

Editing, which can be seamless, arty, jumpy, monotonous, conservative, old-fashioned, stimulating, etc.

Know whether motion itself is used effectively on screen, or whether little happens, and how this affects content.

To evaluate the content of a film, input from others who know the story, subject, or genre is recommended. With them, you will be able to get a good idea as to whether the style of presentation, the choice of imagery, is suited to the subject or message, or whether another style would be more effective.

If the presentation is obscure, the obscurity may be essential to the message. Trust your instincts. If the style is creative, experimental, or radical, it may or may not interfere with the message. If the film is instructional, you must decide on the accuracy or truthfulness of the facts. This can be difficult and may require experience or training: the media are powerful persuaders. If you are left feeling bored, confused, prejudiced, tricked, or drained, these are good indicators of a film's approach to truth.

Some content can be presented only by motion pictures. Your audience will want to know this, especially if the film is a rare or unique document. If the film is not the best medium for the subject, you may want to explore the alternatives, but first you must know them.

Let the prospective film user or instructor tell you what they want to do with the film. Together, you will then be able to decide who is the best audience, how this compares with the intended audience, and whether the film's appeal will be too narrow or specialized. Many films have multidisciplinary or multi-audience potential. Some films assume an interest or background knowledge; others stimulate or create it. The same subject may have a very different treatment in several films, some communicating chiefly by sight or sound, others using sophisticated editing, lighting, multisoundtracks, animation, etc.

Not all instructional films need offer something new. Many films, of course, will lead to other activities: a lesson, discussion, game, or the viewer's own production of a film.

The gray area of ambience taps the film user's own reactions, experience with film (and the other arts), and knowledge of film production. The effective film manager must feel comfortable understanding how a film makes him or her feel and whether the user will share these feelings. Don't be afraid to share your responses to a film with potential users: they are often a great source of information, as long as you respect the user's (possibly very different) reactions.

The direction, writing, acting, or editing may be sophisticated or deliberately naive, heavy or light, careless, pompous, slow, rushed, self-indulgent, restrained, pretentious, etc. Learn the art of describing and inducing reactions to a film. Develop a familiarity with film's many genres. Not all films are works of art: without being told, can you recognize one that is? A film's ambience should lead you to ask whether it appeals primarily to emotion, reason, or imagination (or all three), or whether it will be worth seeing in five or fifteen years.

How you develop and use your film budget will depend on who your users are and the nature of your facility. Whether a film should be rented, leased, or purchased—or bought as a video cassette—will depend on how often it is used and by whom, whether it will be hopelessly dated in five or ten years, what your sources of film acquisition are, and on who is doing the projection. The size of the audience, the importance of image size and clarity, the need to stop or slow the film or replay it, will be factors in deciding on film versus video. Videos, of course, require less storage space, less stringent storage conditions, and are less vulnerable to damage. Most videos are much less expensive than their film counterparts (especially feature films), and many films are now available *only* on video.

A film's frequent use may require frequent repair, rejuvenation, or replacement. Always inspect newly rented or purchased films for damage and color fading. You should not pay for a damaged film. In budgeting, do not be afraid to decide, or to persuade a user, that other, less expensive media may be as effective as film. Explore the many free loan sources: businesses, fire and police departments, hospitals, schools, foreign embassies, and civic groups. To justify your budget, you should have enough projectors, speakers, screens, seats, and maintenance contracts or personnel to warrant expensive rentals or purchases. No film service will be effective without excellent hardware and personnel to back it up.

Whenever possible, films for potential acquisition, and in some instances rental, should be previewed. Often the film distributor will offer a free preview for purchase consideration (if in doubt, inquire), sometimes with an option to keep the print; others charge a minimal fee. Many films can be previewed on television, at film festivals and conferences, and at community events.

Rarely should only one person preview a film if a decision on it is required. A small group of knowledgeable, interested users makes an ideal committee. In some cases, where the film user/buyer knows the work of the filmmaker, or the line of a distributor, he or she may *not* need to preview a title.

Creative interpretation of distributors' catalogs and brochures is recommended, and will tell the experienced selector what he or she needs to know. It is not impossible to evaluate a film intelligently after seeing only 25 percent of it.

There are still many legitimate uses for 8mm and super-8mm film, and you should understand this medium. The cinematography should be appropriate to the content: a small image can't do what a larger one can. Too much shouldn't happen on the screen; many closeups will lose in clarity. Sound and image must be well synchronized. You should know whether to buy silent or sound, optical or magnetic soundtrack film, and whether your audience is familiar with the elements of 8mm filmmaking. You should know when to buy open reel films, film in projection cartridges, or film loops. If you use film loops, the cartridge must be compatible with your projector. It should be durable, easy to repair or replace, and should contain a film lubricant to protect it through frequent use. If you use a single-concept film, the concept should be sufficiently narrowed, and presented clearly and without frills.

Careful attention must be paid to selecting projectors and, to a lesser extent, screens, as successful film utilization depends on the performance of equipment. Projectors may be evaluated by personal inspection, by examining the repair record, by listening to word of mouth, by reading evaluative reports (such as those in *Library Tech-*

nology Reports), by reading catalogs (such as the *Audio-Visual Equipment Directory*), or by talking to sales representatives at conventions and inspecting their displays. In selecting a projector, you must consider the kind of film you are planning to use, the auditorium or room size, how often the projector will be used, your maintenance budget and access to repair persons on and off premises, and who the projector operators may be.

Among the most important factors in selecting projectors are noise of operation, weight, sound quality and ease of operating controls, lamp life and replaceability, whether manual or self-threading, access to the film in midreel (if you need to unthread it), fast-forward and reverse capabilities, safety of operation, convertibility to silent speed (18 fps), focal length of the projector lens (most 16mm projectors have 50mm lenses), ability to freeze-frame safely, and storage area for the cord.

The important factors in selecting 8mm and super-8mm projectors are compatibility with the film cartridge(s) to be used, focal length of the projector lens (which affects the size of the projected image over distance), zoom lens, ease of operation (especially if users will work alone with the film), sound mode, type of projection lamp, and automatic threading capability. The most complete coverage of all aspects of super-8mm hardware may be found in *The Super 8 Book,* by Lenny Lipton.

Projection screens should be chosen according to which film gauge will most often be used, the size and darkness of the screening area, power of the projection lamp, focal length of the projector lens, proportion of viewers who will sit to the sides of the screen, and the purpose for using the film. There is a choice among beaded, matte, lenticular, and super-bright front-projection screens; all have different capacities for image accuracy, brightness, color transmission, and side-view clarity.

Rear-projection units or systems may also be chosen (the audience does not see the projection setup, only the screen), and are especially useful for viewing areas that are confined or difficult to darken completely, as well as for single-concept loops shown on portable viewers.

Evaluative Review Sources

These are works that assess a film's content, technique, or importance, usually to guide potential viewers or users. Judgements may be strong or merely implied. The act of writing about a film makes it difficult to exclude one's personal response completely, however subtle. But the response of a respected evaluator can be a valuable aid in choosing what to show.

PERIODICALS AND SERIALS

American Film
Arts and Humanities Citation Index. (This is also available online, as a computerized data base.)
Audio Visual
Audio Visual Journal
Audio-Visual Communications
Audiovisual Librarian
Booklist
Choice
Cineaste
Cinema/Canada
Classic Images
Communications Information (computerized data base)
Film & History
Film Comment
Film Culture
Film Library Quarterly (recently discontinued)
Film Video News
Film Quarterly
Films & Filming
Films in Review
Instructional Innovator
Jump Cut: A Review of Contemporary Cinema
Library Journal
Library Technology Reports
Literature/Film Quarterly
MLA International Bibliography (also available online, as a computerized data base)
Media & Methods
Media Digest
Media Review
New York Times Film Reviews
Previews (discontinued)
Review of the Arts: Film and Television (also online)
School Library Journal
Science Books and Films
Sight and Sound
Sightlines
Variety

BOOKS

Alvarez, Max Joseph, ed. *Index to Motion Pictures Reviewed by Variety 1907–1980.* Metuchen, N.J.: Scarecrow, 1982.

Artel, Linda, and Susan Wengraf. *Positive Images: Non-Sexist Films for Young People.* San Francisco: Booklegger, 1976.

Barnouw, Erik. *Documentary: A History of the Non-Fiction Film.* New York: Oxford Univ. Pr., 1983.

Batty, Linda, comp. *Retrospective Index to Film Periodicals.* New York: Bowker, 1975.

Brown, Lucy Gregor. *Core Media Collection for Elementary Schools.* New York: Bowker, 1978.

———. *Core Media Collection for Secondary Schools.* New York: Bowker, 1979.

Catalogue of British Film Institute Productions 1951–1976. London: British Film Institute, 1977.

Cyr, Helen W. *A Filmography of the Third World.* Metuchen, N.J.: Scarecrow, 1976.

DeGrazia, Edward, and Roger K. Newman. *Banned Films: Movies, Censors & the First Amendment.* New York: Bowker, 1982.

EFLA Evaluations. New York, Educational Film Library Assn.

Emmons, Carole A. *Short Stories on Film.* Littleton, Colo.: Libraries Unlimited, 1978.

Film Evaluation Guide. New York: Educational Film Library Assn., 1965.

———. *Supplement.* New York: Educational Film Library Assn., 1968.

Film Review Annual. Englewood, N.J.: Jerome S. Ozer, 1983.

Gaffney, Maureen. *More Films Kids Like.* Chicago: American Library Assn., 1977.

———. *What to Do When the Lights Go On.* Phoenix: Oryx Pr., 1981.

Goldman, Eric A., and Nama Frenkel. "Audio-Visual Materials on the Holocaust." In *The Holocaust: An Annotated Bibliography and Resource Guide,* ed. David M. Szonyi. Hoboken, N.J.: Ktav Publishing House and National Jewish Resource Center, 1985.

Gordon, Malcolm W. *Discovery in Film, Book Two: A Teacher Sourcebook.* New York: Paulist Pr., 1973.

Hardy, Phil. *The Western.* New York: William Morrow, 1983.

———, ed. *Science Fiction.* New York: William Morrow, 1984.

Heider, Karl G. *Films for Anthropological Teaching.* Washington, D.C.: American Anthropological Assn., 1977.

Heyer, Robert J., and Anthony Meyer. *Discovery in Film.* Paramus, N.J.: Paulist Pr., 1969.

Holt, Carol Lou, comp. *Annotated Film Bibliography: Child Development and Early Childhood Education.* St. Louis: Child Day Care Assn. of St. Louis, n.d.

Hunt, Mary Alice, ed. *A Multimedia Approach to Children's Literature.* Chicago: American Library Assn., 1983.

Landers Film Reviews. Los Angeles, Landers Assn.

Langer, Lawrence L. "The Americanization of the Holocaust." In *From Hester Street to Hollywood,* ed. Sarah Blacher Cohen. Bloomington: Indiana Univ. Pr., 1983.

Lee, Rohama, ed. *The Film News Omnibus, Vol. 1.* New York: Film News, 1973.

———. *The Film News Omnibus, Vol. 2.* New York: Film News, 1979.

Limbacher, James L. *Sexuality in World Cinema.* Metuchen, N.J.: Scarecrow, 1983.

Loy, Jane M., ed. *Latin America: Sights and Sounds.* Gainesville, Fla.: Latin American Studies Assn., 1973 (CLASP Publication No. 5).

Maltin, Leonard. *Of Mice and Magic.* New York: New American Library, 1980.

———. *TV Movies, 1985–1986 Edition.* New York: New American Library, 1984.

Manchel, Frank. *Film Study: A Reference Guide.* Rutherford, N.J.: Fairleigh Dickinson Univ. Pr., 1973.

Maynard, Richard A. *The Celluloid Curriculum.* New York: Hayden, 1971.

Neher, Jack, ed. *Current Audiovisuals for Mental Health Education.* Chicago: Marquis Academic Media, 1979.

Ohrn, Steven, and Rebecca Riley. *Africa from Real to Reel.* Waltham, Mass.: African Studies Assn. of Brandeis Univ., 1976.

Parker, Barry M. *The Folger Shakespeare Filmography*. Washington, D.C.: Folger Books, 1979.

Parlato, Salvatore. *Films Too Good for Words*. New York: Bowker, 1973.

————. *Superfilms: An International Guide to Award-Winning Educational Films*. Metuchen, N.J.: Scarecrow, 1976.

Peyton, Patricia, ed. *Reel Change: A Guide to Social Issue Films*. San Francisco: Film Fund, 1979.

Rice, Susan. *Films Kids Like*. Chicago: American Library Assn., 1973.

Schrank, Jeffrey. *Media in Value Education: A Critical Guide*. Chicago: Argus, 1970.

Seltz-Petrash, Ann, ed. *AAAS Science Film Catalog*. Washington, D.C.: American Assn. for the Advancement of Science, and New York: Bowker, 1975.

Slide, Anthony. *Films on Film History*. Metuchen, N.J.: Scarecrow, 1979.

Stanley, John. *The Creature Features Movie Guide*. Pacifica, Calif.: Creatures at Large, 1981.

Stephenson, Ralph. *The Animated Film*. New York: A. S. Barnes, 1973.

Sullivan, Kaye. *Films For, By and About Women*. Metuchen, N.J.: Scarecrow, 1980.

Weatherford, Elizabeth, ed. *Native Americans on Film and Video*. New York: Museum of the American Indian, 1981.

Weldon, Michael. *The Psychotronic Encyclopedia of Film*. New York: Ballantine, 1983.

Worsnop, Brenda M., and Chris M. Worsnop. *The Film User's Guide to Canadian Short Films, Vol. 1*. Mississauga, Ont.: Wright Communications, 1979.

Youngblood, Gene. *Expanded Cinema*. New York: Dutton, 1970.

Sources of Sources

In this section, works are listed which lead the reader either to evaluative and nonevaluative sources, or to sources of film distribution, equipment suppliers, or film information.

AFI Factfile. Frederick, Md.: University Publications of America, 1984.

Allen, Nancy. *Film Study Collections*. New York: Frederick Ungar, 1979.

Armour, Robert A. *Film: A Reference Guide*. Westport, Conn.: Greenwood Pr., 1980.

Audiovisual Market Place. New York, Bowker (annual).

Educational Media Yearbook. Littleton, Colo., Libraries Unlimited (annual).

Film Literature Index. Albany, Filmdex (quarterly with annual cumulations).

Gaffney, Maureen, and Gerry Bond Laybourne. *What to Do When the Lights Go On*. Phoenix: Oryx Pr., 1981.

Hoffer, Thomas W. *Animation*. Westport, Conn.: Greenwood Pr., 1981.

International Index to Film Periodicals. London, Federation Internationale des Archives du Film (annual).

Limbacher, James L. "It All Started with D. W. Griffith." *Serials Librarian* 7 (Summer 1983): 67–75.

———. *A Reference Guide to Audiovisual Information.* New York: Bowker, 1972.

Maltin, Leonard, ed. *The Whole Film Sourcebook.* New York: New American Library, 1983.

Manchel, Frank. *Film Study: A Resource Guide.* Rutherford, N.J.: Fairleigh Dickinson Univ. Pr., 1973.

Media Review Digest (formerly *Multi Media Reviews Index*).

Osborne, C. W., ed. *International Yearbook of Educational and Instructional Technology.* New York, Nichols Publishing Co. (annual).

Rehrauer, George. *The Cinema Booklist.* Metuchen, N.J.: Scarecrow, 1972 (*Supplement,* 1974).

———. *The Film User's Handbook.* New York: Bowker, 1975.

———. *Macmillan Film Bibliography.* New York: Macmillan, 1982.

Rowan, Bonnie G. *Scholars' Guide to Washington, DC Film and Video Collections.* Washington, D.C.: Smithsonian Institution Pr., 1980.

Sheahan, Eileen. *Moving Pictures.* New York: A. S. Barnes, 1979.

Sive, Mary Robinson. *Selecting Instructional Media.* Littleton, Colo.: Libraries Unlimited, 1978.

University and College Film Collections: A Directory. New York: Educational Film Library Assn., 1974.

Weaver, Kathleen, ed. *Film Programmer's Guide to 16mm Rentals.* Albany, Calif.: Reel Research, 1980.

Weber, Olga S., comp. *North American Film and Video Directory.* New York: Bowker, 1976.

Nonevaluative Sources

Nonevaluative sources presumably offer no judgment of the materials they present. They are useful chiefly in three ways: they give an idea of what is available on a given subject or genre; they suggest usable materials to those interested mainly in topical coverage; and they suggest titles to be previewed or researched in an evaluative source. Unless a work offers simply a title and a very brief description of a film, it may not be wholly nonevaluative. Descriptions longer than 25 words often imply evaluative information, since the process of translating a film into words is somewhat subjective. Distributor and university catalogs fall into this category.

Following is a list of the basic nonevaluative sources. Others will be found in the "Sources of Sources" section.

Audio-Visual Equipment Directory. Fairfax, Va.: NAVA, the International Communications Industries Assn. (latest ed.)

Audiovisual Materials (Library of Congress Catalogs). Washington, D.C., Library of Congress (quarterly).

AVLINE (Audiovisuals Online). A computerized data base.

British National Film Catalogue. London, British Film Institute (quarterly).

Buteau, June D. *Nonprint Materials on Communication.* Metuchen, N.J.: Scarecrow, 1976.

Canadian Center for Films on Art. *Films on Art.* New York: Watson-Guptill Publications, 1977.

Curione, Maryann, comp. *The Visualization of Anthropology.* University Park, Pa.: Penn State Univ. Audio-Visual Services, 1984.

Daniel, Ronald S. *Human Sexuality Methods and Materials for the Education, Family Life and Health Professions.* Brea, Calif.: Heuristicus Publishing Co., 1979.

Diffor, John C., and Elaine N. Diffor, eds. *Educators' Guide to Free Films.* Randolph, Wis., Educators' Progress Service (annual).

Educational Film/Video Locator. 3rd ed. New York: Bowker, 1986.

Enser, A. G. S. *Filmed Books and Plays.* Lexington, Mass.: Lexington Books, 1985.

Film File 1984–1985. 4th ed. Minneapolis: Media Referral Service, 1984.

Fox, Stuart. *Jewish Films in the United States.* Boston: Hall, 1976.

Graham, Cooper C., et al. *D. W. Griffith and the Biograph Company.* Metuchen, N.J.: Scarecrow, 1985.

Green, Debbie, comp. *Guide to the Collection of the Film Library of the Canadian Institute.* Ottawa: Canadian Film Institute, 1984.

Jones, Emily Strange, ed. *The College Film Library Collection: 16mm Films.* Williamsport, Pa.: Bro-Dart Publishing Co., 1971.

Kone, Grace Ann, ed. *The College Film Library Collection: 8mm Films and 35mm Filmstrips.* Williamsport, Pa.: Bro-Dart Publishing Co., 1971.

——. *8mm Film Directory.* New York: Educational Film Library Assn., 1969.

Limbacher, James L., ed. *Feature Films.* New York, Bowker (biennial).

McClintock, Marsha Hamilton. *The Middle East and North Africa on Film.* New York: Garland, 1982.

Marill, Alvin H. *Movies Made for Television: The Telefeature and the Mini-series 1964–1984.* New York: New York Zoetrope, 1984.

Morris, Peter. *The Film Companion: A Comprehensive Guide to More than 650 Canadian Films and Filmmakers.* Toronto: Irwin Publishing, 1984.

NICEM Guides. Los Angeles, National Information Center for Educational Media (updated irregularly). Series includes:
Index to Black History and Studies—Multimedia
Index to 8mm Motion Cartridges
Index to Environmental Studies—Multimedia
Index to Health and Safety—Multimedia
Index to Nonprint Special Education Materials—Multimedia
Index to Producers and Distributors
Index to Psychology—Multimedia
Index to 16mm Educational Films
Index to Vocational and Technical Education—Multimedia

(Films in the NICEM indexes can also be searched online, on NICEM's computerized data base.)

Niver, Kemp R. *Early Motion Pictures: The Paper Print Collection in the Library of Congress.* Washington, D.C.: Library of Congress Motion Picture, Broadcasting, and Recorded Sound Division, 1985.

Parlato, Salvatore J. *Films Ex Libris.* Jefferson, N.C.: McFarland, 1980.

Reference List of Audiovisual Materials Produced by the United States Government. Washington, D.C.: National Audiovisual Center, 1978 (and 1980 *Supplement*).

Reid, Alison, ed. *Film Canadiana 1979–80.* Ottawa: Canadian Film Institute, 1980.

Sahara, Penelope. *Media Resources for Gerontology.* Ann Arbor: Institute of Gerontology at the University of Michigan, 1977.

Sprecher, Daniel. *Guide to Government Loan Films—16mm.* Alexandria, Va.: Serina Pr., 1980.

Video Source Book. Syosset, N.Y., National Video Clearinghouse (latest ed.)

Weiner, Janet. *How to Organize and Run a Film Society.* New York: Macmillan, 1973.

Winick, Mariann P. *Films for Childhood Educators.* Washington, D.C.: Association for Childhood Education International, 1977.

CATALOGS AND ''FILMOGRAPHIES''

Nonevaluative information may be found in many noncommercially published catalogs. Among the best sources for such catalogs are:

Museums (e.g., the Museum of Modern Art)

Colleges and universities (some of the large film libraries are at Kent State, University of Indiana, Penn State, University of Illinois, University of California at Berkeley)

Major commercial distributors (e.g., Time-Life Video, Films Inc., Budget Films, CRM/McGraw-Hill, Pyramid, Perspective, National Film Board of Canada, Swank)

Specialty distributors (e.g., Resolution/California Newsreel, New Day Films, Cambridge Documentary Films, Research Press, Appalshop, National Geographic, Picture Start)

Local libraries, schools, and cooperatives

''Filmographies,'' lists, and guides are also published—by public libraries, public health and civic organizations, institutes of science, churches, and government agencies. Many professional journals, such as *Film Library Quarterly, Sightlines,* and *School Library Journal,* regularly publish filmographies as well.

MAINTENANCE AND MANAGEMENT

Storage

Films in active collections should be stored at 69 °F (20 °C) ± 1 °, and at 50 °F or lower for long-term storage. Fluctuating temperatures can cause damage. Color fading of Eastmancolor film can be retarded by storing it at 33 °F and 30–40% relative humidity.

Active film collections should be stored at a relative humidity of 30–50%. Very low humidity produces brittleness; over 60% RH promotes mold, shrinkage, and color imbalance.

Store films on an intermediate floor to avoid extremes of temperature and humidity. Use monitoring devices, and air conditioning and dehumidifiers if necessary, as well as smoke and heat detectors.

Use tungsten or fluorescent light tubes, with outer ultraviolet filter sleeves, to avoid light radiation damage. Never store films near direct sunlight.

Reels should be metal and large enough to leave at least ½ inch of space from the edge of the reel to the fully wound film. Reels should be stored in film cans, either plastic or metal, depending on heat and handling. Bent, chipped, or scratched reels will disfigure films.

Most films should be stored on shelves in slitted racks, with space between the reels, at least 6 inches from the floor. Air must circulate freely between reels, shelves, and cabinets. If cans are stored lying flat, no more than eight should be atop one another.

To avoid unnecessary moving of films, store them by accession number (if feasible) so that each film has its own reserved space.

Never keep old, nitrate-base films near acetate-base films. The nitrate base is highly flammable and can chemically deteriorate acetate bases. Never store nitrate-base film in closed containers, or without ventilation.

Films destined for long-term storage and minimal retrieval may undergo conditioned film storage, a process which stabilizes the moisture content of the film in a controlled atmosphere, then seals it in a metal can.

Magnetic soundtrack film should not be stored near a permanent magnet or an electric wire carrying a heavy current.

Care

Try not to touch the film surface—with anything. This is the number-one rule. Fingers are oily and hard objects are abrasive. The projector and the film should be the same temperature before screening; so give them time to warm up from cold storage. Unclean or damaged projector parts will damage films. Make certain the film is wound on the reel correctly (the signs of incorrectly wound films are illustrated in the books mentioned at the end of this section). For most 16mm sound film, the sprocket holes are on the right, and the film comes down over the top of the reel, pointing clockwise. Leaders of contrasting color, at the film's head and tail, should be 5 feet long, and marked to identify the position and the film.

Ideally, films should be inspected and cleaned (usually by machine) after each use or loan and before the first projection of a new film. Follow the directions for operating these machines very closely. Lubricating film is a more complex operation, recommended especially for endless-loop cartridges. If you're cleaning and lubricating film yourself, allow adequate ventilation and drying time before the film is rewound. Some cleaning solutions can destroy magnetic sound tracks; so check this out on a sample of the film. Use a soft, lintless, white cloth, free of fabric fillers, to dry film. And remember: Film cleaning will *not* remove scratches.

REPAIR
Become familiar with the types of film damage: torn sprocket holes, color shifting, blistering, creasing, emulsion scratches, brittleness, shrinkage. Learn the common signs of films improperly wound on reels (often the result of the reel's being bent): curl, spoking, buckle, twist, fluting. Discard badly bent reels.

Broken or damaged film should be repaired as soon as possible, and never used while broken. Splicing may be done by cement or by a variety of tapes and tabs, perforated or unperforated (some splicing machines will perforate the tape as it splices the film). Cement should not be used with ESTAR base film, since it won't hold. Scotch or masking tape should not be used, even temporarily. No part of the splicing tape should jut over the edge of the film. Don't use old cement. Cement splices will take several hours to reach full binding strength.

Become familiar with the causes of poor splices: scraping too little emulsion or binder from the film surface; allowing insufficient drying time; scraping the base unnecessarily; taking too long to bring the spliced ends together after applying the cement; aligning the splicer poorly. Follow the splicing directions accompanying splicing kits and machines to the letter.

8mm and super-8mm cartridge films and film loops are usually sent to the distributor or a lab for repair and lubrication.

Certain types of mild film damage (e.g., light scratches) can be repaired by film rejuvenation in a lab, if it is done well. Fine emulsion and base scratches can be controlled, and most sprocket hole damages repaired. The results of such treatment, though, are only temporary.

You should use caution in deciding whether to rejuvenate a film: it can be expensive, take some time, and different labs do different-quality work. Compare costs from several labs, and have sample work done. Potentially fading color film may be preserved by several techniques that are expensive and generally impractical: through black-and-white separation, cold storage, holography, and copying onto videotape or videodisc. Otherwise, there is virtually no way yet to halt the sometimes swift (5 years) fading of color in Eastmancolor film (which produces those purple and blue movies we see on television). This can affect your decision to purchase and collect color films, as well as your decision to invest in storage, repair, and replacement.

By far the most thorough coverage of film storage and care may be found in Kodak Publication No. H-23, *The Book of Film Care* (Rochester, N.Y.: Eastman Kodak Co., 1983), and in Craig A. Jones' *16mm Motion Picture Film Maintenance Manual* (Dubuque, Ia.: Kendall/ Hunt Publishing Co., 1983).

Management Problems and Solutions

Many claims are made about film; for example, they have an unusually high educational value; they persuade and influence people; they motivate people; they hinder the development of literacy; they can reduce the "failure attitude" some people have toward printed material. Supporters and detractors are easy to find, so a question remains for the film manager or user: Are these claims, or any one of them, true? Judgment on these issues will be affected by one's reading and education, one's experience with using film, one's knowledge of human behavior, one's literacy and reading interests, and how many films one sees. Proponents of media make strong claims for media as a whole, although computers and home video currently head their priorities.

The enormous power of film to attract audiences convinces many that this power is dangerous or unlimited. Many educators, having seen reading fail to attract students, look to the media, and to film, to draw them to the print sources. Other educators blame reading failure on the media, as technology and/or content, and especially television. Many today confuse television programming with film content and format, though we use the two quite differently.

As with any philosophical issue, those most affected by it must make up their own minds what to believe, and commit themselves to at least a temporary resolution of the issue, to avoid further distraction. One's particular type of involvement with film—as buyer, distributor, programmer—will determine much of the orientation toward a resolution.

The choice of which guidelines or criteria to use when selecting films is never inflexible. (The issue is discussed in the section "Special Criteria for Selection.") But even though clear guidelines can be articulated, the matter is often open-ended, subjective, and subject to extraneous pressures. A film's popularity can be a factor, regardless of quality. Quality itself may be a matter of direction, acting, editing, creativity, truthfulness, persuasiveness—though rarely will all these factors be excellent in one film. Response by critics, a film's reputation, and its place in history may need to be considered.

Potential film users may want or have to be involved in film selection, regardless of their expertise. How potential users should be involved in selection can be a sticky issue (though it is relevant to any medium). Sometimes *all* films can be previewed, though it's not always necessary. Who the previewers will be may be a political decision. A community's pressure to show or not to show a film may have to be reckoned with.

Whatever the factors, film selection will vary with experience, and is a source of continuing stimulation to film managers and users. Using rigid guidelines or a single selection criterion will severely restrict the scope and usefulness of a film collection, program, or service.

In using films, you may have to decide *not* to use certain genres, topics, or stories. This is never an easy decision. As with all media, the most obvious problem areas concern pornography and political and religious advocacy (unless special-interest groups are seeking these particular areas). A film manager or user should know his or her audience or clientele well, should understand something about group (and film-viewing) behavior, and must have a clear idea of *why* a particular film is shown. Discussion of the film before or after screening may be appropriate, and the programmer should be prepared to defend his or her choice of film.

The policies and interests of a film manager's parent institution (if any) will have some sway. Whether or not the film user takes a hard line on these matters, the manager should take the time to think them through and be willing to discuss them with all interested film viewers.

You may often have to decide whether to purchase, lease, or rent a film. Of course, many films can't be purchased or leased, except on video, and those that can may be prohibitively expensive. The film manager must consider the nature of the parent collection or institution, and there are many factors affecting such a decision. A film may be used only occasionally, or several times a week. It may lose its effectiveness after two years, or be useful for twenty years. Your film service may be large and rich, or cramped and impoverished; you may have lots of help, or have to do it all yourself, including repairs.

In the long run, owning a film saves money over continuously renting it, unless frequent updating, or a need for multiple copies, are factors. If a film is to be rented or leased (which means owning it, in effect, for a limited period), the various prices and loan conditions of distributors should be investigated. Some films have several distributors; others are distributed only by their creators. Some distributors won't allow you to show your film off premises. The least expensive distributors are usually university film libraries (because of their nonprofit status). Owning or having access to many distributors' catalogs, as well as to source indexes and filmographies, will help you decide to buy or rent, and from whom to buy or rent. And remember, many films are available free of charge through public libraries, corporations, foreign embassies, government agencies, hospitals, professional groups, and public service organizations.

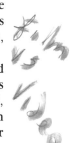

Today, when film managers often must decide whether to buy films or videotapes of films, a trend is developing to buy (and display) everything on video cassette. Many public libraries have demonstrated enormous circulation of feature films on video, as more and more patrons acquire VCRs. Generally, video is less expensive than film, less easily damaged, shows less color fading, is easier to store and replace, and is easier to use than film. So why use film?

Films transferred to video are sometimes poorly transferred, and flaws appear in the image. Their "aspect ratio" may be altered. Sides and tops of films may be cut off. Subtitles may be very difficult to read, or unavailable. Many video releases are more freely edited or cut than the original film. Color is never as sharp. Sound on video monitor speakers is often inferior. Very old films often project poorly on a television screen. And rarely does a television audience become a community. Serious lovers and students of film will be aware of all these factors. Film on celluloid simply presents a better (cleaner, sharper) picture and (so far) sound quality than video, is better suited to large audiences and to the special feeling that accompanies theatrical display.

Many more titles, old movies, subjects, genres, and animations are available on film than on video, and the ambience of a film image—its size, context, sharpness, surrounding darkness—strongly differs from a video image and affects response. The makeup and size of your audience, your budget and storage space, your need for original film imagery, your need to purchase or rent—all will guide you in deciding this issue. The availability and cost of film versus video projection equipment must also be considered.

Many have questioned whether a film library or service needs a specifically trained manager—an audiovisual librarian, a librarian of any kind, a media "expert." The trend is toward specialization and professionalization. However, many institutions have used nonspecialized librarians, nonlibrarians, and nonprofessionals to manage their operations successfully. Film management is less conventionalized than print management and thus (so far) requires a less formalized training background and management style. However, the special expertise necessary for understanding and programming films; for handling projection, storage, and repair procedures; for managing audiences; for knowing the selection, marketing, production, and distribution techniques; and for promoting the unique benefits of film use—all often require a film specialist for optimum management.

Many institutions may have employment guidelines that will settle the matter. Most books and standards of media management recommend having at least one "professional." But the purpose of the film collection or service, its history, the kind of parent institution, and the typical audience will finally determine the level of expertise and authority necessary.

There is little doubt that films should be cataloged, but how to do it is still open to question, for there are many useful systems. Film cataloging efforts have never matched those made on behalf of printed matter: their storage, retrieval patterns, circulation patterns, history, content, and intellectual structure differ strongly. Questions of authorship, subject, and publisher are approached differently with film than with books. Many librarians feel film should be treated like any other medium and painstakingly cataloged and classified, using a battery of specifications. Many try to interfile film catalog cards, and intershelve films themselves, with print materials. Historically, detailed cataloging has facilitated retrieval of print material, and has provided a format for making intellectual distinctions about content and packaging. Since film collections are usually much smaller than print collections, and since they are usually separately shelved (film shelving may be determined by reel size, accession number, film base, or target audience), the methods and problems of retrieval are not always compatible with those for books. Consequently, *AACR2* cataloging doesn't always concern film managers, though it is practiced whenever personnel and institutional needs permit.

Some sort of descriptive cataloging, though, is usually practiced, and many excellent guidelines and standards (see bibliography), including those of *AACR2,* may be applied to idiosyncratic recordkeeping systems. Locally produced filmographies, card catalogs, and indexes are frequently created, and usually serve both manager and clientele

very well. The Library of Congress carefully catalogs its films with Dewey and LC numbers and *AACR2* descriptions; the British National Film Catalog uses the Universal Decimal Classification and its own descriptive style. And there are other, carefully developed systems to choose from, such as the Canadian PRÉCIS system or the system of the International Federation of Film Archives. Many films are of course entered in MARC format on the OCLC data base (nearly 299,000 "Audiovisual Media" were entered on it by 1985). Some films are also searchable by keyword on the RLIN data base.

How funding and budgeting for a film service should be handled depends on the relationship between the service and the parent institution. If film managers control the use of their own budgets, to whom are they accountable? Money must be allocated for repairs, replacement, and duplicate titles, but will film borrowers or users absorb any of these costs if they have caused any damages? There may be a conflict over budgeting priorities between print and nonprint departments; so the need for film will have to be clear.

Maybe a preference for film over, say, video or multimedia will have to be explained. You may be renting out your films (this must be arranged with the film's producers and/or initial distributor); if you are, you must decide what to charge. You must have the hardware to support the software, as well as repair and maintenance personnel. Or does your institution divide these responsibilities among several departments? You should know how to arrange for cooperative film purchasing or rental. These are some of the matters that will underlie all budget proposals.

Guidelines exist for the percentage of the total materials budget that is recommended for film (or nonprint) allocation, as well as for the percentage allocated to repair and replacement, and for the optimum number of films that should be available per school or community population. However, if funding sources are uncertain, dwindling, or threatened, no budgeting standards are likely to carry much weight. The resourcefulness of film managers is well known and can be counted on to cope with a variety of funding problems with aplomb and ingenuity, but their resourcefulness is no excuse for funding sources to ignore or downplay the real, increasing financial needs of responsible film managers. Probably the most carefully developed and monitored management and budgeting standards for film and media services are to be found in the public schools, but there the issue of *film* management is usually but a part of the problem of managing all media, and is subject to strong social and political pressures.

How your films are circulated will depend on who your users are and on how much turnaround time you can work with. Your users may be a small or large community, a public school (or its district), a college, a consortium, special-interest groups, primarily children or businessmen. Each group has its own use habits, and some may be more responsible than others. If a film circulates for a period of ten days, you must judge whether this inconveniences other users. You must consider the matter of overdue fines, damage liability, who will be inspecting and repairing the films.

There is evidence that film circulation is dropping off as videocassettes take over. Nevertheless, film is still very popular, and most borrowers will be careful and grateful for the loan of films.

Films may be shelved in many ways: according to LC or Dewey number, by accession number, or by size, subject, format, or target audience. It doesn't really matter, as long as the method is convenient and observes the rules of preservation. Some libararies give returned films a "next in line" position, regardless of the number of films that are normally ahead of them that are out on loan. Most managers will adapt to their capabilities and opt for a system that either takes the least space or is easiest to retrieve from. How much space you have or cabinets you can afford are also factors.

You may have to decide whether you should train film borrowers or users to use the projector, handle the film, or present a program. If you do, first make certain you have the time—whether you're a good, patient teacher, whether you have staff that can do this for you, whether users want to be taught or be responsible, whether the projector you use is familiar to you and in good working condition, and whether you are prepared for the unexpected breakdowns known to all film managers.

Most film managers who purchase films will need some sort of collection-building policy, if not for themselves, for their backers and users. You will want to consider whether you should concentrate on a particular subject, genre, period; on certain directors or actors; on the needs of your users (or, more difficult to deal with, on their wants). Your collection may simply be eclectic but carefully chosen. Or it may specialize in children's films, films on management training, anthropology, newsreels, local history, health care, Americana, sports, cartoons. You may want the longest or greatest number of films for the money. You may reject all but the highest-quality productions. All these questions of special interests and personal style account for the great variety of film collections across the country.

Some of the standard guidelines on building film collections claim there is an optimum size for a film collection. You may want to consider this. *Guidelines for Audiovisual Materials and Services for Public Libraries,* for instance, issued by ALA, suggests a formula for the number of film prints per population—for example, 400 prints for a population of 300,000 to 500,000, and adding 40 prints a year. ALA's *Standards for School Media Programs* suggests having "access" to 3,000 titles, as well as 500 single-concept 8mm films (this was in 1969). "Access," of course, need not mean "acquisition." Consortia, cooperatives, central film depositories, and public libraries all give schools access to their films.

The number of prints in a collection will be determined by your budget, your needs, and how much you can afford to store and maintain. There is no ideal film collection size. Films are expensive, often hard to locate; film budgets fluctuate; and it is rare that enough films can be bought to satisfy a film manager.

Access to a large variety of films is always beneficial to potential user groups. Most users care little how they get their films.

Film collections are housed in a variety of places; indeed, film "libraries" are rarely recognizable from the outside. Most public schools include them as part of the general "media center," where films are one of many resources. Some smaller colleges do this, but many universities have separate facilities for film storage and service, often administratively unconnected to the library. Many museums, large public libraries, businesses, and public service agencies have separate film departments. Some school districts, counties, and other regional units centralize film purchasing, storage, and service. Some even buy films as a group and erect separate buildings to care for them.

Many question whether film "libraries" necessarily belong in the traditional library setting or need a library-based organization, where acquisition, storage, and service are integrated within one facility. Some organizations put films in one place and film equipment in another. Some academic departments own and manage their own film collections and have the right to deny access to them to other departments. These matters will be decided by a combination of experience, expedience, organizational politics, budgeting priorities, and philosophy. There is no one way to run a film service, but the evidence seems to suggest that the more fragmented the operation and the more dispersed the responsibilities, the less effective the film service will be.

If films leave your premises, whether to near or distant points, you will need an efficient booking and delivery system—perhaps an automated or computerized one. Do you know how to set one up, or where to find someone who can? Your films should be accounted for at all times. If the same film is booked for consecutive periods, you must allow enough turnaround time to accomodate delays, film inspection, and office procedures. The user must know if he or she is liable for loss or damages, wholly or partly. Your collection or institution should consider insurance; rental fees will probably have to include costs of postage, insurance, handling, depreciation. You may wish to pay for outgoing postage. You must select a delivery system: UPS, the regular mail, other private or local messengers, yourself. You must state how the borrower is to return the film. As with many film management issues, the questions often suggest the answers.

A few minor matters of film management remain, and deserve a sentence or two. Films will probably need to be weeded from your collection. When the selection is not obvious, it's usually difficult. The color of the film may have faded to distraction. A film may be hopelessly dated; if it is, you must know how to tell. (Some "dated" films are valuable for that very reason.) The film may be beyond repair or rejuvenation. The entire collection may need to be regularly reviewed for weeding. And you may want to choose from a number of ways of disposing of discarded film: trading, selling, donating.

Given the rise of VCRs, home video, video cassettes, 8mm home videotape, computers, and computer-programmed instruction, you may wonder if it's worth buying 8mm and super-8mm film and film loops. Your users may see 8mm as old-fashioned and irrelevant. Video or small computers may do the job as easily. 8mm programs may be archaic in three years. This is an important issue, and businesses, schools, and public libraries will have different responses to it.

It's expensive but quite possible to convert your acetate-base films to ESTAR-base ones. Because of its great resilience and strength, this thin film base holds up well under heavy use, but tends to wander on the sprockets and presents difficulties with self-loading projectors. Your budget, how often individual titles are used, and how long you want your collection to last will be the deciding factors.

Finally, you may want to consider whether to invest in unusual films—archival footage, old newsreels, locally produced works, amateur films, experimental films. This will depend on the kind of facility you manage, on the needs and interests of your clientele, and, frankly, on your own intersts and ability to generate support for them. Unusual films generally appeal to a select audience, or to film students and scholars. To some they seem peripheral, pretentious, irrelevant to society.

The interested user of such films, of course, appreciates their uniqueness, rarity, and creativity; perhaps enjoys and learns from their weaknesses and biases; and is likely to be a strong supporter of your film service. Don't underestimate how much an average film audience may be surprised and pleased by such films.

Other Concerns

In using and teaching with film, it is important to observe a number of practices regularly and routinely. Before using a film—as obvious as it sounds—you must make certain the projector is working properly, and have an extra projector lamp on hand. Countless film audiences have been angered and frustrated by neglect of this simple guideline. Then load the film to its beginning, so that it starts with its title. Arrange ahead of time for proper darkening of the room or theatre, and see that enough seats are available.

Know the film, preferably through having seen it. Know about its dates, genre, importance, if relevant. Decide whether your audience needs or wants an introduction; if it does, prepare some remarks— remarks, not a lecture. Many audiences resent long, unannounced introductions.

Decide whether your audience needs or wants to discuss the film after seeing it. If it does, prepare some remarks—perhaps invite a guest speaker—that will start the discussion. Know something about group dynamics and how to facilitate discussions, and don't try to extemporize (unless you're very good at it).

Teaching with film requires careful preparation; but many teachers have never learned, or neglect, these guidelines, thinking film can do their job for them. But it must be repeated: See a film before you use it. That way, you'll know whether it's effective, appropriate, up to date, and how it fits into the lesson. Know how to "read" a film— how to recognize its structural elements, how it works on the viewer, what to watch for. Then you can help viewers see it. Show a film again, if it is feasible and necessary. Many film users think this is wasteful, and their audiences learn very little. You may want to arrange for individuals to see a film again on their own time.

Know how a film affects *you,* what it means to you, especially if it is a fictional or persuasive film. Effective use or discussion of a film is often sparked by someone sharing a personal reaction and knowing how to express it. Acknowledge a film's irrational, subliminal, propagandistic, or offensive qualities. Know your resources for locating useful films—local filmmakers, libraries, film cooperatives, businesses, civic groups, and the commercial distributors. Don't rely on only one source. Never underestimate how much is available nor—with work, imagination, and money—accessible. Use film guides and filmographies in planning your lessons. The former are prepared by individuals and experts, rather than by groups or committees. The tastes, knowledge, enthusiasm, prejudices, and obsessions of individuals reveal more about films than blander, more "objective" group reports, and may suggest ways of evaluating a film's usefulness.

In the last decade there has been much talk of film and visual literacy. *Film literacy* is a term used to describe one's understanding of how films communicate, what elements compose the film, how it works. Often the concept of film literacy implies that there is a language, a grammar, or a semiotics of films that differs from those of other media or languages, and that this language is knowable, consistent, and teachable. Skill in understanding film can certainly be acquired, and a jargon for describing film exists and is shared by many. But film literacy differs significantly from print literacy, and even from computer literacy. If you are not literate, you can't read, but if you're not film literate, you may still get a great deal out of seeing a film. (If you aren't "computer literate," you can't program a computer; but you can often operate one.)

The development of a special language for film goes back to Eisenstein and Rudolf Arnheim, and is practiced today by many film critics, theorists, teachers, and filmmakers. A prominent theorist of film semiotics is Christian Metz. Guidance in the use and terminology of film literacy can be found in many sources, most notably in James Monaco's *How to Read a Film* (see bibliography), and is taught on many campuses. Terms such as *montage, mise en scene, two-shot, syntagma, pan, neorealism, jump cut, matte shot,* and *insert* are examples of the vocabulary of film literacy. Many terms describe film genres, film history, persuasion techniques, lighting, sound recording, film stock, camera work, and the many techniques of special effects. While some terms are transferable to "video literacy," videography itself has spawned many new and unique terms irrelevant to filmmaking, such as *switch* or *helical scan.*

The basic elements of film literacy are easily comprehended by the general viewer, provided he or she is given a clear explanation with pertinent illustrations. The more specialized concepts of film literacy should be reserved for more sophisticated audiences or student groups interested in film production and history. The International Visual Literacy Association, which produces a newsletter and conferences, was most recently based at Montgomery College in Tacoma Park, Maryland. It is possible to enjoy and understand a film, however, without any special education in film literacy, especially since television has sensitized so many to the use of visual imagery (although it has deadened many, as well). At the heart of understanding film is a desire and ability to isolate as many elements as possible from the film as a whole, and to see how those elements help to make a film what it is, and have the effect it has.

There are many organizations that gather and disseminate both information about films and the films themselves, and also operate film libraries, sponsor festivals and conferences, publish journals, give training programs, and generally further the interests of filmmaking and film utilization. These organizations often know what new films are available and act as showcases for them at conferences. Information about the major organizations can be found in the *Educational Media and Technology Yearbook,* Leonard Maltin's *The Whole Film Sourcebook, Gadney's Guide to 1800 International Contests, Festivals and Grants in Film & Video,* etc. (see bibliography and ''Sources of Sources'' section). Conference and festival dates, conference locations, and program information can be found in many of the library, audiovisual, and educational technology trade and professional journals. Some of the most important organizations every film manager should know are:

American Archives of the Factual Film
American Film Institute
American Library Association (and particularly three divisions: American Association of School Librarians, Audiovisual Committee of the Public Library Association, and the Library and Information Technology Association)
Association for Educational Communications and Technology (and its many divisions and subdivisions)
British Film Institute
Educational Film Library Association (and the American Film Festival it sponsors)
Film Library Information Council
FILMNET: The Film User's Network
Library of Congress—Motion Picture, Broadcasting, and Recorded Sound Division
Media Center for Children
Motion Picture Association of America
Museum of Modern Art
National Audio-Visual Association
National Audiovisual Center
National Film Board of Canada
National Information Center for Educational Media
National Medical Audiovisual Center
UCLA Film, Television, and Radio Archives

Virtually no university or library school programs offer education specifically for film librarianship, some on the principle that it should not be separated from general or media librarianship. Almost all school media librarians have library school degrees, and so do most academic film librarians, if their film library is part of the main, traditional library. Most other film librarians have backgrounds in educational technology, film studies, media production, public relations, business, and communications, or are self-taught. In 1981, over 91 percent of library schools offered at least one course in nonprint librarianship, with total nonprint courses being 16 percent of all library courses. Over half of these, however, were offered to satisfy state certification requirements for school media personnel. No courses were offered specifically in film services or collection building, though some library students are in programs that allow them to design studies in this area. Twenty-four percent of library school instructors taught nonprint courses in 1981.

Managers of film collections and services generally have multidisciplinary backgrounds and interests, and need considerable resourcefulness in providing titles and services. A common bond, of course, is a strong interest in film and film use. Those who might wish to pursue a career in film library management would be well advised to enroll in a library school that (1) is close to a large film library open to student users; (2) has a program that has flexible course requirements; and (3) is part of a university that offers courses in film and television study and/or production, some of which would be acceptable in satisfying library school requirements. It would not hurt to have some background in video production, history, and services. In addition, students should try to visit as many different kinds of film libraries and organizations as possible—and there are many different kinds—and to try to arrange an internship in one.

ADDITIONAL RESOURCES

In this section are works that were consulted in preparing this chapter and works that cover the many aspects of film, film use, film language, and film distribution. The author would like to stress the importance of a broad background—in books, psychology, mass media, systematics, the history of technology—in attaining the fullest understanding of film's achievement and potential.

Aaron, Shirley L., and Pat R. Scales. *School Library Media Annual.* Littleton, Colo.: Libraries Unlimited, 1983.

AFI Factfile. Frederick, Md.: University Publications of America, 1984.

American Film Institute Catalog of Motion Pictures: Feature Films 1921–1930. New York: Bowker, 1971.

American Film Institute Catalog of Motion Pictures: Feature Films 1961–1970. New York: Bowker, 1976.

Audio-Visual Equipment Directory. Fairfax, Va., NAVA (International Communications Industries Assn.) (annual).

Austin, Bruce A. "Portrait of an Art Film Audience." *Journal of Communications* 34, 1 (Winter 1984): 74–87.

Birdwhistell, Ray L. "The Use of Audio-Visual Teaching Aids." In *Resources for the Teaching of Anthropology,* ed. David G. Mandelbaum. Menasha, Wis.: American Anthropological Assn. (AAA Memoir 95), 1963.

BKSTS Dictionary of Audio-Visual Terms. Boston: Focal Pr., 1983.

Bomar, Cora Paul. *Guide to the Development of Educational Media Selection Centers.* Chicago: American Library Assn., 1973.

Bordwell, David, Kristin Thompson, and Janet Staiger. *The Classical Hollywood Cinema: Film Style and Mode of Production to 1960.* New York: Columbia Univ. Pr., 1985.

Bourne, Tom. "Hollywood in Beverly Hills: The Academy of Motion Pictures Library." *Wilson Library Bulletin* 55 (Jan. 1981): 342–46.

Brady, Anna, comp. *Union List of Film Periodicals: Holdings of Selected American Collections.* Westport, Conn.: Greenwood Pr., 1984.

Brooker-Bowers, Nancy. *The Hollywood Novel and Other Novels about Film 1912–1982: An Annotated Bibliography.* New York: Garland, 1985.

Burns, Ernest D. *Cinemabilia Catalogue Seven.* New York: Cinemabilia, 1980.

Cook, David A. *A History of Narrative Film.* New York: Norton, 1981.

Dayton, Deane K. "Future Trends in the Production of Instructional Materials: 1981–2001." *Educational Communications and Technology Journal* 29 (Summer 1981): 93–100.

DeLaurentis, Teresa, and Stephen Heath. *The Cinematic Apparatus.* New York: St. Martin's, 1980.

Egan, Catherine. "The Great Film Bazaar: Best-Selling Educational Films of the 70s." *Sightlines* 14:21–26.

Ellison, John, ed. *Media Librarianship.* New York: Neal-Schuman, 1985.

Fielding, Raymond. *The American Newsreel 1911–1967.* Norman, Okla.: Univ. of Oklahoma Pr., 1972.

Film Cataloging, Prepared by the Cataloging Commission, International Federation of Film Archives. New York: Burt Franklin, 1979.

"Film Previewing Practices: Seven Experts Tell Their Stories." *Audiovisual Instruction* 24: 14–18.

"Films in Public Libraries." *Library Trends* 27 (Summer 1978): 1–106 (entire issue).

Finnegan, Gregory A. "Memories of Underexposure: Reflections of Women in Film." *Choice* 18 (Sept. 1980): 34–53.

Fleischer, Eugene, and Helen Goodman. *Cataloging Audiovisual Materials.* New York: Neal-Schuman, 1980.

Frost, Carolyn. "Motion Pictures and Videorecordings." In *Cataloging Nonbook Materials: Problems in Theory and Practice,* by Carolyn Frost. Littleton, Colo.: Libraries Unlimited, 1983.

———. "Bibliographic Concepts and Their Application to Nonbook Materials." In *Cataloging Nonbook Materials: Problems in Theory and Practice,* by Carolyn Frost. Littleton, Colo.: Libraries Unlimited, 1983.

Gadney, Alan. *Gadney's Guide to 1800 International Contests, Festivals and Grants in Film & Video* (updated address ed.). Glendale, Calif.: Festival, 1980.

Graham, Cooper C., et al. *D. W. Griffith and the Biograph Company.* Metuchen, N.J.: Scarecrow, 1985.

Gregory, Mollie. *Making Films Your Business.* New York: Schocken, 1979.

Guidelines for Audiovisual Materials and Services for Large Public Libraries. Chicago: American Library Assn., 1975.

Guidelines for Audiovisual Materials and Services for Public Libraries. Chicago: American Library Assn., 1970.

Guidelines for Audio-Visual Services in Academic Libraries. Chicago: Audio-Visual Committee of Association of College and Research Libraries, a Division of American Library Assn., 1968.

Halliwell, Leslie. *Halliwell's Film Guide.* 5th ed. New York: Scribner's, 1986.

———. "A Word on Shape." In *Halliwell's Film Guide.* 4th ed. New York: Scribner's, 1983.

———. "The Decline and Fall of the Movie." In *Halliwell's Film Guide.* 4th ed. New York: Scribner's, 1983.

Harrison, Helen P. *Film Library Techniques.* New York: Hastings House, 1973.

Herrick, Doug. "Toward a National Film Collection: Motion Pictures at the Library of Congress." *Film Library Quarterly* 13 (1980): 5–25.

Hoffer, Thomas W. *Animation.* Westport, Conn.: Greenwood, 1981.

Hutchinson, Joseph Allan. "A Status Study of Educational Media Services in Selected Institutions of Higher Education in the United States." Ph.D. dissertation, Louisiana State Univ., 1981.

Intner, Sheila S. *Access to Media: A Guide to Integrating and Computerizing Catalogs.* New York: Neal-Schuman, 1984.

Langer, Lawrence L. "The Americanization of the Holocaust." In *From Hester Street to Hollywood,* ed. Sarah Blacher Cohen. Bloomington: Indiana Univ. Pr., 1983.

LaValley, Al. "The Great Escape." *American Film* 10 (Apr. 1985): 28–34.

Laybourne, Kit. *The Animation Book.* New York: Crown, 1979.

Library Technology Reports (Nov. 1977): 563–674 (entire issue).

Lipton, Lenny. *The Super 8 Book.* San Francisco: Straight Arrow, 1975.

Katz, Ephraim. *The Film Encyclopedia.* New York: Perigee, 1979.

Knight, Arthur. *The Liveliest Art.* New York: Macmillan, 1957.

McLuhan, Marshall. *The Gutenberg Galaxy.* Toronto: Univ. of Toronto Pr., 1962.

———. *Understanding Media: The Extensions of Man.* New York: McGraw-Hill, 1964.

Magill, Frank N., ed. *Magill's Survey of Cinema, English Language Films, First Series.* Englewood Cliffs, N.J.: Salem Pr., 1980.

———. *Magill's Survey of Cinema, English Language Films, Second Series.* Englewood Cliffs, N.J.: Salem Pr., 1981.

———. *Magill's Survey of Cinema, Silent Films.* Englewood Cliffs, N.J.: Salem Pr., 1982.

_____. *Magill's Survey of Cinema, Foreign Language Films.* Englewood Cliffs, N.J.: Salem Pr., 1985.

Maltin, Leonard. *Selected Short Subjects.* New York: Da Capo Pr., 1983.

Mercer, John. *The Informational Film.* Champaign, Ill.: Stipes, 1981.

Metz, Christian. *Film Language: A Semiotics of the Cinema.* New York: Oxford Univ. Pr., 1974.

Miller, James Grier. *Living Systems.* New York: McGraw-Hill, 1978.

Monaco, James. *How to Read a Film.* New York: Oxford Univ. Pr., 1981.

Munday, Karen S., and John W. Ellison. "A Systematic Examination and Analysis of Non-Print Media Courses in Library Schools." In *Expanding Media,* ed. Deirdre Boyle. Phoenix: Oryx Pr., 1977.

Olson, Nancy B. "Motion Pictures and Videorecordings." In *Cataloguing of Audiovisual Materials: A Manual Based on AACR2,* 2nd ed., by Nancy B. Olson. Mankato: Minnesota Scholarly Pr., 1985.

Ophuls, Marcel. "After the Day After." *American Film* 10 (Nov. 1984): 32–38.

Parlato, Salvatore. "Freeze-Frame: The Educational Film Industry." *Sightlines* 12 (Fall 1978): 25–29.

Peary, Danny. *Cult Movies.* New York: Dell, 1981.

_____. *Cult Movies 2.* New York: Dell, 1983.

Penland, Patrick R. "Films in Libraries." In *Encyclopedia of Library and Information Science* (vol. 8). New York: Marcel Dekker, 1972.

Quinlan, David. *The Illustrated Guide to Film Directors.* Totowa, N.J.: Barnes & Noble, 1983.

Recommendations for Audiovisual Materials and Services for Small and Medium-sized Public Libraries. Chicago: American Library Assn., 1975.

"Reference Publications in Film," a monograph series by G. K. Hall & Co., Boston.

Rehrauer, George. *The Film User's Handbook.* New York: Bowker, 1975.

Rhode, Eric. *A History of the Cinema from Its Origins to 1970.* New York: Hill and Wang, 1976.

Robertson, Patrick. *Movie Facts and Feats: A Guiness Record Book.* New York: Sterling, 1980.

Roud, Richard. *Cinema: A Critical Dictionary.* New York: Viking, 1980.

School Library Media Annual. Littleton, Colo.: Libraries Unlimited, 1983–.

Schramm, Wilbur. *Big Media, Little Media.* Beverly Hills, Calif.: Sage, 1977.

Shipman, David. *The Story of Cinema.* New York: St. Martin's, 1982.

Sive, Mary Robinson. "PRECIS—A Better Way to Index Films." *Sightlines* 13 (Winter 1979/1980): 14–17.

Spehr, Paul C. "Fading Fading Faded: The Color Film Crisis." *American Film* 5 (Nov. 1979): 56–61.

Standards for School Media Programs. Chicago: American Library Assn., and Washington, D.C.: National Education Assn., 1969.

Survey of Film-Video Libraries 1982. New York: Educational Film Library Assn., 1982.

Tarbox, Charles H. *Lost Films 1895–1917.* Los Angeles: Film Classic Exchange, 1983.

Thompson, George Raynor, and Dixie H. Harris. "Army Photography at Home and Overseas." In *The Signal Corps: The Outcome (Mid 1943 through 1945),* by George Raynor Thompson and Dixie H. Harris. Washington, D.C.: Office of the Chief of Military History, U.S. Army, 1966.

Trojan, Judith, and Nadine Covert. *16mm Film Distribution.* New York: Educational Film Library Assn., 1977.

Wheaton, Christopher D., and Richard B. Jewell, comps. *Primary Cinema Resources: An Index to Screenplays, Interviews and Special Collections at the University of Southern California.* Boston: Hall, 1975.

White-Hensen, Wendy, comp. *Archival Moving Image Materials: A Cataloguing Manual.* Washington D.C.: Motion Picture, Broadcasting and Recorded Sound Division, Library of Congress, 1984.

Wiener, Paul B. "On Literacy and Librarians." *Catholic Library World* 54 (Mar. 1983): 303–4.

Woolf, Virginia. "The Cinema" (1926). In *The Captain's Death Bed and other Essays,* by Virginia Woolf. New York: Harcourt Brace Jovanovich, 1950.

Worth, Sol. "The Uses of Film in Education and Communication." In *Studying Visual Communication,* by Sol Worth. Philadelphia: Univ. of Pennsylvania Pr., 1981.

Youngblood, Gene. *Expanded Cinema.* New York: Dutton, 1970.

Diana L. Spirt

ch. 4

Filmstrips

THE MEDIUM
Definition

A filmstrip is a length of 35mm film with sprocket holes on both edges, on which a series of related still pictures, called *frames,* are arranged in a fixed order. The number of frames in a typical filmstrip can vary greatly, from 30 to 50 frames.

Filmstrips are classified as either silent or sound. A silent filmstrip usually has either captions of explanatory text under the pictures or accompanying manuals that contain a running commentary. Captions can also appear on a sound filmstrip. Silent filmstrips are used today primarily for the hearing impaired.

A sound filmstrip generally has an accompanying phonograph record or audiotape, usually a sound cassette. During the last decade, cassettes seem to be the preferred choice. One side of the phonograph records and cassettes packaged in filmstrip sets, usually has an audible signal ("beep") to indicate that the operator should move to the next frame, while the other side is used with equipment that moves the filmstrip automatically by an electronic, inaudible signal. Single cartridges, which contain both the filmstrip and sound tape, are available, and these can be placed in a specially produced projector. There are also filmstrips with an optical sound track on the same film stock as the pictures. Special equipment is required for this type of filmstrip.

Indeed, it is important that the capability of the filmstrip projector match the type of filmstrip. Nevertheless, among the various formats available in projected audiovisual material, the filmstrip remains the most popular and widely used, especially in schools, community colleges, and commercial training courses.

Definitions by Dale, Brown, and Goudket are noteworthy, especially in the historical context.[1] Similarly, the term *filmstrip,* although in common usage today, has been in previous times *filmslides, slide films, Picturols* (trade name), *filmrolls,* and *strip films.*

Brief History

After a history that is longer than most people recognize, audiovisual education became a recognizable field. The filmstrip was part of its early development. Although it is difficult to say that one factor is more important than others in this long, steady race, two significant factors can be isolated: technology and our insatiable desire to control a sometimes hostile environment, philosophically reinforced by the belief of many educators during this period in human perfectibility.

Still pictures were used early in American education. Some teachers had been using visual materials before the turn of the century. The filmstrip had its origin in direct relationship to photographic slides and the filmstrip projector. Three groups can be highlighted as leaders in providing materials from 1900 to 1919: the State Education Department in Albany, New York; the University of Wisconsin Extension Division; and ten administrators in public schools in Chicago. The first two bureaus circulated their slides free on a statewide basis; the latter pooled their resources to establish a similar circuit for their schools. However, until 1915, visual aids were largely limited to the personal resources of individual museums, schools, and other training institutions. Indeed, the first (although unpublished) survey of visual education centers identified 18 between 1905 and 1923. The Keystone View Company of Meadville, Pennsylvania, introduced the first commercial set of slides in 1906; by 1918 it had five different sets on the market. There were at least six other companies dealing in materials and projectors; three in New York, two in Chicago, and one in Davenport, Iowa. The introduction of projection and enlargement aided immeasurably in making visual aids more useful to teachers.

---

1. Edgar Dale, *Audio-visual Methods in Teaching* (New York: Dryden Pr., 1946), 536; James W. Brown et al., *AV Instruction: Technology, Media and Methods* (New York: McGraw-Hill, 1973), 143; Michael Goudket, *An Audio-Visual Primer* (New York: Teachers College Pr., 1973), 30.

The opaque projection of nontransparent materials with flat surfaces had a great impact. It was used widely in elementary schools. Filmstrip *(Picturol)* projection of nonflammable, still film pictures, usually 25 to 50 arranged in sequence, was inaugurated about 1920 by the Underwood brothers. In 1918 a slide-film projector, the Brayco, advertised at $28, appeared. Both were widely adopted because of their ease of use, storage, and cost. From 1920 to 1945, both technology and human institutions, particularly educational, contributed to the increasing use of the filmstrip. In 1923, after a lengthy genesis, the Department of Visual Instruction (later DAVI, now AECT) became a division of the National Education Association (NEA). This served to give national focus to visual materials and to provide a forum for like-minded visual educators. Six deterrents were identified during this period: a scarcity of suitable material; a lack of standards; the high cost of equipment and material; the rigid fire laws (due to the highly flammable early film stock); a scarcity of related school curriculum material; and the lack of electrical circuits in many buildings. In spite of the severe economic and political difficulties during this period, the advancements of technology, combined with the action of educators, provided a platform for the acceptance and popularity of the filmstrip.[2]

Between World War II and 1962, this long-sought solidification was encouraged with the introduction of sound (audio). Filmstrips accompanied by record or tape, predating the cassette format, became popular. Another force in our society was also operating; many visual aids were used simultaneously as toys in the home, and as the public patronized stereopticans, movies, and the radio, educators saw the learning possibilities. Like the current computer situation, this phenomenon helped to eradicate some of the problems, especially availability and cost.

Meanwhile, in 1948, DAVI restated its objectives. The promotion, selection, and evaluation of audiovisual material and cooperation with other agencies were prominent in both its statements and action. Filmstrips assumed a place second only to motion pictures. The American Library Association (ALA) in 1949 published the classic *Audio-Visual School Library Service: A Handbook for Librarians,* by Margaret I. Rufsvold. At the NEA centennial convention in Philadelphia in 1957, the theme was "A New Look at Some Old AV Materials," and filmstrips were included. In 1959, DAVI's publication office noted that Charles F. Schuller's *The School Administrator and His A-V Program*

2. Diana L. Lembo, "A History of the Growth and Development of the Department of Audio-Visual Instruction of the National Education Association from 1923 to 1968" (unpublished dissertation, New York Univ., 1970), *passim.*

was its biggest attraction. The book treated the filmstrip, as well as flat pictures and slides. The H. W. Wilson Company issued a series by Vera Falconer, "Filmstrip Guide," that served for years as a buying guide and complemented the selection and evaluation services in the earlier AV magazines. The outlook for the filmstrip, with the introduction of sound and the provision of bibliographic control, was bright.

At the beginning of the 1950s, it was foretold that instructors would be able to use audiovisual tools, unused or unknown included, with greater effectiveness in the next 20 years. The money that helped to accomplish this came as federal funds, first the National Defense Education Act (NDEA) and later the Elementary and Secondary Education Act (ESEA). Simultaneously, filmstrips received greater coverage in writings on audiovisual materials and in selection and evaluation sources, such as *Booklist, Media and Methods,* and *School Library Journal.* Funds and evaluative sources, together with the increased availability of equipment and electrical circuits in the field, combined to make the filmstrip a commonly accepted medium from 1946 to 1975.

Since 1975, there has been a modest increase for filmstrips in the dollar share of nonbook materials. Filmstrips, usually accompanied by audio cassettes, represent approximately one-quarter of the nonbook market. Technology has continued to provide equipment and materials that have an easy usefulness, even for the most inexperienced. It has also encouraged a sophisticated approach through pacing and sound, to simulate motion.

The availability of suitable materials, particularly related to school curricula and the increasing current-evaluation sources, has made the filmstrip an indispensable part of education. Although the short-tenure *Media Monitor* and *Previews* are out of print (*School Library Journal* has absorbed the latter's evaluation function), *Booklist* continues as an evaluative tool, and *Media Review* is a newcomer. In addition, the hiatus occasioned by the lack of standardization and the high cost of video cassettes (in comparison to the sound filmstrip), together with the economic difficulties of the late 1970s, have helped to maintain the popularity of the filmstrip.

As a fitting (albeit ironic) historical note, 75 color slides, with a 9-minute audio cassette—"The Storage and Care of Films, Filmstrips, Filmloops, Transparencies and Slides"—were produced by the State University of New York at Buffalo and distributed in 1980 by the National Audio-Visual Center. The interest of this national central source strongly suggests that the filmstrip is alive and well. It also mentions filmstrips as the second most-recognized format among the traditional audiovisual formats since the beginning of the visual education movement, although slides had been the first at the turn of the century.

Unique Characteristics

The filmstrip's unquestioned unique characteristic is its ability to *suggest* motion in a predetermined sequence of still pictures. This characteristic has led to its popularity, and also to the next technological step of "showing motion" in its historical successors— film and video.

Advantages and Disadvantages

It is clear from reading the following lists of advantages and disadvantages, which are numerically three to one in favor of the format, why the filmstrip continues to be popular. These enduring factors have been categorized and put in the priority order of most users. The filmstrip:

Is inexpensive to produce, purchase, and ship.

Is available in a wide range of subjects suitable for pre-K to adulthood.

Has easy-to-operate, portable equipment.

Can be developed and produced locally, permitting both the design of materials of temporary interest or immediate importance and the opportunity for creative expression by users.

Is usually accompanied by well-prepared descriptions, guides, and sound (records or tapes).

Cannot get out of order, because of its predetermined sequence.

Relieves the user of assembling, arranging, and refiling a group of slides or other media on the subject of its fixed order.

Can be used by individuals or various-size groups by adjusting the image size (focal length) of the lens.

Makes it possible to present the same material to several groups.

Allows, through its format, for many accepted learning factors: feedback, repetition, review, and inductive reasoning.

Can be employed in a semidarkened room (depending on the wattage of the projector bulb in relation to the size of the room).

Needs less storage space than slides.

Allows intershelving in book-size cartons.

Has protective coating that makes it relatively indestructible.

Can be cut up and used as slides, if torn or damaged.

Can be paced (if silent) to a specific group.

Can be used by several individuals in one room.

Can be used with earphones without disturbing others (if accompanied by sound).

On the other hand, the filmstrip:

Can be restrictive, because of the fixed order.
Becomes dated if one section is outdated before the rest.
May be difficult to repair if torn or damaged.
May be easily lost or stolen.
May present intershelving problems, depending on its packaging.
Can be unimaginative and mediocre.
Can suggest, but cannot display, motion.

SELECTION

Special Criteria

After the general criteria of authenticity, appropriateness, scope, treatment, organization, and physical characteristics are met, the filmstrip format should be examined with reference to special criteria for evaluation and selection. (For further information, see the general selection criteria listed in many of the books in the bibliography at the conclusion of this chapter.) There are four considerations: relationship of the format to the message; organization of the content; technical quality; and educational value.

The content or subject of the filmstrip should be portrayed well, with the suggestion of motion. If the illusion of motion is required by the concept(s), the filmstrip format should not be used. The relationship of the format to the content is a vital rule for all audiovisual material.

The organization is also important. The main idea should be well expressed and logically explained. The objectives should be clearly stated or implied, and immediately available upon analysis. Additionally, the filmstrip should have an obvious purpose and, above all, be current or applicable historically.

The technical quality of the filmstrip should obey the following points. The strip should be well produced in both the visual and audio components. The visuals should be clear, interesting, and suitable. They should vary in style, where appropriate (e.g., photos, graphs, charts, drawings, etc.). There should be an appropriate ratio of closeups to distance shots, satisfying colors, and sufficient images. The audio component should have high fidelity; it should also have clarity (without unintended distortion) and make good use of special effects and, in general, conform to standards of aural presentation. There should be synchronization between sound and images, as well as a suitable integration of verbal and pictorial content. If captioned, the captions should be at the bottom of the frame, well related to the images, and sufficiently large, according to the intended audience.

In considering the educational value of the filmstrip, one should evaluate the strip's potential to stimulate critical thinking. Finally, in determining its educational value, the filmstrip's creativity, imaginativeness, or originality in subject or treatment or both must be considered.

Evaluative Review Sources

Listed in this section are the journals and monographs that represent an overview of the most-used titles that evaluate filmstrips. The *International Index to Multi-Media Information, Landers Film Reviews,* and *Media Review Digest* are widely distributed indexes that bring together evaluative and descriptive reviews of filmstrips, and thus can be very useful in filmstrip selection. (The periodical titles are categorized by the regular or occasional appearance of filmstrip reviews.)

PERIODICALS WITH REGULAR REVIEWS

AV Guide Newsletter
Booklist
Choice
CM: Canadian Materials for Schools & Libraries
Landers Film Reviews

Library Journal
Media and Methods
Media Review
Media Review Digest
School Library Journal
The Science Teacher

PERIODICALS WITH OCCASIONAL REVIEWS

Audiovisual Librarian
Catechist
English Journal
Exceptional Children
Forecast for Home Economics
Instructor

Media in Education & Development
Ohio Media Spectrum
Reading Teacher
SIECUS Newsletter
Top of the News

MONOGRAPHS

International Index to Multi-Media Information. Pasadena, Calif., Audio-Visual Associates (annual). Index to evaluative and descriptive reviews of multimedia.

Ethnic Film and Filmstrip Guide for Libraries and Media Centers: A Selective Filmography.

OTHER SOURCES

Organizational lists, such as ALA/ALSC or YASD's annual list of notable
    filmstrips (e.g., *Especially for Children—Outstanding Audiovisual
    Materials* [ALA/ALSC, 1984] lists materials which bear a copyright date
    of 1981 and 1982).
Journal lists, such as the annual lists in *Booklist, Media Digest, School Library
    Journal,* etc.
Library Technology Reports (ALA) is a bimonthly report on equipment and
    (sometimes) materials.
EPIE Equipment & Materials Reports (Educational Products Information Ex-
    change Institute, Stony Brook, N.Y.) gives reports on equipment and
    multimedia.

Nonevaluative Sources (since 1970)

Included in this section are the most widely known nonevaluative
sources for filmstrips. Both retrospective indexes, like Library of Congress titles, and a current journal, *Instructional Innovator* (AECT), are
given. Both parts of this section, plus publications from ERIC/IR Clearinghouse (Syracuse Univ.), which attempts to offer a wide range of
information on audiovisual materials, and selected U.S. government
publications, which appear occasionally on filmstrips, provide a basic
pool of selection sources for the filmstrip.

PERIODICALS

Educational Technology. Majority of issues contain detailed multimedia prod-
    uct reviews and articles on teaching aids.
Instructional Innovator. Includes notes on new products and materials, to-
    gether with pertinent articles on media.
*Sources: A Guide to Print and Non-Print Materials Available from Organiza-
    tions, Industry, Government Agencies, and Specialized Publishers.* Listing
    of difficult-to-find productions.

MONOGRAPHS

Audio Video Marketplace. New York: Bowker, annual. Includes comprehen-
    sive directory, with addresses, of commercial filmstrip companies.
Educators' Guide to Free Filmstrips. Randolph, Wis.: Educator's Progress Ser-
    vice, annual. Lists commercially sponsored filmstrips.
(National Audiovisual Center [Washington, D.C.]. Any brochures or directories
    from this central source may have valuable selection listings.)
National Union Catalog/Audiovisual Materials (previously titled *National
    Union Catalog/Motion Pictures and Filmstrips,* 1963–72, and *National
    Union Catalog/Films and Other Materials for Projection,* 1973–78.
    Washington, D.C.: Library of Congress, 1979–   . National bibliographic
    listing of multimedia.

NICEM Index to 35mm Educational Filmstrips. Los Angeles: National Information Center for Educational Media, irregular. Retrospective listing of filmstrips, with content descriptions.

MAINTENANCE AND MANAGEMENT

Storage and Care

How filmstrips are kept helps to determine the length of life of the film stock. Consequently, storage and care play an important part economically for those who collect this material. The following list itemizes the most important considerations in active collections. Filmstrip

Is stored (usually if single) in shallow, compartmentalized drawers.

Can be intershelved, singly or in sets, when put in book-sized boxes or in transparent plastic packages.

Should be stored at temperatures between 30 and 70° F. The relative humidity can range from 30 to 50%, with 40% desirable.[3]

Cool, dark storage is recommended by Eastman Kodak, especially for processed color film. It states that filmstrip is best kept on main floors and not in damp basements or hot attics. It also says that a temperature of 21°C (70° F) or less is best, together with a relative humidity between 15 and 50%. A relative humidity of less than 15% should be avoided, because excessive brittleness may result, as well as possible fungus growth.[4]

Should be handled carefully by its edges or leaders.

Must not be cinched while rewinding, because it may result in scratches (although there is protection in the heavy plastic coating of commercially prepared material).

Requires trimming of rough edges before threading.

Should have minor tears repaired with splicing tape.

Should be cleaned after each use with a film cleaner and lint-free cloth. The container should be cleaned at the same time.

Should be checked for damage after each use.

Should be enclosed in plastic containers to avoid damage to the film (and user) from a sharp-edge metal container.

Projection equipment should be covered when not in use. Projector lamps should be handled by their base, and checked to determine

---

3. John Ellison, Gloria S. Gerber, and Susan Ledder, *Storage and Care of Filmstrips, Filmloops, Transparencies and Slides* (Washington, D.C.: Audiovisual Center, 1979).
4. Kodak, E-30, 4.

correct wattage. The lens should be cleaned regularly with lens tissue.

Management Problems and Solutions

Fundamental management questions about filmstrips should be considered. They deal mainly with cataloging and circulating them. After the selection process has been established, these two large considerations must be treated.

SELECTION

Before published selection aids for filmstrips can be used effectively, a basic selection policy should be established. Although such tools can be helpful to the staff, essential concerns must be satisfied to provide a smooth operation. For example, the question "Should the staff involve users in the selection process?" must be addressed and the answer stated.

A list of practical guidelines that will help in the formation of a selection policy appears below. They may help to assure a useful, balanced collection of filmstrips. Some may be familiar, because they are used to induce thoughtfulness about many media; others may be special.

As many of the institution's population as possible should be involved in the selection of materials for purchase. It not only adds new dimensions, but provides insight into use. This sort of participation can also increase interest in the use of all media.

Beyond the principle of satisfying the need of the user, diversity should be sought in most institutions. The key word is *balance*.

Depending on the type of institution, it is wise for the staff to bear in mind any varying levels of visual and audio literacy among the potential users.

In certain institutions, primarily schools, selection for non-users should be considered. Appropriate filmstrip material should be available when the opportunity for use occurs.

A professional (preferably a library media specialist) should have the final approval in purchasing.

It is wise to recognize that censorship is to be avoided. It is also advisable to note reviews and discussions about a filmstrip that is potentially a target for censorship.

The selection process should be as objective as possible. With material that affects one aurally and visually, subjectivity is especially prevalant. Selecting from the user's point of view is helpful in reducing this factor.

Matching the message with the appropriate material is important in the selection of filmstrips. An answer is necessary to the question "Is this medium the most appropriate (and affordable) to carry the contents of the material?"

User demand is the measure that should determine the extent to which there is duplication of materials. Another important consideration is the copyright law. An interpretation of this federal law is available from the Government Printing Office (GPO) or federal depository library.

Selection problems, due to restrictions of space, mandate an examination of more efficient storage, for example, intershelving. Rotating collections among users and retiring little-used material to storage areas, or discarding, should also be explored.

The swift preparation of items for use, particularly topical and requested material, should be attained. Uncataloged material may be considered for circulation when the occasion demands. The aspect of service should be emphasized.

Multiple selection aids should be used. Restricting choices to one or two sources results in filmstrip collections which have less depth than is desired.

A system of continuous review of material is advisable, together with checking basic retrospective sources at least once a year.

Cooperative acquisitions through networking should be explored. Presently, many projects operate on principles upon which others can be built, either as a model or by joining.

Several jobbers and wholesalers have employed media professionals to compile lists of recommended filmstrips. These lists are preferable to publishers' and manufacturers' catalogs, which should be used with great care. Organizations often compile worthwhile lists.

Gifts as possible additions should be welcomed. A "gift policy" should be written to include the appropriateness and disposition of the filmstrip as final criteria.

"Sponsored" materials present another consideration. Many are worth inclusion; however, they should be checked against the criteria of proselytizing and distortion.

CIRCULATION

Where possible, the same circulation procedures that are used for book materials should be used for nonbook materials. As well, filmstrip circulation procedures, based on a cogent policy, should include the equipment that is necessary to use filmstrips. Such a system also promotes the integration of all materials. If affixing a pocket, card, and date-due slip is too difficult (although this method is relatively simple on repackaged filmstrips), an optional means is treating filmstrips like periodicals and keeping the cards on file at the circulation desk.

The circulation of equipment also poses problems. Aside from the decision to circulate equipment for out-of-institution use, there are many decisions that need to be made about them in the institution. For example, a centralized or decentralized method, or some combination of the two, should be decided upon. The rule of thumb in small or medium-sized situations is that equipment, as well as materials, should emanate from a central installation. In most circumstances where there are fewer pieces of equipment than users, requests must be made. These usually take the form of sign-up sheets that include: time needed, requester's name, location of use, type of equipment (filmstrip projector), and pickup time.

Some system for delivery and pickup is obviously needed, and a suitable number of various types of filmstrip projectors for individual use, based on the practical experience of need in the user population, is necessary. Occasionally, a sign-up sheet may be necessary for individual use. This situation, of course, is positive, and demands only that because of increased use, the staff must reexamine the provision of more filmstrip projectors.[5]

Other Concerns

Filmstrips can be used by individuals or by small and large groups. Regardless of the size of the audience, they can and do encourage learning. Although there are literally thousands of commercial filmstrips on various subjects, some—for example, on local history or a specific training method—may require local production.

Principles of presentation, projection, and local production should be stated. Attention to them will help to increase both enjoyment and learning from viewing and listening to filmstrips.

PRINCIPLES OF PRESENTATION
Based on recognized theories that (1) a combination of spoken or printed word and picture is integral in learning, (2) a magnified pictorial image is compelling, and (3) the amount of light (semidarkness

---

5. John T. Gillespie and Diana L. Spirt, *Administering the School Library Media Center* (New York: Bowker, 1983), 302–21.

to darkness) helps the viewer to concentrate on the subject, the following guidelines govern effective use of filmstrips, particularly in group situations. The skill of the presenter in taking advantage of the positive attributes of the filmstrip helps to determine the effectiveness of the filmstrip.

Use the appropriate filmstrip for the objective(s).
Operate the projector well, with or without aid.
Determine the appropriate
    Size of room
    Wattage of projection bulb
    Type of screen
    Magnification (objective)
    Lighting (color filmstrips need more darkness than black and white).
Arrange the environment, especially for viewer visibility and comfort.
Decide, before the presentation, upon the method of repetition, if necessary, and the philosophy behind questions and answers during the presentation (both can be useful if correctly done). The situation will determine the need.
Provide good sound quality for listening. Since silent filmstrips are rarely used now, it is recommended that the principles for the presentation of sound be examined.

PRINCIPLES OF PROJECTION
Although there are many ways to categorize projectors for filmstrips, the following scheme is one way to explain a complex subject in a way that is both descriptive and understandable. However, like everything else, first-hand experience or practice should be mixed with the theoretical, and is therefore recommended.

Types of projectors
    Silent:
        Manual advance knob
        Automatic-remote control
    Sound:
        Combination filmstrip projector and record player (audible and/or inaudible), pulse or "beep" (50 or 1,000Hz)
        Combination filmstrip projector and cassette tape player (as above)
    Others:
        Filmstrip adapter (on slide projector)
        Small "viewers," with rear-screen projection for individuals or small groups

Illumination
   50–1,000 watts (300 watts is usually sufficient for an average-size
   classroom)
Operation
   Except for the largest, projectors are relatively affordable, easy to
   use, lightweight, and portable. Good use suggests that someone
   other than the presenter should operate the equipment.

PRINCIPLES OF PRODUCTION
There are two basic types of filmstrips: photographic and hand-made.
There are also two ways of obtaining filmstrips: commercially and
locally, by in-house production. Filmstrips on many subjects are widely
available from commercial sources. These, of course, should be
evaluated before selection. The staff should use reviews, rather than
the traditional preview print that media producers no longer feel
obliged to release (because of improved bibliographic control):

> The publishers of information and reviews of nonprint media
> need to take a serious look at the markets for their informa-
> tion sources. These are not new words to publishers. Several
> studies have pointed out the deficiencies in the publications
> that review nonprint media. If publications and information
> networks have improved, publishers need to mount extensive
> campaigns to disseminate the improved resources. Media direc-
> tors have, for so long, not depended on publications for in-
> formation that they will not be easily persuaded to change.[6]

If there is a need for a locally produced filmstrip, it can be made
in two ways:
   1. By drawing or writing on a blank 35mm filmstrip.
   2. By photographing, or sending to a special film laboratory,
35mm slides arranged in a desired sequence and numbered. The
photographer, or laboratory, puts the slides into a filmstrip format.
Anyone familiar with a 35mm camera can make the master filmstrip
negative from any series of pictures or drawings. This usually involves
using a copystand with a 35mm single-frame camera. The basic steps
are:
   Detail the idea in writing.
   Outline this idea frame by frame.
   Plan images for each frame.

6. Robert Heinrich and Michael Molenda, "First Annual Survey of the Circulation
of Educational Media to Public Schools" (unpublished report, Indiana University Audio-
Visual Center, Bloomington, 1978), ERIC ED 164 013.

Introduce titles or captions (if necessary).
Arrange frame cards in a storyboard.
Copy these cards with a 35mm camera.
Print the master negative.

ADDITIONAL RESOURCES

Beatty, LaMond F. "Filmstrips." In James E. Duane, ed., *The Instructional Media Library.* Vol. 4. New York: Educational Technical Publications, 1981.

Brown, James W., ed. *Educational Media Yearbook.* Littleton, Colo.: Libraries Unlimited, 1973– .

Cabeceiras, James. *Multimedia Library.* 2nd ed. Washington, D.C.: Academic Pr., 1982.

Cambre, Marjorie A. "Historical Overview of Formative Evaluation of Instructional Media Products." *ECTJ* 29 (n.d.): 3–25.

Croghan, Antony. *Bibliographic System for Non-Book Media.* London: Coburgh, 1979.

Ellison, John, Gloria S. Gerber, and Susan Ledder. *Storage and Care of Filmstrips, Filmloops, Transparencies and Slides.* Washington, D.C.: National Audiovisual Center, 1979 (slide/tape).

Evans, Arthur. "An Evaluation Form that Makes Sense." *Instructional Innovator* 26 (Mar. 1981): 22–32.

Gill, Suzanne L. *File Management & Information Retrieval Systems: A Manual for Managers and Technicians.* Metuchen, N.J.: Libraries Unlimited, 1981.

Gillespie, John T., and Diana L. Spirt. *Administering the School Library Media Center.* New York: Bowker, 1983.

Grove, Pearce S., ed. *Non-Print Media in Academic Libraries.* Chicago: American Library Assn., 1975.

Hicks, Warren B., and Alma M. Tillin, eds. *Managing Multi-Media Libraries.* New York: Bowker, 1977.

Kemp, Jerrold E. *Planning and Producing Audiovisual Materials.* 4th ed. New York: Harper and Row, 1980.

Laird, Dugan. *A User's Look at the Audio-Visual World.* 2nd ed. Fairfax, Va.: National Audio-Visual Assn., 1974.

Library of Congress. *National Union Catalog: A Cumulative Author List, 1958–1962.* Vol. 53. Motion Pictures & Film Strips, Titles, Pt. 1; Vol. 54. Motion Pictures & Film Strips, Subject Index, Pt. 2.

May, Jill P. *Films and Filmstrips for Language Arts: An Annotated Bibliography.* Urbana, Ill.: NCTE, 1981.

Mental Health Materials Center, ed. *Current Audiovisuals for Mental Health Education,* 2nd ed. Chicago: Marquis, 1979.

Nadler, Myra. *How to Start an Audiovisual Collection.* Metuchen, N.J.: Scarecrow, 1978.

Rothwell, Helen de F., comp. *Canadian Selection: Filmstrips.* Toronto: Univ. of Toronto Pr., 1980.

Rufsvold, Margaret I. *Guides to Educational Media.* 4th ed. Chicago: American Library Assn., 1977.

Shaffer, Dale E. *The Filmstrip Collection: Complete Instruction on How to Process and Organize.* Salem, Ore.: By the author, 1972.

Sive, Mary R. *The Complete Media Monitor: Guide to Learning Resources.* Metuchen, N.J.: Scarecrow, 1981.

_____. *Media Selection Handbook.* Littleton, Colo.: Libraries Unlimited, 1982.

_____. *Selecting Instructional Media: A Guide to Audiovisual and Other Instructional Media Lists.* 3rd ed. Littleton, Colo.: Libraries Unlimited, 1983.

Sumer, John. *Slide, Sound, & Filmstrip Production.* Focal Press, 1981.

Thomas, Robert Murray, and Sherwin G. Swartout. *Integrated Teaching Materials: How to Choose, Create and Use Them.* New York: David McKay, 1963.

Weihs, Jean R. "Problems of Subject Analysis for Audiovisual Collections." *Canadian Library Journal* 33 (Oct. 1976): 453 + .

_____. *Non-book Materials: The Organization of Integrated Collections.* 2nd ed. Chicago: American Library Assn., 1980.

Wilson, LaVisa C. *Caregiver Training for Child Care: A Multimedia Program.* Columbus, Ohio: Merrill, 1977.

Wood, Irene. "Evaluating the Media." *Audiovisual Instruction* 20 (Apr. 1975): 6–8.

Wynar, L. R., and L. Buttlar. *Ethnic Film and Filmstrip Guide for Libraries and Media Centers: A Selective Filmography.* Littleton, Colo.: Libraries Unlimited, 1980.

J. Gordon Coleman, Jr.

ch. 5

Flat Pictures, Posters, Charts, and Study Prints

THE MEDIUM

Definitions

These four media—flat pictures, posters, charts, and study prints—can be grouped together under the classification of graphic material. They will, however, be discussed separately in some sections of this chapter because the differences between them are sufficient to warrant this treatment.

Flat pictures are two-dimensional representations of persons, places, ideas, or objects rendered by drawing, painting, or photography which are produced on an opaque backing. Their dimensions may vary considerably, but they rarely incorporate text.

Posters are large, bold designs on opaque backing which incorporate words, shapes, and color and are displayed in a public place to attract and hold attention long enough to convey a brief message.

Charts are opaque sheets which provide summary information, describe relationships, or explain a process through the use of drawings, pictures, symbols, and text. Quite often, charts are incorporated into both verbal and printed presentations in order to add meaning and enhance understanding.

Study prints are visual representations of persons, places, ideas, or objects, accompanied by text and designed for specific instructional purposes. Generally, the text either describes the visual or calls attention to relevant portions of the visual through the use of questions. Though primarily designed for individual use, study prints can be used by small groups of two or three individuals.

Brief History

Flat pictures, produced by painting and drawing, have been in existence since prehistoric times, whereas those produced by photography have only recently come into existence. As paper became more readily available in the 15th century, painting and drawing became more popular and available. In the next century, the *camera obscura* was developed in Italy, but it was only capable of projecting an image onto a piece of paper. Though scientists began the attempt to create permanent images in the early 1700s, it was not until 1826 that the French physicist Joseph Nicéphore Niépce created the first photograph. Soon after, Louis Daguerre perfected this process and produced his pictures, which were called *daguerreotypes.*

Posters have been in existence for several hundred years, having evolved from the handbills and signboards first used for advertising purposes in Europe. The artistic poster, with which we are familiar today, had its origins in early 19th century France. Parisian booksellers and publishers began to use enlarged illustrations as a means to advertise their books in the 1830s.

The development of lithography allowed artists to create vividly colored posters with relative ease and at a nominal cost. Jules Chéret, a French artist, produced the first color poster in 1869, and is often thought to have established the poster as an art form. He believed that the poster needed to be simple and bold so that it could attract attention. To him, the street, not the gallery, was the proper place to display the poster.[1]

The late 19th century ushered in Art Nouveau, which began in France and spread to other countries. Most notable of these artists was Henri de Toulouse-Lautrec, whose work depicted the excitement and frivolity of the Paris cafes. It was also at this time that posters were becoming very popular in the United States. The appearance of Edward Penfield's *Harper's* posters is considered the beginning of the American poster movement.[2]

1. Victor Margolin, *American Poster Renaissance* (New York: Watson-Guptill, 1975), 9–13.
2. Ibid., 9–22.

Soon, because of the vivid colors in the illustrations, posters began to influence fashions, as women adopted the dress styles of the characters depicted in the posters. As with any new art form, the poster was often criticized. Though there was some criticism as to the aesthetic merits of posters, most of the complaints were based on moral grounds; there were some who believed that posters too often depicted lewd or licentious scenes.[3]

Posters have since been used for a variety of purposes, such as recruitment by the military during World Wars I and II. Circuses, the travel industry, and the motion picture industry have used posters extensively for promotional purposes. More recently, the popular-music industry has adopted posters to advertise concerts and record albums.

Charts are closely related to maps, being the forerunner of these representations of land. The first such map was thought to have been created on clay tablets in 2300 B.C. In the 14th and 15th centuries, a navigation chart, called a *portolano,* was used by sailors. They were drawn on sheepskin and showed the outlines of ports and harbors. In the 16th century, Flemish geographer Gerhard Kremer, who used the Latinized name Mercator, developed the map projection which was of much use to sailors. The idea of representing an idea or concept in chart form grew from those early beginnings until we find the four types primarily in use today: tabular or outline charts; flow, organization, or process charts; tree or stream charts; and time-line charts.

Perhaps one could make a case for tracing the history of study prints back to Comenius' 17th century illustrated book *Orbus Pictus,* which used woodcuts to illustrate common objects. However, pairing illustrations with specific written study guides is a fairly recent occurrence. Though this type of media can be used for instructional purposes by any age, the vast majority of study prints produced commercially are intended for use in elementary schools.

Unique Characteristics

The four media formats, grouped together as graphic materials, share many common characteristics. For the most part, they are more alike than dissimilar.

These materials are often available *gratis* or at nominal cost; therefore, the collection of these materials often is not systematic.

The message is always delivered nonverbally, through drawing, painting, photography, or text, or a combination thereof.

3. Ibid.

Generally, each one of these formats is a discretely distinct entity. As such, the sequence in which they are used is often not important, unless they are part of a set. Study prints and occasionally flat pictures can be packaged as part of a set in which the sequence of use is important.

Their purpose is to convey information quickly and efficiently.

Each of these media formats is primarily used by individuals or small groups. Posters, designed to be seen at a distance, can be viewed by many people at once, but each person's interpretation of a poster's meaning is normally an individual matter. When used as part of a presentation, charts are often viewed by large groups.

The content of these graphic materials is quite often ephemeral; thus their value over a period of time is questionable.

In each instance, these graphic materials are developed with a singular purpose in mind.

Advantages and Disadvantages

Among the important and salient advantages are the following:

None of these graphic materials formats requires equipment.

All of these formats are portable and can be easily transported from one locale to another.

As they rely primarily on visual communication, each of these formats can translate the abstract into concrete.

They require no skills on the part of the user, other than possibly basic reading and motor skills, for utilization.

Posters and flat pictures are readily available from a variety of traditional and nontraditional sources at little or no cost.

Each of these formats can be produced and reproduced relatively easily and inexpensively.

Each of these formats is suitable for various age groups and for various purposes.

Charts, posters, and study prints can succinctly summarize and convey information.

Flat pictures and study prints are designed for use by individuals or small groups, whereas charts can be used by individuals or medium- to large-size groups.

Among the important and salient disadvantages are the following:

As a two-dimensional "still" medium, each of these formats lacks depth and motion.

As these formats are primarily designed for a single purpose, they are capable of delivering only a limited amount of information.

Most of the material, especially in poster and chart format, is ephemeral and, therefore, requires more "weeding" than other media formats.

Because of their physical characteristics, it is often difficult to integrate these media formats into the collection.

The physical characteristics of these media are such that specialized storage devices must be employed, thereby possibly limiting user access.

They often require an inordinate amount of time and expense in processing and preservation.

Quite often, they do not lend themselves to normal cataloging and retrieval procedures.

SELECTION
Special Criteria

Because of the ephemeral nature of most of these materials, the content must be correct and up to date.

The content of these formats, especially posters and charts, should be limited to one main point.

Posters and charts are normally perused quickly; therefore, they must be easy to comprehend.

As the name implies, study prints are designed to be looked at and read for a period of time; therefore, they should attract and hold attention. As a rule, posters and charts are not designed for inspection as lengthy or as intense, but they should attract and hold attention.

All four of these media formats should be of adequate size so that they can be understood at a glance. This is especially true for posters and charts.

Because they must be handled by the user, study prints need to be durable.

Posters, charts, and study prints must have legible letters and captions and should contain clear symbols and legends.

Flat pictures and study prints especially need to portray true-size relationships.

All formats should be aesthetically pleasing and employ appropriate use of colors and color contrasts.

All formats should stimulate and/or focus thought.

Evaluative Review Sources

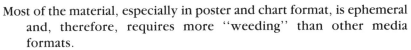
Very few "normal" reviewing sources adequately address these four media formats, except as noted below:
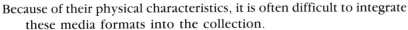

Audiovisual review section of *Library Journal.*
Audiovisual review section of *School Library Journal.*
McCain, Claudia. "Posters for Patrons." *School Library Journal* 21 (Dec. 1974): 24.
Orlin, Lesley E., ed. *Media Review Digest.* Ann Arbor, Mich.: Pierian Pr., yearly.
"Planning for a Print and Poster Collection in Children's Libraries." *Top of the News* 37 (Spring 1981): 283–87.
"Posters-A-Plenty." *Top of the News* 32 (June 1976): 369–72.

Nonevaluative Sources

Titles listed below represent publications since 1970:

Harkheimer, Foley A., ed. *Educator's Guide to Free Health, Physical Education and Recreation Materials.* 18th rev. ed. Randolph, Wis.: Educator's Progress Service, 1985.
Keenan, Linda, ed. *Educator's Index to Free Materials.* 92nd rev. ed. Randolph, Wis.: Educator's Progress Service, 1983.
Nehmer, Kathleen S., ed. *Educator's Grade Guide to Free Teaching Aids.* 27th rev. ed. Randolph, Wis.: Educator's Progress Service, 1983.
Nelki, Andrea. *The Picture Researcher's Handbook.* New York: Scribner's, 1975.
Posters, Charts, Picture Sets and Decals. Washington, D.C.: U.S. Government Printing Office, 1983.
Saterstrom, Mary H. *Educator's Guide to Free Science Materials.* 26th rev. ed. Randolph, Wis.: Educator's Progress Service, 1985.
Shaffer, Dale E. *Educator's Sourcebook of Posters* (437 Jennings Ave., Salem, Ohio 44460), 1981.
Social Responsibilities Round Table of the American Library Assn. *Alternatives in Print.* 6th ed. New York: Neal-Schuman, 1980.
Social Responsibilities Round Table of the American Library Assn. *Alternatives in Print,* 77–78. 5th ed. San Francisco: Volcano Pr., 1977.
Social Responsibilities Round Table of the American Library Assn. *Alternatives in Print,* 73–74. 3rd ed. San Francisco: Volcano Pr., 1973.
Suttles, Patricia H. *Educator's Guide to Free Social Studies Materials.* 25th rev. ed. Randolph, Wis.: Educator's Progress Service, 1985.

MAINTENANCE AND MANAGEMENT

Storage and Care

A storage and care program needs to be undertaken to ensure that the media do not suffer unnecessary damage, to limit the cost of preservation efforts, to limit the loss of information, to extend the life of media, and to increase collection use. Temperature, humidity, and dust are three environmental factors which must be controlled to prolong

Temperature

the life of media. A consistent temperature of 60 to 70°F, a 40 to 50% humidity range, and a dust-free environment will do much to safeguard a media collection.

These media, which generally are not very durable, often require a variety of preservation measures. Posters, flat pictures, and charts can be made more durable when they are mounted on stiff posterboard. Mounting these media with the heat process, using Chartex, or the wet-mounting process, using muslin, will provide a cloth backing for these media, thereby making them more durable. Other types of preservation include sprays and lamination. Items which are of more permanent value can be framed.

These media can be stored in a variety of ways. Large flat items can be housed in metal map-storage cases. Some of the smaller items might be better suited for storage in a filing cabinet, as part of a vertical file, or in a picture file. Framed items can be stored vertically. Study prints, which are produced on sturdy materials, often will not fit into filing cabinets, and require boxes for storage.

Management Problems and Solutions

The media discussed in this chapter present many management problems. Selection and acquisition of these materials is often a serendipitous process due to the fact that many are of such an ephemeral nature. There is very little in the way of bibliographic control with regard to these media, and the prospects for more access to evaluative and nonevaluative sources appear bleak.

As much of this type of media is available *gratis* from corporations, one must be aware of the potential for bias. Therefore, to ensure the development of an objective collection, these media must be examined carefully to detect subtle signs of bias or stereotyping. Obviously, if these media are found to be biased, they should not be in the collection.

Once these media have been acquired, provision must be made so that users can easily locate them. Some of the smaller items, which can be stored in a filing cabinet, could be arranged alphabetically by broad subject headings. Large items, which need to be stored in metal storage cases, could be placed in specific drawers according to subject headings or a classification system. If a general access point is used, such as a card catalog or a card file, references to these media must be included so that the user cannot only determine if the institution has these media, but can also determine where they are.

Concerns related to the circulation of these items must be addressed. Some of the larger items can prove to be somewhat unwieldy and need to be protected from the elements. Items which have been laminated or mounted on muslin or Chartex are somewhat flexible. They can be easily rolled up and placed into tubes, or secured with rubber bands, so that the user can easily transport them. Items which have been framed or mounted on posterboard cannot be handled as easily and are more subject to damage from inclement weather. In such instances, plastic bags should be used to help protect these items.

Of the various media collected, posters, flat pictures, study prints, and charts usually are only of temporary value to a collection. Therefore, the staff must be more diligent in weeding these media from the collection than for other media. Additionally, these media must be inspected more often to detect signs of damage and deterioration.

Other Concerns

These media formats are probably the easiest to prepare. Very little in the way of technical expertise or equipment is required to produce usable materials which fall into this category. Individual posters can be created by using an opaque projector to enlarge an image which can be traced onto a large piece of posterboard or paper. Flat pictures can be found in a variety of places and can be used to produce study prints. About the only real limitation to the local production of such media is the imagination and initiative of the exhibitor.

There are many sources from which some of these media formats can be acquired free of charge. Pictures can be obtained from old magazines and books, pamphlets, advertising material, travel brochures, newspapers, and postcards. Posters and charts are often available from museums, travel agencies, governmental agencies, trade associations, professional organizations, chambers of commerce, theatres, and bookstores.

ADDITIONAL RESOURCES

Abbott, Andrew D., and Rosemary A. Salesi. "Preserve Your Media Collection Today." *Audiovisual Instruction* 24 (Sept. 1979): 29–31.

Barnicoat, John. *A Concise History of Posters: 1870–1970.* New York: Harry Abrams, 1972.

Beatty, LaMond F. *Still Pictures.* Englewood Cliffs, N.J.: Educational Technology, 1981.

Berry, June. "Filing Miscellaneous Materials." *Library Journal* 37 (Feb. 15, 1962): 818–20.

"A Bookstore Sideline: Posters and Prints." *Publishers Weekly* 213 (Jan. 30, 1978): 99–106.

Coplan, Kate. *Poster Ideas and Bulletin Board Techniques for Libraries and Schools.* Dobbs Ferry, N.Y.: Oceana, 1962.

Coty, Patricia Ann. "Organization of Non-print Materials in the Library." *Catholic Library World* 52 (Mar. 1981): 342–43.

Dale, Edgar. *Audiovisual Methods in Teaching.* Hinsdale, Ill.: Dryden Pr., 1969.

Ellison, John W. "Non-book Collections: Storage and Care Practices." *Catholic Library World* 54 (Dec. 1982): 206–9.

Foster, Donald L. *Prints in the Public Library.* Metuchen, N.J.: Scarecrow, 1973.

Goldstein, S., and I. C. Wolfe. *How to Organize and Maintain the Picture/Pamphlet File.* Dobbs Ferry, N.Y.: Oceana, 1968.

Hicks, Warren B., and Alma M. Tillin. *Managing Multimedia Libraries.* New York: Bowker, 1977.

Hill, Donna. *The Picture File.* Syracuse: Gaylord Professional Publications, 1978.

Hill, Joy. *Photo Storage and Retrieval.* Washington, D.C.: ERIC Document Reproduction Service, 1973. ED 107 278.

Ireland, Norma Olin. *The Picture File in School, College, and Public Libraries.* Boston: Faxon, 1952.

Margolin, Victor. *American Poster Renaissance.* New York: Watson-Guptill, 1975.

Miller, Shirley. *The Vertical File and Its Satellites.* Littleton, Colo.: Libraries Unlimited, 1979.

Minor, Ed, and Harvey Frye. *Techniques for Producing Visual Instructional Media.* New York: McGraw-Hill, 1977.

Schonberg, Jeanne. "How to Frame Your Prints." *American Artist* 37 (Nov. 1973): 34–35, 89.

Shaw, Renata V. "Picture Professionalism: Part I." *Special Libraries* 65 (Oct./Nov. 1974): 421–29.

———. "Picture Professionalism: Part II." *Special Libraries* 65 (Dec. 1974): 505–11.

"Sources of Art Prints for Children's Collections." *Top of the News* 37 (Winter 1981): 198–201.

Weihs, Jean, Shirley Lewis, and Janet Macdonald. *Nonbook Materials: The Organization of Integrated Collections.* 2nd ed. Ottawa: Canadian Library Assn., 1979.

Clara L. DiFelice

ch. 6

Holographs

THE MEDIUM

Definition

Hologram is a term applied to the special photographic film or plate which records the amplitude (intensity) and phase (shape of the wave) distributions of a coherent wave, usually light. The word is derived from the Greek _holos,_ meaning "whole," and _gramma,_ meaning "message."

Holography is a technique used to record and reconstruct a hologram. It involves recording, on a special photographic plate or film, the interference pattern of two sets of waves, one termed the _object_ wave and the other a _reference_ wave. Essentially, a coherent light source (generally a laser) is aimed at a prism which splits the beam in two. These beams strike a mirror and then pass through lenses which refract the light, enlarging the beams. One beam, the object wave, reflects off the object being holographed and carries its image to this special photographic plate, where it intersects with the reference beam. The interference pattern of the two beams is recorded in emulsion. Once the plate is developed and the reference beam is reapplied through the back of the plate, the object is re-created where it would have appeared, with all its dimensionality intact.

94

Brief History

Dennis Gabor received the Nobel Prize in Physics in 1971 for his work on the technique of producing holograms. In 1947, building on the theory of light as waves, first expressed by Christian Huygens and later by Thomas Young, Gabor's experiments proved that "the interference of the object wave and of the coherent background or 'reference wave' will then produce interference fringes."[1] With the interference pattern photographically captured on a film or plate, and the reference wave reilluminated from behind, the object wave will reappear. If the object wave carries the pattern of an object, that pattern will re-create the object as an image.

Gabor was attempting to improve upon the images available through the electron microscope. His method proved unusable, however, because there was no light source with a strong enough intensity to provide truly coherent light waves. Additional work on improvement of the theory was done during the early fifties, as well as attempts to create holograms with other wave sources such as X rays and electromagnetic waves. Nothing of significance was produced and research into holograms lapsed.

In 1962 Emmett Leith and Juris Upatnieks, at the University of Michigan, combined the theory of holography with the light waves provided by the laser. Their development of off-axis holograms, in which a light source's beam is split to provide both the reference wave and the object wave, resolved a major problem of double imagery in the early holograms. The strength of the laser's beam also "made it possible to use very fine-grain, low-speed photographic emulsions and to produce large holograms, with reasonable exposure times."[2] Leith and Upatnieks also worked with storing different images on the same film plate by varying the angle of the reference wave.

At about the same time, Yuril N. Denisyuk proposed using layers of emulsion to produce reflection holograms which could be seen in white light. In 1965, G. W. Stroke and A. E. Labeyrie produced the first two-color hologram viewed with white light. These "volume" holograms are made up of the interference patterns embedded in the emulsion. "After development, the complex of layers, illuminated with white light, reflected only a narrow wave band around the original color, because only for this color did the wavelets scattered at the Lippman layers add up in phase."[3]

1. Dennis Gabor, "Holography, 1948–1971," *Science* 28 (1972): 299.
2. Ibid., 303.
3. Ibid., 309.

A further development in the use of holograms occurred in 1965, when scientists working with holography applied interferometrical principles to double-exposure holograms and discovered that fringe patterns would expose defects of manufacturing. An example is the testing of automobile tires for improper bonding of the layers of rubber. A hologram is made of the tire at rest; hot air is blown on it, and another hologram is made on the same photographic plate. Any defect in the bonding of the rubber shows clearly when the fringe patterns are compared. Holographic images are recorded so accurately that this technique can "visualize deformation in a concrete slab caused by the weight of a dime."[4]

In the late sixties, developments by researchers included the 360° hologram and the extremely light-sensitive emulsion, dichromated gelatin. These, along with Stephen Benton's invention of a way to reconstruct transmission holograms by the use of white light (an ordinary high-intensity light bulb), made hologram display much more effective. Lloyd Cross combined many of the new techniques to create the integral hologram. "Integrals are the first practical holographic movies. Each one is really hundreds of holograms made from frames of ordinary movie film, thus making possible a hologram of almost any imagery that can be recorded with a conventional movie camera."[5]

In-depth research has been done in the Soviet Union on the possibility of three-dimensional holographic movies. In 1976, Viktor G. Komar and O. I. Ioshin made remarkable advances in this field. They managed to project a 70mm film for 45 seconds on a "screen made out of elliptical mirrors that directed the image to each individual seat. It showed an actress walking at you with a bouquet of flowers covering her face. But if you moved around in your seat or stood up, you could actually look around the flowers and see her face."[6]

To see this illusion, it is necessary for the viewer to intercept the rays of the hologram itself, not a projection of the light rays emerging from the hologram. One way to do this is by a mirror, but this proved impractical because of the need for a mirror-screen for each member of the audience. The Moscow researchers solved this problem by making the screen itself "a hologram of superimposed mirrors . . . made by exposing a photographic plate the size of the screen to beams diverging from each seat in the theatre and from the point where the image

    4. H. John Caulfield, "The Wonder of Holography," *National Geographic* 165 (1984): 68.
    5. Edward Bush, "Holography: A (General) Technical Guide," *Art and Cinema* 5 (1979): 44.
    6. Sal Manna, "Holography," *Omni* 4 (1981): 168.

was to be formed. When the light rays from the projector impinged on the holographic screen, they came to focus at each seat."[7]

During the seventies, experimentation with holograms moved out of the technical labs and into the hands of the artists. Working with low-cost laser setups, holoartists have taken the techniques of Leith, Benton, Denisyuk and Cross and refined them. With few resources, they have created works that range from surrealistic landscapes to a woman blowing a kiss."[8] (Actually, the integral hologram of a woman blowing a kiss was made by Lloyd Cross.) The repository for a majority of the artistic holograms is the Museum of Holography in New York, which opened in 1976. The variety of exhibitions there and in London, Chicago, and San Francisco have kept holography "in the grasp of the artist and the eye of the public. As a result, a new breed of artist is learning to create images that do not fill simply planes and surfaces, but also space."[9]

A few of the artists, such as Harriet Casdin-Silver, are associated with academia, though not in the fine-arts department. Casdin-Silver was, in 1976, a fellow at MIT's Center for Advanced Visual Studies and an assistant professor of research in Brown University's Department of Physics.[10]

Many physics and engineering departments throughout the country have holography apparatus in their labs and cover the theory of holography in basic courses. Some of the first academic workshops on holography were offered by Tung H. Jeong at Lake Forest College (Illinois). One of his early students was Rosemary Jackson, who founded New York's Museum of Holography. Dr. Jeong has always been an advocate of "holography for the masses,"[11] and was responsible for developing advanced techniques in producing holograms.

Holograms were used as advertisements early in the seventies, most notably the Body by Fisher display for General Motors and Cartier's hologram of a hand holding a diamond bracelet, which appeared outside one of their windows. While not widely exploited since, this form of advertisement presents possibilities for the future as hologram production techniques are refined. A more recent example is the use of

7. "Going to the Roundies (Holographic Motion Pictures)," *Scientific American* 224 (1981): 91.

8. Matthew Tekulsky and Lynn Asinof, "Holography: Laser Pictures That Live," *Science Digest* 89 (1981): 49.

9. Peggy Sealfon, "Holography," *Horizon* 22 (1979): 33.

10. Steve Ditlea, "What Is a Hologram? How Does It Float in Mid-Air . . . And Is It Art?" *Ms* 5 (1976): 34.

11. Manna, "Holography," 38.

small reflection holograms as souvenirs of the 1982 World's Fair. Easily mastered and duplicated in bulk, these plastic, Mylar-backed holograms prove entrancing when first seen.

With the 1980s, holography entered its fourth decade of development. Scientific research and design has matured the industrial application of holographic interferometry; it is used extensively in the testing of manufactured components which must withstand stress. Holographic optical elements—that is, holograms of a lens or mirror— have "proved to be as good, if not better, than the real thing. A large holographic optical element weighs substantially less. . . . Rather than bending the light by its shape, the flat and relatively thin hologram's light-interference pattern bends it."[12]

An example of the use of holograms for this purpose is IBM's checkout scanners for supermarkets. Their ability to focus the laser beam onto the Universal Product Code, despite how the package is passed over the scanner, has provided a strong selling point for checkout systems. These and other examples of holograms' use, "behind the scenes" as it were, prove that holographic techniques and the potential use for holograms continue to be explored by researchers.

Currently, reports about holograms and holographic techniques include reference to computer-generated holograms, X-ray holography, pattern-recognition holographic memory for robots, holographic storage for computer memories, and mass produced foil-incised holograms to thwart counterfeiters of both money and charge cards. These reports show some of the depth of application for a technique that began as a curious exploration of the theory of light waves.

Unique Characteristics

A hologram can capture a moment in time. In essence, it allows the measurement of moving particles from any given instant. With pulsed laser light, the "moment" could be 1 fifty/billionth of a second.

Holograms are images stored on a special photographic plate, without a camera or lens. The plate looks like a series of faint gray lines—not at all like the image.

The hologram's reconstructed image is seen in three dimensions, with great parallax, and the image cannot be felt or held. The image is created in space by focused points of light.

Holograms record accurate microscopic detail. In addition, there is

12. Edward Edelson, "Bizarre New World of Holography," *Popular Science* 214 (1979): 91.

amazing depth of field, as all levels of the image remain in sharp focus. Also, if a magnifying glass appears in a hologram, it will magnify any object placed behind it.

The hologram's plate stores the object's image pattern throughout. Any fragment broken off can be used to reconstruct the entire image, though loss of definition is apparent with smaller portions. This provides extreme durability for the image, making it barely sensitive to scratches and dirt.

Holograms can be used as a method of data storage; theoretically, you could store 10 billion bits per centimeter and provide random access in microseconds. Denseness of storage is limited solely by the photo-sensitive materials currently available.

A stored hologram is wavelength selective. The hologram formed by each wavelength can be retrieved only by that wavelength.

A hologram can be created by any kind of wave where phase and intensity can be recorded: light, sound, microwave, X ray, or computer generated.

A hologram always produces a positive image, regardless of whether the plate is positive or negative.

Advantages

Holograms are three-dimensional images. They allow the viewer to move from side to side or up and down and see a different view from each angle. Visual representation of the image is "rounded off," exactly duplicating the object holographed.

Holograms have a sharp focus for all areas of the image, even if a hologram is of an object not normally seen with visible light, or must be viewed through a microscope.

Holograms can provide spatial orientation; they have been used in training pilots to judge distances.

Holograms can be created with 120° and 360° film planes, allowing the appearance of movement as the viewer circles the hologram.

Holograms can be produced which show both the front and back sides of an object, lending a realism even beyond that provided by three-dimensionality.

Holograms do not require as much careful handling as other film media. Those imprinted on foil are expected to last for some time, with little degradation of the image. Others are virtually impervious to scratches and breakage, due to the redundancy of the information.

Holograms are excellent for teaching scientific principles and abstract concepts; for example, holography demonstrates the principle that vision is an illusion. It is also effective for demonstrating the dif-

ferent wavelengths of light (colors), since an image created with
an argon laser (blue light) appears smaller than the same image
created with a helium-neon laser (red).

Holograms can be utilized in museology, because numerous ancient
objects cannot be handled or displayed for a variety of reasons:
perishability, security, etc. Also, holograms can assist in establishing
the origin and identity of objects, determining their age and state
of preservation.

Holograms can be used in libraries. The main branch can have the real
object or exhibit, while branch libraries have holograms of the object or exhibit.

Holographic movies have the potential of visual realism, because the
quality of the reconstructed image is not affected by the motion
of film through a projected beam. The images would not be
degraded if the film moved irregularly through the projector. The
size of the individual frames making up the holographic movie
would be smaller than those currently in use, leading to a reduction in cost, size of camera, and size of the projector. If frames
were scratched or dirty, it would not be noticeable.

The thickness of the recording emulsion and the hologram's characteristics allow for increased storage capabilities. The images may
be layered throughout the emulsion, and angles at which the image is to be retrieved may be built into a playback mechanism.

Holograms can be made of a "frozen" moment, as small as the pulse
of a laser will allow. Motion otherwise too swift to view can be
stopped and recorded with high resolution.

Holograms have been developed which can be readily duplicated from
the master. They act as a security device for identification purposes,
as proof of validity, and are being examined for further uses along
these lines.

Holograms can become optical lenses which provide a scanning
capability for varied angles. These devices, in use at supermarket
checkout counters, allow for scanning the Universal Product Code
quickly and efficiently, regardless of their size or location.

Holograms provide a means by which two three-dimensional objects
can occupy the same location at the same moment.

Simple holograms can be made in any location where proper care is
taken and motionless equipment and a darkroom are available.

Disadvantages

Holograms are scarce, and tend to be artistic and scientific rather than
educational or commercial at this time.

Many of the holograms currently available are monochromatic, either red or green, depending on the laser used in the recording process. A system for producing holograms in natural color has not been perfected.

Holograms don't convey a sense of bulk or presence; they seem ethereal and insubstantial. Depth of any scene is limited since even thick emulsions provide for relatively few interference points.

image would be useful

Size can be a problem. For most holograms, the plate must be the same size as (or larger than) the object in order to contain the image. If the image is very large, a very large laser must be used to provide the coherent light source. Very large lasers are few and far between, as well as expensive.

The expense of having holograms made to order can be difficult to determine at this time, as there are few firms in the business of producing holograms.

In producing holograms, any motion destroys their accuracy. Even air currents, moving the object, are enough for total blurring if a low-power laser is used to record the image.

Beyond the need for stability, a darkroom is necessary for making holograms, even after purchase of a kit. In addition, high-resolution recording materials can be expensive.

Equipment for producing many holograms is rarely available to artists, due to its expense.

Low-cost holograms exhibit the "speckle effect" whereby the surface of the object appears bumpy, due to the wavelength of visible light.

There is an absence of evaluative sources to aid in the selection of holograms.

Cataloging standards and procedures are still being formulated.

Holograms, to be properly appreciated, must be viewed in a different way from two-dimensional imagery. Users must be educated in the proper way to view holograms.

Holograms cannot be created with natural light. Currently, a laser provides the only light source coherent enough to form the hologram of an object.

Some holograms can only be viewed by looking directly at the film or plate, which limits the size of the audience that can view the image at the same time.

Holograms can have specific playback requirements—for example, a high-intensity bulb at a 45° angle—for viewing a reflection hologram mounted in a specific way.

SELECTION

Special Criteria

Clarity and accuracy of the three-dimensional image are important.
Type and size of the hologram in relation to viewing conditions at the
    institution must be considered.
Relative positions of object and reference beams, as well as the op-
    tical components of the laser setup used in recording, will deter-
    mine the setup for viewing the hologram.
The nature of the light source for recording the image may be impor-
    tant, since some holograms are more easily reconstructed for view-
    ing than others.
Nature of the recording medium—photographic film, dichromated
    gelatin, or another type of emulsion—will determine the ease with
    which the hologram may be viewed.

Evaluative Review Sources

None of the usual evaluative sources cover holograms at this time.
Critical evaluations of a particular artist's works may be available in
art journals, or *Holosphere,* a journal for holography published by the
Museum of Holography in New York. An example of an evaluative re-
view is Peggy Sealfon's article about the Hol-O-Fame exhibit at the
Museum of Holography in 1979.

Nonevaluative Sources

Many companies are working with some phase of hologram production. The following listing provides sources for information about
holograms, as well as availability of holograms.

Ealing Corp.
22 Pleasant St.
South Natic, MA 01760

Edmund Scientific
101 E. Gloucester Pike
Barrington, NJ 08007

Gaertner Scientific Co.
1203 Wrightwood Ave.
Chicago, IL 60614

INTEGRAF
P.O. Box 586
Lake Forest, IL 60045

Jodon Engineering Associates
145-T Enterprise Dr.
Ann Arbor, MI 48103

Multiplex Co.
3221 20th St.
San Francisco, CA 94110

Newport Research Corp.
18235-T Mt. Baldy Circle
Fountain Valley, CA 92708

New York Holographic Lab
34 W. 13th St.
New York, NY 10011

Quantrad Corp.
19900-TS. Normandie Ave.
Torrence, CA 90502

U.S. Laser Corp.
60-TW Prospect St.
Waldwick, NJ 07463

In addition to companies, art galleries and museums are displaying artistic holograms. They can provide holograms, and occasionally they offer seminars on making holograms. The following listing gives addresses of some museums, galleries, and schools which offer information and are a source for holograms:

Buffalo Museum of Science
Humboldt Parkway
Buffalo, NY 14211

Gallery 1134
Fine Arts Research and
    Holographic Center
Museum of the School
    of Holography
1134 W. Washington
Chicago, IL 60607

Holos Gallery
1792 Haight St.
San Francisco, CA 94117

House of Holograms
29291 Southfield Rd.
Southfield, MI 48076

Museum of Holography
11 Mercer St.
New York, NY 10013
(212) 925-0581
    (Offers a traveling exhibition,
    "Through the Looking Glass")

Odyssey Image Center
8853 Sunset Blvd.
Hollywood, CA 90069

Sirens of Light
Goodies Warehouse
200 Second Ave.
Nashville, TN

MAINTENANCE AND MANAGEMENT

Storage and Care

Because holograms are a new medium, there are few accepted practices to follow for their storage and care. For specific requirements, refer to the chapters on photographs, slides, and microforms.

Holograms can be treated like photographs, and stored in a vertical file, cabinet, or drawer.

Place each hologram in a separate pocket or folder.

Holographic plates can be intershelved with books, with a circulation pocket on the outer side of the folder or envelope.

Fingerprints and dust reduce the clarity, but have no significant damaging effects.

At present, it is unknown what effects temperature and humidity have, but the same care should be utilized as with microfiche or slides: no extremes.

If a hologram is recorded on a glass plate, care should be taken to avoid breakage.

If the hologram is mounted, water seeping between the plate and the mount could cause the hologram to fade. Use a barely damp cloth to clean the face of the hologram, and do not rub the cloth against the edges.

Understand the properties of the emulsion used for the hologram and its development processes. Some chemicals can virtually wipe out the hologram's interference pattern, if they come in contact with the plate.

Management Problems and Solutions

Most holograms available at this time are artistic rather than informational, and the uses to which they are put and their place in the collection should reflect this fact. Where people will obviously benefit from the unique qualifications of a hologram, such as the ability to present realia or sculpture otherwise unattainable, the hologram should be selected.

Where holograms act as an information resource of and by themselves—as visual proof of the theory of light waves, for example—there is no doubt that they should be acquired with that purpose in mind. When more than one is acquired—an example of each type of hologram, for instance—then a collection exists. There are also collections of artistic holograms, and collections are established where any other purpose is identified. A portion of the institution's budget should be designated for the purchase and maintenance of the holographic collection, if the need for such has been identified.

Proper identification is achieved by cataloging and processing the holograms for the institution's users. Holograms should be represented in the main catalog with enough detail to thoroughly define the hologram—both subject access and technical information, such as the method used in recording the hologram.

Where no special equipment is needed to view holograms, they should circulate as do other materials in the institution, using existing systems. Policies relating to the use of holograms should duplicate those of other materials—for example, fines for overdues.

Holograms should be treated like other materials: intershelved and interstored with print materials wherever possible. The possibility of maintaining a permanent display area for holograms could be considered where specialized equipment is needed to view them. Projection equipment to access the holograms should be readily available to the users.

When holography becomes more prevalent and simpler in its recording process, it must be considered as a production technique. The place it may hold in the institution will depend on existing policies regarding production. Perhaps users and/or staff will create holograms when recording equipment is readily available. Holograms are being recognized as artistic, educational, and information resources. When any new medium of expression arises, the management problems which accompany it often seem insurmountable. Adapting practices and procedures that are already in place does not always work for new media. On management's side are the experiences associated with the adaptation of other media to a collection: the solutions which worked and those which failed. Before holograms become fully defined as resources, and readily available, solutions should be applied and procedures should be in place for taking advantage of this intriguing medium.

Other Concerns

A written explanation of holography cannot convey the full effect of this unique medium. Unless one actually sees a hologram, the principles at work seem to be couched in terms that are too complex for understanding by nonscientists. Viewing a hologram display, however, creates a sense of wonder which overcomes any deficiency in understanding. Simple acceptance of the phenomenon seems in order. Despite this, the following discussion will attempt to explain the process involved in creating a hologram and will outline the various types of holograms currently available.

Holography is basically a two-step process: recording an object or person and then reconstructing an image of the object or person for display. Holography and photography both use a photo-sensitive material as a recording medium. Light energy, like all other forms of energy in the electromagnetic spectrum, is a wave form that has both amplitude and phase. Conventional photographic film, being an "energy-detection system," records the intensity (square of the amplitude) but not the phase of the wavelength, giving only a two-dimensional representation.

Holography is a method of recording both the amplitude and the phase, thereby storing a three-dimensional representation of the object. This is accomplished by creating what is known as an *interference pattern,* also known as a *difference in phase.* Laser light is coherent—readily in-phase. It is different from ordinary light in that all the light coming out of the laser is of the same wavelength and the light waves are all lined up with each other, trough to trough, crest to crest. Ordinary light is incoherent, out of phase, and of different wavelengths.

In making a hologram, one set of light waves from the laser (the reference beam) is sent uninterrupted to the photographic plate. These waves are still coherent (all of the same length and still lined up) when they arrive at the photographic plate. The other set of light waves (the object beam) reflects off an object, changing its symmetry. This reflected light then falls onto the photographic plate (which consists of fine-grain black-and-white-type emulsion) and meets the reference wave. Where they cross, an interference pattern is created that very accurately resembles the object being holographed. The plate, having been exposed by the light pattern, is developed and a hologram is created.

To view a hologram accurately, it is necessary to reconstruct the image by passing a coherent (laser) light through the hologram. The interference pattern (difference in phase/diffraction pattern), recorded on the hologram, bends the light in a new direction. Because this pattern was formed by using light reflected from the object, the light defracted by the hologram should be identical to the light originally reflected from the object. The viewer is then able to see the tangible object itself, with great depth and parallax.

Where the basic technique for creating a hologram varies, the types of holograms are differentiated mainly by the kind of light needed to view the hologram:

Transmission holograms are viewed by light shining through the hologram.

Reflection holograms are illuminated with white light. Their advantage is that illumination shines on the front of the hologram.

Computer-generated holograms are synthetic holograms, that is, the interference pattern is calculated on a computer and plotted. They can reconstruct light waves reflecting off a nonexisting object.

ADDITIONAL RESOURCES

BOOKS

Butters, John N. *Holography and Its Technology.* London: Peter Peregrinus, 1971.

Caulfield, H. J., and Sun Lu. *The Applications of Holography.* New York: John Wiley, 1970.

Collier, Robert J., Christoph B. Burckhardt, and Lawrence H. Lin. *Optical Holography.* New York: Academic Pr., 1971.

DeVelis, John, and George Reynolds. *Theory and Applications of Holography.* Reading, Mass.: Addison-Wesley, 1967.

Dowbenko, George. *Homegrown Holography.* New York: American Photographic Book Publishing, 1978.

Dudley, David D. *Holography: A Survey.* Washington, D.C.: Government Printing Office, 1973.

Francon, M. *Holography.* Trans. Grace M. Spruch. New York: Academic Pr., 1974.

Hariharan, P. *Optical Holography: Principles, Techniques and Applications.* New Rochelle, N.Y.: Cambridge Univ. Pr., 1984.

Harry, John E. *Industrial Lasers and Their Applications.* New York: McGraw-Hill, 1974.

Jackson, P., and E. A. Bush. *Through the Looking Glass: The Opening of the Museum of Holography.* New York: Museum of Holography, 1977.

Klein, H. Arthur. *Holography.* Philadelphia: Lippincott, 1970.

Kock, Winston. *Lasers and Holography.* 2nd ed. New York: Dover, 1981.

Lehmann, Matt. *Holography: Technique and Practice.* New York: Focal Pr., 1970.

Okoshi, Takanori. *Three-Dimensional Imaging Techniques.* New York: Academic Pr., 1976.

Saxby, Graham. *Holograms: How to Make and Display Them.* New York: Focal Pr., 1980.

Scientific American. *Light and Its Uses.* San Francisco: W. H. Freeman, 1980.

Smith, Howard M. *Principles of Holography.* 2nd ed. New York: John Wiley, 1975.

Stroke, George W. *An Introduction to Coherent Optics and Holography.* 2nd ed. New York: Academic Pr., 1969.

Unterseher, Fred, et al. *Holography Handbook.* Berkeley, Calif.: Ross Books, 1982.

Wenyon, Michael. *Understanding Holography.* New York: Arco, 1978.

ENCYCLOPEDIA ARTICLES

Encyclopedia Americana, 1981, s.v. "Holography."

McGraw-Hill Encyclopedia of Science and Technology, 5th ed., s.v. "Holography."

FILMS

Holography. 16mm, 7 min., 1974. Doubleday Multimedia.

Holography. 16mm, 29 min., 1970. KCET/TV (Los Angeles). Distributed by Public Television Library, 475 L'Enfant Plaza, SW, Washington, DC 20024.

Holography: Memories in Light. 16mm, 21 min., 1985. Arthur Mokin Productions.

Introduction to Holography. 16mm, 17 min., 1972. Encyclopaedia Britannica Educational Corp.

JOURNAL ARTICLES

Anderson, J. "Holography." *Northlight* 11 (1979): 1–41.

Asimov, Isaac. "I Can't Believe I Saw the Whole Thing." *Science* 55 (1972): 25–32.

Barson, John, and Gerry Mendelson. "Holography—A New Dimension for Media." *Audiovisual Instruction* 14 (1969): 40–42.

Bush, Edward. "Holography: A (General) Technical Guide." *Art and Cinema* (Dec. 1979): 41–44.

Buterbaugh, James G. "Holography: Art in an Ephemeral Medium." *Audiovisual Instruction* 24 (1979): 20–21.

Caulfield, H. John. "The Wonder of Holography." *National Geographic* 165 (1984): 364–77.

D'Alleyrand, Marc. "Holograms: Putting the Third D into the Catalog." *Wilson Library Bulletin* 51 (1977): 746–50.

Ditlea, Steve. "What Is a Hologram? How Does It Float in Mid-Air . . . And Is It Art?" *Ms* 5 (1976): 34.

Edelson, Edward. "Bizarre New World of Holography." *Popular Science* 214 (1979): 87–91.

Gabor, Dennis. "Holography, 1948–1971." *Science* 28 (1972): 299–313.

"Going to the Roundies (Holographic Motion Pictures)." *Scientific American* 244 (1981): 86–87.

Goldberg, Norman. "Shoptalk, What Acts like a Lens, Refracts like a Lens, but Has Fewer Curves than Olive Oyl? A Holographic Lens!" *Popular Photography* 89 (1982): 11 + .

Hammona, A. L. "Holography: Beginnings of a New Art Form or at Least of an Advertising Bonanza." *Science* 80 (1973): 484–85.

Hector, Gary. "Sighting Profits in Holography." *Fortune* 107 (1983): 164–68.

Holden, Constance. "Holoart: Playing with a Budding Technology." *Science* 204 (1979): 40–41.

"The Incredible Hologram." *Newsweek* 71 (1969): 41.

Johnson, Claire, and Eleanor Briggs. "Holography as Applied to Information Storage and Retrieval Systems." *Journal of American Society for Information Science* 22 (1971): 187–92.

Kirkpatrick, Larry D., and Mac Rugheimer. "A Holographic Road Show." *Physics Teacher* 17 (1979): 25–31.

Leith, Emmett N., and Juris Upatnieks. "Photography by Laser." *Scientific American* 212 (1965): 24–35.

Lester, Michael C. "Holography: Light Wave of the Future." *Saturday Review: Education* 1 (1973): 58–59.

Lucie-Smith, E. "The Other Day." *Art and Artists* 12 (1978): 28–31.

Lungershausen, Sandy. "Current and Future Uses of Holography." *Biomedical Communications* 11 (1983): 29–33.

Malm, William P. "The Hologram as a Library Resource." *Notes* 32 (1976): 727–33.

Manna, Sal. "Holography." *Omni* 4 (1981): 38 + .

Maxwell, Monty. "Unconventional Photographic Systems: How Will They Change Your Library?" *Wilson Library Bulletin* 46 (1972): 518–22.

Porter, Alan G., and S. George. "An Elementary Introduction to Practical Holography." *American Journal of Physics* 43 (1975): 954–59.

Sealfon, Peggy. "Holography." *Horizon* 22 (1979): 32–35.

Tekulsky, Mathew, and Lynn Asinof. "Holography: Laser Pictures That Live." *Science Digest* 89 (1981): 44–51.

Yavtushenko, Ivan G., and Vladimir B. Markov. "A Museum in a Suitcase: Three-Dimensional 'Replicas' of Works of Art, Produced by the Astonishing Technique of Holography." *UNESCO Courier* 34 (Mar. 1981): 30–33.

A. Neil Yerkey

Ch. 7

Machine-Readable Data Files

THE MEDIUM

Definition

This discussion of machine-readable data files will necessarily include all kinds of computer files: data files, programs, data bases, and data banks. They all exist in the same milieu: computer "software," which includes not only data files as an information resource, but also the programs needed to create and make use of that resource.

Machine-readable files are collections of information coded by methods that require the use of a machine (typically a computer) for processing. Examples are files stored on magnetic tape, punched cards, and magnetic discs.[1] Files may be of two types: programs and data files.

Program files are step-by-step instructions, in machine-readable form, which tell a computer what to do. Depending on the task which the computer is being asked to perform, they may be classified as systems programs, compilers and interpreters, utility programs, and applications programs.

Data files are named collections of all occurrences of a given type of record. They are the raw data which a program manipulates to pro-

---

1. *Anglo-American Cataloguing Rules,* 2nd ed. (Chicago: American Library Assn., 1978), 567.

vide useful information. Data files may be both output from or input to a program. They may be the end product of a processing run, or intermediate storage. In terms of the kinds of information stored in them, data files may be *textual* (correspondence produced by a word processor, full text of literary works, documentation); *numerical* (census data, chemical and physical data, financial and statistical data); *records* (names and addresses, insurance data, class lists, inventory data, business records); or *bibliographic* (periodical references, book cataloging information). (Additional, related definitions are presented later in this chapter.)

Brief History

Since machine-readable data files exist on various storage media, this historical review will focus on the history of those media rather than that of the computer itself. The earliest computers had no external storage; instructions and data were "wired" into the computer, and it had to be "rewired" for each new application. Storage was accomplished simply by saving "wiring boards" for each different application.

The first real storage medium was the punched card, used for input, output, and storage. It was developed by Herman Hollerith, who adapted an idea of Joseph Jacquard's, in which Jacquard used holes in a card to control a weaving loom. Cards and tabulating machines were first used to store, sort, arrange, and print data from the 1890 census. Electromechanical tabulating machines used punched cards for many years before the computer was developed. Following development of electronic computers in the 1950s, cards became the most successful and widely used storage medium. They are still used for many applications, but their use has diminished with the development of discs and the rise of microcomputers. Today, cards are used mainly for temporary transfer of data and as "triggering" data. For example, a library circulation system may have a card in each book which contains only the book's accession number. This card would be used to "call up" the complete book information from disc storage. The same principle is used for a parts inventory or utility usage system, where the bulk of the information is stored on discs, but a card is used to locate desired records.

Magnetic tape was developed in the early 1960s as a faster and more compact way to store information and get it into and out of a computer. Today, tape is used mainly for archival storage and as a convenient medium by which to transfer data from computer to computer. Because tape is a sequential-access medium (records must be read off in the same order in which they were put on and the tape rewound after each use), it is relatively slow and not suitable for transaction-oriented applications in which records must be located rapidly and in random order.

Discs were developed in the late 1960s as a fast, flexible way to get data into and out of a computer. Most modern applications require two things: (1) the storage medium must always be available (online), and (2) records must be retrieved in random, rather than sequential, order. Discs provide those capabilities, and have made possible the myriad data-base applications which are not feasible with tapes or cards.

There has been a drastic change in the way organizations acquire and use machine-readable files. During the 1960s, some commercial and governmental organizations began developing machine-readable data files for their own use or the use of their clients. Large universities and corporations bought or leased these files. The files were transferred physically by mailing tape back and forth. With the advent of sophisticated telecommunications technology, combined with increasing computer capabilities, we entered the "online age" in the 1970s. Increasingly, transfer is being done electronically rather than physically; data files are being *used* rather than *acquired*.

Large organizations create and maintain data files which consist of a combination of internal and external data. Maintenance is usually the responsibility of a data processing department which keeps tapes, cards, and discs in a properly air conditioned environment, following standard data processing organization procedures. Intellectual organization, documentation, and control of data files remain a problem, although there have been attempts at standardizing the procedures.[2] The emergence of microcomputers has complicated this picture. Now, the data processing function is being distributed throughout the organization. Organizations which have had no data processing functions previously are now able to create a variety of data files, most of which are locally produced. They may be shared or sold.

Since the late 1970s, there has been a trend away from file processing and toward data-base processing. With a data-base management system (DBMS), users have access only to the data which they need from a larger body of data which has been gathered to meet many needs.

2. John D. Byrum and Judith Rowe, "An Integrated, User-Oriented System for Documentation and Control of Machine-Readable Data Files," *Library Resources & Technical Services* 16 (Summer 1972): 338–46.

Unique Characteristics

This discussion will focus mainly on the characteristics of the various storage media, and not on characteristics of data files themselves, since the latter are very dependent on the type of data and their application. Characteristics which are expressed as "advantages" or "disadvantages" will be listed in those sections. Following are characteristics which apply to all machine-readable media.[3]

1. Information is digitized in some form of binary coding through the use of holes or magnetized spots.

2. Digitized data can be read only by a machine. An exception is cards which may have equivalent English text printed across the top.

3. Another machine-readable file, a program, must be used to create, manipulate, store, and use; data files are not usable by themselves.

4. Most operating systems have the ability to copy or transfer data.

CARDS

Cards have information coded as combinations of holes punched in cardboard. Electromechanical or optical sensors "read" the presence of holes and send the information to the computer's memory for processing. Other characteristics are:

Data is structured in an 80-column format, 1 column per character.
Cards are readable by humans.
Cards are subject to wear, tear, and moisture, but not to magnetic
    interference.
Cards may be mailed, read, sorted, filed, manipulated, searched, and
    deleted by hand or by electromechanical tabulating machines.
Cards must be read from the beginning of the deck to the end, with
    no random jumping from record to record.
Cards are best for these applications: (a) temporary storage of data,
    until they can be transferred to other media; (b) triggering data,
    to call up full records from a disc; (c) where readable form is im-
    portant to display or collect the data, such as a utility bill.
Cards are rapidly becoming obsolete.

TAPES

Tapes are of two types: (1) large, reel-to-reel tapes, about ½ in. wide and about 2,400 feet long, for use on mainframe and minicomputers; and (2) cassette tapes for use on microcomputers.

---

3. CD ROM is in the developmental stage as a storage medium. For a thorough discussion, see Steve Lambert and Suzanne Ropiequet, eds., *CD ROM, the New Papyrus* (Redmond, Wash.: Microsoft, 1986).

Information is coded as combinations of magnetic spots (character bits) on metal oxide with a plastic or Mylar backing. Data are laid out in 7 or 9 parallel tracks, running the length of the tape. Bits for each character run across the width of the tape. Microcomputers use cassette tapes and store character bits longitudinally.

Tapes are inherently sequential access; records must be read in the same order as placed and there can be no jumping back and forth. The tape must be rewound when the end is reached.

Data must be added to the end of a file; insertions or deletions require creating a new file.

Tapes allow high-density storage. A 2,400-foot reel will store about 46 million characters, or 20,000 pages of text. A microcomputer cassette will store about 500,000 characters (208 pages).

Tapes are best for the following applications: (a) when data are to be processed in the order placed on the file; (b) for cyclical processing (e.g., a monthly payroll); (c) when large numbers of transactions are processed at one time; (d) for archival and temporary storage of large amounts of data.

DISCS

Discs are of three types: (1) hard discs and disc packs, ranging from 5.25 in. to 14 in. in diameter, are metal based and sealed, and provide storage of millions of characters and extremely fast data access; (2) floppy discs, 5.25 to 8 in. in diameter, are on a plastic base, and store hundreds of thousands of characters and provide slower access; and (3) hardened microdiscs, 2 to 4 in. in diameter, in a hard, protective container.

Information is coded as combinations of magnetic spots on metal oxide. Data are laid out in concentric circles called *tracks*.

Data may be accessed randomly or sequentially.

Discs allow relatively high density storage. Mainframe disc packs (about 3 cubic feet) will store 200 million characters. Microcomputer discs will store from 200,000 to 9 million characters. A box of 50 floppy discs occupies about one-half cubic feet and can store about 18.5 million characters of information, equivalent to 4,000 pages of text.

Discs are vulnerable to magnetic interference. Microcomputer floppies are very vulnerable to dust, fingerprints, magnetic interference, and wear.

Discs are best for interactive, real-time systems and those requiring little human intervention.

Advantages and Disadvantages

The first part of this discussion will consider the advantages and disadvantages of using machine-readable files *compared to using equivalent printed sources*. The next part will discuss the advantages and disadvantages of the *various media* relative to each other. General advantages are:

1. Once data are entered onto a storage medium, they may be changed, reorganized, deleted, listed, and copied without retyping. The same data may be used for any number of applications.

2. Data may be transferred from one type of media to another (e.g., tape to disc) and from one computer to another, through cables, mail, or telephone lines. Electronic transfer of data is extremely fast.

3. Machine-readable files take advantage of increasingly sophisticated and inexpensive technology, allowing access and manipulation of data, which otherwise may be prohibitively expensive to obtain and use by manual methods.

General disadvantages of machine-readable data files are:

1. Since machine-readable data cannot be read by humans, there is no way to tell what the medium contains (except with cards), or if the data are intact, through visual inspection. Processing, filing, sorting, and manipulating must be done by the machine.

2. Although costs are decreasing, purchase of hardware requires considerable initial investment, and hardware must be maintained by specialists.

3. Hardware malfunctions may cause catastrophic loss of data or disruptions in organizational functions. Inoperable hardware renders the data useless.

4. It requires a great deal of skill to operate a computer, and even more to write programs and/or create data files.

5. Information stored as magnetized spots is vulnerable and can be easily damaged or lost, often without warning.

6. Most data files contain more information than needed, and it is unprocessed; retrieval of relevant information is complex and often not satisfactory.

Cards are an obsolescent storage medium. Fewer and fewer large computers use cards, except in very special applications. Almost no microcomputers have attached card readers. Even so, their use provides some advantages which make them an attractive medium for some applications. The advantages are:

1. Cards may be preprinted and used as a form. Instructions to the user or key puncher may be printed on the card itself, and they may contain photographs, drawings, and microfilm.

2. Because they are not susceptible to magnetic radiation and are readable by humans, most worn or damaged cards can be reconstructed without serious loss of information. Physically, cards are the most durable medium.

3. Cards are partially a manual medium. They may be filed, deleted, and rearranged without the use of computers. They are more understandable and comfortable to humans.

Some of the disadvantages of cards are that

1. In the past, one card often represented one record, causing an "80 character mentality" in which information had to be squeezed into 80 fixed columns. Card-based systems tend to be inhibiting in terms of data file design.

2. Punching cards is slow, noisy, awkward, and error-prone.

3. Data may be changed or corrected only by repunching the entire card.

4. In comparison to other media, cards provide very slow data transfer. They can be read at about 1,000 per minute, which translates to slightly more than 1,000 characters per second.

5. They are bulky and wasteful of space. One cubic foot of cards will store a maximum of about 58,000 characters, or 14 pages of text.

6. Since cards are becoming obsolescent, data files on cards may have to be converted to other media.

Tapes also are not used as widely as they once were, although they are better than other media for two applications: long-term, archival storage and physical transfer from installation to installation. Storage costs are lower than for discs, and tapes are relatively free from deterioration and damage. Most large computer systems use tapes for backup, archival storage of information, and as a transfer medium.

Tapes have some disadvantages, especially when compared with discs:

1. Data may be added to the end of the file—only. In order to change or delete information, it is necessary to re-create the file. This requires slower, more complex programming operations.

2. Microcomputer cassettes, especially, are slow in transferring data. Mainframe computer-tape transfer rates are much faster, but still slower than discs.

3. Tapes require a great deal of physical handling: mounting, rewinding, shelving, etc.; and cannot be used for high-speed, heavily used, interactive systems.

4. Because of their inherent sequential access, records must be read off a tape in the same order in which they were put on. This does not allow random access or ability to retrieve records through an index.

Discs provide some of the best advantages for day-to-day file management and use. Except for the special applications of tapes (noted above), discs have become the main medium for storage and retrieval of information. Some of their advantages are:

1. Information may be stored, retrieved, changed, deleted, and added easily. Compared to tapes, discs are far more flexible in terms of rearranging and manipulating data.

2. Discs provide extremely fast access (data transfer) because of their inherent capability to retrieve information randomly.

3. Records on discs may be indexed and retrieved in an order different from that in which they were stored. Data may be rearranged and new relationships established as new needs arise.

About the only disadvantage to using discs is that they require relatively more expensive hardware to operate and they are more expensive in terms of cost per data item stored. Microcomputer floppies are very susceptible to damage and loss of data, but this can be overcome with the use of hard discs and by exercising proper care. Another problem with microcomputer discs is that there are no standards for disc formatting, making data transfer difficult across different models of computers. Compatibility is a problem with microcomputers in general.

SELECTION

Special Criteria

This section will cover selection of data files obtained from external sources, and general software for the creation of data files (with emphasis on microcomputer data-base management software). It will *not* cover criteria for selecting data bases which are accessed on telephone networks.[4]

External data files are those obtained from an outside source for use on an in-house computer.[5] A few commercially distributed data files are now available for use on microcomputers, and more can be expected as problems of compatibility, security, quality, and copyright are resolved.[6] Following are selection criteria.

1. A judgment should be made of the relationship of the subject matter to the information needs of the user community to be served.

2. The lease/purchase price and computer start-up/running costs must be weighed against the amount of useful data which will be made available.

3. It should be determined how the time span of the information, completeness, uniqueness, and overlap of the data compare with noncomputerized sources.

4. Timeliness, time lag, and frequency of updates should be compared with other sources.

5. Ease of searching, including the number of access points (i.e., indexing), quality of documentation, and aids to searching the file should be evaluated.

6. How well the data file can be integrated into other information services of the organization is a determining factor in the cost and trouble of implementation.

Data files are rather worthless without appropriate software (programs) to manage and exploit them. Programs may be written in such a way as to manage and use files for a particular application (such as statistical analysis), or they may be generalized file and data-base managers which may serve a variety of end applications. Selection criteria for general applications programs and data-base management systems (DBMS) are as follows:

---

4. Criteria for choosing online data bases and data-base vendors are covered in Ryan Hoover, *The Library and Information Manager's Guide to Online Services* (White Plains, N.Y.: Knowledge Industry Publications, 1980); Ching-chih Chen and Susanna Schweizer, *Online Bibliographic Searching: A Learning Manual* (New York: Neal-Schuman, 1981); and Martha E. Williams, "Criteria for Evaluation and Selection of Databases and Database Services," *Special Libraries* 66 (1975): 561–69.

5. These criteria are described in detail by F. Wilfred Lancaster, *Information Retrieval Systems: Characteristics, Testing and Evaluation* (New York: Wiley & Sons, 1979), 204–17.

6. Lawrence A. Woods and Nolan F. Pope, *The Librarian's Guide to Microcomputer Technology and Applications* (White Plains, N.Y.: Knowledge Industry Publications, 1983), 75–76.

1. A software package should match the scope of your information needs. Consider what information you want to get *out* of the computer and what information is available to put in.

2. If there is not yet a commitment to particular hardware, the needs criteria will be the most important factor in choosing equipment. If equipment is already in place, obviously a program must run on your make of computer. Besides compatibility, you must determine whether you have enough internal memory, appropriate external storage (and what kind: cassette, floppy, hard disc), adequate operating system and compilers, and a proper printer to make effective use of the software.

3. The existence of adequate commercial software and the availability and relative cost of custom programming talent will be a determining factor in deciding whether to write your own programs, buy existing software, or modify software developed by others.

4. Data-base management systems (DBMS) range from simple file managers to sophisticated relational data-base managers. The greater the sophistication, the greater the flexibility and power, but the greater difficulty to learn and use. It is a good idea to determine whether there are training, tutorials, or teaching guides available when you consider a sophisticated DBMS.

5. Capacity, in terms of the maximum number and size of records to be managed, is critical in choosing a DBMS.

6. Valuable data and much time can be lost by a program with hidden "bugs." You should determine whether there are adequate backup and recovery procedures. Also, provisions for data security should be determined.

7. A good applications program or DBMS should have powerful sorting, editing, indexing, and search capabilities. These factors determine how well data files may be exploited.

8. Power and flexibility of reporting capability is important. Some programs allow you to create custom reports, but many limit reports to 80-column, one-line-per-record reports with very little flexibility.

9. If you have files from more than one source, software should have the ability to merge data bases and interface with other files and programs.

Evaluative Review Sources

As the computer has become pervasive, the literature on computer resources has exploded. Although hundreds of software reviews appear in dozens of magazines each month, this section will not attempt to list them all. Instead, it lists the major journals which regularly review data bases and/or software for data file creation and use.

Access: Microcomputers in Libraries	*Information Today*
Byte	*Infosystems*
CIPS Review	*Interface Age*
Compute!	*Library High Tech*
Computer Age	*Library Software Review*
Software Industry Reports	*Online*
Computing Reviews	*Online Review*
Creative Computing	*Personal Computing*
Database	*Popular Computing*
Datamation	*Softside*
Electronic Library	*Software*
Information Processing and	*Software Reviews on File*
Management	*T.H.E. Journal*

Nonevaluative Sources

Most of the following are directories to data bases and data management software. Titles represent publications since 1970.

PERIODICALS
DataBase Alert
Datapro Directory of Software
Data Sources: The Comprehensive Guide to the Information Processing Industry
Monthly Catalog of United States Government Publications

MONOGRAPHS
Association of Computer Users' Software Directory. Springfield, Va.: National Technical Information Service, 1972– (annual).
Capital Systems Group, Inc. *Directory of On-Line Information Resources.* 9th ed. Rockville, Md.: CSG Pr., 1982.
Datapro Complete Guide to Dial-Up Databases. 4th ed. Delran, N.J.: Datapro Research Corp., 1985.
Directory of Computerized Data Files, 1984. Springfield, Va.: National Technical Information Service, 1984.
Directory of Information Management Software: For Libraries, Information Centers, Record Centers. Compiled and edited by Pamela Cibbarelli and Edward John Kazlauskas. Studio City, Calif.: Pacific Information, 1985.

Directory of Online Databases. Santa Monica, Calif.: Cuadra Associates (annual).

Hall, J. L. *Online Bibliographic Databases: A Directory and Sourcebook.* 3rd ed. Detroit: Gale, 1983.

Hildebrandt, Darlene Myers. *Computer Science Resources: A Guide to Professional Literature.* White Plains, N.Y.: Published for American Society for Information Science by Knowledge Industry Publications, 1981.

International Directory of Software, 1983–84. Pottstown, Pa.: Wordtech, Inc., 1983.

The Software Catalog: Microcomputers. Summer 1986 ed. New York: Elsevier, 1986.

Williams, Martha E. *Computer-Readable Databases.* Chicago, Ill.: American Library Assn., 1985 (biennial).

MAINTENANCE AND MANAGEMENT

Storage and Care

All machine-readable files are susceptible to damage and loss of information. For this reason, the cardinal rule for all types of machine-readable media is: *Make backup copies of all important programs and data files.* Keep the original and one backup in fire-resistant, dust-proof, protective containers. Day-to-day work should be done on backup copies, not on the original—assuming that the original is not copy protected; if it is, arrangements must be made to obtain access to replacement copies. A copy of irreplaceable information should be stored at a remote site to minimize loss in case of fire, flood, or theft.

Cards are susceptible to wear, damage, and moisture, but not to magnetic interference. They should be stored in a dry place, perhaps in cabinets which allow them to be kept upright and tightly packed. Cardboard boxes should be avoided for other than *temporary* storage.

Never staple or use metal paper clips on cards. Rubber bands should be avoided for long-term storage; cards react chemically with them, and they cause curling.

Never fold or bend cards. Old or worn cards should be replaced by using a card duplicator.

Tapes are susceptible to wear, dust, folding, stretching, heat, and magnetic interference.

Whether they are used for large computers or microcomputers, tapes should be of the highest quality. Microcomputer cassettes should be designed for digital data; it is not a good idea to use audiotapes for storing computer information.

Store tapes upright in well-sealed plastic reel or cassette cases. Tapes may be stored on open shelves or in cabinets designed for the purpose.

Keep tapes well away from all magnetic fields: motors, bulk erasers, speakers, transformers, magnets.

Do not store tapes in areas where the temperature is high, because the plastic backing is susceptible to melting, stretching, or curling under high temperatures. Between 50 and 80° F is ideal.

Keep tape drives and read/write heads clean. Clean and demagnetize them after each 10–15 hours of use.[7]

About every six months, all tapes should be played through and rewound, whether they have been used or not.

Floppy discs are very susceptible to head wear, dust, heat, fingerprints, and magnetic interference. Hard discs are sealed against environmental problems and are less susceptible to wear or interference. Hardened microdiscs are similar to floppies, but are permanently mounted in a protective container. They are less susceptible to dust and fingerprints, but may be damaged by head wear, magnetic interference, and heat. Most of the following apply to floppy discs.

Always keep discs in their envelopes when they are not in the disc drive.

Store floppies upright in protective containers. Containers should allow the discs to stand loosely, but not lean so as to cause warping. If they are packed too tightly, there is a danger of "magnetic seep," with extraneous data induced from disc to disc.[8] Originals should be kept in fire resistant cabinets.

Do not touch a disc's surface; handle them by the permanent envelope.

Keep discs away from magnets, electric motors, speakers, transformers, and other sources of magnetic radiation.

Do not write on the envelope with a ball-point pen; use a felt-tip marker or write on the label before affixing it to the disc.

Avoid bending floppies, by inserting them carefully in the drive.

Do not expose discs to excessive heat or sunlight. The best storage temperature is between 50 and 80° F.

Keep the disc mechanism clean. Cleaning the read/write head does more to protect discs than the head, and should not be overused. Use a solvent approved for your type of drive after every three to six months of heavy use. *Never* try to clean the discs themselves.

    7. Robert A. Walton, *Microcomputers: A Planning and Implementation Guide for Librarians and Information Professionals* (Phoenix: Oryx Pr., 1983), 13.
    8. Ibid., 18.

Hard discs require care in terms of the environment. They should be used in a room with moderate temperatures (60–95 °F), air conditioning, and a well-regulated power supply.[9] Most hard discs have their own air filtration system, and the manufacturer's suggestions for maintenance should be followed.

Management Problems and Solutions

The use of computers in organizations raises many philosophical and management questions. This review will focus on some of the questions relating to the use of data files within the organization. Larger societal ills and benefits of computers and data banks will *not* be attempted, nor will we consider technical questions relating to computer hardware, operating systems and languages, networking, and the like.

Data files usually require a considerable investment by the organization. They require complex technology and a high level of skill to create, acquire, maintain, and use. For these reasons it may be best to centralize their administration. On the other hand, such a valuable resource may best be distributed and used by whichever departments or organizational units most need the data. Microcomputer data files are most likely to be distributed. Even if the files are distributed, the organization probably should centralize certain aspects of administration, such as purchase, training, and technical assistance.

Especially in the case of distributed files, there is a problem of how, and by whom, data should be changed, added, and deleted. If changes are not done centrally, the organization should develop a plan to ensure the integrity of the data, minimize redundancy, and maintain compatibility with other internal and external files and systems.

In a centralized data base it may be necessary to prevent access to some data, even while encouraging access to other parts of them. Also, some forms of access (such as reading data) may be permitted, while other forms (such as deleting or changing data) will be controlled.

Creation of a new data file or establishment of a service involving data bases requires that many people be trained at many levels. The organization must allow for the cost and time involved. Decisions must be made as to whether users may have unlimited access and how costs will be determined and recovered.

Most external data files are obtained through telecommunication access, but there are still some opportunities to lease or purchase data bases outright. Purchase and lease of commercial data bases is expensive, but once a data base is acquired, the cost per search goes down.

9. Ibid., 20.

Purchase or lease can thus be justified only on the basis of a great deal of use of most of the records in the data base.

Telecommunication access is more of a "pay as you use" situation. Usually, the cost per search is higher, but the total cost is lower for relatively low activity. In addition, problems of compatibility and payment are minimized through telecommunication access; the distributor takes care of ensuring easy access and payment of royalties.

The organization must study the cost/benefit ratio as compared with printed sources. Specifically, the scope and coverage of the data base should be compared with its printed counterpart (if printed counterparts are available), and the cost of retrieving useful information from the data base must be compared with the cost of retrieving that information from other sources. It does little good to have instant computerized access to information if nobody in the organization needs it, if it is already available in familiar sources, if it is out of date or inaccurate, or if it cannot easily be assimilated.

The organization must decide whether to purchase, modify, or custom write software. Often there is no choice. If no satisfactory software exists, it may have to be written from scratch. On the other hand, if the organization does not have programmers and cannot afford to hire them, off-the-shelf software must be purchased. Outright purchase is usually easiest and most economical, but existing software may not meet the needs of the organization. Modification of existing software is difficult and often not successful,[10] and there are problems relating to copyright and licensing. Modification is recommended only for simple enhancements to otherwise good off-the-shelf software. Custom writing is very expensive; it usually costs more and takes longer than anticipated. However, it gives the organization complete control over software design, and may be the only viable solution.

Sometimes a DBMS will serve the data handling needs of the organization. There are many powerful and flexible DBMSs which allow organizations to develop excellent data handling systems. Generally, the more flexible the DBMS, the more expensive and difficult it is to learn and use.

Another management decision is how to integrate old records into the new system. Most organizations work with a constantly expanding base of new data in addition to a large body of old records. A decision must be made whether to enter only the new or, also, to convert the old. This will depend upon how essential and active the old data are, how well they integrate into the new, and whether it is more cost effective to convert or to run with two systems.

10. Woods and Pope, *Librarian's Guide,* 47–48.

Data entry is an exacting, tedious task which requires a great deal of accuracy. Management decisions must be made in terms of setting up temporary or permanent data entry staff and developing procedures for entering, checking, and revising data. There are other options: the organization may use a commercial data entry service, or it may download records from another organization's data files or from a service bureau which sells records for downloading.

Other Concerns

Systems programs (operating systems) direct and coordinate the computer's hardware and control the execution of other programs. Most operating systems are machine dependent (will work on only one model of computer), but they allow other programs to be less machine dependent.

Compilers and interpreters translate "high level" languages like COBOL, BASIC, or Pascal into machine language.

Utility programs are used in conjunction with applications programs to do very specialized tasks, such as sorting, merging, printing reports, and transferring files.

Applications programs are written in a "high level" language to do useful tasks, such as word processing, inventory control, library circulation control, recordkeeping, payroll, and the like.

A *data base* is a collection of multiple records with built-in relationships, structured to allow mutliple users to have access to the data without rearranging them. "Data base" is not just a fancy word for file or a collection of files; it is a collection of files which are self-describing and integrated.[11] (The distinction is subtle but important.)

Data bases are useful in applications in which common data must be shared by many users. Unlike multiple files to meet different applications needs, data bases have little data redundancy, are independent of the programs used to access them, and are controlled in terms of who may add and modify data. They are created and maintained by programs called *data-base management systems* (DBMS). Sometimes a distinction is made between the generic term *data base* and a *data bank,* which is a commercially available data base that conveys news and reference data usually via telecommunications.[12]

11. David M. Kroenke, *Database Processing: Fundamentals, Design, Implementation,* 2nd ed. (Chicago: Science Research Associates, 1983), 9–10.
12. Grace Murray Hooper and Steven L. Mandell, *Understanding Computers* (St. Paul: West Publishing Co., 1984), 471.

Punched cards are a commonly used storage medium in which data are represented by the presence or absence of holes in a specified row- and column-coding scheme. Each set of holes has a distinct meaning, which is translated into machine language for the computer.[13] There are several types, the most common being the 80-column card, which uses a coding scheme developed by Herman Hollerith in 1887 to tabulate the U.S. census. Each column usually represents one character (letter of the alphabet, numeral, or punctuation mark).

Magnetic tape is a narrow strip of oxide-coated material upon which spots are magnetized to represent data.[14] Tapes for large (main- frame) computers are typically one-half inch wide and 2,400 feet long. They will store from 800 to 6,500 characters per inch (equivalent to about 80 punched cards). Microcomputers sometimes use cassettes, which will store about 112 characters per inch.

Magnetic discs consist of a metal or plastic platter, coated on both sides with a magnetic recording material upon which data are stored in the form of magnetized spots.[15] Data are stored in concentric circles called *tracks.* Large computers use hard (metal) discs which are 14 in- ches in diameter. These are often arranged in disc packs of 20 platters each. A disc pack will hold about 200 million characters. Microcom- puters use either hard or "floppy" (plastic) discs which range from 3 to 8 inches in diameter. Floppy discs may hold about 300,000 characters, and small hard discs up to 15 million.

ADDITIONAL RESOURCES

Byrum, John D., and Judith Rowe. "An Integrated, User-Oriented System for Documentation and Control of Machine-Readable Data Files." *Library Resources & Technical Services* 16 (Summer 1972): 338–46.

Chen, Ching-chih, and Susanna Schweizer. *Online Bibliographic Searching: A Learning Manual.* New York: Neal-Schuman, 1981.

"Choosing and Using a Database Management Program." *Creative Computing* (Sept. 1984): special section.

Continental Software. *Tips on Buying Software.* Los Angeles: The Book Co., 1983.

Gorman, Michael, and Paul W. Winkler. *Anglo-American Cataloguing Rules,* 2nd ed. Chicago: American Library Assn., 1978.

Hooper, Grace Murray, and Steven L. Mandell. *Understanding Computers.* St. Paul: West Publishing Co., 1984.

13. Ibid., 479.
14. Ibid., 476.
15. Ibid.

Hoover, Ryan. *The Library and Information Manager's Guide to Online Services*. White Plain, N.Y.: Knowledge Industry Publications, 1980.

Kroenke, David M. *Database Processing: Fundamentals, Design, Implementation,* 2nd ed. Chicago: Science Research Associates, 1983.

Lancaster, F. Wilfred. *Information Retrieval Systems: Characteristics, Testing and Evaluation*. New York: John Wiley, 1979.

Palmer, Roger. *dBase II: An Introduction for Information Services*. Studio City, Calif.: Pacific Information, 1984.

Saffady, W. "Data Management Software for Microcomputers." *Library Technology Reports* 19 (Sept./Oct. 1983): 451–592.

Tenopir, Carol. "In-house Databases I: Software Sources." *Library Journal* 108 (Apr. 1, 1983): 639–41.

_____. "In-house Databases II: Evaluating and Choosing Software." *Library Journal* 108 (May 1, 1983): 885–88.

Walton, Robert A. *Microcomputers: A Planning and Implementation Guide for Librarians and Information Professionals*. Phoenix: Oryx Pr., 1983.

Wanger, Judith, and Robert N. Landau. "Nonbibliographic On-line Data Base Services." *Journal of American Society for Information Science* 31 (May 1980): 172–80.

Williams, Martha E. "Criteria for Evaluation and Selection of Databases and Database Services." *Special Libraries* 66 (1975): 561–69.

Woods, Lawrence A., and Nolan F. Pope. *The Librarian's Guide to Microcomputer Technology and Applications*. White Plains, N.Y.: Knowledge Industry Publications, 1983.

Ernest L. Woodson

ch. 8

Maps

THE MEDIUM

Definition

A map is a visual representation of Earth, at various places and scales, to show topography and thematic distribution of political and cultural phenomena. The main types are road, cadastral, topographic, political, geologic, remote-sensing-imagery, population, soil, climatic, land-use, census, and vegetation maps, and aerial photos and nautical charts.

Brief History

The history of maps and charts must take into account those that are still extant, such as clay tablets, and those that are known only through the literature but have not survived, because of the nature of the materials.

Ancient maps include those used in China, Mesopotamia, and Egypt. The maps of China include topographic, forest, and cadastral maps that go back to 2000 B.C.[1] The Babylonian maps of Mesopotamia are the treasured clay tablets with their circular maps, and the oldest

---

1. Leo Bagrow and R. A. Skelton, *History of Cartography* (Cambridge, Mass.: Harvard University Pr., 1964), 197.

we know about.[2] Egyptian cadastral maps and city plans, drawn on papyrus and other materials, were necessary to describe property that was flooded yearly by the Nile River.

During the Classical period, Greek maps were produced, and two outstanding figures in the history of cartography worked at Alexandria. Eratosthenes measured the circumference of Earth, and Claudius Ptolemy produced world and regional maps in 150 A.D. Ptolemy's work with map projections was significant and his *Geographia,* an eight-volume work dealing with the principles of cartography and mathematical geography, is important to the history of geography and maps.

The next period of map making, the Medieval period, was dominated by Arabic cartography. An Arabic translation in the 9th century of Ptolemy's *Geographia* was important in the continuing development of cartography. An example of an Arabic map is Idrisi's world map of 1154. Later in this period, the Hereford Map *(mappa mundi)* was drawn, in 1290, and the portolan sea chart made navigation and travel itineraries possible in the Mediterranean world and beyond.

The Catalan Atlas of 1375 is an example of maps at the transition of the Middle Ages into the Renaissance. During the Renaissance, Ptolemy's world map, which had come from Greece to Arabia to Italy and Germany, was translated into Latin in the 1470s. This Latin edition of Ptolemy's *Geographia* coincided with printing and European exploration. The cartography that was developed during this period included world maps with advanced information, and examples are Fra Mauro's world map of 1459 and Waldseemuller's world map of 1507, which first used the name America for the New World.

A world map of 18 sheets by Mercator appeared in 1569 in atlas format. Mercator was possibly the first cartographer to use the term *atlas* to describe a collection of bound maps. One of the important landmarks of map making was the publication of Orteluis' *Theatrum* in 1570.

The next period in the history of maps in which big changes occurred can be called the Scientific Revolution or the Modern Age (late 1700s). The emergence of thematic maps, those that illustrate a particular subject, came about during this period. Edmond Halley's maps of physical phenomena, such as winds and ocean currents, are good examples of these early thematic types.

2. Norman J. W. Thrower, *Maps and Man* (Englewood Cliffs, N.J.: Prentice-Hall, 1972), 10.

In conjunction with these developments, Giovanni Cassini made scientific measurements of the Paris meridian. The emphasis on surveying techniques provided the basis of today's maps. Official surveys of countries can be traced back to France during the 17th and 18th centuries.

Mapping in the 20th century has proceeded along parallel lines, with technical advances that allow for quicker updating of maps by aerial photos and other kinds of remote-sensing imagery. Almost all countries have official survey maps which are topographic maps in intermediate and large scales. A similar project (still in progress) is the International Mapping of the World, at the scale of 1:1,000,000.

Unique Characteristics

Grid systems such as latitude and longitude, township and range, and universal transverse mercator are essential for finding locations on a map. The grid size also describes how much area is shown.

Scale is a unique concept to this medium and is part of the cataloging information. It identifies the ratio of distance on the map to distance on the earth, and can be shown on a map in three ways: by a measured bar scale, by a written statement (such as "1 inch equals 1 mile"), or by a fractional scale (such as 1:24,000).

Projection, to transfer the grid system of a globe onto a plane, and representation of the data point by point according to their position on the grid system, are unique to maps.

A language unique to maps includes symbols, lines, colors, names, and spatial relationships, exhibited on the grid to represent reality.

Maps are graphic representations of geographic areas, space, or the universe.

Advantages

The entire surface of the earth can be viewed at a glance.

Maps create a shorthand for visual symbols, and are universally comprehensible.

Maps are easily portable and can be taken into the field or laboratory, with no special equipment required for their use.

Maps can be mass produced. They are generally inexpensive and often free, as when acquired under government depository status.

Maps provide the clearest means of identifying direction, distance, and landmarks.

Almost everyone is familiar with maps.

Maps can present either a comprehensive or selective picture of a subject.

Disadvantages

Interpretation of maps requires a certain amount of skill.

Most maps are not cataloged and thus cause problems for bibliographic control.

Loose sheets maps are easily damaged when they are browsed, then refiled into map cases.

Because of their visual attraction, they are often stolen.

Maps are difficult to photocopy, and color is usually lost.

Maps vary tremendously in format: some are folded; others are sheets; many are in atlas form, thus creating disadvantages for storage, bibliographic control, and reference service.

Distance is distorted on all maps; therefore some knowledge of the projection is required.

When a scale is given for a small-scale map, it is usually accurate only along certain lines or between certain points.

It is difficult to represent relief on flat maps.

SELECTION

Special Criteria

The reputation of the publisher can be an important factor, since the overall accuracy of a map's representation of reality may be difficult or impossible for the selector to ascertain.

The amount of detail on a map should be sufficient, not confusing or overwhelming.

Color (if any) should be properly registered.

The area covered by a map should be suitable to specified user needs.

The scale of the map should be appropriate for the detail necessary to convey the desired information. Generalization is greater on smaller maps.

The scale and legend should be indicated clearly.

The printing should be clear, without blurring.

Place names should be spelled correctly.

If the map portrays political data, check for recent changes in political boundaries and place names.

Symbols should be adequately explained.

Special features, such as mileage charts, should add to (not detract from) the primary focus of the map.

Paper used for printing should be durable enough to withstand the map's intended use.

Commercial vendor's maps may be more expensive than similar maps available from government agencies; compare prices.

Evaluative Review Sources

PERIODICALS

American Cartographer
  (American Congress on
  Surveying and Mapping)
*Annals of the Association of
  American Geographers*
Australian Geographer
  (Geographical Society of New
  South Wales)
Canadian Cartographer
  (Canadian Association of
  Geographers)
Cartactual
Cartographic Journal
  (British Cartographic Society)
Cartographica
Cartography
Geographical Journal
  (Royal Geographical Society)
Geographical Magazine
Geographical Review
  (American Geographical
  Society)

Geography
  (Geographical Association)
*Information Bulletin of the West-
  ern Association of Map
  Libraries*
Irish Geography
  (Geographical Society of
  Ireland)
Journal of Geography
  (National Council for
  Geographic Education)
New Zealand Journal of Geography
  (New Zealand Geographical
  Society)
Professional Geographer
  (Association of American
  Geographers)
*SUC Bulletin: Bulletin of the Society
  of University Cartographers*

Nonevaluative Sources

PERIODICALS

Bibliography and Index of Geology
*Bulletin of the American Congress
  on Surveying and Mapping*
*Bulletin: Special Libraries
  Association, Geography and
  Map Division*
Current Geographical Publications

GeoAbstracts
*New Geographical Literature and
  Maps*
*Publications of the Geological
  Survey*
Scottish Geographical Magazine

BOOKS

Allin, Janet, comp. *Map Sources Directory*. Toronto: Office of Library Coordination, Council of Ontario Universities, 1978.

Carrington, David K., and Richard W. Stephenson, eds. *Map Collections in
  the United States and Canada: A Directory*. 4th ed. New York: Special
  Libraries Assn., 1985.

Catalog of Aeronautical Charts and Related Publications. Riverdale, Md.:
  National Ocean Survey, Distribution Division, 1981.

Geo Katalog. Stuttgart, West Germany: Geocenter Verlagsvertrieb GmbH
  (annual).

Guide to USGS Geologic and Hydrologic Maps. McLean, Va.: Documents Index, 1983.

Index to Maps in Books and Periodicals. Boston: G. K. Hall, for American Geographical Society, 1976.

Index to Topographic Maps. Reston, Va.: U.S. Geologic Survey, 1981.

Library of Congress and Research Library of the New York Public Library. *Bibliographic Guide to Maps and Atlases.* Boston: G. K. Hall, 1984.

Nautical Chart Catalog. Riverdale, Md.: National Ocean Survey, Distribution Division, 1981.

University of Illinois, Map and Geography Library. *Biblio.* 1986.

Winch, Kenneth L., ed. *International Maps and Atlases in Print.* 2nd ed. New York: Bowker, 1976.

World, United States and Historical Maps. 11th ed. Rockville, Md.: National Ocean Survey, 1980.

Map Sources

The National Cartographic Information Center takes orders for maps produced by the U.S. Geological Survey and directs users to appropriate governmental agencies, when necessary:

National Cartographic Information Center
U.S. Geological Survey
507 National Center
Reston, VA 22092

Two vendors that attempt to meet all map needs are:

Edward Stanford Ltd.
12–14 Long Acre
London WC2E 9LP, England

Geo Center
Internationales LanderKartenaus
    GmbH.
Postfach 800830
DT Stuttgart 80, West Germany

Following is a list of selected commercial and association map publishers:

American Map Co.
1926 Broadway
New York, NY 10023
(212) 595-6582

Denoyer-Geppert Co.
5235 N. Ravenswood Ave.
Chicago, IL 60640
(312) 561-9200

Hubbard Scientific Co.
1946 Raymond
Northbrook, IL 60062
(312) 272-7810

A. J. Nystrom and Co.
3333 N. Elston Ave.
Chicago, IL 60618
(312) 463-1144

Royal Geographical Society
1 Kensington Gore
London SW7 2AR, England

George F. Cram Co.
P.O. Box 426
Indianapolis, IN 46206
(317) 635-5564

Hammond Inc.
515 Valley St.
Maplewood, NJ 07040
(201) 763-6000

National Geographic Society
17th and M Streets N.W.
Washington, D.C. 20036
(202) 857-7000

Rand McNally
10 East 53rd St.
New York, NY 10022
(212) 751-6300

Royal Scottish Geographical Society
1 Randolph Crescent
Edinburgh EH3 7TU, United
  Kingdom

MAINTENANCE AND MANAGEMENT

Storage and Care

The storage and preservation of maps, charts, relief models, aerial photos, and globes is a difficult aspect of a map collection because of the variety of formats and sizes of map materials. The basic approach to storing an active map collection must be what can be called the *multifaceted approach*. Many different types of storage need to be used in order to protect the maps and, at the same time, allow for browsing and retrieval.

The following paragraphs cover most of the possibilities, although there are other methods that some map librarians invent to solve this basic requirement of a map collection.

Steel map cases, for storing maps horizontally, are the most-used method for map collections in North America. Most topographic and thematic maps can be stored by this method.

Steel file cabinets are necessary for aerial photos, road maps, city plans, maps in folders (such as geologic field guides), and indexes for topographic series maps.

Large wall maps need a sizable area where they can be placed vertically to avoid damage.

Atlases need wide shelving where they can be placed horizontally to prevent damage to the binding. (Older atlases of greater value meet the same requirements as rare books for storing and preservation.)

Globes can stand on top of map cases or tables, and thus are not a problem for most map collections (provided space is available).

Special provision must be made for plastic relief models. They should be hung separately, where they will not be damaged by having anything laid on top of them. A system such as the one at the Library of Congress's Geography and Map Division works well for optimum preservation, where models are hung by hooks and wires.

Mylar encapsulation is a cheap way to preserve valuable maps, and to prevent damage to indexes that are used a great deal.

Taping edges with masking tape will help prevent wear and tear on maps.

Priority use areas need to be identified in order to put fewer maps in heavily used drawers. For example, instead of averaging 300 maps per drawer, place 100 per drawer in a much-used area, and 350 to 400 per drawer where you have identified less use.[3]

If maps are being circulated through a central automated system, the map librarian needs to advise the circulation department of the special problems of care for this material. Also, the librarian should check to see how the maps are handled when returned to the circulation department. (Many people treat maps like newspapers, if they have not had experience with this medium.)

Proper temperature and humidity levels will decrease the rate of chemical damage to the collection. Temperatures should be controlled between 65 and 75° F and the humidity level should be between 50 and 60%.

Ultraviolet rays in sunlight and in artificial sources are destroyers of paper. Window panes near the collection should be of special glass or protected with ultraviolet filters. Coated tubes or plastic shields should be used with fluorescent lighting.

Deterioration begins for a map as soon as it is made, so the staff must begin preservation as soon as the map arrives. People, rodents, insects, and improper storage are responsible for mechanical damage that is evidenced in missing sections, folds, and tears. Acid in the paper, reacting to light, heat, and humidity, causes chemical damage. Discoloration and brittleness are indications of chemical damage.

Unintentional damage can result from inadequate staff training and improper orientation for the user. The basic rule of no smoking, eating, or drinking should be followed by user and staff when working with maps. This reduces the attraction for insects and prevents stains, burns, and smoke damage.

3. Mary Larsgaard, *Map Librarianship* (Littleton, Colo.: Libraries Unlimited, 1978), 156.

Management Problems and Solutions

Since maps are bountiful and many are available at reasonable prices from government agencies, a map collection can quickly outgrow its space. Thus it is imperative that there be a collection-development policy to specify what types of maps will be acquired. The policy should delineate which geographical areas will be collected, the chronological limits of coverage, what formats will be included (i.e., wall maps, flat maps, raised relief maps, globes, etc.), types of topical maps, and the standard scale for the collection. These decisions will be based on the institution's resources and user needs. The collection policy should be in writing, and should be periodically reevaluated with necessary revision.

Special storage cabinets are a necessity for flat maps, and although many maps can be acquired inexpensively, the cabinets themselves may be costly. Wooden cases are generally more expensive than steel cases, and steel cases may be sturdier in the long run. Steel cases are also lighter than wood. Many modern map libraries are using steel cabinets for these reasons. Cases must be selected with great care, as they will house the collection for many years to come.

Storage areas for globes, atlases, folded maps, and similar materials should also be provided in the map collection area, if these materials will be included in the collection. Book shelves and filing cabinets will suffice for most of these materials. Wall maps, which are usually rolled for storage, will need special attention because of their size. Tube files may be purchased for wall maps, and these files can be stored vertically or horizontally, depending on the size of the storage space available.

Acceptable locations for map collections must satisfy the stress factor or bearing weight of the floor of the building, caused by the weight of the maps and cases. The weight of the maps and traditional steel cabinets can range from 100 to over 300 pounds per square foot. Architects and planners should be made aware of the stress which a map collection can create.

Because of the large size of maps, user space and technical processing space must have large tables and work areas. Larsgaard suggests a minimum of 10 square feet, and up to 35 or 50 square feet, should be provided for each map user. The work area for processing should be large enough to hold a table at least 6 feet by 4 feet.[4]

The purpose of a map collection can be either an archival or an open circulating collection. The main concerns regarding these two different approaches include the cost of the maps, security of the col-

4. Ibid., 209.

lection, intended use of the information, and the philosophy of the institution.

If maps are to be circulated, mailing tubes can be provided for housing flat maps. Maps which have been mounted onto a backing material are best left unrolled and protected in flat boxes or large envelopes, with stiff boards on either side of the map.

The bibliographic control and retrieval of maps is an important function of the collection, and is largely based on the decision whether to catalog the entire collection, or only the thematic and not the topographic maps, or something in between. Experts on this subject within map librarianship write that cataloging gives the map librarian bibliographic control. A map catalog has the additional value of reducing wear and tear on the maps.[5] Theoretically, if unlimited funding were available, every map and atlas in the collection would be officially cataloged by a system such as the Library of Congress MARC format.

Extended reference service can best be accomplished if the supporting materials in cartography are housed in the map room. These supporting materials include journals, atlases, catalogs, and reference books. Map librarians and geographers realize that more complete reference service can be provided by having all the cartographic materials in one collection.

The management decision on how much material can be centralized depends to a large degree on two factors. One is where the map collection is housed within the institution, and the other is the existing makeup of the collections of the entire institution.

One of the unique characteristics and problems of map collecting is the impossibility of acquiring maps that are "classified" by the military. These include detailed, large-scale maps of many countries, such as Turkey, Bolivia, the Soviet Union, and the United States. This is a management problem that seems to have no solution at the present time.

Thousands of maps are added each month to map collections, and this presents a major ongoing problem of storage and care. The way that libraries successfully handle this challenge is similar to their response in other areas of the information center. The possibilities include adding more cases to house the sheet maps. Another strategy is to eliminate duplicate or older maps. A third consideration is maps on microforms, as in the U.S. Geological Survey open-file reports.

The cartographic literature is not full of articles on how to solve this dilemma, but the solutions that map collectors seem to be im-

5. Ibid., 91.

plementing are the following. Adding more map cases is the best method to attack this problem, if the funding and space are available. The unique visual tool that is a map is best expressed as a sheet map on paper, according to this author. Older maps should not be discarded, however, because they are so valuable for historical research; but many *duplicate* maps can be eliminated from the collection. For example, duplicate topographic maps of certain states can be eliminated if they are of low priority in the collection development policy.

What about microforms for maps? The number of maps on microfilm and microfiche is increasing because of the obvious advantages of cost and storage. One type of map that has been successful as a microform is nautical charts, though there are many disadvantages to this format. For example, they are difficult to consult for details,[6] and loss of color of course detracts from the symbolism that is so important on thematic maps. More research is needed on the problem of distortion in the final product.

Other Concerns

Map series is a group of maps which generally have the same specification or some common characteristic, such as scale.

Map scale refers to the size of a feature on a map, compared to the size of the same feature on Earth. The larger the scale, the closer the map comes to being the same size as on Earth; the smaller the scale, the greater the difference between the size of a feature on the map compared to its size on Earth. *Large-scale* maps show small areas in great detail. *Small-scale* maps show large areas in a very generalized form.

Cadastral mapping and surveying refers to the establishment of land boundaries and subdivisions, primarily for the purpose of describing property or defining ownership.

Topographic maps, usually at scales of 1:4,000,000 to 1:20,000,000, include such information as elevation and terrain (illustrated by contours, layer tints, or shaded relief), and/or railroads, cities and towns, regional drainage patterns, selected spot elevations, and locations of historical or archeological interest.[7] They cover individual countries, states, or regions.

6. Roman Drazniowsky, *Map Librarianship: Readings* (Metuchen, N.J.: Scarecrow, 1975), 387.

7. Judith Tyner, *The World of Maps and Mapping: A Creative Learning Aid* (New York: McGraw-Hill, 1973), 22.

Political maps display political boundaries, capital cities, political affiliations, place names, and selected physical features.

Thematic maps normally illustrate one particular subject, such as agriculture, economics, vegetation, temperature, or rainfall. They may be *qualitative,* showing a particular quality such as soils, climate, or vegetation, or they may be *quantitative,* illustrating statistical data.

Special-purpose maps include ocean basin maps, graduated-circle maps, time zone maps, aeronautical charts, nautical charts, geologic maps, weather maps, road maps, city maps, recreation area maps, historical atlas maps, space photomaps, lunar charts, computer-drawn maps, flow maps, distribution maps, and orthophotomaps (enhanced photographic images in correct orthographic position).

ADDITIONAL RESOURCES

Bagrow, Leo, and R. A. Skelton. *History of Cartography.* Cambridge, Mass.: Harvard University Pr., 1964.

Brown, Lloyd A. *The Story of Maps.* Boston: Little, Brown, 1949.

Cobb, David A. "Selection and Acquisition of Materials for the Map Library." *Drexel Library Quarterly* 9 (1973): 11–25.

Crone, G. R. *Maps and Their Makers.* 4th ed. London: Hutchinson, 1968.

Drazniowsky, Roman, ed. *Map Librarianship: Readings.* Metuchen, N.J.: Scarecrow, 1975.

Fisher, H. T. *Mapping Information.* Cambridge, Mass.: Abt, 1982.

Larsgaard, Mary. *Map Librarianship.* Littleton, Colo.: Libraries Unlimited, 1978.

Le Gear, Clara E. *Maps: Their Care, Repair, and Preservation in Libraries.* Washington, D.C.: Library of Congress, 1956.

Monmonier, Mark S. *Maps' Distortion and Meaning.* Washington, D.C.: Assn. of American Geographers, 1977.

Nichols, Harold. *Map Librarianship.* 2nd ed. London: Clive Bingley, 1982.

Raisz, Erwin. *General Cartography.* 2nd ed. New York: McGraw-Hill, 1948.

Ristow, Walter W. *The Emergence of Maps in Libraries.* London: Mansell, 1980.

Thrower, Norman J. W. *Maps and Man.* Englewood Cliffs, N.J.: Prentice-Hall, 1972.

Tooley, R. V. *Maps and Map-Makers.* 4th ed. London: Crown, 1970.

Tyner, Judith. *The World of Maps and Mapping: A Creative Learning Aid.* New York: McGraw-Hill, 1973.

Marilyn L. Shontz

Microforms

THE MEDIUM

Definition

The term *microform* is applied to all forms of microreproduction on film or paper (e.g., microfilm, microfiche, microopaque).[1] Microforms are generally viewed by individual users at specially designed machines, or "readers," which provide the needed magnification.

Micrographics is the term for the overall technology in the creation and use of microforms.[2]

A *microimage* is a reproduction of an object, such as a source document, which is too small to be read or viewed without magnification.[3]

Brief History

Although treated as a novelty until the 1920s, microforms originated much earlier. John Benjamin Dancer, an English scientist, known as the "father of microphotography," began to experiment with and manufacture microproduced novelty texts as early as 1839. In 1853 he successfully sold microphotographs as slides to be viewed with a

1. Heartsill Young, ed., *The ALA Glossary of Library and Information Science* (Chicago: American Library Assn., 1983), 145.
2. Joseph L. Kish, Jr., *Micrographics: A User's Manual* (New York: John Wiley, 1980), 1.
3. Young, *ALA Glossary,* 145.

microscope. Utilizing Dancer's techniques, a French optician, Rene Dagron, was granted the first patent for microfilm in 1859. He also began the first commercial microfilm enterprise, manufacturing and selling microphotographic trinkets. Dagron, in the fall and winter of 1870–71, during the Franco-Prussian War, demonstrated a practical use for microforms when carrier pigeons were used to transport microfilmed messages across German lines to the besieged city of Paris.

The first practical commercial microfilm use was developed by a New York City banker, George McCarthy, in the 1920s. He was issued a patent in 1925 for his Checkograph machine, designed to make permanent film copies of all bank records. The device used motion picture film and a conveyor belt to photograph checks before they were returned to bank customers. In 1928 Eastman Kodak bought McCarthy's invention and began to market it under Kodak's Recordak Division. By 1933 there were over 700 machines in American banks. With a perfected 35mm microfilm camera, Recordak in 1935 expanded and began filming and publishing the *New York Times* in microfilm.

Two significant events in 1938 hastened the use of microforms for archival preservation in American libraries and institutions. Because of rapid deterioration of the newsprint original and the numerous difficulties in storage and use of newspapers, Harvard University Library began its Foreign Newspaper Microfilm project. Today this project continues, sponsored by the Association of Research Libraries, and the microform masters are stored at the Center for Research Libraries in Chicago. This same year also saw the founding of University Microfilms by Eugene Power. He had previously microfilmed foreign and rare books, but in 1938 his work became a commercial enterprise as he expanded into microfilming doctoral dissertations.

Although World War II slowed the growth of institutional applications of the new microfilming industry, microphotography was still used extensively for espionage and for regular military mail. To conserve space, letters going overseas (and vice versa) were sent on microfilm, with a V-Mail or "hardcopy" being produced and forwarded at the receiving side. The war also brought a threat of destruction to the records of civilization. This threat added an urgency to the microfilming of records, documents, archives, and collections. During the closing war years and the immediate postwar years, there was a flurry of microfilming by occupying nations.

After the war, the idea of using microforms for active information systems, and not just for preservation of materials, was proposed. Vannevar Bush[4] and Fremont Rider[5] both envisioned libraries utilizing microforms as active information sources as well as a storage medium. A lack of standardized formats, the poor quality of reading devices, and the emphasis in the industry on commercial business applications all emerged as obstacles to the concept. However, increased funding and improved technology in the late 1950s and 1960s encouraged academic libraries and research libraries to continue to expand their activities in the area of microforms.

The 1970s brought a general decrease in library finances, along with a rapidly growing information society and computer industry. Limited funding, coupled with the information explosion, forced libraries and institutions and their users to microforms as an alternative to bulky, expensive print materials. Improved film, readers, viewers, reader-printers, and the advent of portable or lap readers made this money-saving choice more acceptable. However, user reluctance remained a strong deterrent to microform use.

The improved technology of the 1970s also increased COM, or computer output microform, applications. Microforms produced directly from a computer are being used to produce parts catalogs, hospital and insurance records, telephone listings, college catalogs, patent records, publisher's catalogs, and library catalogs. Some large institutions have begun producing their own COM publications in-house, with smaller institutions utilizing commercial service bureaus. A summary of services offered and criteria for selection of a service bureau have been offered by Hoberg.[6]

Advanced technologies which extend the basic COM process are available now. State of the COM art technology and applications for today's office are summarized by Suiter.[7] CIM (computer input microform) uses optical character reader equipment (OCR) to scan print documents and convert them automatically to digital information on magnetic computer tape. This technique speeds up the process of data entry, eliminates human error, and allows permanent storage of data in a microformat. Microfacsimile transmission is especially useful for large data files which must be maintained in remote locations and updated frequently. With microfacsimile, digitalized microimages can be

4. Vannevar Bush, "As We May Think," *Atlantic Monthly* (July 1945), 106–7.

5. Fremont Rider, *The Scholar and the Future of the Research Library: A Problem and Its Solution* (New York: Hadham Pr., 1944).

6. Richard P. Hoberg, "Expanding Roles for the Micrographics Service Company," *Journal of Information and Image Management* 18 (Apr. 1985): 8–11 + .

7. H. G. Suiter, Jr., "COM and the Evolving Office," *Journal of Information and Image Management* 17 (Nov. 1984): 14–23.

transmitted through a telecommunications network and output as COM microforms.

COM microforms can also be used in word processing and electronic mail applications to make permanent copies of transmissions. For existing large files of microforms, CAR (computer assisted retrieval) can retrieve information from individual microforms through a computer index. Although costs for these technologies are still high, the costs of CAR systems have recently decreased 15–20 percent, with the capabilities of the systems doubling.[8]

Videodisc and optical disc technologies are new areas of experimentation for the storage and retrieval of data. Several manufacturers are offering such systems currently.[9] Videodisc can combine for storage and publishing both still and moving pictures, while optical disc stores digital data. Badler and Grills[10] and Kish[11] both comment on the high costs of optical disc technology when compared to microforms and on the probability of these costs remaining so in the foreseeable future. Veaner[12] and Chadwyck-Healey,[13] in analyzing the status and future of videodisc technology, agree that its limitations and costs will keep it from competing with microforms for permanent storage. Chadwyck-Healey summarizes the outlook for microformats: "Microforms have a future not only in the short term but probably in the more distant future as well.[14]

Unique Characteristics

In usage, microforms are viewed primarily by individuals rather than by groups. In addition, the format can serve two main purposes in organizations: records can be purchased and stored for research and archival reasons; and/or current institutional records can be produced, stored, and utilized in microforms.

8. Robert D. Atkins, "Computer-Assisted Retrieval: Cost of CAR Goes Down, Productivity Goes Up," *Journal of Information and Image Management* 18 (May 1985): 33–34.

9. David T. Bogue, "Micrographics Prognosis for 1985," *Journal of Information and Image Management* 18 (Feb./Mar. 1985): 16.

10. Mitchell M. Badler and Caroline M. Grills, "Micrographics and the Optical Disk Challenge," in *1982–83 International Micrographics Sourcebook* (New Rochelle, N.Y.: Microfilm Pub., 1982), 356–57.

11. Joseph L. Kish, Jr., *Micrographics: A User's Manual* (New York: John Wiley), 169.

12. Allen B. Veaner, "Incredible Past, Incredible Future," *Library Resources and Technical Services* 26 (Jan./Mar. 1982): 52–56.

13. Charles Chadwyck-Healey, "The Future of Microform in an Electronic Age," *Wilson Library Bulletin* 58 (Dec. 1983): 270–73.

14. Ibid., 270.

Unique in their characteristics:

Microreproductions can be made on either opaque or transparent backgrounds.

Microforms can be produced, stored, and used on roll film or flat film.

Film polarity for black-and-white microforms can be positive or negative.

The use of color film is the exception, because of expense and shorter shelf life.

The actual size ratio of the microreproduction to the original can vary, requiring corresponding magnification for proper viewing.

Microforms can be produced on a high-quality archival film, which assures the institution of the permanence of its collection and records.

A complete description of the various types of microforms is found in the "Other Concerns" section, near the end of this discussion.

Advantages and Disadvantages

Advantages and disadvantages of microforms relate to equipment and space requirements, costs, collection development, and provision of services.

ADVANTAGES

Microforms conserve storage or shelf space by requiring 90–95 percent less space than the print equivalents.

Purchase of microforms can reduce binding costs of serials, costs of document storage, mailing or shipping costs in acquisitions and interlibrary loan, replacement costs for missing or damaged items, and acquisition costs, as the microform copy is usually less expensive than its print equivalent.

Collection development needs are furthered through the purchase of microforms because a wide range of materials are available in microforms; rare and out-of-print materials can be made more widely available; microforms can retain the clarity and readability of the original; and an extensive permanent collection can be made available when archival quality film is purchased, properly cared for, and stored.

Using microforms can improve both services to users and administrative functions. For users, microforms are easily converted back to print with reader-printer access; they can be quickly and easily updated or replaced; and they are less likely to be mutilated or removed from the collection. The ease and rapidity of replacement is also helpful in fulfilling administrative functions such as microform catalog updating. With the proper equipment, microforms can also be duplicated from one microformat to another, or be incorporated into computerized retrieval systems and word processing systems.

DISADVANTAGES

Although there is a considerable saving of storage space with the use of microforms, additional institutional space is necessary for specialized equipment. The types of equipment required depend on the microformats chosen, the planned uses for them, the reduction ratios, and the need for producing paper copies. A specialized physical environment, which includes proper lighting, special furniture, temperature control, humidity control, and air circulation control, is also needed for use and storage of microforms.

Cost savings obtained from the purchase of microforms are somewhat offset by additional expenses incurred. In addition to the original costs of specialized equipment and the continuing costs of environmental control, equipment maintenance costs are a factor. There may also be added costs with duplication of current print sources, along with the microform source, as with some serial publications.

Difficulties encountered when purchasing micorforms for collections include understanding the variety of standards used in the production of microforms, evaluation of large sets prior to purchase, and the lack of color film images available for most uses because of the expense and technical problems involved. Historically, there has also been a lack of bibliographic control of microforms, both internal indexing/labeling as well as external description and listings. This can make access to the microforms in an institution's collection difficult.

Microform use in institutions has encountered resistance from both staff and users. Fatigue, eyestrain, difficulty in browsing, difficulty in locating information, difficulty in comparing documents, limitation to in-house use, and intimidation by the technology have all been identified as problems. Administrators also encounter problems related to the copyright law and its restrictions on duplication, as well as the legality of microform records.

SELECTION

Special Criteria

In the selection process,[15] collection managers should consider:

Microforms must be compatible with the existing microforms collection and with available equipment. Reduction and magnification

15. A thorough discussion of microform evaluation can be found in Allen Veaner's *The Evaluation of Micropublications: A Handbook for Librarians* (Chicago: American Library Assn., 1971).

ratios, type of microformat, storage requirements, and standards which were followed in the manufacturing process should all be considered.

The type of film stock—silver halide, diazo, or vesicular—should be selected according to the intended uses of the microform. Silver halide film has been determined by the American National Standards Institute to have an indefinite shelf life if properly cared for and stored.

As color film is more expensive but not permanent, the need for black-and-white or color film should be evaluated.

The polarity of black-and-white film must be considered. With reader-printer equipment, negative polarity will produce the traditional black image on a white background in paper copy; while positive polarity film will produce a white image on a black background. Some reader-printers will produce a traditional copy from either positive or negative film polarity.

The sharpness and completeness of the microimages when viewed should be considered, as well as the clearness and readability of paper copies when produced at a reader-printer.

All packaging and containers should be certified free of harmful chemicals.

The ease of use, including eye-readable headings, frame numbers, indexing on the film, and the availability of print indexes, should be considered prior to purchase.

When large microform sets are purchased, all of the following must be considered: the publishing schedule, the date of termination, the completeness of the set, the availability of replacement parts, and the pricing of individual parts and the total set. In addition, the selector should determine the availability of individual titles from the set for preview, evaluation, and/or purchase.

Evaluative Review Sources

PERIODICALS
International Journal of Micrographics and Video Technology
Library Technology Reports
Microform Review
Serials Review

BOOKS
Cumulative Microform Reviews 1972–1976. Westport, Conn.: Meckler, 1979.
Microform Review; Cumulative 10 Volume Index 1972–1981. Westport, Conn.: Meckler, 1982.
Napier, Paul A., comp. *Index to Micrographics Equipment Evaluations.* Westport, Conn.: Meckler, 1982.

Saffady, William, ed. *Micrographics Equipment Review*. Westport, Conn.: Meckler, 1978– (annual).

Nonevaluative Sources

PERIODICALS
Datapro Reports on Office Systems
Journal of Information and Image Management
National Preservation Report

BOOKS
Dodson, Suzanne Cates, ed. *Microform Research Collections: a Guide*. 2nd ed. Westport, Conn.: Meckler, 1984.
Guide to Microforms in Print, Subject Guide to Microforms in Print, and *Microforms in Print: Supplement*. Westport, Conn.: Meckler, 1975– . Annual.
Guide to Micrographic Equipment. Silver Spring, Md.: National Microfilm Association, 1975– .
Index to Microform Collections. Ed. Ann Niles. Westport, Conn.: Meckler, 1984.
International Microforms in Print: A Guide to Microforms of Non–United States Micropublishers. Westport, Conn.: Microform Review, 1974/75– .
International Micrographics Source Book. New Rochelle, N.Y.: Microfilm Pub., 1972– . Biennial.
Microform Market Place. Westport, Conn.: Microform Review, 1980– . Biennial.
Microforms Annual. Elmsford, N.Y.: Microforms International Marketing Corp. Annual.
Micropublishers' Trade List Annual. Westport, Conn.: Meckler, 1977– . Annual.
National Register of Microform Masters. Washington, D.C.: Library of Congress, Cataloging Distribution Service, 1965– . Annual.
Newspapers in Microform. Washington, D.C.: Library of Congress, Cataloging Distribution Service, 1973– . Annual.
New York Public Library Register of Microform Masters: Monographs. New York: The Library, 1983.
Serials in Microform. Ann Arbor: Xerox University Microfilms, 1972– . Annual.

MAINTENANCE AND MANAGEMENT
Storage and Care

Microforms in active collections are subject to attack by molds and fungi, as well as discoloration, brittleness, cracking, scratches, and tears. Protection from these types of damage requires proper storage and care, including control of temperature and humidity; control of chemicals, light, and dust; proper storage containers and cases; and adequate protection during use.

The recommended temperature for a microform storage area is 68–70° F, with a constant relative humidity of 40–50%. It is essential to have accurate, periodic readings in all sections of the storage area.

Ultraviolet light from the sun or from fluorescent lights will cause deterioration of both silver halide and diazo type films. In addition, silver halide film can be affected by chemical fumes or chemicals such as paint, ammonia, and peroxides. The chemical in fingerprints (uric acid) makes it essential that microforms always be handled by the edges. Dirt and dust particles on any microformat can cause scratches both during use and in storage. Air circulating in the microforms' storage area should be continuously filtered to eliminate dust and other pollutants.

The microforms' storage area should be located away from outer walls, direct sun, windows, air vents, and radiators. Storage cabinets, cases, and drawers should be metal. All individual containers should be metal, plastic, or acid-free paper. In addition, all plastic reels, clips, rubber bands, and string ties used should be certified chemical free. Most microforms are stored vertically and may be tightly packed in drawers or cases. However, reel microfilm should be stored loosely, wound on reels to avoid scratching.

Because scratches and tears are most likely to occur during use, all users should be instructed in the care of microforms and proper equipment use. Users should be requested to report any damage they encounter. Ideally, microforms should be inspected for damage after each use. A regular program for inspection of the microform collection, and maintenance and inspection of all equipment, should be established. Protective containers should be used for circulation.

A checklist, devised and tested, can be used by an institution's staff to assist in the evaluation of their microform storage and care practices. Available as an ERIC document (ED 181 883), readers can evaluate practices in which they are currently engaged, as well as those they need to undertake.[16]

Management Problems and Solutions

Microforms are now being utilized in all types of institutions for both specific administrative tasks and for document storage and use. The

16. John W. Ellison, Gloria S. Gerber, and Susan E. Ledder, *Microforms: Storage and Care Self-Evaluation Form* (Amherst: State Univ. of New York at Buffalo), ED 181 883, 1979.

Broward County Main Library in Fort Lauderdale, Florida, is an example of a library which has incorporated microforms extensively into all areas of its operations. Designed as a reference and research facility, the Main Library has its card catalog, major periodical indexes, and 40 percent of all of its holdings on microfiche or microfilm. In addition, technical services functions are completely automated.[17]

Problems which have been reported by institutions who utilize microforms can be categorized as those related to the collection, those related to user acceptance, those related to administrative tasks, and special problems such as bibliographic control, standardization, copyright, and the legality of microform records.

COLLECTION DEVELOPMENT AND MICROFORMS

Materials published in microformats include journals, newspapers, and other serials; government publications; legal materials; music; out-of-print monographs; proceedings; manuscripts; technical reports; records and archival materials; bibliographies and union catalogs; catalogs, directories, and listings. The majority of micropublications are republished in microform from the original print version. However, an increasing amount of material is originally published in microformat. *Publishers' Catalog Annual* (Meckler Publishing), a yearly compilation of current publishers' catalogs, is an example of a bibliographic source being published in microfiche only. National Technical Information Service (NTIS) and Educational Resources Information Clearinghouse (ERIC) are both government-sponsored agencies, publishing original technical reports and documents in microfiche.

Collection managers are faced with decisions regarding microforms which affect the development and use of their collections. For institutions with extensive backfiles of serials, the decision to switch to microforms can mean savings in storage space and binding costs, as well as greater file integrity. Purchasing republished materials in microformats can expand a collection to include rare and out-of-print materials and print materials whose hardcopy prices are prohibitive. Also, directories and catalogs, available in both print and microformat, are more readily and easily updated when the microformat is purchased. Finally, as many materials are now available in microformats only, the intensity and depth of a collection can be determined by their inclusion or exclusion.

Cooperative efforts in the areas of microform collections and preservation have significantly increased the quantity of materials

17. Jeanne Nikolaison and Ray Nikolaison, "Microforms Dominate," *Journal of Information and Image Management* 18 (Feb./Mar. 1985): 32–35.

which are accessible to users. After a lag in the 1970s, several major cooperative projects have emerged in the 1980s.[18]

In 1981 the Major Microform Survey, completed by the Association of Research Libraries (ARL), identified items of greatest interest to research libraries. Based on the results of the survey, OCLC, with the cooperation of ARL, began a shared cataloging project with the purpose of increasing user access to significant microforms.[19] After a two-year study, the Research Libraries Group also began a cooperative microform project in 1983. Funded by the National Endowment for the Humanities (NEH) and the Mellon Foundation, RLG chose United States monographs, 1876–1900, to begin its brittle-books-preservation microfilming project.[20]

The Office of Preservation, established by the National Endowment for the Humanities in January 1985, has been charged by that organization with providing national leadership in preserving humanities resources and making them more accessible to scholars. The Office has stated that the Endowment will devote "significant funding" to cooperative efforts in preservation.[21] In addition to assisting RLG's brittle-books project, it has a priority project of its own in the U.S. Newspaper Project. In the initial phase of the Newspaper Project, selected sites in various states are entering comprehensive and complete bibliographic records into the CONSER data base through the OCLC online computer system. A later phase of this same project will include microfilming of selected newspaper titles.[22]

USERS AND MICROFORMS

An area of great concern to institutions and producers is the lack of acceptance by users of microforms. Salmon summarizes research about user resistance to microforms, categorizing the difficulties as poor cataloging and indexing; lack of portability; difficulties in equipment use (such as noisy and hard to manipulate); poor image quality, with scratches, smudges, and missing or reversed pages; physical fatigue and eye fatigue; and use problems, such as taking notes, making notes on the document, flipping pages, and comparing two or more documents.[23]

18. Nancy E. Gwinn, "The Rise and Fall of Cooperative Projects," *Library Resources and Technical Services* 29 (Jan./Mar. 1985): 84.

19. "OCLC's Major Microforms Project," *Microform Review* 13 (Fall 1984): 232–33.

20. Gwinn, "Rise and Fall of Cooperative Projects," 85.

21. Jeffrey Field, "The Role of the National Endowment for the Humanities' Office of Preservation in the National Preservation Effort," *Microform Review* 14 (Spring 1985): 81.

22. Gwinn, "Rise and Fall of Cooperative Projects," 85.

23. Stephen R. Salmon, "User Resistance to Microforms in the Research Library," *Library Scene* 8 (June 1979): 24–29.

This identified user resistance was the topic of a study by Whitmore, completed in 1980. She hypothesized that a microform-user instruction program in two academic libraries would improve user attitudes and acceptance of microforms. The experimental groups who viewed a slide/tape program about microforms *did* exhibit slightly more positive attitudes toward microforms than did the control groups. Whitmore concluded that user education could assist in changing negative attitudes.[24]

Boss and Raikes stated that most difficulties with microforms are the result of inadequate facilities planning and operation. They produced guidelines which provide assistance for collection managers who wish to make the best and most efficient possible use of microforms in their institutions.[25] Hall and Michaels also maintain that the "best possible viewing environment is a particularly important element of a successful microform operation."[26] The guidelines they have developed are for a regular microform reader maintenance and repair program. Both sets of guidelines, if implemented, could result in improved user satisfaction.

Another approach to improving microform use and acceptance in institutions is proposed by Eichhorn. She suggests that a uniform set of standards for public service is needed, and recommends five steps for the development of these standards in local institutions.[27]

ADMINISTRATIVE TASKS

Microforms have been used by institutions for various administrative purposes, such as keeping circulation records, acquisition records, and card catalog production. Saffady discusses some of these applications.[28] However, prior to initiating such applications, the collection manager makes some decisions regarding media and system selection.

Choosing the right type of media is an important element in using microforms for administrative tasks. Artlip discusses making a choice between microforms and newer media applications now available, such as optical or magnetic disc, giving the strengths and limitations of

---

24. Marilyn Whitmore, "Microforms and the User: The Relationship of a Microform Instruction Program to User Acceptance" (Ph.D. dissertation, University of Pittsburgh, 1980).

25. Richard Boss and Deborah Raikes, *Developing Microform Reading Facilities* (Westport, Conn.: Microform Review, 1981), 13.

26. Hal W. Hall and George H. Michaels, "Microform Reader Maintenance," *Microform Review* 14 (Winter 1985): 24–34.

27. Sara Eichhorn, "Standards for Public Service of Microform Collections," *Microform Review* 13 (Spring 1984): 103–7.

28. William Saffady, *Micrographics* (Littleton, Colo.: Libraries Unlimited, 1978), 22.

each.[29] Dodson takes the more traditional microfilm and discusses the effects of light, heat, humidity, scratches, and longevity of the three main types of film: silver, diazo, and vesicular. Implications for collection managers who must choose the right film type for a specific purpose are given.[30]

Collection managers are faced with the task of evaluating and selecting micrographics systems which will meet their institutional and user requirements. Meyer offers a list of considerations in choosing such a system:

> type of input
> nature of the information to be stored
> how the information will be used
> overall system cost
> speed and ease of document retrieval
> need to disseminate the information to several locations
> capability and cost of making duplicates, either in another
>   microform or on paper
> frequency with which the file is changed or updated
> need for file integrity
> storage density
> anticipated means of reading and duplication at central and/
>   or remote locations
> compatibility with other information systems such as data
>   processing[31]

System selection could also involve a decision to contract with a micrographics service company. Such agencies offer a wide variety of services which could replace some or all in-house activities. Hoberg offers a summary of micrographics service agencies and discusses criteria an institution should use in the selection of such an agency.[32]

COM (computer output microform) is a major type of system utilized in administrative functions. A current overview of COM system applications for information storage and retrieval in the modern office is presented by Suiter, who maintains that "image management on film will be here for a long time to come." Latest developments in computer-aided design (CAD), data-base management, computer-

29. Paul M. Artlip, "How to Choose the Right Media: Optical, Magnetic, or Microfilm," *Journal of Information and Image Management* 18 (Sept. 1985): 15–17 + .
30. Suzanne Cates Dodson, "Microfilm—Which Type, Which Application?" *Microform Review* 14 (Spring 1985): 87–98.
31. Ellen T. Meyer, ed., *An Introduction to Micrographics: A Consumer Handbook* (Silver Spring, Md.: National Micrographics Assn., 1980), 8.
32. Hoberg, "Expanding Roles for the Micrographics Service Company," 8–11.

assisted retrieval (CAR), word processing, and the personal computer are presented.[33]

The availability of Library of Congress MARC records and bibliographic data-base records for individual institutions on magnetic tape has influenced many institutions to convert from the standard card catalog to a COM microform catalog. Computer magnetic-tape records can be used with a COM recorder and a mainframe computer to produce microfilm or microfiche catalogs. This option for a COM catalog is discussed by Diaz,[34] Saffady,[35] and Malinconico.[36] A Library Catalog Cost Model has been developed by King Research and tested in 72 libraries.[37] This computer cost model compares 12 alternatives to maintaining the standard card catalog. Seven of the alternatives include some use of a COM catalog.

SPECIAL PROBLEMS

Special management problems which have developed, related to microforms, include those with standardization, bibliographic control, copyright, and legality of records.

A lack of standardization of film types, film sizes, frame patterns, and reduction/magnification ratios has plagued microforms' users since the beginning years. Only recently have industrywide standards been adopted and voluntarily adhered to by producers.

The membership of the Agency for Information and Image Management (AIIM), formerly the National Micrographics Association (NMA), represents both users and producers of microforms. It is the organization primarily responsible for developing and proposing industry and national standards in the United States. Based on a consensus of the members, it makes recommendations to the National Information Standards Organization (Z39) of the American National Standards Institute (ANSI). If the deliberations lead to adoption as a national standard, the committee further submits its recommendation to the International Standards Organization (ISO) for possible adoption as an international standard. Kidd has compiled a listing of the micrographic standards of AIIM.[38] Current standards deal with roll film and fiche formats,

33. Suiter, "COM in the Evolving Office," 14–23.

34. Albert J. Diaz, ed., *Microform in Libraries: A Reader* (Westport, Conn.: Microform Review, 1975).

35. William Saffady, *Computer-Output Microfilm: Its Library Applications* (Chicago: American Library Assn., 1978).

36. Michael Malinconico and Paul J. Fasana, *The Future of the Catalog: The Library's Choices* (White Plains, N.Y.: Knowledge Industry Pub., 1979).

37. Robert R. V. Wiederkehr, *Alternatives for Future Library Catalogs: A Cost Model* (Rockville, Md.: King Research, 1980).

38. Harry B. Kidd, "Micrographics Standards in Libraries," *Microform Review* 13 (Spring 1984): 93–102.

quality of resolution and density, and storage conditions for archival purposes. Also available from AIIM is its *Standards Set,* which is published as a two-volume loose-leaf binder to facilitate continuous updating.

Bibliographic control, like standardization, has been and is a serious concern to institutions, their staffs, and users. A 1972 study by the Association of Research Libraries noted bibliographic control of microforms as a "foremost need."[39] Both internal and external bibliographic control are discussed. Internal bibliographic control includes eye-readable legends, numbered frames, labeling of boxes or containers, and adequate indexing of contents, both indexing on the film itself and the availability of print indexes. External bibliographic control includes the availability and quality of descriptive cataloging information as well as local, national, and international bibliographic listings.

While internal bibliographic control through the various microform producers has improved, external control is still far from adequate. Because of the lack of quality cataloging information, many institutions acquire and maintain microform collections without the descriptive information which could provide optimum access for users and staff. Three major national efforts to improve external bibliographic access are in process. The first is by the Library of Congress, which is including *The National Register of Microform Masters* in its future plans for automation of the *National Union Catalog.* Online MARC Catalog records of the microform masters will then be more readily available to institutions through utilities such as OCLC.[40]

A second project, the U.S. Newspaper Project, funded by the National Endowment for the Humanities, has as its initial phase placing complete bibliographic records in OCLC through CONSER.[41] OCLC also has its own Major Microforms Project, which encourages the Association of Research Libraries to add microform records to the OCLC data base.[42]

The current copyright law (PL 94-553, 1978) presents a legal problem for collection managers. Two aspects of noncompliance exist: (1) microrepublishing without obtaining copyright permission, and (2) illegal copying by users. Grills notes that "to date there are no land-

39. Felix Reichmann and Josephine M. Tharpe, *Bibliographic Control of Microforms* (Westport, Conn.: Greenwood Pr., 1972), 3.

40. "Future of the National Register of Microform Masters," *Library of Congress Information Bulletin* 41 (Mar. 12, 1982): 82–84.

41. Gwinn, "Rise and Fall of Cooperative Projects," 85.

42. "OCLC Major Microforms Project," 232.

mark cases in the microform copyright controversy."[43] Illegal copying has been made more possible and likely by new technology, such as the reader-printer. The Copyright Clearance Center was established to facilitate implementation of the law, but, as compliance is voluntary, its success has been limited. There is still a need for producers, users, and publishers to develop a mutually workable copying system.[44]

Institutions can also be faced with the issue of the legality of microform records. Because of questions related to presenting filmed reproductions of documents in a court of law, various state and local government agencies have adopted guidelines for preserving and storing documents. Some institutions use a certificate of authenticity for verification of records.[45]

Other Concerns

1. *Microfilm,* or "roll microfilm," is a continuous strip of microimages on unperforated photographic film. Common widths are 16mm and 35mm, but 8mm, 70mm, and 105mm widths are also available. In length, microfilm is usually 100 feet, although it can be several thousand feet. The first and last few inches are blank (a "leader"), although they may contain eye-readable bibliographic data. Microfilm is usually wound on a reel, but may be placed in cartridges or cassettes for ease of use, file security, and protection.

   Two major categories or frame orientations exist:

   Vertical or *cine mode,* in which pages or frames form one long column of images, perpendicular to the edges of the film, as in motion picture film, and

   Horizontal or *comic mode,* in which pages or frames are positioned in comic strip style, with one long row of images parallel to the edges of the film.

   In addition, frames may be simplex, with one page per frame, or duo, duplex, or duo-duplex, with two or more pages per frame.

2. *Microfiche,* or "fiche," is a flat sheet of photographic film, usually 4 × 6 inches or 3 × 5 inches, with rows and columns of microimages in a grid pattern. With eye-readable identification of contents in the heading, microfiche can be filed vertically in drawers for easy access to individual fiche.

43. Caroline M. Grills, "Micropublishing in the '80s under the Revised U.S. Copyright Law," *Journal of Micrographics* 14 (July 1981): 14.
44. Ibid., 16.
45. Kish, *Micrographics,* 148.

3. *Ultrafiche* is a microfiche which contains microimages reduced to 90 times (or more) smaller than the original print.

4. An *aperture card,* or "image card," is similar to the standard computer punch card, with one or more windows or cut-out spaces in which segments of microfilm are mounted. One major use is for recording and storing engineering drawings.

5. A *film jacket,* or "jacket," is a flat, transparent plastic sleeve with channels into which pieces of microforms can be inserted. They are usually a standard 4 × 6 inch size and allow the jacket to accept strips of 35mm or 16mm film, providing a combination of sizes in a single format.

6. A *microopaque* can be either a microcard or a microprint, and consists of microimages printed on heavy opaque card stock which can be printed on both sides. Because of the opaque characteristic, microopaques require specialized equipment for viewing.

Other special characteristics of microforms—eight in all—include:

1. *Polarity,* or the light/dark relationship in a microimage. Film produced by a direct image process will produce a positive polarity microform—one with a light background and dark images. Film produced by a reversed image process will produce a negative polarity microform—one with a dark background and light images.

2. Three major types of film are used in the manufacture of microforms:

    Silver halide film, or "silver film," combines silver and a member of the halogen family in either a direct or a reverse process to produce microimages. It was the first type of film used and is the only one for which national standards have been developed. Silver film is considered to be permanent, of archival quality, and is recommended for preservation projects.

    Diazo film is produced by a direct image process, using diazonium salts, ammonia, and light to produce microimages. Diazo film is less expensive and more quickly produced than silver film.

    Vesicular film is usually produced by a reverse image process which uses heat and ultraviolet light to produce microimages. This newest type of film is also less expensive and quickly produced, but is highly susceptible to image loss at high temperatures.

3. The *reduction ratio* of a microform is the ratio which indicates the number of times the original image has been reduced through the filming process. All three designations, 18x, 18:1, 18 to 1, could

be used to indicate an image which was reduced to 1/18 its original size. Reduction ratios have been categorized as follows:

Low—up to 15x
Medium—up to 30x
High—up to 60x
Very high—up to 90x
Ultra high—90x and higher

4. The *magnification ratio* is the opposite of a reduction ratio. It is normally used to indicate the power of a lens in a microreader, viewer, or reader-printer.

5. *Resolution* is defined as the sharpness of a microimage. Quality and degree of resolution can be determined by checking a Resolution Test Chart, on the first frame of a microform.

6. *Contrast* is the tonal difference (high and low brightness) between the light and dark areas in a microimage.

7. The term *generation* refers to the relationship between the original or camera film master (the first generation) and the copies made from it. A copy which has been made from the first-generation master is termed *second generation,* and so on. With each generation there may be a loss of resolution or image quality.

8. *Computer output microform,* or COM, is the process by which the binary signal output, directly from a computer, is converted by COM recorder equipment to an analog signal, which is then processed as microimages. The output from the COM process is normally microfilm or microfiche.

ADDITIONAL RESOURCES

Artlip, Paul M. "How to Choose the Right Media: Optical, Magnetic, or Microfilm." *Journal of Information and Image Management* 18 (Sept. 1985): 15–17 + .

Assn. of Information and Image Management. *Standards Set.* Silver Springs, Md.: The Assn. 1971–   .

Avedon, Don M. "Microforms as Library Tools." *Library Trends* 30 (Fall 1981): 253–65.

Bahr, Alice Harrison. *Microforms: The Librarians' View, 1978–79,* 2nd ed. White Plains, N.Y.: Knowledge Industry Pub., 1978.

Boss, Richard, and Deborah Raikes. *Developing Microform Reading Facilities.* Westport, Conn.: Microform Review, 1981.

Chadwyck-Healey, Charles. "The Future of Microform in an Electronic Age." *Wilson Library Bulletin* 58 (Dec. 1983): 270–73.

Cruse, Larry, and Sylvia B. Warren, eds. *Microcartography: Applications for Archives and Libraries.* Santa Cruz, Calif.: Western Assn. of Map Librarians, 1982.

Diaz, Albert J., ed. *Microforms and Library Catalogs: A Reader.* Westport, Conn.: Microform Review, 1977.

Dodson, Suzanne Cates. "Bibliographic Control of Microforms: Where Are We Today?" *Microform Review* 12 (Winter 1983): 12–18.

———. "Microfilm—Which Type of Application?" *Microform Review* 14 (Spring 1985): 87–98.

Dranov, Paula. *Microfilm: The Librarians' View, 1976–77.* White Plains, N.Y.: Knowledge Industry, 1976.

"Dukane MDP Microfilm Reader: LMM Excel Microfilm Reader." *Library Technology Reports* 21 (May/June 1985): 209–29.

Eichhorn, Sara. "Standards for Public Service of Microform Collections." *Microform Review* 13 (Spring 1984): 103–7.

Ellison, John W., Gloria S. Gerber, and Susan E. Ledder. *Storage and Care of Microforms* (slide). Washington, D.C.: National Audiovisual Center, 1979 (66 slides with cassette).

———. *Microforms: Storage and Care Self-Evaluation Form.* Amherst: State Univ. of New York at Buffalo, 1967, ED 181 883.

Fair, Judy H., ed. *Microforms Management in Special Libraries: a Reader.* Westport, Conn.: Microform Review, 1979.

Farrington, Jean Walter. "Video Disc: A Versatile New Storage Medium." *Serials Librarian* 7 (Winter 1982): 35–40.

Fleischer, Eugene B. *A Style Manual for Citing Microform and Nonprint Media.* Chicago: American Library Assn., 1978.

Folcarelli, Ralph J., Arthur C. Tannenbaum, and Ralph C. Ferragamo. *The Microform Connection: A Basic Guide for Libraries.* New York: Bowker, 1982.

Gabriel, Michael R., and D. P. Ladd. *The Microform Revolution in Libraries.* Greenwich, Conn.: JAI Pr., 1980.

Grills, Caroline M. "Micropublishing in the '80s under the Revised U.S. Copyright Law." *Journal of Micrographics* 14 (July 1981): 13–16.

Gunn, Michael J. "Current Developments in Colour Microform Technology." *Microform Review* 14 (Winter 1985): 21–23.

Hall, Hal W., and George H. Michaels. "Microform Reader Maintenance." *Microform Review* 14 (Winter 1985): 24–34.

Hawken, William R. *Evaluating Microfiche Readers: A Handbook for Librarians.* Washington, D.C.: Council on Library Resources, 1975.

Hernon, Peter. *Microforms and Government Information.* Westport, Conn.: Meckler, 1981.

Hoberg, Richard P. "Expanding Roles for the Micrographics Service Company." *Journal of Information and Image Management* 18 (Apr. 1985): 8–11+.

Kidd, Harry B. "Micrographics Standards in Libraries." *Microform Review* 13 (Spring 1984): 93–102.

Kish, Joseph L., Jr. *Micrographics: A Users Manual.* New York: Wiley, 1980.

"Library Announces Policy on Cataloging Microreproductions." Library of Congress Information Bulletin 40 (July 31, 1981): 245–46.

Luther, Frederic. *Microfilm: A History 1839–1900*. Barre, Mass.: Barre Pub., 1959.

Lynden, Frederick C. "Replacement of Hard Copy by Microforms." *Microfilm Review* 4 (Jan. 1975): 15–24.

Melin, Nancy J. *Serials and Microforms: Patron Oriented Management*. Westport, Conn.: Meckler, 1983.

Meyer, Ellen T., ed. *An Introduction to Micrographics; A Consumer Handbook*. Silver Spring, Md.: National Micrographics Assn., 1980.

"Microfiche Readers for Libraries." *Library Technology Reports* 19 (May/June 1983): 221–327.

"Microform Reader Printers for Libraries (Test Report)." *Library Technology Reports* 20 (Nov./Dec. 1984): 711–862.

National Micrographics Assn. *Glossary of Micrographics*. Silver Spring, Md.: National Micrographics Assn., 1980.

_____. *How to Select a Microform Reader or Reader-Printer*. Silver Spring, Md.: National Micrographics Assn., 1974.

Nikolaison, Jeanne, and Ray Nikolaison. "Microforms Dominate." *Journal of Information and Image Management* 18 (Feb./Mar. 1985): 32–35.

Norris, Charles I. "Integrated Office Systems: The Paperless Office." *Journal of Micrographics* 13 (May/June 1980): 23–26.

Reichmann, Felix, and Josephine M. Tharpe. *Bibliographic Control of Microforms*. Westport, Conn.: Greenwood Pr., 1972.

Resources and Technical Services Division. *Guidelines for Handling Library Orders for Microforms*. Chicago: American Library Assn., 1977.

_____. *Microforms in Libraries: A Manual for Evaluation and Management*. Chicago: American Library Assn., 1985.

Rice, E. Stevens, and Heinz Dettling. *Fiche and Reel: A Guide to Microfilm and Its Use*. 4th ed. Ann Arbor: University Microfilms International, 1980.

Rubin, Jack. *A History of Micrographics: In the First Person*. Silver Spring, Md.: National Micrographics Assn., 1980.

Saffady, William. *Computer-Output Microfilm: Its Library Applications*. Chicago: American Library Assn., 1978.

_____. *Micrographics*. 2nd ed. Littleton, Colo.: Libraries Unlimited, 1985.

Salmon, Stephen R. "User Resistance to Microforms in the Research Library." *Library Scene* 8 (June 1979): 24–29.

Schleifer, Harold B. "The Utilization of Microforms in Technical Services." *Microform Review* 11 (Spring 1982): 77–92.

Spigai, Frances G., and Brett B. Butler. "Micrographics." In *Annual Review of Information Science and Technology*. Vol. 11. Ed. Martha E. Williams. Washington, D.C.: American Society for Information Science, 1976. 59–106.

Spreitzer, Francis. *Selecting Microform Readers and Reader Printers*. Silver Spring, Md.: Assn. for Information and Image Management, 1983.

Suiter, H. G., Jr. "COM in the Evolving Office." *Journal of Information and Image Management* 17 (Nov. 1984): 14–23.

Veaner, Allen B. *The Evaluation of Micropublications: A Handbook for Librarians.* Chicago: American Library Assn., 1971.

———. "Incredible Past, Incredible Future." *Library Resources and Technical Services* 26 (Jan. 1982): 52–56.

———. "Micropublication." In *Advances in Librarianship.* Vol. 2. Ed. Melvin J. Voight. New York: Seminar Pr., 1971. 165–86.

Whitmore, Marilyn P. "Microforms and the User: The Relationship of a Microform Instruction Program to User Acceptance." Ph.D. dissertation, University of Pittsburgh, 1980.

Williams, Robert F., ed. *Legality of Microfilm: Admissability in Evidence of Microfilm Records* (looseleaf). Chicago: Cohasset Assoc., 1980.

Kathleen M. Tessmer

Ch. 10

Models

THE MEDIUM

Definition

Model: A tangible three-dimensional representation of an object.

The model may be larger or smaller than, or identical in size to, the object it represents. An object represented by a model may exist in the real world; may be a prototype of a real-world object (e.g., an architect's model of a building); or may represent an object with no real-world counterpart (e.g., a *Star Wars* spaceship).

The above definition excludes the hologram, which is three-dimensional, but it is a projected visual representation of an object rather than a tangible representation. The word *model* is often used to indicate theoretical or abstract models as well as tangible objects. Theoretical or abstract models are not considered here.

Brief History

The earliest models known were figures carved and fashioned by people in primitive societies. Some were fetishes which had religious significance for their makers.

The oldest historical records of modelmaking date to the Egyptian culture of 4000 B.C. The Egyptians buried many meticulously carved models in royal tombs. The models were placed in the tombs along with real items to provide comfort for the spirit or *ka* of the dead person. These were so precisely fashioned that they provide a mirror of everyday life, recording minute details of dress, domestic life, and occupations. Much of what we know of other ancient cultures was learned through models placed in tombs.

In 17th century France, Jean Baptiste Colbert, minister of marine under Louis XIV, ordered that a scale model be made of each ship built for the French navy. These later were placed in a maritime museum, Musée de la Marine, Paris, where they may still be studied today. Models such as these are valuable for historical research.[1]

Making and collecting models has been a pastime for hundreds of years. Every age has had an interest in making models of means of transportation. Models of horses and chariots have been found in ancient tombs. Some of the earliest ship models were of galleys and sailing ships. Model trains were eagerly collected following the introduction of the steam engine and are still popular today. After the spectacular airplane flights of the 1920s, display airplane models as well as flying models and gliders also became popular.[2]

All these, as well as automobile models and models of farm machinery, have their collectors today. Model rocketry clubs were formed before the space program was established. But models are not only hobby or collector's items, they have been and are used in a wide variety of settings.

Military models were used extensively to plot troop and transport movements and to plan strategy during the Second World War. Realistic aircraft and airplane models helped to teach identification of allied and enemy vehicles. Mockups were devised for training programs in the army and navy and for training factory workers in defense factories.[3] Present-day military training makes use of scale models, mockups, and full-scale models to teach weaponry, navigation, strategy, and tactics.

Model making is important today in the manufacture of ships, automobiles, and aircraft. The planning begins on paper; next, scale models are constructed and tested. Aircraft and automobile aerodynamics are tested in wind tunnels. Hull designs of ships are tested in ship-model basins, which can produce wind and wave actions of various kinds. After scale models of automobiles are tested, full-scale mockups are made and, finally, a working prototype.[4]

1. "Model," *Encyclopedia Americana* (Danbury, Conn.: Grolier, 1984), 290–91.
2. Morris Ozer, "Modelmaking," *Encyclopedia International* (New York: Grolier, 1976), 186.
3. Edgar Dale, *Audio-Visual Methods in Teaching* (New York: Dryden Pr., 1946), 88–90.
4. "Model," *Encyclopedia Americana,* 291–94.

Models are also important in architecture, urban planning, layout of industrial plants, and civil engineering projects such as bridges and dams.

The use of models in study and teaching is not limited to recent times. A scholar named Gerbert used wood and leather spheres for the study of astronomy in the 11th century. Models, called "illustrated manikins," were used in France in the early 19th century. The medical college at Albany (N.Y.) imported one in 1841, which Mark Hopkins, president of Williams College, determined to purchase for his college.[5] He is among the many educators who have emphasized the use of materials which could be touched and manipulated.

From the "audio-visual teaching method" textbooks of the 1950s to the "instructional technology" textbooks of the 1980s, the use of models for instruction has been a part of teacher education and training. However, over the past 30 years, the amount of time and attention given to the use of models has decreased as new media formats and technologies have proliferated. This means that although a wide variety of models are in use at all levels and in all kinds of instructional settings, less and less attention is devoted to the use of models as an instructional medium.

Unique Characteristics

The model is usable when the object itself is physically too large, too small, too dangerous, too delicate, or too remote to be handled or examined.

The model can provide a three-dimensional representation of objects inaccessible due to space or time, for example, dinosaur models (past), planetariums (distance and breadth of space), orbiting cities (future).

The model can provide concrete examples of concepts such as "shelter" by three-dimensional representations of buildings that vary as much as cathedrals, pyramids, wigwams, and pueblos.[6] The model can provide a three-dimensional representation of a process which occurs over a considerable area of space and/or a relatively long period of time, for example, the movement of the sun around Earth.[7]

While models, holograms, and realia all show interrelationships in three dimensions, only models and realia provide tactile input. The

5. Edgar Dale, *Audio-Visual Methods in Teaching,* rev. ed. (New York: Holt, Rinehart and Winston, 1954), 81.
6. Dale (1946), 217.
7. Ibid., 217–18.

model may be handled and/or manipulated repeatedly in ways not possible with the original object; for example, a crayfish can only be taken apart once, a model many times.

Advantages

Models are a familiar format. Children's toys are often models taken from real life (e.g., dolls and doll houses, cars, trucks, trains, and boats). Adults often are involved with model building or collecting. Homes may be decorated with miniatures or art replicas.[8]

Models "offer a sense of depth, thickness, height, and width,"[9] making it possible to understand concepts and relationships in more concrete ways than any other media format except realia.

The model offers a firsthand experience if the real item is too fragile, too large, too small, too dangerous, or too distant to be examined.

Models offer opportunities for tactile learning. Because they can be touched and repeatedly manipulated, they provide enhanced sensory learning.

Opportunity for repeated examination can strengthen and reinforce learning.

Significant features of objects may be emphasized or enhanced in models.

Complex objects may be simplified.

Models are, for the most part, durable and will last for many years.

Models can be constructed by users or instructors.

Users can construct models as part of an integrated learning experience requiring research, planning, construction, and evaluation.

Disadvantages

Users not familiar with the real item may not truly understand the size and proportions of the model. Any inconsistencies of color, scale, or shape may mislead or confuse the user.

Models may oversimplify.

Purchased models may be too expensive for small institutions. In this case, sharing through some sort of network should be considered.

Some models are difficult to reassemble.[10]

8. James Cabeceiras, *The Multimedia Library,* 2nd ed. (New York: Academic Pr., 1982), 203–4.

9. Phyllis J. Van Orden, *The Collection Program in Elementary and Middle Schools,* (Littleton, Colo.: Libraries Unlimited, 1982), 176.

10. Ibid.

Models constructed in-house may not be as well made or durable as
    commercially available models.
Construction of models may be costly in terms of time and materials.
The size of some models may limit their use with a group.[11]
Storage may be a problem with models that are heavy or bulky.

SELECTION

Special Criteria    good point

GENERAL

Models should be selected and used based upon need:

A two-dimensional representation may be sufficient if the third dimen-
    sion is not important to comprehension.
Select a model if the third dimension is important and the original item
    is unsuitable for use, due to unavailability, fragility, size, etc.
The cost should be appropriate to the probable educational benefit to
    be derived. Models constructed by users may be less costly
    monetarily, but may require a large investment of time.
Construction of models is indicated if an educational benefit is expected
    as a result of model construction.

The size should be appropriate for type of use. Models intended
for use with groups need to be large enough so all can see essential
features clearly. Smaller models may only be suitable for individual
or small-group learning situations.

Exact-scale models should of course be true to scale. The scale
should be clearly indicated, preferably on the model itself. Models not
made to exact scale should not be disproportionate or misleading.

Color should be used in appropriate ways rather than randomly
(i.e., to reproduce the color of the object in nature, to highlight specific
features, etc.). Some inexpensive models may be represented in color
in dealers' catalogs, but arrive as kits of blank plastic pieces with instructions for painting.

Parts of models should be clearly labeled or keyed to a list of
features in accompanying documentation. Labels on the object itself
should be legible, yet not distract from the model itself.

Types of models should be selected with regard to the complexity or simplicity desirable for a particular group of users; for example,

11. Ibid.

globes for younger users need not have all the features older users require.

Dissectible models should not only be easy to take apart, but should also be easy to reassemble. Replacement parts should be available at reasonable cost. Occasionally, replacement information may be included with parts lists provided with an item. Replacement information is not ordinarily indicated in supplier catalogs.

Working models should work smoothly and be sturdy enough to tolerate repeated use. Written directions should be provided, either on the item itself or in accompanying documentation. Accompanying documentation should include any special maintenance or safety procedures.

Preview before purchase is always advisable. Institutions which may lend or allow examination of models are listed below. A special caution is necessary with regard to inexpensive plastic models for educational use. These should be purchased only after preview or on a 30-day return basis, as they are often made from brittle material which cracks after only one or two uses.

GLOBES

Size. Globes for classrooms range from 8 to 24 inches in diameter. Most classroom globes are 12 or 16 inches, with a trend toward the 16-inch size for group use. The 8-inch globes are useful for individual work.

Material. Most globes today are constructed of lightweight, high-impact material. Metal globes will dent if dropped and are comparatively heavy. Transparent, slate-surface, and plastic globes can be marked on. Inflatable globes take up little storage space and can be written upon; with proper care to avoid puncture, they are quite durable.

Mounting. Cradle mounts allow globes to be rolled freely or completely removed from their stand for examination. A half- or full-meridian mounting is preferable to a mounting which merely permits the globe to spin on a rod attached through the South Pole.

Types. Relief, with raised surfaces; political, designed to show country and city boundaries; physical-political, which include political divisions, but emphasize land and ocean features; blank-slate or outline globes, with surfaces suitable for marking and erasing.

Additional criteria. Look for "accuracy in area sizes, shapes, directions, and distances; clarity of boundaries, special orientation lines, physical features and legends; non-glare, protective transparent coating."[12]

12. Warren B. Hicks and Alma Tillin. *Developing Multi-Media Libraries,* 2nd ed. (New York: Bowker, 1970), 132.

Evaluative Review Sources

No selection source regularly and systematically evaluates models. Evaluations of models may occasionally appear in issues of the following journals:

Booklist. Evaluates material for all ages.
Curator. Includes information and articles on techniques and technology of model making, criteria for evaluation of models and sources for models.
Curriculum Review. Evaluates instructional material for grades K–12.
Instructor. Evaluates instructional material for grades K–12.
Media Review Digest. Reviews appearing in journals may occasionally be located through this source.

Nonevaluative Sources

There are no separate selection lists for models; in addition, models are rarely included in general audiovisual lists. Most of the standard instructional resources and audiovisual reference sources do not include listings for models, mockups, dioramas, or three-dimensional objects. For example, among those sources which might be thought to include all of these formats, but do not, are *Educational Media Yearbook*,[13] *NICEM Index to Producers and Distributors*,[14] and *AudioVideo Marketplace*.[15]

A limited number of model sources may be found through the following works:

Audiovisual Marketplace: A Multimedia Guide. New York: R. R. Bowker Co., 1180 Avenue of the Americas, New York, NY 10036 (annual).
Sive, Mary Robinson. *Selecting Instructional Media: A Guide to Audiovisual and Other Instructional Media Lists.* 3rd ed. Littleton, Colo.: Libraries Unlimited, 1983.
In this work, models and mockups are grouped with realia, specimens, games, and toys under the heading "Manipulative Materials." Annotations do not indicate which sources, if any, include models or mockups.

To locate models of various kinds and types, consult publishers' catalogs. (Development of your own card file or data base containing information about suppliers and their models is highly recommended.) The following list of producers and suppliers was compiled from a wider list of suppliers known to the author through direct experience or recommended by others. The list excludes sources of collector and hobby models, but is based upon direct examination of producers' and

13. *Educational Media Yearbook, 1973–* (New York: R. R. Bowker, Annual).
14. *NICEM Index to Producers and Distributors* (Los Angeles: National Information Center for Educational Media/NICEM Irregular).
15. *Audiovisual Market Place* (New York: R. R. Bowker, Annual).

suppliers' current catalogs. Suppliers who did not respond to a request for a current catalog are not included. The mailing addresses which follow this section were current as of March 1984.

Producers and Suppliers

Those judged to have the most comprehensive model offerings, based on examination of the catalogs received, are:

Carolina Biological Supply Co.   Nasco
Central Scientific Co.   Schoolmasters Teaching Aids
Curriculum Productions Co.   Ward's Natural Science
Hubbard Scientific Co.   Establishment

Producers and Suppliers by Subject

Suppliers are listed under a category only if their offerings in that category were judged to be significant in relation to those of other suppliers.

ANATOMICAL MODELS (HUMAN)
Carolina Biological Supply Co.   Nasco
Central Scientific Co.   Nystrom
Denoyer-Geppert   Spenco
George F. Cram Co.   Ward's Natural Science
Hubbard Scientific Co.   Establishment

ART AND ARTIFACT REPRODUCTIONS (THREE-DIMENSIONAL)
Alva Museum Replicas   Metropolitan Museum of Art

BIOLOGICAL MODELS
Carolina Biological Supply Co.   Nystrom
Central Scientific Co.   Schoolmasters Teaching Aids
George F. Cram Co.   Ward's Natural Science
Hubbard Scientific Co.   Establishment
Nasco

FOOD
Audiovisual Enterprises   Nasco

FOSSIL REPRODUCTIONS
Carolina Biological Supply Co.   George C. Page Museum Shop of
Central Scientific Co.   La Brea Discoveries

Hubbard Scientific Co.
Nasco

Schoolmasters Teaching Aids
Ward's Natural Science
  Establishment

GEOLOGICAL MODELS
Carolina Biological Supply Co.
Central Scientific Co.
Hubbard Scientific Co.

Nasco
Schoolmasters Teaching Aids

GLOBES AND RELIEF MAPS
ABC School Supply
Carolina Biological Supply Co.
Central Scientific Co.
George F. Cram Co.
Hubbard Scientific Co.
National Geographic

Nienhuis Montessori
Nystrom
Rand McNally
Replogle Globes
Schoolmasters Teaching Aids

MATHEMATICAL MODELS AND MANIPULATIVE MATERIALS
ABC School Supply
Central Scientific Co.
Creative Publications
Creative Teaching Associates
Cuisenaire Co. of America

DLM Teaching Resources
Educational Teaching Aids
Gamco
Nienhuis Montessori
Schoolmasters Teaching Aids

MECHANICAL MODELS
ABC School Supply
Carolina Biological Supply Co.
Central Scientific Co.

Childcraft Education Corp.
Nasco
Schoolmasters Teaching Aids

MONEY
Creative Publications
DLM Teaching Resources

Educational Teaching Aids
Gamco

PLANETARIUMS
Central Scientific Co.
Denoyer-Geppert
Hubbard Scientific Co.

Nasco
Nystrom
Schoolmasters Teaching Aids

ROCKET MODELS
Carolina Biological Supply Co.
Nasco

Schoolmasters Teaching Aids

WEATHER MODELS
Carolina Biological Supply Co.
Central Scientific Co.
Hubbard Scientific Co.

Nasco
Schoolmasters Teaching Aids

Addresses of Producers and Suppliers

ABC School Supply, Inc.
6500 Peachtree Industrial Blvd.
Norcross, GA 30071

Alva Museum Replicas
140 Greenwich Ave.
Greenwich, CT 06830

Audio-Visual Enterprises
911 Laguna Rd.
Pasadena, CA 91105

Carolina Biological Supply
2700 York Rd.
Burlington, NC 27215

Central Scientific Co.
2600 S. Kostner Ave.
Chicago, IL 60623

Childcraft Education Corp.
20 Kilmer Rd.
Edison, NJ 08818

Creative Publications
3977 East Bayshore Rd.
P.O. Box 10328
Palo Alto, CA 94303

Creative Teaching Associates
5629 E. Westover
P.O. Box 7766
Fresno, CA 93747

Cuisenaire Co. of America, Inc.
12 Church St.
New Rochelle, NY 10805

Curriculum Production Co.
Dept. 4, Box 457
Churchville, PA 18966

Denoyer-Geppert Co.
5235 Ravenswood Ave.
Chicago, IL 60640

DLM Teaching Resources
One DLM Park
P.O. Box 4000
Allen, TX 75002

Gamco Industries, Inc.
P.O. Box 310D9
Big Spring, TX 79720-0022

George F. Cram Co.
301 S. LaSalle St.
P.O. Box 426
Indianapolis, IN 46206

Educational Teaching Aids
159 West Kinzie St.
Chicago, IL 60610

Gessler
900 Broadway
New York, NY 10003

Hubbard Scientific Co.
P.O. Box 105
Northbrook, IL 60062

Metropolitan Museum of Art
Museum Special Service Office,
Box 700
Middle Village, NY 11379

NASCO
901 Janesville Ave.
Fort Atkinson, WI 53538

National Geographic Society
16th and M Sts.
Washington, DC 20036

Nienhuis Montessori USA, Inc.
320 Pioneer Way
Mountain View, CA 94041

Nystrom
3333 Elston Ave.
Chicago, IL 60618

Page Museum Shop
5801 Wilshire Blvd.
Los Angeles, CA 90036

Rand McNally & Co.
P.O. Box 7600
Chicago, IL 60680

Replogle Globes
1901 N. Narragansett Ave.
Chicago, IL 60639

Spenco Medical Corp.
P.O. Box 8113
Waco, TX 76714-8113

Schoolmasters Teaching Aids
745 State Circle
P.O. Box 1941
Ann Arbor, MI 48106

Ward's Natural Science
   Establishment
3000 E. Ridge Rd.
Rochester, NY 14626

For a comprehensive list of companies which make models, consult *Thomas Register of American Manufacturers* (New York: Thomas Publishing Co.), an annual publication found in most library reference collections. Models are listed under the following headings:

Dioramas
Figures & Forms: Display
Figures: Lead
Models: Anatomical, Biological & Zoological, etc.
Models: Automobile
Models: Display
Models: Electronic Product & Production Equipment
Models: Experimental Work, to Order, for Inventors
Models: Geographical, School
Models: Geometrical, School
Models: Marine
Models: Molecular
Models: Plant Layout
Models: Plastic
Models: Prototype
Models: Scale

Local Sources

The following types of institutions may be contacted to identify models which might be shared at the local level. Staff in these institutions may be asked for specific recommendations and for names of suppliers they have found reliable. Sometimes local institutions participate in networks which share union lists of media.

Public libraries may lend museum replicas of sculptures and artifacts. Many museums have education programs which use (and which may lend) models suitable for use by individuals and groups.

Hobby shops carry several types of model kits and may be willing to special-order items not regularly carried in stock. They are a good source of construction material for making models.

Public school districts often have union lists of audiovisual media. Regional education agencies in many states have lists of materials, including models, available for loan to schools in their area. Colleges, universities, and community colleges use models in classrooms and laboratories for teaching subjects ranging from chemistry and botany to automotive repair. Models are usually not listed in academic library catalogs, with the exception of curriculum libraries of colleges of education. Contact departmental offices for information.

MAINTENANCE AND MANAGEMENT

Storage and Care

Institutions differ in the ways that they store models. Museums and libraries often place models on display or intershelve them with other material on the same subject. Sturdy items, requiring little or no manipulation, may even be placed on tables or in carrels where they can be studied and used without special supervision.[16] In contrast, departments and individuals generally prefer to keep models stored out of sight, in cupboards or closed storage areas, so that they do not distract or divert attention when they are not in use.

The name of the manufacturer or supplier should be written inconspicuously on the model itself. The name of the institution acquiring the model should be stamped or engraved on the item in a place which will not be distracting. Mark individual, separate pieces in the same way as the model, to the extent practicable.

If the original container is flimsy, transfer the model to a container which will hold it more securely. Small models may be stored in containers such as boxes. Plastic or vinyl zip-top bags may be used to keep small pieces together. Transparent vinyl bags can cover and protect large models, yet allow them to be visible. A colorful picture or diagram from an unsuitable original container may be attached to the new container so that the contents are readily apparent. The outside of any container should be labeled. Attach an inventory of parts to the inside of the container or to the base of the model itself. In formally cataloged collections, a copy of the catalog card may be attached to the model or the container and a classification number recorded on each separate piece of the model. Store documentation such as teacher's guides with the item.

PREPARATION FOR USE OF MODELS

All parts should be clearly identified.

If possible, a master copy of the key or diagram which identifies parts or features of a model should be stored in a separate file. A duplicate copy should be kept with the model.

16. Cabeceiras, 208.

Provide a copy of a key or diagram identifying parts or features for individual or small-group use.

Persons using models before a group should know the model well enough so that they are able to indicate significant features without referring to a key or diagram.

PREPARATION FOR USE OF CUTAWAY AND DISSECTIBLE MODELS

Verify that all parts are present.

The order for assembly or disassembly of multipart models should be readily apparent to individual or small-group users. If not, instructions should be provided.

Persons using models before a group should know the model well enough so that they can take it apart and reassemble it without reference to a key or diagram.

PREPARATION FOR USE OF MOCKUPS AND WORKING MODELS

Be sure the working model is operational. Verify that all parts are present and in working order.

Check for presence and condition of any supplies used with the model (e.g., light bulbs, fuel, or other chemicals).

Rehearse before demonstrating a working model to a group.

Be certain that individual and small-group users are instructed in safety procedures and know how to operate working models to avoid injuring themselves or damaging the model.

Management Problems and Solutions

Models may either be selected centrally or by departments or individuals within an institution. This affects organization, storage, and budget. Departments and individuals may guard models closely and be averse to sharing material. Models that are purchased by departments or individuals are often stored out of sight, in cabinets or storage rooms, and only emerge for use at rare intervals.

Without central organization or management, some potential users will not know the organization owns the model, let alone where it is located. Unnecessary duplication of purchases will occur if there is no accessible central file or list of models owned by the institution. The model itself may be located away from the central location, yet still be accessible, if a central record is available.

Organization of the file can be as simple as a handwritten list or as complex as a computer data base. If the organization has a library, models should be cataloged in the same way as books, filmstrips, and other media formats. Information on descriptive cataloging of models, globes, and dioramas can be found in several works. *Access to Media: A Guide to Integrating and Computerizing Catalogs*, by Sheila S. Intner, is a comprehensive guide to the planning required to integrate all types of audiovisual material into library catalogs. *The Anglo-American Cataloguing Rules,* second edition (*AACR2*), prescribes in detail how to catalog models according to the code adopted by major libraries in most English-speaking countries.

Other helpful sources for cataloging and processing these formats include *Nonbook Materials: The Organization of Integrated Collections*, by Jean Riddle Weihs, and *Cataloging, Processing, Administering AV Materials: A Model for Wisconsin Schools*, which provides suggestions for processing, housing, circulation, and care of models. *Cataloging Nonbook Materials: Problems in Theory and Practice*, by Carolyn O. Frost, compares recommended practices in *AACR2* and in Weihs' book. *Problems in Bibliographic Access to Non-Print Materials* is a report of Project Media Base of the National Commission on Libraries and Information Science, which investigated the feasibility of a network of audiovisual resources and the major barriers to such a network. Models were among the media included in a media inventory survey done for the report. The report provides both background and recommendations.

A model with pieces will need to be checked before and after each use to be sure that it is complete. Inevitably, over time any material with parts and pieces requires replacement of lost or damaged parts. If replacement parts are not available, the entire item may be rendered useless.[17]

Durability, size, and expected future utility may determine whether models produced in-house are made part of the permanent collection or treated as ephemeral materials.

Models that are circulated from central locations should be properly packaged for safe transit. Borrowers need to be made aware of their responsibility for proper care and use, as well as informed of their liability in case of loss or damage. Some institutions charge a user fee to cover cost and maintenance of items such as models, sculpture, or artifacts. Written policies which specify loan conditions and penalties are recommended.[18]

17. Joy K. Moll and Patricia Hermann, "Evaluation and Selection of Toys, Games, and Puzzles: Manipulative Materials in Library Collections," *Top of the News* 21 (Nov. 1974): 88.

18. Cabeceiras, 208.

Other Concerns

There is considerable ambiguity in the use of the word *model* in reference sources, in books about nonbook materials, and in publishers' catalogs. Often, no clear distinctions are made between *models* and *realia*. *Realia*, in this handbook, is defined as the term used to describe the object itself, "the real thing"—not a representation. Sometimes both models and realia are found listed under the terms *Objects* or *Three-Dimensional Objects*. At other times, models are included under the terms *Realia* or *Three-Dimensional Objects*.[19] It is important for searchers to realize that they must search for models under the terms *Objects, Realia, Three-Dimensional Objects,* and also under specific types of models.

Library catalogs do not have one heading under which all types of models may be found, but expect the searcher to look for a specific type of model. For example, the following terms represent a partial listing of subject headings for models found in the catalogs of libraries using Library of Congress subject headings:

Architectural models
Astronomical models
Biological models
Chemical models
Engineering models
Geometric models
Geological models
Historical models
Hydraulic models
Hydrologic models

Mathematical models
Military miniatures
Miniature craft
Models and modelmaking
Relief models
Ship models
Surface, models of
Wind tunnel models
Zoological models[20]

Searching for "Models" in publishers' catalogs, library catalogs, indexes, or data bases can be extremely frustrating for yet another reason: some of the terms listed above are used to refer to both tangible, three-dimensional models and abstract, theoretical models.

TYPES AND KINDS OF MODELS
As Haney and Ullmer point out, "the definitions of these terms encountered in audiovisual literature are not precisely uniform."[21] The

19. Irene Wood, "Audiovisual Services," *ALA World Encyclopedia of Library and Information Services* (Chicago: American Library Assn., 1980), 60; Leonard Montague Harrod, *The Librarians' Glossary and Reference Book of Terms Used in Librarianship, Documentation and the Book Crafts,* 4th ed. (Boulder, Colo.: Westview Press, 1977).

20. *Library of Congress Subject Headings,* 9th ed. (Washington: Library of Congress, 1980).

21. John B. Haney and Eldon J. Ullmer, *Educational Communications and Technology,* 3rd ed. (Dubuque: Wm. C. Brown, 1980), 32.

definitions given below were compiled from many sources and are those generally agreed upon. No single source lists every type of model given here.

Diorama. A diorama is a "miniature three-dimensional scene intended to represent a real-life scene. It usually consists of figures or objects set on a stage which has a background painted to suit the setting." Some museum dioramas have nearly life-sized figures. Proportions of structures and backgrounds may be distorted in order to enhance perspective and create an illusion of greater depth. Dioramas are often built as classroom projects. They may illustrate great battles, scenes from literature, or typical interiors or exteriors of buildings, such as Victorian mansions or television stations.[22]

Globe. "A spherical representation of the earth, a celestial body, or the heavens."[23]

Nonworking model. Also known as the *static model* or *solid model*, this type of model has no moving parts, even if the original does have parts which move.[24] It represents the original in appearance, but not in function or operation. Examples include animal life, such as insects or birds; imitation food, such as hamburgers or fruit; historic buildings, such as Mount Vernon or the Eiffel Tower; historic weapons, such as guns, cannon, and spears.[25] The solid model often gives a general impression, with distracting details omitted.[26]

Partially working model. A model in which the operation or function of only certain parts is represented; for example, an engine model in which only the pistons move; a life-sized model of an infant for cardio-pulmonary resuscitation (CPR) in which the "lungs" are inflatable.

Working model. A model which shows what the original does, how it operates and functions.[27] Many children's toys fall in this category (e.g., road-building equipment, farm machinery, kitchen stoves, etc.). In instructional settings, working models include weather models, inventions such as the telephone and telegraph, periscopes, water pumps, oil derricks, etc.[28]

22. Murray R. Thomas and Sherwin G. Swartout, *Integrated Teaching Materials: How to Choose, Create and Use Them* (New York: David McKay, 1963), 430.

23. *Webster's Ninth New Collegiate Dictionary* (Springfield, Mass.: Merriam-Webster, Inc., 1983), 521.

24. Cabeceiras, *The Multimedia Library,* 205.

25. Thomas, 424–25.

26. Martha F. Meeks, *Models for Teaching* (n.p.: The Visual Instruction Bureau. Division of Extension. The University of Texas, 1956), 6.

27. Cabeceiras, 205.

28. Thomas, 428–29.

Mockup. "A full-sized structural model built accurately to scale chiefly for study, testing or display."[29] Mockups are often simplified in some way: eliminating some details in order to highlight essential functions or parts.[30] The driver-training simulator is a mockup familiar to many. LINK Navigation Trainers are used to simulate real-life flying conditions, and move in response to the pilot's operation of the controls.[31] Mockups are used to "show interrelationships of parts, to demonstrate operations, processes, or procedures involving many parts."[32]

Cut-away or cross-sectional model. A cut-away model provides a way of representing the interior of a model, which would not ordinarily be visible, for example, a cut-away of a turbine, to show the rotating blades; a cross-sectional model, illustrating geological formations where petroleum is found; a cross-section of a ship, showing the cabins, cargo space, and engine rooms. Cut-away models show the user internal construction and give an idea of the parts which make up the whole.[33]

Dissectible or build-up model. Dissectible models are constructed with removable sections which may be taken apart and put back together again. The "human torso," with removable vital organs, is of this type. These models "effectively demonstrate the relationships and functions of the various parts."[34]

Original form. Original forms are models which show how something will work or look before it is actually made. Architects' models of proposed buildings may be made to a small size; designers of new coins first construct models which are larger than the actual coin will be. Sometimes the material used may be different than that in the real item. Plastic may represent glass; painted wood may mimic metal.[35]

Exact model. An exact model is exact in almost every detail, except for enlargement or reduction.[36] The exact model may also be made of materials different from the original, and is often used where the original is perishable, fragile, rare, or expensive. Examples include

29. *Webster's Ninth New Collegiate Dictionary,* 762.

30. James W. Brown, Richard B. Lewis and Fred F. Harcleroad, *A-V Instruction: Materials and Methods,* 2nd ed. (New York: McGraw-Hill, 1964), 421.

31. Ibid., 301.

32. Meeks, 9.

33. Ibid., 8.

34. Ibid.

35. Ralph R. Knoblaugh, "Model Making," *World Book Encyclopedia* (Chicago: World Book, 1983), 572.

36. Cabeceiras, 204–5.

models of food, soft-bodied insects, and famous gems.[37] The exact model may also be called a *miniature* if made of material identical to the original (see "Miniature," below).

Replica. A close reproduction or facsimile of an object,[38] a replica may be exactly the size of the original or may be a scale model. A replica may also be referred to as an *exact model*, and may sometimes be classed as *realia*.[39]

Exact-size model. This is a replica which is precisely the size of the original, but may not reproduce all the features of the original.

Scale model. The scale model may be larger or smaller than the original, for example, a globe representing the Earth, a scale model of a famous sailing ship. Scale models help users see details and relationships more easily.[40] The scale model should always be labeled with regard to its scale.[41]

Miniature. An item which is "made of the same material and which can perform the same function as a larger version" is known as a *miniature*, rather than a *model*.[42]

ADDITIONAL RESOURCES

This list includes only works published since 1970. Separate works on models are scarce, and deal primarily with model making or model collecting as a hobby—a category represented but not exhaustively treated in this bibliography. Older editions of works, referring to models in an instructional context, often provide more detailed discussion of models than more recent editions.

Evaluation Criteria, Acquisition, Use

Anderson, Ronald H. *Selecting and Developing Media for Instruction*. 2nd ed. New York: Van Nostrand, 1983.
    Chapter titled "Physical Objects—Real Things" provides instructional objectives and useful checklists. *On-job training, hands-on training,* and *simulation training* are defined; however, realia, mockups, and models are not clearly distinguished, which leads to discrepancies between section headings and the terms used in the discussions following those headings.

Brown, James W., Richard B. Lewis and Fred F. Harcleroad. *A-V Instruction: Technology, Media and Methods*. 6th ed. New York: McGraw-Hill, 1983.

37. Meeks, 6.
38. *Webster's Ninth New Collegiate Dictionary,* 999.
39. Cabeceiras, 206.
40. Meeks, 6.
41. Cabeceiras, 204.
42. Ibid., 205.

Models are discussed in a chapter titled "Real Things, Models, and Demonstrations." The emphasis is upon construction of models; nine recipes are provided for plastic mixtures such as plaster of paris and casein glue. Suggestions are given for use of sand tables and for construction of dioramas, contour maps, and models with motion.

Cabeceiras, James. *The Multimedia Library: Materials Selection and Use.* 2nd ed. New York: Academic, 1982. 202–8.

The chapter titled "Models, Realia, and Games and Simulations" includes sections identifying types of problems and criteria for selection and utilization of models.

Cummins, Thompson R. "Diorama." *Unabashed Librarian* 36 (1980): 32.

This is a one-page illustrated "how-to."

Erickson, Carlton W. H., and David H. Curl. *Fundamentals of Teaching with Audio-Visual Technology.* 2nd ed. New York: Macmillan, 1972. 89–92.

Suggestions for using models in the classroom.

Haney, John B., and Eldon J. Ullmer. *Educational Communications and Technology: An Introduction.* 3rd ed. Dubuque: Wm. C. Brown, 1980.

Models and mockups are discussed in a brief section within a chapter titled "Object Media."

Hicks, Warren B., and Alma Tillin. *Developing Multi-Media Libraries.* 2nd ed. New York: Bowker, 1970.

Includes brief sections on selecting, cataloging, and physical processing of globes and dioramas. Descriptive cataloging information has been superseded by *Anglo-American Cataloguing Rules*, 2nd ed.

Knoblaugh, Ralph R. "Model Making," *World Book Encyclopedia.* Chicago: World Book, 1983. 571–72.

"Model," *Encyclopedia Americana.* Danbury, Conn.: Grolier, 1984. 290–94.

Ozer, Morris. "Modelmaking." *Encyclopedia International.* New York: Grolier, 1976. 186–89.

Thomas, James L. *Turning Kids on to Print Using Nonprint.* Littleton, Colo.: Libraries Unlimited, 1978.

Chapter titled "Dioramas" provides strategies for planning and producing dioramas and includes sections on materials and estimated costs.

Van Orden, Phyllis J. *The Collection Program in Elementary and Middle Schools: Concepts, Practices and Information Sources.* Littleton, Colo.: Libraries Unlimited, 1982.

———. *The Collection Program in High Schools: Concepts, Practices and Information Sources.* Littleton, Colo.: Libraries Unlimited, 1985.

In this and in the companion work (listed above), advantages and disadvantages, selection criteria, and collection considerations for models, sculpture, toys, and globes are presented in a chapter titled "Criteria by Format: Multisensory Materials."

Weihs, Jean. *Accessible Storage of Nonbook Materials.* Phoenix: Oryx Pr., 1984.

Wittich, Walter A., and Charles F. Schuller. *Instructional Technology: Its Nature and Use.* 5th ed. New York: Harper & Row, 1973.

_____. *Instructional Technology: Its Nature and Use.* 6th ed. New York: Harper & Row, 1979.

Models are discussed in a chapter titled "Three Dimensional Teaching Materials."

Woodbury, Marda. *Selecting Materials for Instruction: Media and the Curriculum.* Littleton, Colo.: Libraries Unlimited, 1980.

A chapter titled "Toys and Other Manipulatives" provides useful criteria for manipulative materials. Information on models is nearly hidden in a chapter titled "Pictorial Media."

Cataloging of Models

Anglo-American Cataloguing Rules. 2nd ed. Chicago: American Library Assn., 1978.

Frost, Carolyn O. *Cataloging Nonbook Materials: Problems in Theory and Practice.* Ed. Arlene Taylor Dowell. Littleton, Colo.: Libraries Unlimited, 1983.

Hohenstein, Margaret, et al. *Cataloging, Processing, Administering AV Materials: A Model for Wisconsin Schools.* 3rd rev. ed. Madison: Wisconsin Library Assn., 1981.

Intner, Sheila S. *Access to Media: A Guide to Integrating and Computerizing Catalogs.* New York: Neal-Schuman, 1985.

Comprehensive guide to integrating audiovisual collections in small and medium-sized libraries.

Project Media Base. *Problems in Bibliographic Access to Non-print Materials: Final Report.* A project of the National Commission on Libraries and Information Science and the Assn. for Educational Communications and Technology. Washington, D.C.: Superintendent of Documents, U.S. Government Printing Office, 1979.

Soulier, J. Steven. *Real Objects and Models.* Englewood Cliffs, N.J.: Educational Technology Publications, 1981. (The Instructional Media Library, vol. 12)

Brief history; useful in subject areas, local production, care and storage.

Weihs, Jean Riddle, Shirley Lewis, and Janet Macdonald. *Nonbook Materials: The Organization of Integrated Collections.* Ottawa: Canadian Library Assn., 1979.

Nancy Bren Nuzzo

ch. 11

Music Scores

THE MEDIUM

Definition

A music score is the written or printed format of a musical work in which all the parts of the participating voices and/or instruments that are supposed to be heard simultaneously appear on different staffs, one aligned above the other. In descriptive cataloging the term is not applied to music for one performer (e.g., solo piano, unaccompanied violin, etc.). Depending upon its size and intended use, a score may also be called a complete, full, open, orchestral, or performance score, or a conductor's score when the edition is large enough for that purpose. Scores reduced in physical size are called miniature score, pocket score, or study score. Scores edited for rehearsal or performance include close score, conductor's score (band), condensed score, organ-vocal score, piano reduction, piano score, piano-vocal score, short score, and vocal score. In a general description of library materials, all music editions are sometimes referred to as scores, as distinguished from books about music, or sound recordings.[1]

1. Suzanne E. Thorin and Carole Franklin Vidali, *The Acquisition and Cataloging of Music and Sound Recordings: A Glossary* (New York: Music Library Assn., 1984), 17.

Brief History

A discussion of the history of music scores must take into account the development of music notation, the types of music which are written down, the various formats in which music can appear, and the history of music printing. These are not isolated developments, but interrelated factors which continue to change, and determine the physical appearance of a piece of music.

The vocal and instrumental parts that appear on separate staffs of a music score are individual lines of music notation. Although the symbols of standard modern notation have been in use since about 1600, their roots can be traced to the symbols of Greek and Oriental speech recitation, or ecphonetic notation.[2] From about the 9th century, shorthand-like neumes, symbols which indicate the shape of a melody, were used by members of the church as they disseminated chant. The melodies had been learned by rote; the neumes above the text did not indicate exact pitch but were reminders of the relative rise and fall of the melody. By the year 1200, neumes had taken on square and diamond shapes, staff lines had been added, and the notation was used not only for church music but for secular music as well. Following a century of particularly rapid development, notational principles were revised by Philippe de Vitry in his treatise *Ars Nova* (ca. 1320) and a new period of refinement was ushered in.[3] The developments of this period "provided the premises for the notation of the following six hundred years and, in large measure, enabled composers to think as creative artists, unencumbered by the inherent clumsiness of the tools of their art."[4]

Until the development of the motet in about 1225, polyphonic (multipart) music was notated in score form with the parts lined up one above the other. The individual parts of a motet, however, were notated in their entirety, one following the other on the page. This arrangement was more practical for the motet form because the upper voices were texted and moved with many rapid notes; the lower voices moved more slowly and with few notes, and required less space on the page.[5] This format was also easier to print, as were later partbooks where individual parts were issued in separate books.

---

2. Willi Apel, "Notation," in *Harvard Dictionary of Music,* 2nd ed. (Cambridge, Mass.: Belknap Pr. of Harvard Univ. Pr., 1969), 578.
3. Ibid., 579.
4. Lloyd Ultan, *Music Theory: Problems and Practices in the Middle Ages and Renaissance* (Minneapolis: Univ. of Minnesota Pr., 1977), 74.
5. Apel, "Score," in *Harvard Dictionary of Music,* 759.

No matter how the parts were aligned on the page, they were written by hand until the 15th century. Until 1501, early music printers, who *were* encumbered by the inherent clumsiness of their tools, limited their output to liturgies (which contained a single voice part) and books with musical examples.[6] Their methods included movable type and woodblocks, and frequently either the lines of the staff or the notes themselves were added by hand to solve the problem of correctly lining up those two elements. Multiple impressions, where the notes and staff were printed one at a time, were used with great success by Ottaviano dei Petrucci and others, but this was a costly and time-consuming process.

Two 16th century developments provided for the printing of music with a single impression: the use of type elements, which contained both the note and the adjacent pieces of the staff, and the use of engraved plates. The disadvantages of the first method were its inflexibility and the uneven appearance of the result. In the mid-18th century, Breitkopf, a Leipzig printer, successfully used type with even smaller components (e.g., note heads, stems) that yielded an improved appearance. Engraved music was pleasing to the eye, but the expenses of copper plates and costly labor were disadvantages. Other metals, such as pewter, were also used; such softer metals allowed the faster method of using punches to mark the plates. Late in the 17th century, Alois Senefelder invented the process of lithography, which from its beginning was associated with music printing but did not replace the practice of engraving music.

Together with variations of the lithographic and engraving processes, today's methods include photography, dry transfer, and the use of music typewriters and computers. Modern-day scores have changed as well—some compositions contain few, if any, musical notes. "Chance" compositions may consist solely of written instructions to the performer; others may contain charts, mylar sheets, or pieces of fur. Scores for electronically produced music may be instructions for re-creating the composition or they might be graphic representations of the sounds produced. These and other diversities are a challenge both to music publishers and to institutions that choose to acquire music scores.

Music has a long history of collection in libraries and other institutions, from 7th century monastic collections to present-day national music information centers. The growth of musicology during the 20th century has stimulated the growth of music collections and of organiza-

6. A. Hyatt King, *Four Hundred Years of Music Printing* (London: British Museum, 1968), 9.

tions that are concerned with their development, including several cooperative projects that focus on identifying the location of important source materials.[7]

Unique Characteristics

Music notation is a universal language in the sense that it crosses traditional language barriers, yet to understand it requires special training and knowledge.

Music scores are visual instructions for the creation of aural events, and their realization requires the intervention of one or more performers. Nevertheless, users who are unskilled in performance but can read music are able to study and understand scores.

Advantages

Music scores are usually considered a permanent, not ephemeral, item in the institution's collection.

Because music does not become outdated like literature in rapidly advancing fields, a quality edition of music will retain its value over many years.

Disadvantages

Music is expensive and time-consuming to acquire, process, and handle.
Most music comes unbound and requires special binding techniques.
Special knowledge is needed to catalog music.
Individual performance parts receive hard use, are easily lost, and are difficult to replace.
It may be necessary to purchase several editions of a single musical work in order to satisfy the study and performance needs of users.
Music is outside the scope of most book dealers, making it necessary to order music through specialized music dealers.
The lack of bibliographic control and the preponderance of titles for a single musical work invite duplication in the collection.
Recently composed music may be available for hire only, or be published in small runs that go out of print quickly.

7. Rita Benton, "Libraries: Introduction," *New Grove Dictionary of Music and Musicians* 10:719–25.

SELECTION

Special Criteria

The objectives of the institution, the scope and intended use of the collection, and the sophistication of its users are particularly important factors in selecting music.

The period of composition (e.g., Medieval, Romantic, Contemporary) and the medium of the work (i.e., the performing forces for which it was written) will help identify works that are outside the scope of the collection or that are needed to achieve a balanced collection.

The reputation of the composer and the work may be considered. When reviews of a particular work are unavailable, the composer's reputation is especially important.

The performing difficulty of the work may be a factor in performance collections.

The selection of one edition of a work over another may be based on its format (e.g., whether it is a score or performance parts); the quality and quantity of editorial notation; the quality of printing, paper, and binding; and the language of text.

The selector may wish to consider the presence of a recorded version of the work in the institution's sound recordings collection.

Evaluative Review Sources

The following lists recommend works that should be contained in a basic music collection.

Krummel, Donald W. "Musical Editions: A Basic Collection." *Choice* (Apr. 1976): 179–94.

Music Library Assn. Committee on Basic Music Collection. *A Basic Music Library*. Ed. Robert Michael Fling. Chicago: American Library Assn., 1983.

GENERAL REVIEWS[8]

Music and Letters	*Notes: The Quarterly Journal*
Music Review	*of the Music Library*
Musical Times	*Association*

REVIEWS FOR PARTICULAR INSTRUMENTS OR AREAS OF INTEREST

Clavier	*Instrumentalist*
Early Music	*Piano Quarterly*
Guitar Review	*Woodwind-Brass and Percussion*

8. Music reviews can be found in the many publications devoted to a particular instrument, as are such instrument society organs as *The Horn Call, International Trumpet Guild Journal,* and *The American Recorder.* Those that are listed are just a sample of what is available.

Nonevaluative Sources

Titles below represent publications since 1970. There is no single comprehensive bibliography or catalog of music scores. Many needs can be met by consulting national bibliographies, lists of music for particular instruments, and publishers' catalogs.[9]

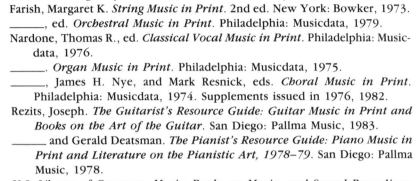

British Catalogue of Music. London: British Library, 1957– .

Farish, Margaret K. *String Music in Print.* 2nd ed. New York: Bowker, 1973.

_____, ed. *Orchestral Music in Print.* Philadelphia: Musicdata, 1979.

Nardone, Thomas R., ed. *Classical Vocal Music in Print.* Philadelphia: Musicdata, 1976.

_____. *Organ Music in Print.* Philadelphia: Musicdata, 1975.

_____, James H. Nye, and Mark Resnick, eds. *Choral Music in Print.* Philadelphia: Musicdata, 1974. Supplements issued in 1976, 1982.

Rezits, Joseph. *The Guitarist's Resource Guide: Guitar Music in Print and Books on the Art of the Guitar.* San Diego: Pallma Music, 1983.

_____ and Gerald Deatsman. *The Pianist's Resource Guide: Piano Music in Print and Literature on the Pianistic Art, 1978–79.* San Diego: Pallma Music, 1978.

U.S. Library of Congress. *Music, Books on Music, and Sound Recordings.* Washington, D.C.: Library of Congress, 1953– .

MAINTENANCE AND MANAGEMENT

Storage and Care

"Musical scores are usually purchased unbound, and the method of binding them varies according to their form, the use to be made of them, and the permanency of the collection."[10]

Music bindings should be sewn through the fold so that the music will lie flat for study or performance.

In a performance-oriented collection, all the music for one work should be kept together but not bound in a single volume, so that individual parts may be used for performance. In a collection used principally for study, a work comprising a score (e.g., a keyboard part with other instruments notated) and one or more parts may be divided so that the score is available for use without the parts.

Folders with pockets on the inside of the cover may be used when the music comprises two or more parts, with one part sewn into the folder and the others inserted into the pockets. Thick or numerous

9. For a comprehensive list of current publishers' catalogs, consult George R. Hill, "Music Publishers' Catalogues," in *Notes.* This is a regular feature of the journal.

10. Ruth Wallace, ed., *The Care and Treatment of Music in a Library* (Chicago: American Library Assn., 1927), 48.

parts should be stored in portfolios which stand on the shelves like bound volumes, or be laid in horizontal, hinged boxes. The individual parts should be sewn into flexible, protective covers.[11]

Because of its format, some music cannot or should not be bound. Single parts are often formatted to facilitate easy page turns during a performance and can be rendered useless by binding. Contemporary compositions often come in single pages that are to be spread out during a performance. Such items should not be attached to their protective covers.

Label all parts and indicate on the folder or portfolio the number of parts contained.

Shelves for music need to be wider and spaced farther apart on the uprights than shelving for books. Twelve-inch shelves, spaced 15 inches apart, will accommodate the depth and height of most scores.[12]

Additional storage may be needed for oversize scores. Widely spaced shelves will accommodate bound volumes, but flat storage, such as map cases, may be needed for unbindable scores in unusual formats.

Miniature scores may be segregated from the rest of the collection to facilitate shelving and prevent their dislocation among larger volumes.

Management Problems and Solutions

Institutions that decide to acquire music scores acquire a score of management problems as well. Different institutions will come up with various solutions that work, based on the mission and users of the institution, and financial and historical considerations. The following is a discussion of five fundamental areas that are affected by the decision to acquire music scores.

The selection of music is complicated by the fact that a single musical work may be published in several editions—as a facsimile of the composer's manuscript, as a volume in the complete works of the composer, as a separately published full score, miniature score, piano reduction or arrangement, as performance parts, or as one work in a collection of many composers' works. The nature of the collection will reflect the mission of the institution and the needs of its users, and will affect decisions made in the selection process. A collection used mainly for research, such as might be found in a large university,

11. Much music can be pamphlet-bound in-house. Consult Joan O. Falconer, "Do-It-Yourself Music Binding," *Wilson Library Bulletin* 48 (1973): 332–35, for a description of the technique.

12. Robert Michael Fling, *Shelving Capacity in the Music Library,* Music Library Assn. Technical Report No. 7 (Philadelphia: Music Library Assn., 1981), 7–17.

will contain scholarly editions, complete critical editions of composers' works, and facsimiles of important sources in foreign libraries. There would be no attempt to collect scores in languages other than the original, or sets of parts for performance.

A collection used for study, as might be found in a college library, will need multiple copies of works in the standard repertoire (most conveniently in miniature score), historical anthologies, and English translations of vocal works. A conservatory's collection would emphasize performing editions. There, a work might be available in several editions which reflect various editors' tastes or are arrangements of the original. A collection used for recreation would probably include song books, children's music, and recent anthologies of popular music or sheet music.

Naturally, there will be crossover among these different types of collections: recreational collections will include some study scores and performance editions; study collections may contain some facsimile or performance editions. Whatever the nature of the collection, it is a factor in the choice of repertoire and edition which can be determined by examining the objectives of the institution. A selection policy based on these objectives is absolutely essential in order to build a collection that supports those goals. Guidelines for selecting popular music, archival materials, and performance editions will be especially useful in the selection process.

The selection of scores should be by a staff member with musical training, in consultation with members of the institution's music department, if one exists. Such users of the collection should be encouraged to contribute their "want" lists; the staff can then select those titles which conform to the institution's selection policy.

The process of acquiring music requires attention to detail. Ideally, the person who acquires scores will have some musical knowledge and will be responsible only for acquiring music materials. Less-than-ideal situations prevail, however, and where there is a central acquisitions department or position responsible for acquiring all types of materials, the special requirements of music scores must be made clear.

The most immediate problem is that general book vendors rarely supply music scores. The acquisitions department will need to go through a music dealer or buy directly from the publisher. The department may need different procedures or separate files for score orders. For example, if the general in-process order file is arranged by title, many score orders would fall into large groups with titles like "Concerto," "Symphony," etc. A composer-title arrangement is better. When ordering music, it is essential to describe the desired format accurately (e.g., miniature score, piano-vocal score, set of parts) and verify that what is subsequently received conforms to what was ordered.[13]

Out-of-print music may sometimes be obtained by requesting the publisher's permission to photocopy a copy existing elsewhere. A form for this purpose has been prepared by the Music Publishers' Association of the United States and reprinted in issue 58 (Sept.–Oct. 1984) of the Music Library Association *Newsletter*.

For all but the smallest collections, formal music training is essential for the staff member who catalogs scores. The position requires a knowledge of music history, the ability to read music, and foreign-language skills. While the necessity of having such a specialized staff member adds to the overall cost of handling music scores, such a person will be well qualified to catalog music literature and recordings as well. Ideally, this person will work in the vicinity of the music collection, especially if it is far removed from the central cataloging department.

If the choice of a classification scheme for scores has not already been made, the nature of the collection and the use to be made of it are important factors to consider.[14] In cataloging, another consideration is the degree to which anthologies of music are to be analyzed. The solution here will reflect the amount of available staff time and the availability of printed indexes to such anthologies.

The generic nature of music titles (e.g., symphony, concerto, sonata) is a consideration when designing or selecting an online catalog. For example, an author-title search that uses the first four letters of the author's (composer's) name and the first four letters of the title will not be specific enough for music. In such a case, a user looking for William Schuman's *Symphony no. 3* will end up with all of Schuman's, Shumann's, and Schubert's symphonies. The solution is to include the music collection staff in the selection or design process.

If the binding or bindery preparation of music is not done by the music collection staff, the person responsible must be trained to understand the characteristics listed under "Storage and Care" (above). In-house pamphlet binding is time consuming, but is one area where trained students can be used effectively.

---

13. Some problems of ordering music, as well as some helpful suggestions, are described in H. P. Dawson and B. R. Marks, "The Ordering and Supply of Sheet Music," *Brio* 2 (1965): 8–10.

14. Four classification schemes for scores are evaluated by Olga Buth in "Scores and Recordings," *Library Trends* 23 (1975): 427–50.

In determining the location of the music collection—within a general collection, in a separate department, or in a separate building—the nature and mission of the parent institution will give rise to certain management considerations. A small collection may be integrated into the general collection, but a medium to large collection is best housed in a separate area, with books and periodicals about music, microforms of music or music literature, and musical recordings. The wisdom and practicality of this arrangement have been eloquently defended by Rita Benton.[15]

In brief, the user of music materials must frequently consult a combination of literature, microforms, scores, and recordings, and is better served when they are housed together. Especially in institutions that support a music department, the score collection is very important to a specialized group of users, and it is to their advantage to have it nearby. However, those advantages must be weighed against the disadvantage of being separated from the general collection, whose users may not be aware of the existence of a score collection, and the risk of alienating the collection's staff and users from the general body of users, staff, and administration.

If the scores are to be part of a general collection, their special shelving requirements may create problems if the collection is shifted or expanded. In all cases, institutions that collect rare materials, such as composers' manuscripts or first editions, will want to keep them in a controlled environment, or at least one that is secure.

Other Concerns

Circulation policies may need to be adjusted for music. The loan period for music scores can follow the institution's general policy, with several exceptions. Certain types of scores, such as volumes in the complete edition of a composer's works, monuments of music (*Denkmäler*), and other historical series, may be considered reference works and their use suitably restricted. Rare materials should be used only under supervision.

Materials intended for performance should have an extended loan period to allow for the time needed to prepare the work for performance. Performers cultivate the habit of marking up their music, and the institution should set a policy regarding the condition in which music is to be returned. For example, the policy might state that marks may be made in pencil but must be erased before the music is returned.

15. Rita Benton, "The Nature of Music and Some Implications for the University Music Library," *Fortes Arbis Musical* 23:53–60.

If the collection is to be used primarily for study, and performance from the scores is discouraged, gift items may successfully be used as an adjunct collection for performance. This problem arises mainly with piano and vocal music; fortunately, many gifts fall into these categories.

Reflected in all these areas is the advantage of having a musically trained staff. More than materials in other disciplines, music scores require special knowledge for understanding, and to select, acquire, and catalog them requires specialized training. In situations where the institution has a music department, music collection staff should encourage the participation of the department in collection development and policy decisions. Often, the person responsible for overseeing the music collection will act as a liaison between the department and the general administration, and can benefit from the support of a music collection committee, composed of interested users. The department should be encouraged to offer monetary as well as moral support, to offset the extra expense of handling music scores and to appease the administration.

ADDITIONAL RESOURCES

Apel, Willi. *Harvard Dictionary of Music*. 2nd ed. Cambridge, Mass.: Harvard Univ. Pr., Belknap Pr., 1969.

Benton, Rita. "The Nature of Music and Some Implications for the University Music Library." *Fontes Artis Musicae* 23:53–60.

Bradley, Carol June. *Manual of Music Librarianship*. Ann Arbor: Music Library Assn., 1966.

———. *Reader in Music Librarianship*. Washington, D.C.: Microcard, 1973.

Buth, Olga. "Scores and Recordings." *Library Trends* 23 (1975): 427–50.

Dawson, H. P., and B. R. Marks. "The Ordering and Supply of Sheet Music." *Brio* 2 (1965): 8–10.

Duckles, Vincent. *Music Reference and Research Materials: An Annotated Bibliography*. 3rd ed. New York: Free Pr., 1974.

Falconer, Joan O. "Do-It-Yourself Music Binding." *Wilson Library Bulletin* 48 (1973): 332–35.

Honea, Ted. "Music . . . A Binding Challenge." *New Library Scene* 4/3 (June 1985): 1.

Jones, Malcolm. *Music Librarianship*. London: Clive Bingley, 1979.

King, A. Hyatt. *Four Hundred Years of Music Printing*. London: British Museum, 1968.

New Grove Dictionary of Music and Musicians. Ed. Stanley Sadie. 20 vols. London: Macmillan, 1980.

Smith, Elizabeth E., and Ruth T. Watanabe. "The Music Library in Its Physical Aspects." *Library Trends* 8 (1960): 604–13.

Thorin, Suzanne E., and Carole Franklin Vidali. *The Acquisition and Cataloging of Music and Sound Recordings: A Glossary.* New York: Music Library Assn., 1984.

Wedgewood, Mary. "Avant-garde Music: Some Publication Problems." *Library Quarterly* 46 (1976): 137–52.

Donald L. Foster

ch. 12

Original Art

THE MEDIUM

Definition

"Art," wrote the English poet and art critic Sir Herbert Read, "is most simply and most usually defined as an attempt to create pleasing forms. Such forms satisfy our sense of beauty and the sense of beauty is satisfied when we are able to appreciate a unity or harmony of formal relations among our sense-perceptions."[1]

Over the centuries, artists have used many different techniques to create art that will "satisfy our sense of beauty." For the purpose of this book, however, we will limit our examination to those art media that are most often collected, stored, displayed, and lent to users by institutions. These various media—oil paintings, original prints, watercolors, gouache, pastels, drawings, sculpture, and the original crafts—will be defined and briefly explained at the end of this chapter.

Brief History

The oldest surviving examples of art are the pictures of bison, bulls, horses, reindeer, and other animals painted on cave walls in southern France and northern Spain by nomadic artist-hunters of the *Paleolithic*

---

1. Herbert Read, *The Meaning of Art* (Baltimore: Penguin, 1949), 16.

Age (15,000 to 10,000 B.C.). According to anthropologists, these pictures were used as hunting magic and totem animals. Primitive man also decorated his weapons and tools, and later his clothing, pottery, and baskets; still later, he adorned himself with ornamented bone and bead jewelry.

The *Egyptian and Mesopotamian Periods* (3000 to 1100 B.C.) began with the development of the great city cultures in the river valleys of the Nile, Tigris, and Euphrates. During this period, the visual arts became institutionalized for the first time and were separated into the three main branches of painting, sculpture, and architecture. Architecture was gigantic in scale and proportion, and contained huge bas-reliefs and murals representing stylized human figures, usually related to death and afterlife. Egyptian art, in particular, centered on the rulers, or Pharaohs. The minor arts (jewelry making, weaving, pottery, etc.) were popular, displaying an elaborate sense of ornament and decoration.

The *Greek and Roman Periods* (3000 B.C. to 400 A.D.) had their beginnings on the island of Crete (3000–1100 B.C.) with the colorful wall and vase paintings of the Minoans. Cretan artists worked first with traditional geometric forms, which soon evolved into more natural figures, including priests and priestesses, bulls and bull fighters, dolphins and other fish. On the Greek mainland, influences from Egypt, Mesopotamia, and Crete—as well as from northern Europe—gave rise to three-dimensional art forms. Sculpture and bas-reliefs were the basis of the first laws of proportion and beauty; art became humanized as gods and goddesses began to take on human forms. In the Late Roman Period (200 B.C.–400 A.D.), figures became even more realistic, and builders of the period began to construct utilitarian architecture on a grand scale, erecting religious, public, and private structures of various kinds. The most dynamic architectural developments were the huge brick and concrete arches and vaults, which revolutionized the use of interior space.

Many of the artists of the *Early Christian Period* (300 to 400 A.D.) were pagans who continued the Greek and Roman styles, but with an emphasis on spiritual motifs. Symbols took precedence over realism and spiritual expression over physical beauty. Fresco and mosaic techniques were popular; in architecture, simplicity was the dominant factor.

Byzantine Art (500 to 1000 A.D.) reached its height during the middle of the 6th century, when Constantinople became the center of artistic activities. Oriental influences were seen in the ornamental, two-dimensional surfaces of art. Mysticism became more evident, with special emphasis placed on symbolic representation. Small, portable icons, encrusted with precious metals and stones, were a creative outlet for artists of the period; manuscript illumination, mosaic art, and panel painting also became popular.

Beginning with the *Carolingian Period* (750–850), continuing through the *Pre-Romanesque Period* (850–1000), and culminating in the *Romanesque Period* (1000–1175), religious art continued to be the chief means of expression. This was most evident in the proliferation of illuminated manuscripts, ornate crucifixes, colorful mosaics, and elaborate church metalwork. Religious stone carvings became a prominent part of church architecture and monumental sculpture found new favor. Emotionalism and mysticism were essential ingredients in the arts of the 9th and 10th centuries.

The high point of Christian church architecture came in the *Gothic Period* (1140 to 1500), when all other arts were subordinate to cathedral building. Stained glass became popular and an essential part of church building. Sculptures were detached from the walls, so to speak, to become three-dimensional pieces instead of mere supports. The Madonna and Child was the favorite motif in paintings of the period. The arts moved toward a more realistic representation and closer to nature, yet were still religious in subject matter.

The *Renaissance* (1420 to 1600) was a period of rebirth in the arts, with artists "returning" to ancient Greece and Rome for inspiration and emphasizing the human figure and the natural world. The Renaissance saw the introduction of oil painting directly on canvas and the scientific mixing of colors. For the first time, painters succeeded in representing three-dimensional space on two-dimensional surfaces. During the High Renaissance (16th century), printmaking rose to a new respectability; in oil painting, landscapes replaced the human figure in importance. Many individual styles developed during the Renaissance. The famous Renaissance artists include Botticelli, Durer, Giorgione, Giotto, da Vinci, Michelangelo, Piero della Francesca, Tintoretto, and Titian.

Baroque Art (1600 to 1730), an essential part of the Counter Reformation, was a reaction to the arts of the Late Renaissance (Mannerism) that were becoming more and more confusing to viewers. During the Baroque Era, painters replaced excesses with simpler subjects and with an emphasis on balance and harmony. Art appealed to the emotions and was more easily understood by viewers. Popular subjects of the time were saints, martyrs, church fathers, and mythological figures. Light and shadow took the place of bright colors, giving pictures a more dramatic interest. Despite the striving for simplicity, this was a complex period of contrasting styles, represented in the works of artists such as Bernini, Caravaggio, El Greco, Hals, Poussin, Rembrandt, Rubens, Tintoretto, Valasquez, Van Dyck, and Vermeer.

During the *Rococo Period* (1700 to 1800) art shifted from the religious to the secular; geographically, from Italy to France. Artists like Watteau, Boucher, and Fragonard, and later David and Gainsborough, turned from religion and mythology to everyday subjects. Colors were light and bright; paintings were light-hearted, sentimental, and picturesque, depicting garden scenes, court ladies, and genre portraits of various kinds.

In the *Nineteenth Century*, Paris remained the center of the art world and became the battleground for a quick succession of revolutionary movements and schools. The Romantics, led by Delacroix and Géricault, were the first on the scene, followed by Manet and the Realists, then by the Impressionists, who emphasized the play of light and color on the surface of objects, followed by the Post Impressionists (Cézanne, Gauguin, and Van Gogh), who spearheaded the 20th century reaction against the Impressionists and other 19th century movements. The experimenting of Cézanne and the Post Impressionists became the basis for a long line of daring 20th century art movements. The 19th century saw the revival of the engraving and etching techniques and the development of lithography as an art form.

The *Twentieth Century* is characterized by the multiplication of art movements. Artists began to experiment with different subjects, forms, and color combinations and worked in mixed media of all kinds. Original prints became popular, especially with collectors—both individual and institutional. The arts and crafts movement had a rebirth. Oil and watercolor painting, drawing, and sculpture experienced a continuing rise in popularity. Original works of art were sold in galleries, book stores, auction rooms, and department stores and were displayed in museums, libraries, schools, businesses, corporate offices, factories, restaurants, churches and synagogues—everywhere people congregated, including the home.

Unique Characteristics

Art is a direct communication between artist and viewer.

Art communicates the highest aesthetic values of our culture.

Art reflects the history of man and his environment through the eyes of the artist in an aesthetically and uniquely personal way.

Art, the oldest means of communication, is still available today for us to experience; it is centuries older than the written word.

Art communicates through a wide variety of visual elements: line, color, form, tone, texture, space.

Art can be appreciated on many levels, and appreciated on a different level each time it is viewed.

The monetary as well as the aesthetic value of quality works of art increases with time.

Each art object is unique and can only be reproduced, never duplicated.

Advantages

Original works of art are unique, which means that each institution will own the *only* copy of each piece it acquires.

Quality works of art increase in value and are, therefore, an excellent institutional investment.

Benefits received from viewing original art works are immediate. Yet art is something that one can return to, over and over, for renewed enjoyment and appreciation.

When works of art are put on display, they can greatly enhance an institution's appearance and image.

With proper handling, art works last indefinitely, even when lent to users.

The study of original works of art is the best way to learn about art and art appreciation.

If the institution lends works of art, users can have original art in their homes without incurring the expense of ownership.

Many "outside" activities (traveling exhibits, craft demonstrations, exhibits by local artists, classroom tours, etc.) can be easily incorporated into the institution's original art program at little or no cost.

Original works of art complement other institutional holdings and programs, such as books about art, art lectures, AV presentations, and institutional tours.

Original works of art can be used to reach users not easily reached through books and other materials. For example, mobile art exhibits can be sent to community centers, nursing homes, day-care centers, hospitals, and even to the homes of shut-ins. Also, minorities who understand little or no English and preschoolers who have not yet learned to read can appreciate original works of art.

Disadvantages

Because each work of art is one of a kind, each is irreplaceable if lost or destroyed.

Because each work of art is unique, it is difficult to know the value of any particular piece at any given time.

The institution must often absorb extra expenses for storage and display facilities, insurance and security measures, and the framing and handling of art works.

Because of the nature of original art works, not all items can be lent to users.

Original works of art are not available through traditional book and nonbook sources.

Staff members must have special knowledge and appreciation to select and properly care for original works of art and to interpret the institution's collection to users.

SELECTION

Special Criteria

Select works that are convenient for framing, storage, display, circulating, and handling.

Select pieces that are in top condition. Always check for abuse, misuse, damage, wear and tear.

At least at first, limit the selection of art to specific media (original prints, local crafts, oil paintings, sculpture) and/or to specific artists, periods, styles, subject matter, or combinations of these— for example: 20th century original prints by local artists on western subjects.

Don't try to build a complete collection in any area. Instead, strive for a balanced collection within each specialty.

Emphasize the works of local artists. Local artists (and local users) should be the first consideration when planning and developing an institution's art program.

Select quality pieces that are characteristic of each artist's best-known period and style. It's better to collect a few recognizable, quality works than many idiosyncratic works of doubtful quality.

Don't buy specifically with investment in mind. Although original works of art are an excellent long-term investment, concentrate mainly on artistic value.

Consider user needs, including the needs of various segments of the community (minority groups, children, senior citizens, artists, students, etc.).

Buy only from reputable dealers and trustworthy sources. If there are no art dealers in the area, order through dealers' catalogs. Other sources include art fairs and shows, art associations, antique shops, auction houses, and of course the artists themselves.

Make gifts a basic part of the selection policy. Encourage donations, both cash and art works, from organizations and individuals, including the artists themselves. Be cautious, however, about accepting "vanity" gifts from "Sunday painters."

Establish a special line-item budget allocation for original art. If this is impractical, the book, AV, or other budget can be used, perhaps with loan and overdue fees as a supplement.

In writing, establish an art selection policy for the institution. Include in the policy any restrictions on media, styles, subjects, and periods of art to be collected and state the emphasis the collection is to take.

Know the art market, including availability of works, prices, and popular artists and styles.

Visit places where original works of art are sold, created, and exhibited (including artists' studios), to learn about the art world.

Consult experts in the field (museum curators, art critics, local artists, art teachers, dealers) whenever questions arise about selection criteria.

Consider establishing a committee to help in the selection of art works. The committee could include staff members as well as community artists, teachers, curators, and other art experts.

Evaluative Review Sources

Each original work of art is one of a kind, which means that only the more expensive works, created by well-known artists, will be evaluated in journals and other sources, and then only indirectly. In short, review sources for individual works of art do not exist.

The value of a work of art, both monetary and aesthetic, is based—more than anything else—on the latest recorded offering or sale by a dealer, auction house, or artist of a similar work by the same artist or by an artist of similar reputation and creative abilities. The chief selection authority for original works of art is, therefore, "comparison shopping," based upon

1. The selector's aesthetic appreciation of original art works
2. The reputation of the artist and his works
3. Advice from experts in the art community
4. Past purchases of works of similar quality, size, and subject matter, created by the same artist or by an artist of similar reputation and abilities
5. Continual perusal of art books, exhibition catalogs, magazine articles, and dealers' catalogs about the artist and his works (or similar artists and works) and about the art world in general.

Nonevaluative Sources

The lack of evaluative sources for original art makes nonevaluative sources indispensable, if only to help sharpen the selector's judgment. Nonevaluative sources include the following:

Books on art, artists, art history, and the selection and appreciation of art are essential guides. A cross-section of titles is included in "Additional Resources" (below).

Art periodicals feature articles on art and artists, and provide gallery and dealer announcements and ads. The most popular periodicals are *Art in America, Artnews, Arts Magazine, Print Collector's Newsletter,* and *American Artist.*

Exhibition catalogs represent an ongoing review of the arts. The chief tool for selecting exhibition catalogs is a quarterly publication, *The Worldwide Art Catalogue Bulletin*, which contains brief descriptions of all major American and European art exhibition catalogs.

Dealers' catalogs are essential. Because there are no jobbers for original art, dealers and galleries have become the chief source. Their names and addresses can be found in most art magazines, as well as *Fine Arts Marketplace, Art in America: Annual Guide to Galleries, Museums, Artists.*

Art groups and associations, national and local, are excellent sources of information on art and art selection. Check local phone directories and the regional art magazines for the names of art groups in the area. *American Art Directory* and *Fine Arts Market Place* contain national listings.

Auction houses are another source. The annual *International Auction Record* lists the principal auction houses of the world, auction dates, and—most important for the institutional collector—the prices collected each year from the sale of over 40,000 works. Although prices are for the most expensive works auctioned each year, they provide a basis for selecting works of the better-known artists.

Galleries, museums, dealers, and art supply and frame shops can serve as another up-to-date source of information on art. Curators, dealers, and shopowners who sell, buy, and exhibit original works of art on a day-to-day basis have valuable firsthand knowledge of art collection and selection.

Local artists themselves are an excellent resource for information on collecting and selecting original works of art.

MAINTENANCE AND MANAGEMENT

Storage and Care

Designate a special area of the institution, preferably a separate room, as the art storage/work area.

Include in this area the following furnishings: desk and chairs; typewriter and office supplies; one or more work tables; filing, tool, and supply cabinets; storage facilities for frames, mats, and similar materials; shelving for reference materials; equipment and facilities for cleaning, framing, matting, and repairing art materials (including running water); storage facilities for original art.[2]

Store like objects together. For ease of storage, identification, and handling, try to arrange paintings, sculptures, prints, pottery, and other art works by category, and then by size.

Keep storage, work, and display areas clean, well ventilated, and free of clutter.

Handle art works as little as possible. The more you move a piece, the more you risk damage.

Handle art works with clean hands. Dirt and perspiration can cause permanent damage.

Plan what you're going to do *before* you touch a work of art. Know the nature of the work, and where and how you're going to move, store, or display it.

At least once a year, inspect each work of art for deterioration and damage. Also inspect every piece each time it is moved.

Consider all works of art as irreplaceable. Treat each piece as if it were the most valuable object in the institution.

Store all art objects at least 1 ½ inches off the floor, in shelves, bins, cabinets, or trays.

If damage occurs, collect and save for restoration all detached fragments, including paint chips, torn corners, broken pieces, and fabric strands.

Leave major cleaning and restoration to the experts.

Don't subject art to extreme temperature change. A uniform 70° F is ideal, and good air conditioning is essential, especially for works of art on paper.

Never allow the humidity to go above 70% (50% is best). High humidity can cause mildew.

2. Raymond Harrison, *The Technical Requirements of Small Museums* (Ottawa: Canadian Museums Assn., 1969), 23.

Keep art objects away from direct sunlight. Even indirect sunlight and strong fluorescent or other artificial light can fade colors and accelerate the degeneration of art works.

Guard against air pollution. Sulphur dioxide is particularly dangerous, especially to works of art on paper. The best prevention is a good air conditioning system.

Watch out for insects. Bookworms, cockroaches, silver fish, and termites are just as destructive to art works as they are to books and nonbooks. The best precaution is a dry, air conditioned, well-ventilated, properly lighted, and soundly constructed building.

Know local laws and ordinances concerning the destruction and theft of art works.

Make sure that the institution's insurance policy covers all original art works in the collection.

Install (if necessary) window and door locks, electric alarm systems, fire extinguishers, and other security and safety measures.[3]

Keep accurate, up-to-date records on all pieces—if possible, photographic records.

Know where each art work is at all times—on loan, in storage, on display, wherever.

Never display or circulate a damaged or soiled art work; this can encourage even more damage.

Inventory art holdings periodically, and at least daily for items on display.

Observe these special guidelines for paintings:

Do not carry paintings on one side or by the frame. Instead, carry with one hand beneath and one hand on the side of the frame.

The best way to store paintings is on sliding screens. The units can be hung from tracks attached either to the ceiling or to a free-standing structure.

Otherwise, store paintings in plywood bins in an upright position. You can construct the bins yourself—a foot or so wide and tall enough to accommodate standard-size pictures.[4]

Avoid stacking paintings on top of each other. If stacking is unavoidable, be sure to separate paintings by corrugated cardboard or another protective material.

3. Joseph Chapman, "Physical Security," in *A Primer on Museum Security,* ed. Caroline K. Keck (Cooperstown: New York State Historical Assn., 1969), 1–13.

4. E. Verner Johnson and Joanne C. Horgan, *Museum Collection Storage* (Paris: Unesco, 1979), 34–35.

Avoid touching the surface (or even the backs) of paintings. It's a good idea to protect the back of each painting with cardboard or other backing.

Store paintings framed. This avoids moving paintings into and out of frames.

Cover stored paintings with canvas, cardboard, or other material to protect the surfaces. Pad bins and other storage areas to protect the frames.

When displaying pictures, place rubber or cork bumpers at the bottom corners of the back of each frame. This prevents dust streaks and allows air to circulate behind the pictures, and also helps to keep pictures straight. The pressure of the frame against the wall will hold the bumpers in place.

Observe these special guidelines for sculpture, crafts, and other three-dimensional works:

Never carry sculpture, ceramics, and other objects by their projecting parts, such as handles, arms, edges, or rims. Support each piece by the bottom, with one hand, and by the side with the other.

Do not handle or carry more than one object at a time. Also, know exactly what you're going to do with a piece before you touch it.

Do not allow any part of a work of art to protrude beyond the edge of its tray, box, shelving, drawer, or other storage area or container.

Line storage boxes, shelves, and cabinets that contain fragile objects with padding.

Do not overcrowd storage boxes or shelving. Separate each item in a box or tray with thick, absorbent materials, making sure that the pieces do not touch each other.

Handle pottery and other fragile items on cushioned surfaces: soft cloth, velvet, cotton padding.

Avoid opening containers or removing objects from shelves to identify individual pieces. Instead, identify the outside of each container, drawer, and shelving area that holds an art object.

Observe these special guidelines for textiles:

Keep rugs, costumes, wall hangings, and other textiles away from direct sunlight. Even prolonged exposure to natural light can weaken fibers and fade colors.

Keep storage and display areas clean and fumigated. Wool, silks, and other animal fabrics are especially susceptible to attack by insects.

Clean stains and restore damaged fibers as soon as possible. The longer you let a stain remain on a fabric, the more difficult it is to remove; the longer you allow broken threads to remain broken, the more difficult they will be to restore.

Keep sharp objects away from textiles, whether in storage, on display, or in transit. Remove metal pins, rings, wooden dowels, and other objects from textiles when they are stored.

Develop a periodic cleaning program for fabrics. Even with careful handling and proper storage, textiles accumulate dust.

Avoid folding textiles, which can weaken the fibers. Roll, hang, or keep fabrics in a flat position in storage. If you *must* fold, use crumpled, acid-free tissue paper in the folds, fold lightly, and never fold in the same creases.[5]

Observe these special guidelines for prints and other works of art on paper:

Never stack original prints on top of each other, unless they are protected by guard sheets or placed in plastic envelopes.

Store unframed prints in standard print containers (solander boxes), portfolios, map cabinets, or other flat files.

Store framed prints by hanging them on pegboard panels, walls, or screens; or stand them vertically in plywood bins. Do not store original prints in their frames for extended periods.

Never pick up a print by the frame or by the edge of the mat. Use both hands.

Do not scrape anything across the surface of a print or drawing. Be especially careful when stacking works of art on paper.

Mat all prints and other works of art on paper, both to enhance their looks and to protect against damage. Do the matting yourself or have it done professionally.

Mat prints with a backboard that supports the print and a frame board with a window to display the print. Hinge the two boards by a linen tape along the top and place the print between the two hinged boards so that the image will be displayed through the window (see Figure 1).

Use only quality materials when matting a print, especially any materials that touch the print. Use 100 percent rag matboards, hinges made from Japanese mulberry paper, and vegetable paste. Also use proper-size frames and sturdy hardware (screw eyes, picture hooks and wire) which are neither too heavy nor too light to do the job.[6]

5. Frieda K. Fall, *Art Objects: Their Care and Preservation,* vol. 1 (Washington, D.C.: Museum Publications, 1967), 101–11.

6. Francis W. Dolloff and Roy L. Perkinson, *How to Care for Works of Art on Paper* (Boston: Museum of Fine Arts, 1971), 25–30.

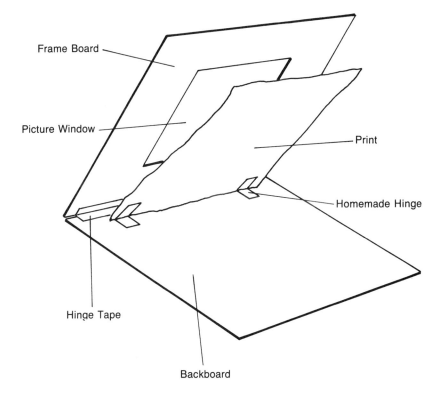

Figure 1. Standard Print Mat

Never trim the margins of an original print to fit a mat or frame. Always cut the mat, or switch frames.

Frame all prints that are to be displayed or circulated. You can buy ready-mades, or pay for custom framing, or do the framing yourself.

Don't "overframe" original prints. Commercial quick-change frames work well for temporary framing, made either of natural wood or metal, in basic colors of black, gold, or silver.

A properly framed print should include the frame (with screw eyes affixed to the back of the frame and twisted picture wire between the eyes), glass (or Plexiglass), matted print, and a lightweight backing which, if in a permanent frame, has been sealed to the frame around the edges to keep out dust and dampness (Figure 2).

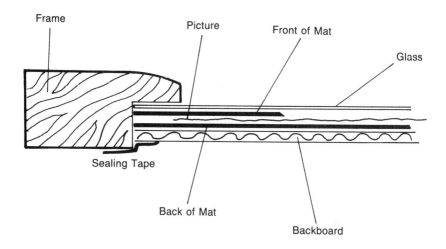

Figure 2. Cross-Section of Framed Print

Management Problems and Solutions

The institution's art program should be supervised by a member of the staff who has an understanding and appreciation of art. Duties include establishing an acquisitions policy and overseeing the selection of individual works of art; organizing storage, work, and display areas; supervising the framing, matting, and preparation of art works; establishing bibliographic control and security systems for the works; coordinating related institutional services; developing a budget and overseeing expenditures; and interpreting the program to users and to other staff members.

Art works do not lend themselves to the same organization, subject emphasis, and classification systems that books and other media do. In most cases, a simple accession or control numbering system works best, with inventory sheets to describe the individual pieces. On each sheet would be listed the artist's name, title of the work, medium, and a brief description of the work, including dimensions, condition, and color. Also indicate whether or not the artist's signature or initials appear on the piece and include any acquisition information required by the institution, such as price, donor's name, date and place of purchase.[7]

    7. Donald L. Foster, *Prints in the Public Library* (Metuchen, N.J.: Scarecrow, 1973), 77–79.

Identification markings should be placed on all original works of
art, especially if the pieces are to be lent; be careful, however, not to
mar the appearance. You can mark the *backs* of picture frames and
the *backs* of the canvases. Also, place ownership stamps on original
prints, watercolors, and drawings, preferably on the backs in the lower
right- or left-hand corners. Use a brown or light-color ink so that the
markings will not spread or show through the paper. Also, place ownership markings on three-dimensional art objects, either on the bottom
of each piece or in some other unobtrusive spot.

Works of art should be displayed in a place in the institution that
will provide maximum exposure and adequate security. This could be
in the lobby or near the main entrance; or pieces could be scattered
throughout the institution: in corridors, meeting rooms, foyers, offices,
branches.

It's a good idea to rotate art works being displayed, so that users
will see the institution's entire collection and to "rest" individual
pieces. The length of time that any group of works should be left on
display is about one month.

The institution can also provide "traveling exhibits" for schools,
galleries, libraries, and other groups and agencies in the area. This is
an excellent way to advertise the art program and at the same time
serve the community. Make sure, however, that host institutions have
adequate security and that they will provide proper care of the works.

The institution can sponsor community exhibits. This might include local art competitions; displays of arts or crafts of teenagers, senior citizens, and other groups; shows of individual artists and art
groups; and displays of "for sale" works of art dealers and associations.

To give meaning to the display and also to leave a more lasting
impression on viewers, exhibits should be set up around clearly defined
and unifying themes. A typical theme might be the works of a certain
artist or group of artists, a specific subject or period of art, or simply
the institution's latest acquisitions.

Avoid all-encompassing exhibits. It is better to have a few well-
chosen, good-quality, representative works that are tastefully displayed
than a bewildering jumble of unrelated works. If possible, arrange the
exhibit so that it tells a story.

Support the exhibit with book and nonbook materials. The exhibit
might include a guest lecturer, a slide-tape presentation, or a brief tour
of the institution, emphasizing available books and other materials in
the collection. Provide a catalog of the exhibit, even if it is only a listing
of the works on display and a reading list.

Be sure to label each work of art on display. Type (or print) one
label for each piece. Minimum information would be the artist's name,

title of the work, and medium. Other information might include the date of execution, donor's name or special purchase fund, name of the institution, and identification number.

Display paintings, prints, and other flat works on the walls and approximately at eye level, with larger pieces placed proportionately higher so they can be viewed at a distance. Children's art should be at a level where they can view the display comfortably. Also consider the handicapped. This might require ramps, easy-access display areas, or extra-wide aisles and doorways.

When hanging pictures, strive for an attractive presentation, the best possible support for each piece, and the most effective conservation methods. Besides hooks nailed into the wall, you can use pegboards, picture-rail hooks, panels attached to pressure poles, and portable screens. You can also place works on the tops of bookstacks, on floor or table-top easels, and in glass cases. Three-dimensional works should be on pedestals or shelves, with smaller items locked in display cases. Floodlights can be set up to ensure adequate lighting. See that there are no obstacles obstructing viewers, and be sure to mark *clearly* whether or not the works on display are to be touched.

You will want to maintain the same climatic conditions in display areas as you do in storage areas. Keep works out of direct sunlight, in uniform temperatures of around 70° with humidity below 70, and in surroundings free of dust, dirt, and insects. Try to avoid displaying original works of art near radiators, heating or air vents, or on damp outside walls.

Provide for as much mobility as possible, so that the layout can be easily changed. Consider, for example, using mobile shelving, pegboard panels, or display cases with wheel- or ball-type casters.

In order for users to receive maximum benefit from an institution's art collection, individual works should be made available for home appreciation. Most institutions charge a small circulation fee, perhaps 50¢ to $1. Fees will depend on the type and value of the works and on the economics of the community being served by the institution. Try to keep the art-loan system compatible with the institution's other systems, using (if possible) regular loan cards and charging machines. There may be pieces that, because of format, cost, size, or rarity, will have to remain in the institution.

Unless you have a large loan collection, you will probably need to place a limit on the number of items that can be borrowed. One item per person (or 2 or 3 per household) for one or two months, with no renewals, is about right. Although all users should be included in the loan program, the institution will want to apply restrictions on who can check out the works. Children, for example, might be allowed to borrow items only when accompanied by an adult, or through a school or other sponsoring institution.

Once the collection is established, other institutions in the community (schools, nursing homes, libraries) should be allowed to take advantage of the loan program. Here again, restrictions should be established, especially if large portions of the collection could be tied up for extended periods.

The institution will probably want to establish regulations on overdues and set fines for late returns and damaged pieces. Users might even be asked to sign a ''statement of responsibility,'' agreeing to pay for any damage or loss, and perhaps a small deposit should be required for each loan. It's also a good idea to phone the borrower or send a reminder notice a week or so in advance of the due date.

The institution should circulate only framed pictures and provide users with sturdy carrying containers such as foam-padded canvas bags or cardboard boxes, either home made or purchased from an art or library supply house. Also state in writing the art-loan policies; legal liabilities; overdue, loss, and damage fines; and other information relevant to the care, transportation, home display, and preservation of art works.

Facilities should be provided in the circulation area for storing works that are waiting to be picked up or returned to the storage area. Staff members who work with original art should become familiar with the proper care and handling of loan items. Automatically, they should inspect all outgoing and incoming works, noting any damaged or soiled areas.

Rental-purchase plans are popular in many institutions. One of the best ways to initiate such a plan is to ask local artists to lend their works to the institution. The institution would then lend the works to users for a small fee, and also make the pieces available for purchase. The rental fee could be applied toward the purchase price if the piece is bought.

A promotion program should be developed. The institution might start, for example, with an exhibition of the loan collection publicized through photo-articles in the local newspapers. Also post signs and pass out flyers at the loan desk, explaining the program and perhaps even listing the works to be lent.

Other Concerns

Painting can be defined as the art of reproducing scenes on two-dimensional surfaces by means of lines and colors. *Oil painting* is the art of covering with a tool (usually a bristle brush), on an absorbent surface (usually a canvas), layers of pigments that have been ground on linseed or other oil. *Watercolor* is painting with pigments mixed with water, usually applied to paper with a brush. *Gouache* (also called *poster painting*) is painting with watercolors that have been rendered opaque by the addition of white pigment. *Pastel* is painting on paper with crayons made from dry, powdered colors, mixed with just enough gum to bind. *Drawing* is the tracing of a picture on paper by making black marks with a charred willow twig. *Charcoal* is often used for making preliminary sketches for oil, watercolor, or another painting technique.

Sculpture is three-dimensional art (or art in relief), created by either *carving out* a material such as stone or wood (i.e., removing waste material until the form is created); *modeling* (or building up) materials from a lump of material, such as clay, wax, or plaster; or *assemblying* (or joining together) prefabricated materials, as in welded metal construction. An especially popular assembly technique is *kinetic sculpture*, which is the joining together of mechanically moving parts actuated by a motor, hand crank, or natural process. The most popular kinetic sculpture is the *mobile*, a free-standing assembly made of natural and/or abstract objects, usually suspended on wires and moved by a combination of air currents and its own structural tensions.

Printmaking is the technique of creating an image with a knife or other instrument on a wood block, metal plate, stone, or other material; then inking the surface; and, finally, transferring the image onto a paper, cloth, or other material through direct contact with the inked surface.

The artist can create either an unlimited number of prints ("unlimited edition") or a specific number of prints ("limited edition"). In a limited edition, the artist creates a specific number of impressions which he or she usually signs and numbers at the bottom left-hand corner of each print. (The notation 8/25, for example, means that the print is number 8 in a total edition of 25.) To be an "original print," the finished print must be signed and numbered by the artist, or at the very least approved by him or her.[8]

The *relief process* (woodcuts, linocuts, wood engravings) is a printmaking technique in which the artist cuts away unwanted parts of the surface of the material to make the picture *stand out* in relief. In the *intaglio process* (etching, drypoint, aquatint, mezzotint), the artist incises a picture with tools or acids on a metal plate, which causes the picture to appear *below* the surface of the material. In the *planographic*

---

8. Joshua B. Cahn, *What Is an Original Print?* (New York: Print Council of America, 1967), 9.

process (lithography), the artist draws an image with a grease-base crayon or ink upon the surface of a block of limestone and transfers the picture onto paper with a printing press. In the *stencil process* (serigraphy and silk screen), the artist cuts out patterns of paper or other material, places the cut-out material on a printing surface of paper or cloth, and then applies color with a squeegee or similar tool to create a picture or design.[9]

Craft making is the making of articles that are artistic and that also serve a practical purpose. The various skills involved in craft making include woodwork, metalwork, pottery, weaving, and the manipulation of metals, plastics, and other materials. Crafts that are popular today include the making of tapestries, rugs, macramé, clothing, furniture, pots and other kitchen ware. The chief difference between original crafts and other art media (i.e., between the applied and the fine arts) is that in original crafts aesthetic appreciation is subservient to the function of the object.

ADDITIONAL RESOURCES

Arnason, H. H. *History of Modern Art*. 2d ed. Englewood Cliffs, N.J.: Prentice-Hall, 1977.

"Art Loan Collections." *Library Journal* 99 (May 1974): 1258–61.

Bebeau, Gordon. "Circulating Art Collections." *Wisconsin Library Bulletin* 62 (May 1966): 168.

Broxis, Peter F. *Organizing the Arts*. London: Bingley, 1968.

Cahn, Joshua B. *What Is an Original Print?* New York: Print Council of America, 1967.

Cunha, George M. *Conservation of Library Materials*. Metuchen, N.J.: Scarecrow, 1972.

David, Carl. *Collecting and Care for Fine Art*. New York: Crown, 1981.

Dolloff, Francis W. *How to Care for Works of Art on Paper*. Boston: Museum of Fine Arts, 1971.

Donson, Theodore B. *Prints and the Print Market: A Handbook for Buyers, Collectors, Connoisseurs*. New York: Crowell, 1977.

Eagle, Joanna. *Buying Art on a Budget*. New York: Hawthorn, 1969.

Ellsworth, Rudolph C. "Renting Art." *Canadian Library* 24 (Mar. 1968): 534–35.

Fall, Frieda K. *Art Objects: Their Care and Preservation*. Washington, D.C.: Museum Publications, 1967.

Faure, Elie. *History of Art*. Garden City, N.Y.: Garden City Pub., 1937.

Foster, Donald L. "A Picasso in Every Library." *Wilson Library Bulletin* 37 (Sept. 1962): 58–60.

9. Carl Zigrosser, *A Guide to the Collecting and Care of Original Prints* (London: Arco, 1966), 5–7.

———. *Prints in the Public Library*. Metuchen, N.J.: Scarecrow, 1973.

Gardner, Helen. *Gardner's Art through the Ages*. 7th ed. New York: Harcourt Brace Jovanovich, 1980.

Goldman, Judith. "Print Criteria." *Art News* 70 (Jan. 1972): 48–51.

Gombrich, Ernst H. *The Story of Art*. 12th ed. New York: Phaidon, 1972.

Goodhope, Jeanie. "The Library: Showcase for Teenage Talent." *Top of the News* 35 (Spring 1979): 291–93.

Harrar, H. Joanne. "Photographs, Pictures, and Prints." In *Nonprint Media in Academic Libraries*, ed. Pearce S. Grove. Chicago: American Library Assn., 1975.

Harrison, Raymond. *The Technical Requirements of Small Museums*. Ottawa: Canadian Museums Assn., 1969.

Janson, Horst W. *History of Art*. 2nd ed. New York: Abrams, 1977.

Johnson, E. Verner, and Joanne C. Horgan. *Museum Collection Storage*. Paris: Unesco, 1979.

Kay, Jane H. "Boston's Public Library: A Keeper with Many Keys." *Art in America* 59 (Jan. 1971): 78–81.

Keck, Caroline K. *How to Take Care of Your Paintings*. New York: Scribner's, 1978.

———, ed. *A Primer on Museum Security*. Cooperstown: New York State Historical Assn., 1969.

King, Antoinette. "Conservation of Drawings and Prints." *Special Libraries* 63 (Mar. 1972): 116–20.

Kujoth, Jean S. *Readings in Non-Book Librarianship*. Metuchen, N.J.: Scarecrow, 1968.

Ligocki, Michael. "Regional Art as a Library Service." *ALA Bulletin* 55 (Nov. 1961): 882–84.

Luckey, Carl F. *Official Guide to Collector Prints*. Florence, Ala.: House of Collectibles, 1976.

Netherland, Lynda M. "The Walls Were Bare." *Louisiana Library Assn. Bulletin* 37 (Summer 1974): 48–53.

Pacey, Philip. *Art Library Manual: A Guide to Resources and Practice*. New York: Bowker, 1977.

Read, Herbert. *The Meaning of Art*. Baltimore: Penguin, 1949.

Robb, David M. *Art in the Western World*. 4th ed. New York: Harper & Row, 1963.

Rosenbaum, Lee. *The Complete Guide to Collecting Art*. New York: Knopf, 1982.

Samuels, Peggy. *Everyone's Guide to Buying Art*. Englewood Cliffs, N.J.: Prentice-Hall, 1984.

Schneider, Gerald. *The Intelligent Art Buyer's Guide*. Silver Spring, Md.: Art for Love and Money, 1980.

Schonberg, Jeanne. *Questions to Ask Your Framer*. Los Angeles: Tamarind Lithography Workshop, n.d.

Shapiro, Cecile, and Lauris Mason. *Fine Prints: Collecting, Buying, and Selling*. New York: Harper & Row, 1976.

Smith, Frances. "The Art Department Gallery: San Antonio Public Library." *Texas Library Journal* 46 (Spring 1970): 17–18.

Smith, Merrily, ed. *Matting and Hinging of Works of Art on Paper.* Washington, D.C.: Library of Congress, 1981.

Stephenson, Genevieve A. "Some Notes on the Care of Prints and Photographs at the National Portrait Gallery." *Picturescope* 20 (Winter 1972): 174–79.

Sutherland, Thomas A. "Art in a Public Library." *Southeastern Librarian* 16 (Summer 1966): 101–2.

Swartzburg, Susan G. *Preserving Library Materials: A Manual.* Metuchen, N.J.: Scarecrow, 1980.

Vershbow, Arthur. *Print Collecting Today: A Symposium.* Boston: Public Library, 1969.

Zigrosser, Carl. *A Guide to the Collecting and Care of Original Prints.* London: Arco, 1966.

Mildred Knight Laughlin
and Patricia Ann Coty

ch. 13

Overhead Transparencies

THE MEDIUM

Definition

An overhead transparency is an image on a transparent background which can be viewed by transmitted light, either directly or through projection. The major types of overhead transparencies are clear acetate (on which information is drawn with a pen or grease pencil), thermographic (produced by heat process), diazo (produced by ammonia process), and electrostatic (produced by xerography). Overhead transparencies are usually mounted on cardboard frames, and may include overlay transparencies in addition to a base transparency. They are usually projected for group viewing by an overhead projector.

Brief History

As early as 1692, "magic lanterns" were used in the projection of drawn transparencies on an exterior screen. Later, the projection of horizontal images was discovered.

Transparencies became an important nonbook visual resource when they were developed by the Armed Forces in World War II as a training device. Industry extensively adopted the use of overhead transparencies for teaching purposes in the late 1940s, and early television studios used them for newscasts and weather reports. Schools did not generally adopt transparencies for visual presentation until the

214

1960s because the cost of the projection equipment was prohibitive. When the size and cost of the projectors were reduced, the transparency emerged as a valuable and widely used device for visual presentations.

An innovation in transparency preparation involved the creation of the impression of movement, by applying light-polarizing materials directly to the transparency surface. A rotating disc of polarizing material is then placed in the light beam (attached to the projector), which produces the effect of motion and pattern on the screen. A patterned belt can be attached to the projector to give the illusion of flow for printed transparencies.

Many improvements and new techniques have been made which encourage transparency preparation at the local level. Companies such as 3M provide transparency masters for photocopy machine duplication. Film is available which allows color to be produced with a thermal copy machine. Through the use of carbon film, local producers can type directly onto film to produce transparencies. Fine felt-tip pens now allow greater control of the width and thickness of letters drawn directly on a sheet of clear acetate. Colored plastic cutouts, moved by the user on a projected transparency, can suggest movement or show the effect of change. The exactness of copy through machines such as the Thermofax make overlay preparation (using sequential displays) less time consuming.

Commercial packaging has also been improved, facilitating storage and use. Transart, for example, produced "Flipatran," a spiral book system which facilitates both presentation and storage of local and commercial transparencies. Kits which include transparencies, such as the Milliken packages, also contain spirit masters, perforated transparencies, and notes.

Transparencies have been used primarily in group settings. However, they have been made more accessible and usable through the recent development of an easel-type lightbox.

Unique Characteristics

Overhead transparencies are media designed for projection, but large enough to be viewed with the unaided eye. Overhead transparencies are unique among projected media in that they may be manipulated by the presenter while being presented, by using one or more of the following methods: writing directly onto the transparency; using "progressive disclosure" to cover parts of the transparency with opaque paper, and revealing parts of the transparency in stages; using transparent overlays so that successive details can be added to the transparency; or by projecting silhouettes of objects placed on the stage of the overhead projector.

Advantages

The many advantages of overhead transparencies for use in group presentations have made them a popular medium, especially in educational situations.

Overhead projectors are relatively inexpensive, portable, and simple to operate. Equipment for projection is available in most institutions.

During the use of overhead transparencies, the presenter faces the audience while controlling the transparencies, which are legible to both the audience (as projected) and the presenter (on the overhead projector). Since the presenter faces the audience, he or she can maintain eye contact with the group, facilitating communication. The presenter can also use the overhead transparencies as a presentation outline.

Material can be added to, or removed from, the overhead transparency during the presentation. Color or other markings can be added while the transparency is being projected, to highlight specific points. These markings can later be removed from the transparencies, if nonpermanent ink is used.

The presenter can point to a portion of the transparency with a finger or other small object, and have the portion silhouetted on the screen.

The presenter can control the order of presentation and the amount of time spent on each segment, altering the order or speed of presentation as the need arises. Presentations can be easily modified by adding or removing transparencies.

Transparent overlays allow the progressive development of a concept. Progressive disclosure of information can also be achieved by the use of opaque material (i.e., paper), laid over the transparency and advanced down the page line by line, or by cardboard "windows" affixed to the transparency frame.

Overhead transparencies can be used effectively in normal room light, since the overhead projector lamp is so bright. This allows the audience the ability to take notes, and encourages better communication between the presenter and the audience than does projection in a darkened room.

The illusion of motion can be added to overhead transparencies by use of a circulating disc of polarized material on the projection equipment, and by overhead transparencies which contain light-polarizing materials on their surface.

Opaque shapes or objects, or translucent objects such as compasses and rulers, can be projected by placing them on the projector stage.

A wide variety of overhead transparencies are available for purchase from commercial vendors.

Overhead transparencies are easy and inexpensive to produce, requiring only a grease pencil or felt-tip pen and a sheet of acetate. They can be made, quickly and easily, both by young people and adults. A high degree of creativity is allowed in local production.

Paper copies of the transparency can easily be made on a photocopier for distribution to the audience, and can serve as the basis for notetaking.

Using a roll of acetate, the presenter can write the material for a total presentation in one continuous series, and it can be stored on the roll for reuse. Inexpensive attachments for overhead projectors allow the presenter to mount the roll on the projector, for continuous feed.

The overhead projector can serve as a "projected blackboard" for lectures, allowing the presenter to project impromptu notes as the need arises.

Disadvantages

The size of the overhead transparencies, and lack of standardized packaging, may present storage problems. Transparencies are usually mounted on cardboard frames, about 10 ¼ by 11 ¾ inches, making them an odd size for storage in filing cabinets and on shelves.

Overhead transparencies may be easily damaged or destroyed.

Large-size (minimum ¼ inch) print on overhead transparencies is necessary for the audience to read the text easily. Locally produced transparencies often neglect this rule, especially when made from typewritten masters. The very ease with which amateurs can create overhead transparencies can have disastrous results, for poorly produced transparencies can greatly detract from an otherwise good presentation.

Incorrect positioning of the overhead projector or screen can result in distortion in the projected image, known as *keystoning*. The keystone effect is especially common with overhead projection, because the projector is normally set up very close to, and far lower than, the screen. This effect can usually be eliminated if the top of the screen can be tilted forward, or if the projector can be raised to the level of the screen.

The audience's view of the projected overhead transparency may be partially blocked by improper positioning of the projector and/or the presenter, since they remain in the front of the room during the presentation.

The effectiveness of overhead transparencies may vary greatly, depending on the talents of the presenter. The sequence of presentation and any oral description of the subject matter are controlled by the presenter.

In general, use of overhead transparencies is limited to group presentations. Since transparencies usually contain limited visual information, which is meant as a supplement to an oral presentation, they do not lend themselves well to independent study.

Within a presentation, it may be difficult for the presenter to locate earlier transparencies when discussion necessitates review. This is, however, true with other projected visuals as well.

Overhead transparencies cannot communicate motion well, and are basically a still medium. Although motion can be simulated by the use of light-polarizing materials, producing such transparencies locally can be difficult. Even with properly produced materials, the simulated motion is limited in its effectiveness.

The widespread availability of overhead projectors can lead to their overuse as a substitute for the chalkboard or other more appropriate visual media.

Color transparencies may be more expensive than similar 35mm slides, so care in selection is necessary.

SELECTION

Special Criteria

Many of the criteria leading to the selection of overhead transparencies as the preferred medium for particular situations are criteria for projected visuals in general. Having identified projected visuals as a requirement, considerations such as cost, portability, flexibility, and commercial or local availability of materials may point to overhead transparencies as the preferred medium. At this point, a decision as to whether needs can best be met by local production or by the purchase of commercially produced transparencies must be made. Factors such as cost, complexity of the material, need for color, artistic abilities of local production staff, and the time available for development of in-house materials or purchasing of commercial materials will affect the decision whether to produce or purchase overhead transparencies.

The criteria listed below can, for the most part, be applied to either locally or commercially produced transparencies.

The overhead transparency format should be the *best* choice for presentation of the material.

In a set of transparencies, the majority should be usable in the institution.

Information in the transparencies must be logically sequenced and organized, current, and reliable.

The technical qualities of the transparency should be pleasing to the eye, omitting irrelevant information, limiting text, and presenting a well-spaced, uncluttered, effective message. Lettering must be adequate in size and style, so that the projected image will be legible to the audience. This is best tested by actual projection of the material in conditions under which it will likely be used.

Overlays should be included where sequential presentation of the content would improve the transparency's effectiveness. If there are overlays, they must be in correct registration, with double hinges holding them to the frame.

The overhead transparencies should be designed to encourage audience interest and participation.

Transparencies should have durable mounting and packaging, and should be well labeled to permit easy identification.

When overhead transparencies are selected or produced, special attention must be given to the textual matter (if any). When text is used, a maximum of six or seven words per line, with a maximum of five or six lines, is a good rule of thumb. Cluttered transparencies which attempt to convey too much text at once are unsuitable.

Letter size is extremely important for overhead transparencies. Letters shold not be less than 1 inch high for every 30 feet of viewing distance. Letter size for *any* text should never be less than ¼ inch high. Whatever lettering is used, the transparency should be tested for legibility under conditions of actual use.

Large clear areas on a transparency can result in a brightness on the screen which is uncomfortable to view, but a sheet of tinted acetate can be placed over the original transparency in such a case. For locally produced transparencies, consider colored acetate for producing the transparency.

Evaluative Review Sources

There is no single source for consistent evaluations of overhead transparencies, but many of the professional library and educational publications include reviews of transparencies on an occasional basis. The following publications include transparencies among the media they evaluate:

PERIODICALS
Media Review Digest
School Library Journal
School Library Media Quarterly

BOOKS
Brown, Lucy Gregor. *Core Media Collection for Elementary Schools.* New
    York: Bowker, 1978.
_____. *Core Media Collection for Secondary Schools.* 2nd ed. New York:
    Bowker, 1979.
        These texts recommend materials that have been favorably reviewed
    or evaluated, including transparencies.
Sive, Mary Robinson, comp. *The Complete Media Monitor: Guides to Learn-
    ing Resources.* Metuchen, N.J.: Scarecrow, 1981.
        Recommended media, including transparencies, for all grade levels.
Winkel, Lois, ed. *The Elementary School Library Collection: A Guide to Books
    and Other Media, Phases 1–2–3.* 14th ed. Williamsport, Pa.: Bro-Dart,
    1984.
        Recommends quality media for elementary school use.

Nonevaluative Sources

The titles below represent current, in-print sources for locating
overhead transparencies. While they may include annotations in their
citations for transparencies, they do not include reviews or other
evaluative information.

PERIODICALS
Audiovisual Materials

BOOKS
Educational Media Catalogs on Microfiche. Hoboken, N.J.: Olympic Media
    Information. Semiannual updates.
        A comprehensive collection of catalogs of audiovisual software
    distributors (over 400). Includes the contents of the catalogs. Valuable
    for identifying the types of materials that are commercially available.
Index to Educational Overhead Transparencies. 6th ed. Los Angeles: National
    Information Center for Educational Media, 1980.
        Known to those in the field as one of the NICEM indexes, this vol-
    ume is a comprehensive listing of over 5,000 overhead transparencies from
    more than 200 producers. All subjects and grade levels are included. Most
    have short annotations and information about intended audiences.

MAINTENANCE AND MANAGEMENT
Storage and Care

Storage conditions for all overhead transparencies:

1. Transparencies should be stored away from direct sunlight or heat sources.
2. Temperature of 70° F is best, with relative humidity of 50%.
3. Avoid all sources of dust and danger of scratching. Storage facilities should protect the edges of the transparencies and their frames from damage.

Storage facilities for unmounted transparencies:

1. Can be hole-punched ring binders, with a plain sheet of paper between each transparency.
2. May be between transparent plastic protectors in a binder file.
3. May be a vertical file or a special cabinet, together with mounted transparencies.

Storage facilities for mounted transparencies:

1. May be mounted on cardboard or pressboard, to protect the surface and facilitate ease in handling.
2. May be appropriate envelopes, for base and overlays together.
   a. Plastic envelopes may add to the dust problem, but allow viewing without removal.
   b. Manila envelopes may add to the danger of scratching the transparencies.
3. May be modular cabinets, equipped with a lighted panel for viewing.
4. May be a legal- or x-ray-size vertical file.
5. Storage shelves or boxes, divided into narrow slots.
6. May be sturdy boxes, or intershelved with other materials, or housed on shelves organized by type of media.
7. Can be transparent folders, suspended from filing rods.

Storage methods for transparency sets:

1. If they are already in boxes or binders suitable for shelving, transparencies may be interfiled with other media or isolated by type.
2. They may be separated for individual use, if appropriate, and filed with other single transparencies.

Care of transparencies:

1. Transparencies should be handled only at the edges.

2. If possible, they should be inspected after each use and wiped with a clean, slightly dampened cloth.

3. Transparencies should not be allowed to become wet, except for erasing a transparency produced with water-soluble ink.

4. If a transparency is to be written on a great deal, it should be covered with a clear acetate sheet, and writing can be done on the sheet instead of directly on the transparency. In this way, repeated writing and cleaning will not damage the original transparency.

Management Problems and Solutions

Not all problems regarding transparencies will be applicable to every institution that uses transparencies, nor will one solution necessarily be appropriate for any other user. Each problem must be examined in terms of initial cost, staff time, relationship to the objectives of the institution, and response to the users of this medium. However, general statements can be made to address managerial question areas.

Users should be systematically involved in the selection and production of overhead transparencies. This is especially true for this medium because transparencies tend to be closely interrelated to lecture presentations; they are not usually designed to stand alone as a teaching tool. Suggestions for purchase should be solicited from potential users of the materials. All potential purchases should be reviewed by those who will likely have use for them.

Transparency masters or commercially produced transparencies should be purchased if they succinctly address the unique needs of the institution's users. Often, commercially produced transparencies cannot be identified which approach a concept in the exact way needed by the user. Then, local production will be an appropriate alternative. Local production may also be preferred in cases where time or cost create restrictions.

Reviewing tools are less easily located for transparencies than for other media, but it is imperative that the staff have access to existing tools and use them diligently. When possible, previewing is productive because it allows the user to try out concept presentations before purchase, and allows a trial under actual conditions.

The storage of transparencies offers a unique problem because of their odd size. Mounted overhead transparencies are often as large as 10¼ by 11¾ inches, so they may not fit easily into standard storage systems. Certainly, storage decisions depend upon space, use, cost, and user preferences. In all instances, the classification and storage must allow easy retrieval by the user. This necessitates inclusion in the information retrieval source of a classification system, or at least a subject access, directing the user to appropriate transparencies. Most staff now recognize the need to classify commercially produced transparencies in the same manner as books, but locally produced transparencies present serious problems of time for classification and accessible storage.

When appropriate, all transparencies produced by the staff or with institution materials should be housed in a central location. When transparencies are produced at the request of an individual, that person often wants to retain them in his or her office or classroom. This would prevent use by others, and often results in loss of the transparencies through misplacing them or the user leaving the institution. By storing transparencies in a central location, they are made available to others who may have the same needs. Multiple copies of locally produced transparencies can be made inexpensively, allowing the interested individual to retain a set, as well as providing a set for storage in the central location.

If a decision is made to interfile overhead transparencies with books and other media collected by the institution, it should be based on the perception that this storage approach enhances retrieval. Other factors in such a decision will be available space, storage potential, storage facilities that would be needed if other options were pursued, and budgetary constraints. If overhead transparencies are interfiled with other media, they should be stored in sturdy, protective boxes, and shelves must be adjusted to adequate height to hold the boxes. When possible, all transparencies should be mounted, as this enhances use and deters damage.

The circulation of transparencies outside the institution depends entirely on the local situation. If the storage mode allows adequate packaging to protect circulated materials and the equipment needed for projection is readily accessible, the decision to circulate should be made. There is no inherent reason why transparencies should not circulate as freely as other materials held by the institution. Circulation periods should be based on the characteristics of the collection and its users.

Production of transparencies is a responsibility that should be accepted and encouraged by staff. From simple production with felt-tip pens on clear plastic or acetate to more sophisticated approaches, the results often satisfy the unique needs of the user (not available in commercially produced materials) and at a low cost. In addition, the sense of pride in product is often a motivating device, especially when young people are involved. However, in-service workshops and one-to-one assistance are necessary if the products are to be technically satisfying. If possible, the institution's budget should cover the supplies for more than one type of transparency production, since different methods of production offer diverse results. Animation materials and equipment may not be cost effective, so this should be carefully considered before decisions to purchase them are made.

Other Concerns

A number of relatively simple methods exist for local production of overhead transparencies. In an institution where overhead transparencies are heavily used, it would be wise to consider investing in the equipment and materials needed to produce high-quality transparencies on site. This may be especially important if there is often a need for overhead transparencies of very specialized subjects which cannot be easily purchased. Equipment and materials investments may be very cost effective over the long run.

Some of the methods of overhead transparency production include:

1. *Hand-prepared transparencies directly on acetate.* The user may apply grease pencils; fine- and broad-tip felt pens in a variety of colors, and either permanent or water-based; transparent, color, dry-transfer letters; or transparent color tape on sheets of clear or tinted acetate or plastic. Most permanent-ink, felt-tip pens will adhere to acetate, but if the ink is opaque, the pen markings may project as black rather than the expected color. Test the results of pens and pencils before investing a great deal of time creating transparencies that may not have the desired results.

   Most water-soluble pens do not adhere to acetate, but special water-soluble pens are available from supply houses which *can* be used on acetate. The advantage to this type of pen is that the material on the transparency can be easily erased by wiping with a damp cloth.

   It is especially important that users of rolls of acetate on the overhead projector be aware of the permanency of the pen they are using. Permanent inks are very difficult to remove from acetate, and unless the user intends to retain the whole roll of acetate for reuse, grease pencils or water-soluble pens should be used.

2. *Diazo.* This process produces brilliantly colored transparencies, but it is rarely used because other processes are much less time consuming. Diazo transparencies are prepared by placing diazo film

on a master and exposing the film to ultraviolet light, then exposing the film to ammonia vapor.

3. *Picture transfer lift*. In this process, clay-based color or black-and-white magazine pictures, printed on clay-coated paper, are applied face down to a clear, adhesive-backed acetate using a roller, laminating machine, or dry-mount press to obtain a tight seal. After the acetate-covered picture is soaked in water for a few minutes, the paper is peeled away from the acetate, upon which the picture now remains. Without the paper backing, the acetate-backed picture is now translucent, and can be projected on an overhead projector.

    Most popular magazines are produced with clay-coated paper, so this technique offers a quick and easy way to create overhead transparencies, especially for coverage of current events.

4. *Dye transfer*. A spirit duplicating machine is used to transfer the image from a master to frosted acetate. The product is then sprayed with clear lacquer to make it transparent.

5. *Thermal process*. This procedure involves putting heat-sensitive film and a master prepared with india ink, soft-lead pencil, good typewriter ribbon, or black printing ink through a thermal copier, such as the Thermofax. Images from the master are transferred onto the acetate by the heat of the thermal process.

6. *High-contrast photograph*. Utilizing high-contrast film, processing the negative with high-contrast developer, and enlarging the negative on a large sheet of high-contrast film, the negative can be used as an overhead transparency. A positive transparency can also be prepared, or the diazo process can be used to create duplicate transparencies, in color if desired.

ADDITIONAL RESOURCES

Books

American Assn. of School Librarians, ALA, and Assn. for Educational Media and Technology. *Media Programs District and School*. Chicago: American Library Assn., 1975.

Brown, James W., Richard B. Lewis, and Fred F. Harcleroad. *AV Instruction*. 6th ed. New York: McGraw-Hill, 1983.

Bullard, John R., and Calvin E. Mether. *Audiovisual Fundamentals*. 3rd ed. Dubuque: Wm. C. Brown, 1984.

Green, Lee. *501 Ways to Use the Overhead Projector*. Littleton, Colo.: Libraries Unlimited, 1982.

Heinich, Robert, Michael Molenda, and James D. Russell. *Instructional Media.* 2nd ed. New York: Wiley, 1985.

Kemp, Jerrold E. *Planning and Producing Instructional Media.* 5th ed. New York: Harper, 1985.

National Audio Visual Assn. *Basic Tips on Producing and Using Overhead Transparencies.* Fairfax, Va.: National Audio Visual Assn., 1981.

Overhead Projection Guide. Fiskerville, R.I.: Arkwright, 1980.

Satterthwait, Les. *Graphics, Skills, Media and Materials.* Dubuque: Kendall-Hunt, 1977.

Sparks, Jerry D. *Overhead Projection.* Englewood Cliffs, N.J.: Educational Technology Pub., 1981.

Thomas, James L. *Nonprint Production for Students, Teachers and Media Specialists.* Littleton, Colo.: Libraries Unlimited, 1982.

Thompson, Anthony H. *Guide to the Production and Use of Audio-Visual Aids in Library and Information Science Teaching.* Paris: Unesco, 1983.

Journal Articles

Anderson, Donald, and Catherine Lumbattis. "Development of Instructional Strategies for Large Group Instruction Accounting Classes." *Journal of Business Education* 59 (Nov. 1983): 56–65.

Bohning, Gerry. "Teaching with Transparencies." *Voc Ed* 59 (Aug. 1984): 38–39.

Boswell, D. A. "Evaluation of Transparencies for Psychology Instruction." *Teaching of Psychology* 7 (Oct. 1980): 171–73.

Hall, Candace Catlin. "Use of a Type Size Transparency in School Libraries and Media Centers." *Education of the Visually Handicapped* 11 (Winter 1979–80): 112–17.

Johnson, Roger. "Overhead Projectors—Basic Media for a Community College." *Audiovisual Instruction* 23 (Mar. 1978): 21–22.

Jones, J. Rhodri. "Getting the Most Out of an Overhead Projector." *English Language Teaching Journal* 32 (Apr. 1978): 194–201.

Kunka, Robert L., and Alice Kirkman Kunka. "The Use of Overhead Transparencies in Pharmacy Education." *American Journal of Pharmaceutical Education* 47 (Spring 1982): 68–70.

Locker, Kitty. "Teaching with Transparencies." *ABCA Bulletin* 40 (Sept. 1977): 21–27.

McCormack, Alan J. "A Method for Making Color-Lift Transparencies." *American Biology Teacher* 44 (Jan. 1982): 40–41.

Marie Bruce Bruni

ch. 14

Pamphlets

THE MEDIUM

Definition

A pamphlet is a brief treatment of a subject issued as a separate publication, most often with a binding of paper set flush with the pages. It is an "occasional" publication which often represents the most recent and/or current information available on a subject. Pamphlets are not intended to be exhaustive in coverage, but supply the user with specific information.

Brief History

The word *pamphlet*, as we know it today, was first used in the 14th century to distinguish a short booklet from a book. Originally, the word comes from "Pamphilus, seu de Amore," a Latin poem published in this form in the 1100s. The primary purpose of pamphlets was to distribute material on topical issues of a polemical and propagandist nature. Their popularity increased after the invention of the printing press and they began to circulate throughout Europe.

During the religious controversies of the 1500s, pamphlets were widely used in England, France, and Germany. Martin Luther was an early and effective user of pamphlets. The use of pamphlets spread, and they were utilized by authors during the Elizabethan Age and in

France by critics of the government. By 1660, at the time of the Restoration in England, pamphlets had lost ground to newspapers and periodicals, but they again became important as political weapons during the Glorious Revolution of 1688. Pamphlets were widely used in the 1700s in the United States, primarily for political purposes. The 1800s saw a continued use of pamphlets in Europe and America, mostly on political themes.

Although few pamphlets have achieved lasting literary merit, there are notable exceptions. John Milton's *Areopagitica*, Thomas Paine's *Common Sense*, Hamilton, Jay, and Madison's *The Federalist Papers*, and Edmund Burke's *Reflections on the Revolution in France* are but a few.

The 1900s have brought a change in the use of pamphlets. Although still used for partisan propaganda on many occasions, their content has changed primarily to information on topical concerns.

Unique Characteristics

Pamphlets are inexpensive, or free, and proliferate in today's society. Since they cover such a broad range of subjects, when pamphlets of general interest are found, they can be ordered in quantity and given away to users.

Advantages and Disadvantages

Pamphlets are relatively inexpensive, or free, and provide current information to update other sources. Often pamphlets give concise information on one topic. On the other hand, they can explore one topic in depth, if required.

Large numbers of pamphlets can be obtained for free distribution. Since pamphlets are relatively inexpensive to produce, groups can compile information that will be of local interest to a community. Pamphlets are easily gathered at meetings, conventions, and institutions, making them readily accessible to a growing collection.

Pamphlets have frequently caused problems in information centers because of their disadvantages. Pamphlets are usually unbound, or bound with a soft cover, and come in a multitude of shapes and sizes, making them difficult to shelve. There are few centralized sources for pamphlet acquisitions, even though a few pamphlet jobbers exist. Ordering, classifying, and weeding pamphlets is labor intensive, and a collection requires a vigorous and regular weeding program to cull out-of-date material since it is often of temporary value.

Information on the organization of pamphlets has largely been ignored; consequently, little is available. Cataloging is usually by broad subject classification, making bibliographic access difficult. Vertical files are often overstocked and are difficult to manipulate. Users may be reluctant to use materials stashed away in file drawers. When pamphlets are stored in piles, instead of files, access becomes difficult if it is necessary to sort through a large mass. If pamphlets are filed out of sight of the user, he or she may not think of them as a source of information. Or, if pamphlets are thought of, they may not be easily located.

Another problem with pamphlets is that they are easily stolen. Frequently the most interesting will "disappear" from a collection. Finally, paper used for pamphlets is often acidic or of poor quality, contributing to a fast deterioration.

SELECTION

Special Criteria

1. Pamphlet material should be factually accurate.
2. Choose a variety of viewpoints on controversial topics.
3. Staff should not spend more time on acquisition than a pamphlet is worth.
4. During selection, consider whether the pamphlet is necessary, and whether it adds something to the collection not just as easily accessible in a book or periodical.
5. Avoid anonymous pamphlets.

Evaluative Review Sources

PERIODICALS
Booklist
U*N*A*B*A*S*H*E*D* Librarian

BOOKS
Gotsick, Priscilla, et al. *Information for Everyday Survival: What You Need and How to Get It*. Chicago: American Library Assn., 1976.
Newsome, Walter L. *New Guide to Popular Government Publications for Libraries and Home Reference*. Littleton, Colo.: Libraries Unlimited, 1978.

Nonevaluative Sources

Titles listed below represent publications since 1970:

PERIODICALS

*Consumer Information Catalog: A Catalog of Selected Federal Publications
of Consumer Interest*
Library Journal
Monthly Catalog of United States Government Publications
Monthly Checklist of State Publications
Public Affairs Information Service Bulletin
*Sources: A Guide to Print and Nonprint Materials Available from Organiza-
tions, Industry, Government Agencies, and Specialized Publishers*
Vertical File Index

BOOKS

*Alternatives in Print: An International Catalog of Books, Pamphlets,
Periodicals, and Audiovisual Materials.* San Francisco: Glide, 1971– .
Annual.
Educator's Guide to Free Guidance Material. Randolph, Wis.: Educators' Prog-
ress Service. Annual.
*Educator's Guide to Free Health, Physical Education and Recreational
Materials.* Randolph, Wis.: Educators' Progress Service. Annual.
Educator's Guide to Free Science Materials. Randolph, Wis.: Educators' Prog-
ress Service. Annual.
Educator's Guide to Free Social Studies Materials. Randolph, Wis.: Educators'
Progress Service. Annual.
Educator's Guide to Free Teaching Aids. Randolph, Wis.: Educators' Prog-
ress Service. Annual.
Educator's Index of Free Materials. Randolph, Wis.: Educators' Progress Ser-
vice. Annual.
Free and Inexpensive Learning Materials. Nashville: George Peabody College
for Teachers. Biennial.
United States. National Center of Child Abuse and Neglect. *Catalog of NCCAN
Publications.* Washington: U.S. Government Printing Office, 1983.
──────. National Clearinghouse of Alcohol Information. *Publications Order
Form.* Rockville, Md.: U.S. Government Printing Office, 1983.
──────. National Clearinghouse for Drug Abuse Information. *Publications
Listing.* Kensington, Md.: U.S. Government Printing Office, 1983.
──────. Small Business Administration. *Free Management Assistance Publica-
tion.* Fort Worth: U.S. Government Printing Office, 1980– .
United States Geological Survey. *Popular Publications of the U.S. Geological
Survey.* Alexandria, Va.: U.S. Government Printing Office, 1967– .
Van Zant, Nancy P. *Selected U.S. Government Series.* Chicago: American Li-
brary Assn., 1978.

Other Sources

Many popular periodicals can supplement these sources. Examples are:

Good Housekeeping's "The Better Way."
Changing Times: The Kiplinger Magazine, "Things to Write For."
Byte, "Reader Service."
Saturday Evening Post, "The Post Reader Service Center."

These are just a few of the many periodicals that offer pamphlets in a regular column. Don't stop there, because pamphlet sources can occur almost anywhere in a periodical—as part of a feature story, a regular column, or even in advertisements. Be on the lookout everywhere for sources for pamphlets.

MAINTENANCE AND MANAGEMENT

Storage and Care

Pamphlets have been housed in both open and closed file boxes which are interfiled with books on the shelf. They have also been housed in file cabinets.

Interfiling with books is advocated by staff, who also favor the same classification system for all materials in the institution. Not only pamphlets, but all nonbook materials (films, tapes, slides, etc.) are interfiled. There are some disadvantages to this system, such as:

All items must be cataloged.

Emphasis on specifics is no longer possible. "Fineness" of identification, which is unique to so many pamphlets, is lost.

For most institutions, it is physically and economically impossible to disperse pamphlets to exact positions among books. A determination of housing one or two pamphlets in a box, or having them bound, must be made. Consideration must also be given for pamphlets dealing with the same subject that will be added regularly.

Segregated housing of pamphlets is usually the preferred method of storage. They are placed in folders and then into filing cabinets. Because the method is simple and can be applied to all sizes of pamphlets, consistency is maintained. This also speeds the addition of new materials to the file.

It is important that the cabinet be of heavy steel construction, with blocks or compressors to keep individual folders erect. Suspension folders are best. They are suspended from tracks which are easily installed in standard file drawers. Because the folder glides on tracks along both sides of the drawer, filing is greatly simplified and expedited. All identifying tabs remain at eye level, so that folders are easily found.

Should pamphlets be shelved, either with books or separate from them, pamphlet boxes must be provided to prevent the loss of the smaller ones. These boxes should be labeled with major subject heading or classification number. In some cases, the contents of the box may be listed on it.

If pamphlets are stored in a special area, it should be located near the circulation department and be easily accessible.

An unbound publication suffers more from exposure to sunlight, artificial light, and air than a bound one. It is also more sensitive to dust and handling, and more easily removed from the institution or lost. Therefore, a valuable pamphlet may warrant binding. One must be careful, however, to avoid binding pamphlets with acidic materials, as acid will advance deterioration after a short time.

Institutions circulating unbound pamphlets should provide manila envelopes to protect them.

Management Problems and Solutions

Pamphlets can provide information that is current and sometimes available nowhere else. In order to do that, however, the organization and maintenance of the file requires an investment of time and staff. The first thing to consider is the ordering of pamphlets and how it will be done. Use of a jobber may be considered, or acquisitions may be assigned to one staff member. It is necessary to develop a procedure to be used if the ordering is done by a staff member. Perhaps the simplest method is a postcard with a standardized format for routine free requests. It saves a great deal of time and postage.

Some pamphlet sources may require a different procedure, such as a letter and SASE to get a pamphlet, or inclusion of a small charge, but this may be dealt with as the need arises. If the pamphlets being requested are issued regularly, it would be advantageous to be on a mailing list for future publications.

Jobbers will not always accept orders for free publications, and others often take an extremely long time to receive. Since pamphlets are free, inexpensive, and often of dated value, the time invested in acquiring, cataloging, and storing them should not exceed their worth.

It is best to assign responsibility for the pamphlet collection to one individual, to provide continuity and organization. Current and continuing sources of information for pamphlets should be maintained in a file, such as a 3 by 5 inch card file, so that sources can be added or deleted as necessary. As pamphlets are ordered, a simple system of noting title of pamphlet, cost (if any), sources, and date ordered may be written on a 3 by 5 card and kept in a separate outstanding order file. When the material is received, the card can be discarded. (There are varying opinions as to whether records of orders should be kept, but records can avoid duplication of efforts in an area that can quickly become labor intensive for something of passing value.)

Once material has been received, the easiest and most frequently used method of cataloging is by subject category. Subject headings can be broad or specific, depending on the nature of the pamphlet and its intended usage. The pamphlet collection is generally housed in file folders and arranged alphabetically in file cabinets, with a separate subject index to provide easier access. Copies of this index should also be available at other locations within the institution so that the files and their contents are easily accessible to the users.

Other methods of storage include boxes, binders, and filing directly on shelves with books. Boxes are often cumbersome—and tend to be overlooked and stacked somewhere difficult to get to. Binders are not always appropriate because of the varying sizes and formats of pamphlets, as well as poor quality of paper in many pamphlets. Interfiling with book stock often becomes complicated because it requires full cataloging for access, and many pamphlets are difficult if not impossible to catalog. Additionally, their different sizes make them easy to misplace, difficult to shelve, and hard to locate.

Pamphlets and the information they contain can quickly become obsolete, so it is necessary to conduct a vigorous and thorough weeding of the collection at least once a year—preferably twice a year, if time permits. Providing users with accurate information should be of primary importance when using pamphlets as sources of information. Pamphlets should also circulate, as do other materials from the collection, for the same amount of time as everything else. Many users find that information contained in pamphlets is easier to use, and they should have the same amount of time to use them as they do other materials.

Depending upon the size of the institution and the size of the pamphlet file, it may become necessary to have more than one file. For example, separate files may be needed for local history, government documents, and generalized collections. It may even be necessary to house them in different locations within the institution.

A regular program of acquisitioning and developing a pamphlet collection should be pursued to provide the institution's users with information that is current, topical, and often not available elsewhere. Not only is it important to develop this collection, but it is just as important to maintain a good subject index for access, for without it, the information is lost. Equally important is allowing the staff to become familiar with the collection, so that it becomes second nature to refer to the pamphlet collection as a source of information.

From the viewpoint of the user, it is necessary to make the pamphlet collection as easily accessible as possible, to override any uncomfortable feelings in approaching it. From the management standpoint, the time invested in developing and maintaining a pamphlet file can be returned many times over, as long as that collection is kept current, the staff knows and uses it, and any barriers for the potential user have been removed. The pamphlet collection can provide an institution with sources of information that make its functioning more efficient, more timely, and more satisfactory to its users.

Other Concerns

Pamphlet files can be quite flexible. Pamphlets are good for supplementing a book collection when there is a temporary surge in demand in specific subject areas.

Pamphlets can be housed with other materials such as leaflets, charts, maps, pictures, newspaper clippings, individual issues of magazines, small paperback books, and other items. It is up to the discretion of the staff to determine if the integration of this material is the easiest method of storing it and making it accessible to users.

ADDITIONAL RESOURCES

Adelman, Jean S., and Mildred S. Myers. "Pamphlets." *Encyclopedia of Library and Information Science*. Vol. 21. New York: Marcel Dekker, 1977.

Bator, Eileen. "Automating the Vertical File Index." *Special Libraries* 71 (Nov. 1980): 485–91.

Bernhardt, Frances S. *Introduction to Library Technical Services*. New York: H. W. Wilson, 1979.

Brodus, R. N. *Selecting Materials for Libraries*. 2nd ed. New York: H.W. Wilson, 1981.

Cabeceiras, James. *The Multimedia Library*. New York: Academic Pr., 1978.

Clinton, A. *Printed Ephemera: Collection, Organisation, and Access*. London: Bingley, 1981.

Condit, Lester. *A Pamphlet about Pamphlets*. Chicago: University of Chicago Pr., 1939.

Dean, J. F. "In-House Processing of Paperbacks and Pamphlets," *Serials Review* 7 (Oct. 1981): 81–85.

Ford, Stephen. *Acquisition of Library Materials*. Chicago: American Library Assn., 1973.

Gronlund, M. "Pamphlets—A Question of Format." *U*N*A*B*A*S*H*E*D Librarian* 42 (May 1982): 9–10.

"Have You Tried the Vertical File?" *Georgia Librarian* 19 (May 1982): 9–10 + .

Ireland, Norma Olin. *The Pamphlet File in School, College and Public Libraries*. Boston: F. W. Faxon, 1954.

Katz, William A. *Collection Development: The Selection of Materials for Libraries*. New York: Holt, Rinehart and Winston, 1980.

Kouns, Betty. "Clippings and Sweet Talk for Free Information." *Library Journal* 104 (Apr. 15, 1979): 897.

Landau, Thomas, ed. *Encyclopedia of Librarianship*. 3rd rev. ed. New York: Hafner, 1966.

Lerner, F. "Classified Vertical File." *U*N*A*B*A*S*H*E*D* Librarian* 26 (1978): 3–4.

Miller, Shirley. *The Vertical File: A Handbook of Acquisition, Processing, and Organization*. 2nd ed. Littleton, Colo.: Libraries Unlimited, 1979.

Moon, I. B. "Free and Inexpensive Materials." *Collection Building* 3 (1981): 67–73.

Reid, David. "Ephemera and Local Studies." *New Library World* 80 (Spring 1979): 174–76.

Reisinger, C., and R. J. Barth. "To Build or Not to Build: Planning and Building a Resources File." *Illinois Libraries* 61 (Oct. 1979): 702–5.

Reynolds, Judith. "Pamphlets in Public Libraries: A Survey of Selection and Handling." *Wisconsin Library Bulletin* 75 (May 1979): 133–35.

Schleicher, Linda. "Pamphlets Find New Home." *Wyoming Library Roundup* 35 (Jan. 1980): 57–58.

Schweibish, Gertrude F. "We Sell Pamphlets." *U*N*A*B*A*S*H*E*D* Librarian* 18 (1976): 29.

Shaffer, Dale Eugene. *The Pamphlet Library: Use of the Sha-Frame System*. Salem, Ohio: Shaffer, 1972.

Sheperd, Leslie. *The History of Street Literature*. Detroit: Singing Tree Pr., 1973.

Spencer, M. D. "Pamphlet Collection Development." *Bookmark* 41 (Winter 1983): 91–98.

Swartzburg, S. G. "Preservation of Pamphlets." *U*N*A*B*A*S*H*E*D* Librarian* 28 (1978): 5.

Tarlton, S. M. "Give Those Freebies the Attention They Deserve." *South Carolina Librarian* 25 (Fall 1981): 10–11.

Taylor, Mary. *School Library and Media Acquisitions Policies and Procedures*. Phoenix: Oryx Pr., 1981.

Thorpe, Stephen. "Leaflets for Information." *Library Association Record* 83 (Sept. 1981): 434–35.

Vickers, S. C. J., and D. N. Wood. "Improving the Availability of Grey Literature." *Interlending Review* 10 (Oct. 1982): 125–30.

Woodbury, M. L. "Free Materials and Their Costs." In *Selecting Materials for Instruction*, vol. 2. Littleton, Colo.: Libraries Unlimited, 1980.

Lee David Jaffe

ch. 13

Phonograph Records

THE MEDIUM

Definition

The phonograph record has taken a half-dozen distinct forms in its long history, and time and popularity have contributed to a general confusion of terminology. As used in this chapter, the term *phonograph record* includes any format that consists of a turning surface with a wave-form groove which vibrates a stylus to produce sound. This covers all the cylinder and disc formats of various speeds, sizes, and materials. Each applies the same basic principle for sound recording and reproduction.

Phonograph, *gramophone,* and *record* are common terms for the phonograph record. Technically, *phonograph* refers to the cylinder format and *gramophone* to the disc. *Record* is an abbreviation of either phonograph record or recording.

The different formats are identified by their playing speed, playing time, and size. Each may be known by several different names.

The currently produced formats are the 7- and 12-inch, microgroove phonograph records. The 12-inch disc is commonly called an *LP*, for "long playing," or a *thirty-three*, for 33⅓ revolutions per minute (rpm), the speed at which it is played. The 7-inch disc is usually called a *single* because it has room for one song on each side, or a *forty-five,* as in 45 rpm.

236

A phonograph record player or phonograph is also called a *changer* or *turntable*, depending upon features and the mood of the marketing department. They are basically the same device: a platter turning at a specified rate and an arm positioning a playing stylus on the phonograph record's surface. Players vary greatly in features and in the configuration of their parts.

The phonograph record rides on a turning *platter*, and the disc's center hole a spindle. *Stylus* has replaced *needle* (it was once a cactus thorn) as the term for the part that rides inside the phonograph record groove. The stylus is connected to an electromagnetic cartridge, or pickup, which translates the vibration into weak electrical signals. The cartridge rides over the disc at the end of a tone arm, which positions the stylus on the phonograph record, ensures even and exact pressure of the stylus in the groove, and serves as a conduit for the wires from the cartridge to the amplifier.

Brief History

EARLY YEARS

Thomas Edison is commonly credited with inventing the phonograph record in 1877. However, Charles Cros, a French inventor, described the device in a paper he delivered earlier that same year. That Edison chose *phonograph*—Cros' term—for his talking machine and that he may have had access to Cros' writing raise questions about Edison's claim.[1]

The argument may be moot since a prototype of the phonograph was built and in use twenty years earlier. Leon Scott developed the "phonauthograph" in 1857 to study sound waves. Using a megaphone with a bristle attached to its narrow end to scratch lines on a rotating cylinder, Scott recorded sound waves visually.[2]

Edison was awarded a patent in 1878 for his cylinder phonograph player. His original machine used a rotating cylinder, covered with tin foil to record the sound, and a sharp needle attached to the narrow end of a cone to etch and replay the groove. Wax later replaced tin, allowing recordings to be erased with a sharp blade, and molded shellac superseded was to permit mass production.

In 1888, Emil Berliner patented the Gramophone, a record player using discs. After an initial period of chaos, the playing speed was stan-

1. Gerald Gibson, "Sound Recordings," in Pearse S. Grove, ed., *Nonprint Media in Academic Libraries* (Chicago: American Library Assn., 1975), 79–80.
2. "Sound Recording, Transmission and Reproduction," in *New Grove Dictionary of Music and Musicians* (London: Macmillan, 1980).

dardized at 78 revolutions per minute and the needle was made to move from the outside edge to the center. The Gramophone eventually succeeded Edison's player as the machine of choice.

Acoustical recording suffered from the limited tonal range and instrumentation it could record. For instance, piano could not be recorded convincingly. Despite this drawback, a respectable selection of music was available on disc by 1925.[3]

The infant technology began to make changes in the music world. Recording greatly increased the music that people heard. In the days before radio, phonograph records were the major source of music for many people. Recordings of historical importance were made and preserved for posterity. Performances could now be repeated, studied, compared, and copied. Performers realized additional fame and income through record sales.

The phonograph record made music into an industry which formed the core of today's entertainment industry. The early phonograph record companies—Columbia, Victor, Deutche Grammophon Gesellschaft, EMI, and Pathe—would later move into filmmaking, radio, television, publishing, electronics, and computers. These original phonograph record companies are still at the heart of that industry.

ELECTRONIC ERA

Some of the phonograph record's sound quality problems were answered when microphones and amplification, technologies spun off from radio, came to recording. A wider range of instrumentation could be recorded with better balance among the instruments. The new technology rendered the body of existing recordings obsolete.

LONG-PLAYING RECORDS

Introduction in 1948 of long-playing, microgroove phonograph records, made of durable polyvinyl chloride, solved two of the medium's greatest limitations: the 78 rpm disc was made of brittle shellac, and had a playing time of less than 5 minutes. Vinyl has the added advantage of extreme smoothness, reducing surface noise in playing.

Columbia Records marketed a 12-inch, 33⅓ rpm disc, and RCA Victor followed with a 7-inch, 45 rpm format. The 20-minute per side Columbia disc—called the *LP*, for "long-playing"—won the day, with the 45 regulated to shorter, pop music.

3. "Gramophone," in *New Grove Dictionary of Music and Musicians* (London: Macmillan, 1980).

TAPE RECORDING

Magnetic tape, though invented shortly after the phonograph record, became available for studio production only after World War II. Previously, performances were recorded directly on a disc which could not be edited or altered. Tape permitted more flexibility in the studio, extending what could be recorded and what could be done with it.[4] Finished tapes can be transferred to disc after studio editing.

STEREO, QUADRAPHONIC, AUDIOPHILE, AND DIGITAL

Stereophonic records were introduced in 1957. The advantage of stereo is a more natural reproduction of concert hall ambience, and it has become the standard mode of recording in all sound formats. Stereo requires two amplifiers (usually housed together) and two speakers or special headphones.

Quadraphonic sound, introduced in the early 1970s, tried to go stereo two steps better with simulated reflected sound adding front and back to stereo's left and right. The phonograph record-buying public apparently did not believe that the doubtful benefits justified the extra cost. Problems with establishing an industry standard added to consumers' hesitation. Few phonograph records were issued in "quad," and it died quietly.

Audiophile phonograph records are specially recorded and mastered (or "pressed") to produce a higher-quality disc. Special pressings have been made from the beginning, but the most recent technique is a response to competition from other sound-recording media. Direct-to-disc recording, remastering, half-speed mastering, precision stamps, special vinyl formulations, and limited pressings amount to going back and doing it right the second time, since the recipients of these ministrations tend to be tried and true popular hits. The audiophile phonograph records appear to be an effort to squeeze the final bit of capability from the phonograph record and hold on to the market.

Digital recording appeared in the 1970s. As far as the phonograph record is concerned, digital is a studio technique. While a performance or a new audiophile master may be recorded digitally on tape, the material will be translated to analog signals for phonograph record release. The digitally recorded master imparts better fidelity to the final, analog phonograph record, which is labeled as a *digital disc.*

Noise reduction, once thought unnecessary for phonograph records, was introduced recently as a response to the increasing sound quality of cassette tapes and the formidable challenge of compact discs.

---

4. Brian Eno, "The Studio as a Compositional Tool" (unpublished lecture).

As with quadraphonic sound, the public has not responded warmly because of questionable benefits and additional costs. It has not caught on and its future is in doubt.

PROGNOSIS AND SPECULATION
The phonograph is more than 100 years old, and in that time it has changed most of its features. The original phonograph record and player have little in common with their modern counterparts. It has also changed the way we produce and listen to music. Once a curiosity, it has become one of the most prominent features of our culture.

The phonograph record set a very tough standard against which other sound-recording media would be measured and, until recently, rejected. The recent emergence of strong competitors is a signal that they have met, and perhaps surpassed, that standard.

At stages in its development, the phonograph offered improvements worth the cost and inconvenience of retooling and replacing the existing collections and equipment. The change to disc, then to the vinyl LP, and most recently to stereo were marked by nothing less than a turnover of the repertoire. Neither quadraphonic sound, nor noise reduction, nor audiophile quality was sufficient inducement to warrant the wholesale abandonment of existing collections and equipment that followed more significant innovations.

It is the cassette tape and compact disc that are experiencing the boom that the phonograph record enjoyed in the past. The momentum is apparently with these other formats. This has been aided by the availability of studio tape masters, which were used to produce phonograph records and can just as easily serve the other formats.

It would be too easy, and probably irresponsible, to pronounce the doom of such a long-lived and capable medium as the phonograph. We cannot rule out a technological rescue (though the smart money would have it going the other way). Whatever may happen, the phonograph record will survive. The investment in collections and equipment, especially production equipment, cannot be easily dismissed. However, the phonograph record's commercial future will be a lot more limited than its past.

Unique Characteristics

The phonograph record is the only recording medium that uses mechanical vibrations to record and reproduce sound, and it is the only sound-recording medium whose equipment is not portable.

Some companies are marketing portable phonograph record players—units small and light enough to be carried easily, but not capable of playing a disc while moving. Functionally, the phonograph record is not portable.

In recording, a cutting stylus carves the phonograph record surface. Reversing the process, the playing stylus passes down the cut groove and transmits the ensuing vibration to the amplifier. Despite many changes in records and players, the stylus and groove are basic to the phonograph.

The stylus-and-groove technology sets limits on the phonograph record's capability, including making them extremely sensitive to movement. Motion changes the stylus' contact with the groove, possibly causing it to jump out of the groove entirely. Even vibrations in supporting surfaces or the surrounding air can be added to the recorded signals and affect sound quality.

Advantages

The phonograph owes its popularity and commercial success to good sound quality, a wide selection of titles, and reasonable prices. Institutional collectors look for the same qualities, but may also be interested in characteristics of no interest to the average consumer. These may include:

Permanence. The inability of the phonograph to record may have hurt it in the marketplace, but re-recordability is rarely an advantage to a phonograph record collection. In fact, the permanence of the medium is an advantage.

Random access. Selections can be played in any order and repeated without first listening to the adjacent material. Visible bands on the phonograph record help locate selections. Some turntables can locate and play selections automatically. For students, researchers, lecturers, or demonstrators interested in specific selection, this attribute is an advantage. Phonograph records can also be played linearly.

Availability. More recorded material is available on phonograph records than on any other audio medium. Time has also helped build a repertoire of size and historic importance far greater than other media can offer. The implications for the selector are obvious: the phonograph record format offers more opportunity for collection building.

Cost. The phonograph has a slight price advantage over cassette tapes and a sizable advantage over compact discs. However, phonograph record prices are increasing faster than cassette prices, and the cost of turntables is rising while the price of a cassette deck is decreasing.[5]

5. U.S. Bureau of the Census, *Statistical Abstract of the United States, 1984* (Washington, D.C.: Superintendent of Documents, 1984), 226, 777.

There are cost considerations other than unit price. The amount and kind of use a collection receives affect the long-term costs and the soundness of the investment. Phonograph records can be expected to give less use, and therefore value, in circulating collections.

Fidelity. The phonograph record offers excellent sound production. Though it has been challenged in this area recently, its sound quality can still be ranked among its advantages.

Familiarity. The phonograph is a common technology, familiar and nonthreatening. It can be introduced in a wide variety of settings.

Installed base. The turntables and records already in homes and institutions give the phonograph inertia. The investment in existing collections and equipment cannot be ignored. Also, the great sound collections are still on phonograph records.

Production threshold. The equipment for mastering and manufacturing phonograph records is simple and cheap enough to allow a small cottage industry to operate and release out-of-the-mainstream material into the market. This ease of access, which has brought us the earlier ethnic and folk recording booms, promises that future small and startup efforts will be available on phonograph records.

Disadvantages

Fragility. The sensitivity of phonograph records to poor handling (detailed in "Storage and Care") is a big disadvantage.

Ease of use. Largely because of its handling requirements, the phonograph record is less easy to use than other audio formats. This is a disadvantage especially in collections used by children and those with physical disabilities.

Playing time. The upward limit on a phonograph record's playing time is set by its diameter, turning speed, and groove size, which are standard. Cassette tape and compact disc have longer playing times, allowing greater capacity and flexibility in recorded material.

Nonportability. Phonograph records cannot be played while moving. For institutions, portability is not a direct concern, but users may prefer formats which can be played in a wider variety of settings.

Dead-end technology. If the phonograph record has inertia, the competition has momentum. We can expect few significant improvements in phonograph record technology, while the competition promises many. This could affect availability of material on record. Phonograph record and turntable sales are already falling while cassette and compact disc sales are climbing.[6]

6. Ibid.

SELECTION

Special Criteria

Phonograph records serve a wide variety of purposes and audiences. Accordingly, the resources used in selection are of three general types: general catalogs, subject-oriented listings, and guides relating to specific purposes.

There is to date no comprehensive listing of phonograph record releases. While the *Schwann* and *Phonolog* guides may be the best general catalogs available, they are limited in coverage and accuracy. With the *AACR2* and MARC formats for sound recordings only recently established, the major bibliographic utilities are far behind in providing the needed access.

Subject-oriented listings dominate the resources available to phonograph record selectors. These focus almost exclusively on musical programs. Review sources cover music from every possible perspective, with classical and pop recordings receiving the most attention. Specialty publications pick up the slack in other areas.

For professionals such as educators, trainers, and librarians organizing collections and programs, sources are limited in coverage and currency. The mainstay National Information Center for Educational Media's *Index to Educational Records* was last issued in 1980, and even that is out of print. (A new edition is promised.) Some areas have no guide, or only hopelessly out-of-date special resources are available. Coverage of phonograph records in the library literature is embarrassingly spare.

With the exception of the United Kingdom and Germany, access to information about foreign releases is very difficult. "Small press" phonograph record companies may occasionally get some of their releases listed or reviewed in major selection tools, but generally they rely on specialty publications covering their subject area or on promotional mailings. Ralph Records maintains a computerized bulletin board called "Big Brother." Unlike some other media, previews of phonograph records are rarely available.

Against this backdrop of meager resources is the daunting task of sifting through the enormous output of a popular medium.[7] The emergence in the last decade of two strong competitors in the sound-recording field further complicates the responsibility for selecting phonograph records. As the cassette tape and compact disc continue to show increasing strength in the consumer market, the process will probably become more complicated and difficult.

7. Ibid., 226.

Before anything else, consider the appropriateness of the material to the collection. The next criteria is to establish the aptness or usefulness of the program in the form of a sound recording. In fact, very little is recorded which will not find a place in some collection or another, but whether it should be selected for a particular collection is another matter. The last determination is which of the three available audio formats from which to select the material.

Selection of phonograph records is now extremely prejudiced by the availability of cassette tapes and compact discs. Obviously, when a title is offered in only one format, or the selector is able to buy one of each or is limited to single format, the issue is much simpler. For most current titles, however, selectors usually have a choice of three formats offering exactly the same material. The key often is the intended audience and use.

Select a phonograph record over a cassette tape for teaching and demonstration use or when excellent sound quality is required and when portability and special handling needs (as with disabled people) are not at issue. Select a phonograph record over a compact disc when users are expected to provide their own playback equipment and, again, when portability is not needed.

Select a phonograph record over a cassette and a compact disc when price is a consideration, when you are reasonably certain of being able to protect the collection, and when familiarity with the medium is important.

Evaluative Review Sources

PERIODICALS

Absolute Sound
American Music
American Record Guide
Audio
Billboard
Black Music and Jazz Review
Bluegrass Unlimited
Blues Link
Blues Unlimited
Booklist
*Cadence: The American Review
    of Blues and Jazz*
*Canadian Composer/Compositeur
    Canadien*
Cash Box
Circus Magazine

Clavier
Coda
Creem
Down Beat
Early Music
English Dance and Song
Ethnomusicology
Fanfare
Folk Music Journal
Folk Review
Gramophone
Guitar Player
Hi-Fi News and Record Review
High Fidelity
JEMF Quarterly
Jazz Journal International

Journal of American Folklore
Keyboard
Library Journal
Melody Maker
Music and Musicians
Music Journal
Musical Times
Musician
New Records
Notes: Quarterly Journal of Music Library Association
Opera Journal
Opera News
Opera Quarterly

Ovation
Record
Record Collector
Record Review
Records in Review
Rolling Stone
School Library Journal
Sing Out! Folk Song Magazine
Spin
Stereo Review
VOYA: Voice of Youth Advocates
Wilson Library Bulletin
Young Children

BOOKS

Bookspan, Martin. *Consumer's Union Reviews Classical Recordings.* Mount Vernon, N.Y.: Consumer's Union, 1978.

Fox, Charles, Peter Gammond, and Alun Morgan. *Jazz on Record: A Critical Guide.* Westport, Conn.: Greenwood Pr., 1978.

Gambaccini, Paul, and Susan Ready, comp. *Rock Critics' Choice: The Top 200 Albums.* New York: Quick Fox, 1978.

Greenfield, Edward, Robert Layton, and Ivan March. *The New Penguin Stereo Record and Cassette Guide.* New York: Penguin, 1982.

———. *The Penguin Stereo Record Guide.* 2nd ed. New York: Penguin, 1977.

Harris, Kenn. *Opera Recordings: A Critical Guide.* New York: Drake Pub., 1973.

Harrison, Max, Charles Fox, and Eric Thacker. *The Essential Jazz Records.* Westport, Conn.: Greenwood Pr., 1984.

Lyons, Leonard. *The 101 Best Jazz Albums: A History of Jazz on Records.* New York: Morrow, 1980.

Marsh, Dave, and John Swenson, eds. *The New Rolling Stone Record Guide.* New York: Random House/Rolling Stone Pr., 1983.

———. *The Rolling Stone Record Guide: Reviews and Ratings of Almost 10,000 Currently Available Rock, Pop, Soul, Country, Blues, Jazz, and Gospel Albums.* New York: Random House, 1979.

Opera on Record. Ed. Alan Blyth, discographies compiled by Malcolm Walker. New York: Harper and Row, 1982.

Records in Review. Great Barrington, Mass.: Wyeth Pr., 1955– . Annual.

Tudor, Dean, and Nancy Tudor. *Grass Roots Music.* Littleton, Colo.: Libraries Unlimited, 1979.

INDEXES

Education Index
Jazz Index
Magazine Index

Media Review Digest
Music Index
New York Times Index

Popular Music Periodicals Index
Popular Music Record Reviews
  (or *Annual Index to . . .*)
R.I.L.M. Abstracts
Readers' Guide to Periodical
  Literature

Record and Tape Reviews Index
Record Ratings: Music Library
  Association's Index of Record
  Reviews

Nonevaluative Sources

Titles listed below represent publications since 1970.

PERIODICALS
Gramophone Classical Catalogue
Gramophone Popular Catalogue
Gramophone: Spoken Word and Miscellaneous Catalogue
The New Schwann
Phonolog Reporter

BOOKS
British Music Yearbook. New York: Schirmer, 1975– . Annual.
Brown, Lucy Gregor. *Core Media Collection for Secondary Schools*. 2nd ed. New York: Bowker, 1979.
Cohen, Aaron I. *International Discography of Women Composers*. Westport, Conn.: Greenwood Pr., 1984.
Coover, James B., and Richard Colvig. *Medieval and Renaissance Music on Long-Playing Records: Supplement, 1962–1971*. Detroit: Information Coordinators, 1973.
Delaunay, Charles. *New Hot Discography: The Standard Directory of Recorded Jazz*. Ed. Walter E. Schaap and George Avakian. Hackensack, N.J.: Wehman Brothers, 1966.
Ethnic Recordings in America: A Neglected Heritage. Washington, D.C.: American Folklife Center, Library of Congress, 1982.
Fellers, Frederick P., comp. *The Metropolitan Opera on Record: A Discography of the Commercial Recordings*. Westport, Conn.: Greenwood Pr., 1984.
Find That Tune: An Index to Rock, Folk-Rock, Disco & Soul in Collections. Ed. William Gargan and Sue Sharma. New York: Neal-Schuman, 1984.
Hodgins, Gordon W. *The Broadway Musical: A Complete LP Discography*. Metuchen, N.J.: Scarecrow, 1980.
Hoffmann, Frank W., comp. *The Cash Box Singles Charts, 1950–1981*. Metuchen, N.J.: Scarecrow, 1983.
Indiana University. Archives of Traditional Music. *A Catalog of Phonorecordings of Music and Oral Data Held by the Archives of Traditional Music*. Boston: G. K. Hall, 1975.
International Music & Opera Guide. London: Tantivy Pr.; New York: New York Zoetrope, 1977– . Annual.

Jasen, David A. *Recorded Ragtime*. Hamden, Conn.: Archon Books, 1973.

Johnson, Harry Alleyn, ed. *Ethnic American Minorities: A Guide to Media and Materials*. New York: Bowker, 1976.

Lee, Dorothy Sara. *Native North American Music and Oral Data: A Catalogue of Sound Recordings, 1893–1976*. Bloomington: Indiana Univ. Pr., 1979.

Lynch, Richard Chigley. *Musicals! A Directory of Musical Properties Available for Production*. Chicago: American Library Assn., 1984.

Merriam, Alan P. *African Music on LP: An Annotated Discography*. Evanston, Il.: Northwestern Univ. Pr., 1970.

Moses, Julian Morton. *Collectors' Guide to American Recordings, 1895–1925*. New York: Dover, 1977. (Reprint of 1949 ed.).

Multimedia Materials for Afro-American Studies: A Curriculum Orientation and Annotated Bibliography of Resources. Ed. and comp. Harry Alleyn Johnson. New York: Bowker, 1971.

National Information Center for Educational Media. *Index to Educational Records*. 5th ed. Los Angeles: National Information Center for Educational Media, Univ. of Southern California, 1980.

New York Library Assn. Children's and Young Adult Services Section. *Recordings for Children: A Selected List of Records and Cassettes*. 4th ed., rev. New York: The Section, 1980.

Nite, Norm N. *Rock On: The Illustrated Encyclopedia of Rock n' Roll*. New York: T. Y. Crowell, 1974–78.

Nordquist, Joan. *Audiovisuals for Women*. Jefferson, N.C.: McFarland, 1980.

Pitts, Michael R., and Louis H. Harrison. *Hollywood on Record: The Film Stars' Discography*. Metuchen, N.J.: Scarecrow, 1978.

Recorded Sound. ARS Electronics, 1984.

Roach, Helen Pauline. *Spoken Records*. 3rd ed. Metuchen, N.J.: Scarecrow, 1970.

Rust, Brian A. L. *The American Dance Band Discography, 1917–1942*. New Rochelle, N.Y.: Arlington, 1975.

———. *The Complete Entertainment Discography, from the Mid-1890s to 1942*. New Rochelle, N.Y.: Arlington, 1973.

Sprecher, Daniel. *Guide to Educational Recordings*. Alexandria, Va.: Serina Pr., 1971.

Stahl, Dorothy. *Discography of Solo Song: Supplement, 1975–1982*. Detroit: Information Coordinators, 1984.

———. *A Selected Discography of Solo Song: Supplement, 1971–1974*. Detroit: Information Coordinators, 1976.

Taylor, L. C. *Resources for Learning*. 2nd ed. Harmondsworth, England: Penguin, 1972.

MAINTENANCE AND MANAGEMENT
Storage and Care

NATURE OF PHONOGRAPH RECORDS AND FACTORS AFFECTING THEIR DURABILITY

The life span of a phonograph record depends upon the record itself and the world in which it exists. A record by itself, isolated from the real world of dust, heat, and jelly sandwiches, will last a long time. To those in the business of putting phonograph records into the real world, the question is how to mitigate the damage.

One work is consistently cited as the foundation for all discussion of phonograph record care: *The Preservation and Storage of Sound Recordings*,[8] which presents a detailed analysis of phonograph records and the requirements for effective storage.

Composition of Records

The phonograph record's chemical and physical nature has a direct bearing upon its longevity. Since the phonograph record captures and returns sound by means of a groove exposed on the record's surface, physical changes to the disc affect sound quality and shorten the useful life of the recording.

Under a microscope, a phonograph record's grooves appear as steep canyons, with many irregular turns. Each turn, no matter how subtle, corresponds to a sound. Wearing of the groove removes sound from the recording. Additions to the groove, in the form of dust, smoke particles, and scratches, will produce unwanted sounds.

The flatness of the disc promotes even contact between the playing stylus and the walls of the groove. A warped phonograph record literally throws the stylus upward, sometimes out of the groove, only to be slammed down, with damaging force, at some other point.

Modern phonograph records are made of polyvinyl chloride (PVC). PVC is a thermoplastic, meaning that it is formed, and re-formed, by heat. It expands when heated, but conducts heat poorly. Like many plastics, PVC accumulates and holds static electricity easily.

Pure PVC is not chemically stable, especially in the presence of heat, moisture, oxygen, and ultraviolet light (e.g., sunlight). Added stabilizers inhibit deterioration. The life span of a phonograph record therefore partly depends on retention of the stabilizer.

The plastic is flexible enough to absorb and recover from the stresses applied during playing and gentle mishandling, yet it is so soft that it may be irreparably damaged by even slight carelessness.

Record life also depends on the quality of manufacture and of the materials used in the disc. Poor-quality PVC and filters, residues, and impurities shorten the phonograph record's life. A poorly pressed or mishandled record may be permanently warped, or will skip and not be playable from the first.

---

8. Pickett, A. G., and M. M. Lemcoe, *The Preservation and Storage of Sound Recordings* (Washington, D.C.: Library of Congress, 1959).

Given these conditions, institutions must look to proper storage and care to affect the usable life of their collections. Any record, regardless of the quality of its manufacture, will last its potential lifetime only through proper care.[9]

Harmful Substances and Conditions

Foreign material, heat, moisture, frequent variation of temperature or humidity, physical stress, light, air, and biological agents will damage phonograph records.

Foreign material. Dust and microparticles (including smoke residues) on the surface of a record are the most common problem in record care. Aside from the obvious aural evidence of dust on a record (the pops and clicks you hear), its continued presence will lead to permanent damage to the groove.

The playing stylus accumulates and drags the particles down the groove, carving away its walls and damaging the stylus. Once dust is at the bottom of the groove, it is hard to remove. Dust may also contain chemical reagents, such as acids, which can destabilize or damage the plastic.

Dust is attracted by the static charge on the record. It holds the dust fast, even against attempts at cleaning. The longer a record is in the open, the more dust it will collect. Some cleaning methods push dust deeper into the grooves. Oily fingerprints hold dust to the record. Pressure or rubbing force dust deeper into the grooves.

Heat. While extreme temperatures will melt a record, even moderate heat, such as generated by sunlight, can render a phonograph record unplayable. PVC's high rate of expansion when heated and its low heat conductivity cause the part of the record directly affected to expand while neighboring areas do not, causing warping and shearing of the plastic.

Moisture. Moisture is not a direct threat to stabilized PVC, but it is a medium for other agents. Air pollutants, such as sulphur dioxide, combine with moisture to form acids. Fungi, which feed on older record materials and grow on packaging, benefit from moisture. A dry environment inhibits all of these agents.

Low temperature and humidity. Cold or dryness is not always good for phonograph records. Cold causes the plastic to contract and become brittle, and is often accompanied by high humidity and con-

9. Ibid., 5–52; Myron Berger, "Record Cleaners and the Real World," *High Fidelity* 30 (July 1980): 44–46; B. J. Webb, "Component Interfaces: Stylii/Dirt Grooves," *Audio Amateur* no. 4 (1978): 28–30, 31.

densation on the record and packaging. Cycling of cold and heat results in a contraction/expansion cycle that damages the recording.

A dry environment promotes static, which in turn attracts dust. A constant temperature of 60 to 70° F and relative humidity of 45 to 65% is recommended—also accounting for human comfort in a work environment.[10]

Physical stress. A phonograph record may be damaged through relatively light stress. Leaving a record on an uneven surface, under uneven pressure, or leaning without support will warp it. A phonograph record can be "audibly scratched" by rubbing it against almost any surface. Since such handling may be commonplace, the greatest danger is in the cumulative effect.

Another source of stress is inherent in *playing* the record. A tone arm's few grams translate into hundreds of pounds of pressure per square inch at the tip of the stylus. Rebounding from wall to wall in the grooves, the stylus will reach speeds over 100 miles per hour.

Design of the player and its components and the resilience of polyvinyl chloride mitigate much of this stress. Maladjustment and incompatibility of components will damage a recording at its heart. Wear may not be immediately audible, but it will be progressive and permanent.

Light. Light causes both physical and chemical changes in the record. Ultraviolet light deteriorates PVC. Even stabilized PVC can be damaged by the heat that light generates. Exposure to light should be kept to a minimum.

Air. Oxygen deteriorates PVC. Other chemicals in air are corrosive and will combine with moisture to form acids which will damage stabilized PVC. Exposure to air also promotes the accumulation of dust.

Biological agents. Fungi will grow on record packaging and on food and fingerprints left on the disc by careless handling. The byproducts of these colonies will etch the record. Damage is irreversible. Access to the disc, warmth, humidity, moisture, oxygen, and mishandling promote fungal growth.

CARE AND HANDLING

Phonograph record care involves four areas of activity: shelf storage, handling, playback, and maintenance. Recommended procedures, established in each area, take into account the nature of discs and the environmental hazards. Guidelines for record care can be very simply stated:

---

10. Pickett and Lemcoe, *Preservation and Storage of Sound Recordings,* 7.

Never handle or rub record surfaces.

Keep phonograph records in a cool, dry, smoke-free environment, with constant temperature and humidity control.

Do not expose records to sunlight or air longer than necessary for use.

Clean records before and after use.

Store records in inner sleeves within cardboard jacket.

Records should be stored upright, but not leaning, to prevent warps.

Play records on equipment which is properly adjusted and in good repair.

These basic guidelines will provide for reasonable record life. More detailed guidelines include the following.

Shelf storage. Room temperature and humidity should be constant. Sixty to 70° F and a relative humidity of 65 to 75% are recommended.[11] Smoking should be prohibited in storage areas. Do not place the records in sunlight. Take steps to reduce dust in storage and listening areas. The records should be stored on edge, weighted lightly to prevent warps. Do not pack records tightly.

Retain the original cardboard jacket and inner sleeve for storing phonograph records, but discard plastic "shrink" wrap, which will warp the disc. Always store discs in the inner sleeve and jacket, with the sleeve's opening up, to prevent the record from accidentally falling out and to deter airborne dust from getting at the record. Replace the inner sleeve in the jacket while the record is being played, again for protection from dust.

Lost inner sleeves should be replaced, as well as damaged cardboard jackets and sleeves—not repaired. Plastic outer jackets, while they help preserve the cardboard jacket, do nothing for record care. They may actually promote damage from heat, and the manila inner sleeves are unsuitable.

Handling. Polyvinyl chloride is easily scratched, so great care must be taken whenever handling a disc. Do not touch the record surface. Handle discs by supporting, not gripping, the edge and the paper center label. Do not allow the phonograph record's surface to contact any surface except the packing inner sleeve and the phonograph record player's turntable mat. Other surfaces are likely sources of inadvertent scratches and dust. Do not rub or slide the disc on any surface.

Bow out the sides of the cardboard jacket so that it does not rub the phonograph record's surface during removal and pull the record out by a corner of the inner sleeve. Reach into the inner sleeve and

11. Ibid.

lift the record out, supporting the disc at the edge and label. Place the record on the player by supporting opposite edges. Reverse this procedure to return the record to its packing.[12]

Clean records on removal and again before returning them to their jackets (see "Maintenance," below).

Playback. New lightweight and flexible materials allow the stylus to track the record grooves more accurately and with less wear, but components must be carefully selected, in proper adjustment and good condition. The price of good equipment is an investment in the preservation of the collection.

Maintain equipment regularly. Precise calibration is important. Cartridges should be installed at the factory, or by the retailer or a trained technician. Styli should be examined and cleaned regularly, and worn or damaged styli should be replaced immediately. Other calibrations— tracking weight, skating—which will affect record wear should be checked frequently.

Records should be cleaned before and after playing. Use antistatic mats or conductive brushes to reduce the static electric charge created by cleaning, handling, and playing a disc. Keep the player's cover closed, except to place or remove a record.

Maintenance. "Treating" records, to clean them or to impart or maintain certain characteristics, is controversial. It divides the phonograph record world along the lines of near-religious fervor. There is no definitive answer.[13]

One side maintains that record polyvinyl chloride can be improved upon. It proposes a variety of liquid cleaners, polishers, lubricants, antistatic solutions, and preservatives. Some coat the surface while others bond with and change the chemistry of the PVC. There are dramatic and convincing results from many of these products, but many others are useless and potentially harmful. Choose record-care supplies with great care.

The least-is-best school rejects anything that changes the record chemistry. It says that alcohol-based solutions and detergents remove stabilizers from PVC and accelerate deterioration. Wet-cleaning methods, with the notable exception of the Keith Monks machine, only serve to wash particles to the bottom of the groove and leave mold-promoting moisture.

12. David Ranada, "How to Handle Records," *Stereo Review* 47 (Sept. 1982): 62–63.

13. Berger, "Record Cleaners and the Real World," 44–46; Webb, "Component Interfaces: Stylii/Dirt/Grooves," 28–31; Robert Long, "Record and Tape Care Products That Really *Do* Work," *High Fidelity,* 32 (Nov. 1982): 38–41; "Phonograph Prescriptions: Do They Work?" *High Fidelity* 30 (May 1980): 46–50.

This camp proposes mechanical cleaning and care. Brushes, sometimes dampened with water or solutions, remove dust from the record surface. Ion guns, conductive turntable mats, and carbon fiber brushes bleed off static electricity. Again, tests reveal that certain of these products perform better than others, and some are best left alone.

Each institution will have to adjust cleaning procedures to local conditions—humidity and temperature variation, cleanliness of the storage environment, size of the collection, frequency of use—but regular and thorough cleaning of phonograph records, by whatever means, must be done. Have circulating records, especially prone to mishandling, cleaned on their return. Provide the selected equipment, training, and adequate time for this task.

Repairs to records are rarely effective. Scratches are permanent, though some companies promote products to minimize or eliminate record scratches. Records warped by heat, if the damage is not severe, may be repaired.[14] Records warped by careless storage may be restored to their original condition by simply placing them back in the record rack, between other records, and waiting a few weeks to a few months, depending on the severity of the warp. Some accessories reduce the effect of warps during playing.

Such storage and care guidelines, if not already implemented, should be added to the institution's program at the earliest possible date. Plans for bringing procedures up to standard should be integrated into the development of the institution's program, including the drafting of future budgets, replacement of equipment, selection and design of new facilities, staff training and awareness, user education, and administrative support.

While full implementation may be a remote and frustrating goal, any improvement in handling and storage will have immediate rewards. Many care requirements for phonograph records cost little or nothing. If cleaning equipment is on hand, require that it be used. Rearrange furniture to get record racks away from windows. Have cooling and heating system filters and grates cleaned. Teach staff how to handle discs, and have them instruct users.

The investment in the current and future collection may carry weight in requests for major funding for storage and care. Regardless of how remote such goals may be, do not abandon them. Keep administrators aware of the need. Failure to properly maintain, care for, and store phonograph records renders the process of acquiring, cataloging, and shelving the collection a series of futile activities.

14. Peter Dobbin, ''Waging War on Warps, *High Fidelity* 31 (Nov. 1981): 50–53.

Management Problems and Solutions

This discussion addresses two problems concerning phonograph record collections that are raised (but not answered) elsewhere in this chapter: public access to the collection and changes in the sound-recording industry.

USER ACCESS

The phonograph record's legendary fragility and sensitivity to poor handling present management with a series of problems. At every stage of a phonograph record's life in the collection, from selection to weeding, the medium's susceptibility to damage must be accommodated. Management can respond to most of these problems by implementing the recommendations in the section "Storage and Care."

User access to the collection cannot be resolved with simple mechanical responses. The question pits the two opposing tendencies against each other at a particularly sensitive point: the phonograph record's handling requirements cry out for sequestering the collection, while it is equally compelling to argue that the collection is there to be used.

If staff members are not self-compelled by the need for public access, users may raise the issue. Phonograph records are a very common medium, and users may not take kindly to restrictions. Further, they may have a justified need to browse the collection, to examine individual discs and to listen to them on their own equipment in a setting of their choosing.

Such use makes it virtually impossible for management or staff to maintain the integrity of the collection and safeguard the information it contains. The side for preservation would argue to limit access to the phonograph records as much as local conditions will allow. Close the stacks and do not permit the collection to circulate. Have items, requested from a public catalog, played from the staff area to listening stations in the facility. This ensures that only trained staff members handle discs in a controlled environment, using properly maintained equipment.

This response is based upon a very severe view of the use and value of the collection. It is possible to compromise and still maintain some control. There are many degrees between one extreme and the other. The stacks may be kept closed to the public, to limit handling and permit more control of the storage environment. In-house circulation allows some supervision of use and control of the equipment. Requiring borrowers to be trained before taking phonograph records out of the facility gives the minimal assurance that users know how to handle phonograph records.

Management must find the right balance between access and security for each collection. Local interests and political considerations will almost always be heard. It is the manager's responsibility that collection development and preservation also have a place in the decision.

THE NEW RECORDING INDUSTRY
The shift of the sound-recording industry away from dependence upon the phonograph record, discussed in "Brief History," offers another challenge to management. In production, the phonograph record is now merely another end product, created from the same studio master as its competition. That competition is giving the phonograph record the first real challenge of its career.

The norm several years ago was to release everything on phonograph record and make selected items available on the other formats, after the phonograph record had tested the market. Now, cassettes and compact discs are released on a near-equal footing with the phonograph record. The increased availability of both formats is visible in music stores. Cassette tapes and equipment showed tremendous growth in sales since the late 1970s, while phonograph record and player sales have been declining during the same period.[15]

More significant is the difference in capability and how that may affect content of material released on the rival formats. For example, the cassette release of David Byrne's *The Catherine Wheel* (Sire, 1981), took advantage of tape's longer playing time and contained the full score; the phonograph record release included only the songs.

The phonograph record has been around so long that popular music has been shaped in its image. New music is usually not released until there is enough to fill an LP. Material is excised, if there is not enough room on the phonograph record. A hit song is rarely longer than three and a half minutes, the capacity of a 45 single. The phonograph record's limits do not have to be music's limits.

Cassettes and compact discs have capacities and abilities that are not available from the phonograph record. It is only a matter of time before more musicians and recording companies start to produce more material that will not fit on a phonograph record. When this happens, the phonograph record will be left far behind.

A shift away from the phonograph record could occur very quickly, with disastrous results particularly for the manager not in touch with the trend. The problem is then how to be aware of developments in

15. U.S. Bureau of the Census, *Statistical Abstract of the United States, 1984* (Washington, D.C.: Superintendent of Documents, 1984), 226, 777.

this and related industries, and anticipate changes that will affect the collection.

The sure solution is expansion of the phonograph record collection's jurisdiction to include all recorded formats, including sound, video, and machine-readable data. Technical developments of the past few years have led to some overlap among these areas and the future promises a greater interdependence of recording technologies. Responsibility for managing the recorded-sound collection will increasingly require expertise in a variety of other fields. This position will also afford the flexibility of collecting in whatever format is offered or most appropriate to the material presented.

A less aggressive response is a thorough and ongoing education in information technology. A knowledgeable manager will be aware of important developments and be able to advise upper management and confer with managers of other, related collections in order to coordinate activities.

ADDITIONAL RESOURCES

American Library Assn. Library Technology Program. *Evaluation of Record Players for Libraries, Series II: A Report Based on a Study Conducted for the Library Technology Project by United States Testing Company, Inc.* Chicago: The Assn., 1964. [LTP Publications, No. 8.]

American Library Assn. Library Technology Project. *The Testing and Evaluation of Record Players for Libraries: A Report Based on a Study Conducted for the Library Technology Project by Consumers' Research, Inc.* Chicago: The Assn., 1962. [LTP Publications, No. 5.]

Assn. for Educational Communications and Technology. Information Science Committee. *Standards for Cataloging Nonprint Materials.* 3rd ed. Washington, D.C.: The Assn., 1972.

Ballard, John. "Rock Record Reviewing Sources." *Top of the News* 34 (Spring, 1978): 287–89.

Batten, Joseph. *Joe Batten's Book: The Story of Sound Recording; Being the Memoirs of Joe Batten.* London: Rockliff, 1956.

Berger, Myron. "Record Cleaners and the Real World." *High Fidelity* 30 (July 1980), 43–46.

Berliner, Emile. *Three Addresses.* Washington, D.C.: s.n., 1913.

Bettini Phonograph Laboratory. *Bettini Micro-phonograph and Records: [catalogue] June, 1898.* Stanford: Archive of Recorded Sound, 1965. [Reprint Series, Stanford Univ. Libraries, Publication No. 1.]

Bibliographic Control of Nonprint Media. Ed. Pearce S. Grove and Evelyn G. Clement. Chicago: American Library Assn., 1972.

Briggs, Gilbert Arthur. *Sound Reproduction.* 3d ed., rev. and enl. Idle, Bradford (England): Wharfedale Wireless Works, 1953.

Cabeceiras, J. *Multimedia Library: Materials Selection and Use.* 2nd ed. Orlando, Fla.: Academic Pr., 1983.

Carnegie Corp. of New York. *A List of 953 Records, also 149 Scores and 82 Titles of Books Contained in the Sets of Music Study Material for Use in Colleges.* New York: The Corp., 1938.

Century of Sound: 100 Years of Recorded Sound, 1877–1977. Ed. Ihor Todoruk. Montreal: Studio 123, 1977.

Chew, V. K. *Talking Machines, 1877–1914: Some Aspects of the Early History of the Gramophone.* London: H.M.S.O., 1967.

————. *Talking Machines.* 2nd ed. London: H.M.S.O., 1981.

City of London Phonograph and Gramophone Society. *Ninety Years of Recorded Sound: An Exhibition, 31st July to 11th August, 1967 at the Lecture Hall, Gresham College, London.* Bournemouth (England): The Society, 1967.

Colby, E. "Sound Scholarship, Scope, Purpose, Function and Potential of Phonorecord Archives." *Library Trends* 21 (July 1972): 7–28.

"Collecting Popular Music." Tim LaBorie, issue ed. *Drexel Library Quarterly* 19:1(Winter 1983).

Columbia Graphophone: Cylinder & Disc. Bournemouth (England): Talking Machine Review, 1974.

Columbia Phonograph Co. *The Graphophone, 1906.* New York: A. Koenigsberg.

Conference on the Phonograph and Our Musical Life (Brooklyn College, 1977). *The Phonograph and Our Musical Life: Proceedings of a Centennial Conference, 7–10 December, 1977.* Ed. H. Wiley Hitchcock. New York: Institute for Studies in American Music, Dept. of Music, School of Performing Arts, Brooklyn College of the City University of New York, 1980. [I.S.A.M. Monograph 14]

Crabbe, John. *Hi-Fi in the Home.* 4th ed. London: Blandford, 1973.

Curtis, Robert. "Revolution Now? Classical Music Recordings & Compact Discs." *Library Journal* 111 (May 1, 1986).

Daily, Jay Elwood. *Organizing Nonprint Materials: A Guide for Librarians.* New York: M. Dekker, 1972.

Dearling, Robert, and Celia Dearling. *The Guiness Book of Recorded Sound.* Enfield (England): Guiness Books, 1984.

Delaunay, Charles. *Hot Discography . . .* Edited by Hot Jazz . . . 1940 ed. Corrected and reprinted in U.S.A. New York: Commodore Record Co., 1943.

Disc Recording and Reproduction. Ed. H. E. Roys. Stroudsburg, Pa.: Dowden, Hutchinson & Ross, 1978. Distributed by Academic Pr. (N.Y.). Benchmark Papers in Acoustics, 12.

Dobbin, Peter. "Waging War on Warps." *High Fidelity* 31 (Nov. 1981): 50–53.

Dolan, Robert Emmett. *Music in Modern Media: Techniques in Tape, Disc and Film Recording, Motion Picture and Television Scoring and Electronic Music.* New York: G. Schirmer, 1967.

Dressler, Diane Grace. *A Music Record Library for Preschool Children.* Master's thesis, Columbia Univ., 1970.

Dusting Off a Little History: Spring Type Phonographs. 1st ed. Yorba Linda,
  Calif.: Phonograph Collectibles (18242 Timberlane, Yorba Linda 92686),
  1981.
Edinburgh. Royal Scottish Museum. *Phonographs & Gramophones: A Com-
  memorative Catalogue of the Exhibition Held at the Royal Scottish
  Museum from 2nd July–2nd October 1977 to Celebrate the Centenary
  of Thomas Edison's Invention of the Phonograph.* Edinburgh: The
  Museum, 1977.
Edison Phonograph: The North American Phonograph Company. New York:
  A. Koenigsberg, 1975. (Historical Facsimile Ed., No. 24)
Edison (Thomas A.) Inc. *Edison Phonographs: For Cash or on Easy Payments.*
  New York: A. Koenigsberg, 197?.
_____. *Instructions for the Management and Operation of Edison's Speak-
  ing Phonograph.* New York: A. Koenigsberg, 197?.
_____. The Phonograph and How to Use It: Being a Short History of Its In-
  vention and Development, Containing Also Directions, Helpful Hints, and
  Plain Talks as to Its Care and Use, etc. Including Also a Reprint of the
  Openeer Papers and Phonograph Short Stories. New York: A. Koenigsberg,
  1971 (facsimile ed.).
Electric and Musical Industries Limited. *The EMI Collection.* 2nd ed.
  Bournemouth (England): Talking Machine Review, 1977.
Fleisher, Eugene B., and Helen Goodman. *Cataloging Audiovisual Materials:
  A Manual Based on the Anglo-American Cataloging Rules II.* New York:
  Neal-Schuman, 1980.
Fothergill, Richard, and Ian Butchart. *Non-book Materials in Libraries: A Prac-
  tical Guide.* 2nd ed. London: Clive Bingley, 1984.
Frost, Carolyn O. *Cataloging Nonbook Materials.* Littleton, Colo.: Libraries
  Unlimited, 1983.
Frow, George L. *The Edison Disc Phonographs and the Diamond Discs: A
  History with Illustrations.* Sevenoaks (England): G. L. Frow, 1982.
Gaisberg, Frederick William. *The Music Goes Round.* New York: Arno, 1977
  [1942].
Gelatt, Roland. *The Fabulous Phonograph, 1877–1977.* 2nd rev. ed. New
  York: Macmillan, 1977.
Girard, Victor, and Harold M. Barnes. *Vertical-Cut Cylinders and Discs: A
  Catalogue of All "Hill-&-Dale" Recordings of Serious Worth Made and
  Issued between 1897–1932 Circa.* London: British Institute of Recorded
  Sound, 1971.
Gramophone Co. *The Auxeto Gramophone.* Dundee (Scotland): City of Lon-
  don Phonograph and Gramophone Society, 197?.
Gronow, Pekka, comp. *The Columbia 33000-F Irish Series: A Numerical
  Listing, with an Artist Index Compiled by Bill Healy and a Title Index
  Compiled by Paul F. Wells.* Los Angeles: John Edwards Memorial Foun-
  dation at the Folklore and Mythology Center, Univ. of California, 1979.
  [JEMF Special Series No. 10.]
Haggin, Bernard H. *Music on Records.* New York: Oxford Univ. Pr., 1938.

Hazelcorn, Howard. *A Collector's Guide to the Columbia Spring-Wound Cylinder Graphophone, 1894–1910*. New York: APM Pr., 1976.

Henry Seymour (firm). *Sound-Reproducing Accessories [the Catalogue of] Henry Seymour, 544 Caledonian Road, London, N.7*. Bournemouth (England): Talking Machine Review, 1971.

Hurst, P. G. *The Golden Age Recorded: A Collector's Survey*. New and rev. ed. Lingfield (England): Oakwood Pr., 1963.

Intner, Sheila S. *Access to Media: A Guide to Integrating and Computerizing Catalogs*. New York: Neal-Schuman, 1984.

Jewell, Brian. *Veteran Talking Machines: History and Collectors' Guide*. Tunbridge Wells (England): Midas Books, 1977.

Kaufman, Judith. *Library of Congress Subject Headings for Recordings of Western Non-Classical Music*. Philadelphia: Music Library Assn., 1983.

Koenigsberg, Allen. *Edison Cylinder Records, 1889–1912, with an Illustrated History of the Phonograph*. 1st ed. New York: Stellar Productions, 1969.

Long, Robert. "Record and Tape Care Products That Really *Do* Work." *High Fidelity* 32 (Nov. 1982): 38–41.

Lydon, Michael. *Boogie Lightning: How Music Became Electric*. New York: Da Capo Pr., 1980.

Mak, William. *Rights Affecting the Manufacture and Use of Gramophone Records*. The Hague: Martinus Nijhoff, 1952.

Marty, Daniel. *The Illustrated History of Talking Machines*. Trans. Douglas Tubbs. Lausanne: Edita, 1981.

McWilliams, Jerry. "Sound Recordings." In Susan G. Swartzburg, ed. *Conservation in the Library*. Westport, Conn.: Greenwood Pr., 1983. 163–84.

Media and Microcomputers in the Library: A Selected, Annotated Resource Guide. Ed. Evelyn H. Daniel and Carol I. Notowitz. Phoenix: Oryx Pr., 1984.

Michigan State Library Services. *Spoken Word Recordings*. Lansing, Mich.: State Library Services, 1974.

Miller, Russell, et al. *The Incredible Music Machine*. London: Quartet Books, 1982.

Mitchell, Ogilvie. *The Talking Machine Industry*. London, New York: Sir I. Pitman & Sons, 1922.

Moogk, Edward B. *Roll Back the Years: History of Canadian Recorded Sound and Its Legacy: Genesis to 1930*. Ottawa: National Library of Canada (distributed by Information Canada), 1975.

Moore, Jerrold Northrop. *A Voice in Time: The Gramophone of Fred Gaisberg, 1873–1951*. London: Hamilton, 1976.

Myers, Kurtz. *Index to Record Reviews: Based on Material Originally Published in Notes, the Quarterly Journal of the Music Library Association between 1947 and 1977*. Boston: G. K. Hall, 1978.

National Information Center for Educational Media. *Index to Educational Records*. Los Angeles: Univ. of Southern California, 1971. 72, 75, 80.

National Phonograph Assn. *Proceedings of the 1890 Convention of Local Phonograph Companies*. Introduction by Raymond R. Wile. Reprint ed. Nashville: Country Music Foundation Pr., 1974.

Nonbook Materials: A Bibliography of Recent Publications. Ed. Hans Wellisch. College Park: College of Library and Information Services, Univ. of Maryland, 1975.

Non Print Media in Academic Libraries. Ed. Pearce S. Grove. Chicago: American Library Assn., 1975. [ACRL Publications in Librarianship, No. 34]

Olson, Nancy B. *Cataloging of Audiovisual Materials: A Manual Based on AACR2.* Mankato: Minnesota Scholarly Pr., 1981.

Pathé Frères. *Pathé Frères London Ltd.: Phonographs, Cylinders and Accessories.* S.1.: s.n., 197?.

The Phonograph and How to Use It; Being a Short History of Its Invention and Development, Containing Also Directions, Helpful Hints and Plain Talks as to Its Care and Use, etc. Including Also a Reprint of the Openeer Papers and Phonograph Short Stories. New York: Press of A. Becker, 1900.

"The Phonograph and Sound Recording after One-Hundred Years." Ed. Warren Rex Isom. *Audio Engineering Society Journal* 25 (Oct./Nov. 1977): 656–897.

Phonographs & Gramophones: A Symposium Organised by the Royal Scottish Museum in Connection with the Exhibition of Phonographs and Gramophones and the Centenary of the Invention of the Phonograph by Thomas Alva Edison: Held in the Royal Scottish Museum, Chambers Street, Edinburgh, on Saturday 2nd July 1977. Edinburgh: Royal Scottish Museum, 1977.

Pickett, A. G., and M. M. Lemcoe. *The Preservation and Storage of Sound Recordings.* Washington, D.C.: Library of Congress, 1959.

Prescott, George B. *The Speaking Telephone, Talking Phonograph and Other Novelties.* Ann Arbor, Mich.: University Microfilms, 1980.

Present Information with Audio Recordings. Center for Vocational Education, Ohio State Univ. Athens, Ga.: American Assn. for Vocational Instructional Materials, University of Georgia, 1977.

Proudfoot, Christopher. *Collecting Phonographs and Gramophones.* 1st American ed. New York: Mayflower Books, 1980.

Ranada, David. "How to Handle Records." *Stereo Review* 47 (Sept. 1982) 62–63.

Read, Oliver, and Walter L. Welch. *From Tin Foil to Stereo: Evolution of the Phonograph.* 2nd ed. Indianapolis: H. W. Sams, 1976.

Readings in Nonbook Librarianship. Ed. Jean Spealman Kujoth. Metuchen, N.J.: Scarecrow, 1968.

Rogers, JoAnn V. *Nonprint Cataloging for Multimedia Collections: A Guide Based on AACR2.* Littleton, Colo.: Libraries Unlimited, 1982.

Rosenthal, Murray P. *How to Select and Use Record Players.* Rochelle Park, N.J.: Hayden Book Co., 1979.

Schroeder, Don, and Gary Dare. *Audiovisual Equipment and Materials: A Basic Repair and Maintenance Manual.* Metuchen, N.J.: Scarecrow, 1979.

Seibert, Donald. *The MARC Music Format: From Inception to Publication.* Philadelphia: Music Library Assn., 1982.

Sive, M. R. *Media Selection Handbook*. Littleton, Colo.: Libraries Unlimited, 1983.

Smart, James Robert, and Jon W. Newsom. *"A Wonderful Invention": A Brief History of the Phonograph from Tinfoil to the LP: An Exhibition in the Great Hall of the Library of Congress in Celebration of the 100th Anniversary of the Invention of the Phonograph*. Washington, D.C.: Library of Congress, 1977.

The Story of Edison Bell, Being a Succinct History of Edison Bell Efforts and Activities Dating from the Invention of the Original Talking Machine Down to the Year of Grace 1924. Bournemouth (England): City of London Phonograph & Gramophone Society, 1967.

Swartsburg, Susan G. *Preserving Library Materials: A Manual*. Metuchen, N.J.: Scarecrow, 1980.

Tewksbury, George E. Introduction by Thomas A. Edison. *A Complete Manual of the Edison Phonograph*. Sevenoaks (England): G. L. Frow, [1979?].

Tillin, Alma M., and William J. Quinly. *Standards for Cataloging Nonprint Materials: An Interpretation and Practical Application*. 4th ed. Washington, D.C.: Assn. for Educational Communications and Technology, 1976.

Webb, B. J. "Component Interfaces: Stylli/Dirt/Grooves; or Disc Maintenance: Ends & Means." *Audio Amateur* (1978): 28–30, 32.

Weihs, Jean R. *Accessible Storage of Nonbook Material*. Phoenix: Oryx Pr., 1984.

_____ et al. *Nonbook Materials: The Organization of Integrated Collections*. 2nd ed. Ottawa: Canadian Library Assn., 1979.

Who Is Who in Music. 1941 Ed. A Complete Presentation of the Contemporary Musical Scene, with a Master Record Catalogue. Chicago, New York: Lee Stern Pr., 1940– .

Whyte, Bert. "Giving Records the Brush-Off." *Audio* 66 (Nov. 1982): 20, 22.

Wilson, John Steuart. *The Collector's Jazz: Traditional and Swing*. 1st ed. Philadelphia: Lippincott, 1958.

Wimbush, Roger, comp. *"The Gramophone" Jubilee Book*. Harrow (England): General Gramophone Publications Ltd., 1973.

Young, J. Lewis. *Edison and His Phonograph*. Bournemouth (England): Talking Machine Review [1970].

Clara L. DiFelice

ch. 16

4|8

Photographs

THE MEDIUM

Definition

Photograph is a term applied to either the image produced on a sensitized film by its exposure to light, or a printed reproduction of that image. The word is derived from the Greek *phos*, meaning "light," and *graphos*, meaning "written."

Photography is a technique used to record permanent images of objects on an emulsion by chemical means, after the emulsion has been changed by exposure to radiation, usually light waves, emitted by or reflected from an object. Photography is referred to variously as a technology, a science, and an art. Essentially, a camera and lens combination is used to focus and capture the light rays reflecting off an object onto film. The film, when developed with the proper chemicals, yields a negative image of the object. Light is again used to convert the negative image into a positive reproduction upon a sensitized paper. The paper, also developed with chemicals, presents the original image, either with tones of black, white, and gray or in reproduced colors.

Brief History

The history of photography is a history of the scientific and technical advancement of a theory about light, which emerged as early as the 5th century B.C. and was alluded to by Aristotle, Bacon, and Leonardo da Vinci, among others. The earliest commentary dealt with the projected image created by light shining through a small hole onto a wall. This theory was confirmed with the construction of the *camera obscura* as a device of benefit to artists interested in presenting graphic reality. Experimentation with the machinery of photography continued even as it generated the desire to capture the image in some permanent manner. During the 18th century, theoretical and practical explorations of the chemical properties of silver nitrate, which darkened with exposure to light, provided a basis for further developments.

The history of photography continues with the almost simultaneous announcements by Jacques Daguerre in France and William Fox Talbot in England of their processes by which the images formed in the camera could become a permanent record. Daguerre's process resulted in the unique positive image, the *daguerrotype*, whereas Talbot's provided a negative image repeatable indefinitely in a positive print, known as the *calotype*. From this point forward, developments in chemical processing affected glass plate, film, and paper negatives and positives. Mechanical and technical enhancements of the camera and its lens systems, as well as the evolution of numerous accessories for the photographer, have continually shaped the industry, technology, and art known as photography.

Photography's evolution became an interlinkage of developments mainly in England, France, and America. News of the possibilities being explored traveled quickly in a world increasingly interested in scientific and technical advancement. Photography's first impact was upon artistic endeavor, both attracting and repelling artists whose livelihood depended upon their ability to interpret and present reality. There is little doubt that photography began to shape the role of art in society, or that art determined the uses of photography. Portraiture became the bread and butter for many photographers. At first, the long exposures necessary with daguerrotypes made portrait taking a painful process for the sitter. By the mid-1840s, however, developments led to an easier portrait session and daguerrotype establishments were set up in urban centers while roaming daguerrotypists captured likenesses throughout America, England, and eastern Europe. Seemingly, everybody enjoyed looking at themselves, and today we view multitudes of unnamed people captured in the daguerrotype, the tintype, the collodion/albumen paper print or its glass version, the ambrotype. The success of the celebrity portrait and its many offshoots, including fashion photography, is due to society's fascination with the portrait photograph.

Photographs of people expanded our view of ourselves, and photographs of places made possible the expansion of our view of the world.

Landscape photography, explored in daguerrotypes with panoramic views, but more in the replicable calotype, began in the early years of photography's development. Its use in the travel spots of the world created a record of views of both urban and rural landscapes long since changed. Photography became recognized as a truly useful tool, both as a documentary and artistic one, with these views. They range from archeological sites in the Mideast to unexplored territories in the American West. Despite the burdens associated with "portable" darkrooms and bulky cameras, many expeditions included photographers throughout the mid-1800s. Landscape photography, as demonstrated by these early practitioners, has evolved into, among other things, the ubiquitous postcard and calendar art.

When we think of the way a photograph, snapped at the finish line, can determine the outcome of the Kentucky Derby, we participate in one of the earliest beliefs associated with photography: that it can present an objective reality, a factual view that documents an event. This is the photography that in the 1850s and 1860s presented the ongoing developments of industrial activity as well as the events which became news. The results of Matthew Brady's studio photographers on the fields of the Civil War, using the newly developed collodion technique, were forerunners of the documentary photograph and today's photojournalism.

By the turn of the century, the developments in photography were responding to needs expressed by the photographers, ranging from the dry plate to artificial lighting to smaller cameras and the possibilities of capturing color and motion. George Eastman's introduction of the Kodak camera in 1888 had a definite impact on the growth and development of the photographic industry, creating a consumer market responding to the fascination of "snapshots." For photographers interested in the documentary aspects, and those beginning to explore artistic expression, the technological changes highlighted new possibilities for using photography. With the invention of the halftone photoengraving process, the place of photography in the world became assured. This provided the ability to reproduce photographs while printing text in a relatively inexpensive manner; essentially, it created advertising and photojournalism, the chronological sequencing of the picture story, and a new role for portraiture.

Fine-art photography could be said to have begun with the presentation of great art and sculpture in the 1850s. Photography's ability to reproduce artwork created the study of art history and allowed access to collections scattered throughout the world, many privately controlled. Also at this time, the use of photography as art was being explored by several painters' attempts to define an aesthetic for the

new medium. From the 1890s onward, artistic photography, with its
attendant critical activity, began to define a role for photography
as art.

Currently, photography is ever present and allows for the expansion of our vision of the world from microscopic levels to beyond the
limits of our space. In 1857, Lady Elizabeth Eastlake wrote an article
in response to some of the criticisms then appearing regarding the subject of photography as art.

> Photography is the purveyor of such knowledge to the world.
> She is the sworn witness of everything presented to her
> view. . . What are her representations of the bed of the ocean,
> and the surface of the moon—of the launch of the Marlbo-
> rough, and of the contents of the Great Exhibition—of Charles
> Kean's now destroyed scenery of the 'Winter's Tale,' and of
> Prince Albert's now slaughtered prize ox—but the facts which
> are neither the province of art nor of description, but of that
> new form of communication between man and man.[1]

Unique Characteristics

The photograph is a single image which can present a concept. The
camera can record a moment in time, an object or person, preserving
the image in both negative and positive representation.

The photograph is comprehensible without the aid of projection
equipment or other media.

The photograph can reproduce fine detail with complete accuracy,
and convey texture, size, and a variety of subjective and objective images of reality.

Photography provides an exact and repeatable image.

Various sizings of the image are possible for the photographic print
made from the negative.

Modifications throughout the printing process can change the final
photograph without harming the original negative. These can lead to
the same image being conveyed in any variety of forms, usually artistic by design.

The photographic negative allows for the reproduction of the image by a variety of means into an original print, a newspaper photo,
or a book illustration.

1. Lady Elizabeth Eastlake, ''Photography,'' *Quarterly Review* 101 (Apr. 1857),
reprinted in Beaumont Newhall, *Photography: Essays & Images* (New York: Museum
of Modern Art, 1980), 93–94.

Advantages

Photographs are visual images which can translate abstract ideas and historic events into a realistic context.

Photographs can generate interest, stimulate curiosity and the imagination, and clarify the meaning of abstract concepts.

Photographs can reproduce detail and make visible those things which cannot be viewed by the unassisted eye. Microscopic photography and telescopic photography allow us to see details never before viewed.

Photographs can be used individually or in groups; they are easily viewed, without special equipment; and they are easily understood, without explanation.

Photographs have a strong historic value, preserving an event as it happens.

Photographs can be easily produced for specific purposes.

Photographs can be easily reproduced and duplicated, allowing for any number of viewers and ensuring the image will last through time.

Photographs can be combined effectively with any variety of media.

There are many sources of free or inexpensive photographs. Collections may be developed in any type of institution for relatively little investment.

Fine-art photography can increase in value over time.

Photographs are easily circulated. They can be small and lightweight, even when mounted for protection, and can be duplicated when a negative is available, in the event of damage or loss.

Equipment and facilities for producing photographs can be cheap and readily available, ranging from an Instamatic camera, with development provided through the local drugstore, to a high-quality 35mm camera with a telephoto lens, and a develop-it-yourself darkroom at a local camera shop.

Disadvantages

The fragility of negatives and photographic prints can require special environmental conditions for storage to ensure preservation.

Historic photographs or unique works of art cannot be used in their original form; they must be copied for any type of active collection.

Photographs and negatives may not be erased and reused, they must be stored. The readily available photograph can lead to bulky and inaccessible collections.

Photographs cannot be viewed by sight-impaired users.

Photographs may be easily overlooked as information resources by users because they are so prevalent in our lives.

Photographs are a flattened, two-dimensional representation of reality.

With the exception of instant prints, photography can require investment in equipment and a darkroom for producing on-site photographs.

SELECTION

Special Criteria

The clarity, accuracy, and overall quality of the image is of particular importance in the selection of photographs.

The type and size of the photograph must be considered in relation to the intended use.

The age of the photograph and whether it is a "vintage print" (produced within a short time of the photograph being taken), a copy print, or an original print should be considered.

The mechanics of producing the photograph (type of camera and film used, method of development, type of light and speed at which the photograph was exposed) may have an impact on the future use of the photograph.

Additional criteria may depend upon the individual photograph and how it matches the nature of the overall collection. Criteria for archival/historical collections will vary from those for artistic or general collections.

Evaluative Review Sources

Of the media review journals, *Previews* occasionally included evaluations of photographs. Professional journals in any number of fields may include evaluations of readily available photographs. Fine-art photography is reviewed in art journals and other photography publications, such as *Popular Photography* (in the "Shows We've Seen" column).

American Photographer profiles photographers and their pictures. *Photographics: A Collector's Newsletter* is an art and investment publication for serious collectors of photography.

Nonevaluative Sources

In comparison with other media, photography may be said to have the widest variety of applicable uses. As a primary source of documentary information, the photograph permeates such fields as advertising, journalism, medicine, science, and a host of others. The possible sources for photographic materials are as numerous as they are varied. Titles listed below represent publications since 1970.

Free Stock Photography Directory. New York: Infosource Business Publications, 1978– . Annual.
A Handlist of Museum Sources for Slides and Photographs, by Sharon Petrini and Troy-Jjohn Bromberger. Santa Barbara: Univ. of California, 1972.
World Photography Sources. New York: Bowker, 1981– . Biennial.

Photograph Collector, *U.P.A. Journal*, and *Visual Resources* are journals which can suggest sources of photographs. Check the latest edition of *Photographer's Market* for tips on where to acquire photos (it is published annually by Writer's Digest Books of Cincinnati).

In addition to the above, Richard Blodgett's appendixes on "Resource Materials" and "Where to Buy Photographs" provide valuable information regarding dealer's catalogs and auction houses as markets for fine-art photography (see "Additional Resources"). A complete listing of photography dealers can be obtained from:

Assn. of International Photography Art Dealers, Inc., Box 1119, F.D.R. Station, New York, NY 10022.

MAINTENANCE AND MANAGEMENT
Storage and Care

Photographs are a fragile medium. They can be damaged by light, dampness, heat, air pollution, careless handling, improper framing, and adverse storage conditions. In spite of this, original daguerrotypes and calotypes and early photographs have survived for many years. It is possible to find many photos from the turn of the century still in a trunk in an attic. Glass-plate negatives and many early photographs can be easily restored to their original clarity by a skilled photo technician. This ability to restore negatives allows for copy prints of photos which may otherwise vanish from existence.

Photographs should be stored in a vertical file, cabinet, or drawer. Sulphur-base products should be avoided: cardboard, wooden boxes, rubber bands, wooden frames, cheap photo albums. The best storage containers are baked-on-enamel steel filing cabinets or archive-quality storage boxes, such as Hollinger or Solander boxes.

Temperature and humidity should be controlled. Temperature should be as low as tolerable, certainly below 65° F (if a separate storage room is available) and humidity should be in the 30–40% range, or at least below 50%. Silica gel is *not* recommended as a dehumidifier under well-kept storage conditions. It is better to set aside a small room and use a portable electrical refrigeration-type dehumidifier.

Handle negatives, glass plates, and photographs only by the edges; never touch the image surface. Care must be taken to avoid fingerprints, since oil and acids from the hand will cause damage. When working with photographic materials, wear cotton gloves.

Store negatives in strips, in Mylar or cellulose triacetate envelopes, one per envelope. Since negatives are unlikely to be used to a great extent, their care and storage should follow the guidelines for archival storage of photographic materials.

Unmounted photographs should be protected by Mylar sleeves. These sleeves allow for examination of both the front and back of the photograph. Hollinger paper envelopes can be used, if cost proves a barrier to using Mylar.

Mount photographic prints, to protect them and facilitate handling, on 100% rag museum board which is nonacidic and free of impurities which could eventually damage the print. Dry mounting with dry-mount tissue is adequate. Never use rubber cement. Unmounted prints should be separated from each other by museum-quality, acid-free archival paper.

Use glass when framing prints, since the long-term effects of Plexiglass are still unknown. If glass breakage is possible, which is far more likely to damage the print, frame with Plexiglass. Frame with a mat, so that the photograph does not touch the glass.

Rotate photographs from storage to display to allow rest from exposure to light. Stack any photographic materials being stored on their edges, never flat, and never on top of each other.

Identify photographs with separate labels wherever possible. Never write on the back of a photograph with anything except a soft-lead pencil, lightly wielded. Try to identify color prints with the type of process used to develop them, the type of film, and the date the print was made. Color photographs will fade after twenty years, and this kind of identification will enable duplicate printing to be planned for and effected.

Photographs can be intershelved if mounted within a hinged mat, the surface of the photo fully protected by a cover mat. Circulation pockets and identifying labels can be placed on the outside of the mat.

Care should be taken to "understand" the emulsion on any historic photograph. Exposure to some common chemicals can destroy photographs which used early processes. Historic photographs should be represented in the collection by copy prints. A copy print with a slight amber or yellow tone to the photographic paper can convey the age of the photo, and is an effective way to present historic photographs.

Management Problems and Solutions

With the wide range of photographs available to an institution, establishing guidelines is necessary in developing the collection to its usable potential. Obviously, some collections are self-selective, such as fine-art photography, a local history photo collection, or a local newsphoto collection; these provide examples of collections which can have easily understood guidelines. An institutional photo archive is another example. Still, since photographs are so prevalent, a decision must be made about how much of the institution's resources should go to developing the collection. Highly defined collections allow for better management of resources in selecting photographs than collections with a universal scope. The selection of valuable historic or artistic photographs may lead to problems with the expense of care and preservation of these materials.

Where photographs fit the defined collection guidelines and/or act as unique information resources, they should be acquired. A portion of the institution's budget should be designated for the purchase and maintenance of a photographic collection. Sources of acquisition include auction houses, art galleries and dealers, local and national news agencies and photographic libraries, and gifts from users, businesses, and service agencies in the community. One can even request a photograph of the president from the White House. A photographer can be placed on the institution's staff to provide photographs as needed. Amateur snapshots may be considered and should be scrupulously examined if offered for their unique value of time, object, or place. Any historic photographs, particularly of a local nature, should be sought from their owners. Offer to provide copy prints, and assure owners that by depositing their photographs with a responsible institution they ensure the photographs will not be lost or fade away with time. If the original cannot be acquired, request permission to make a copy print for the institution's collection. Collect documentation from the owners regarding the photograph.

Proper identification of the material is achieved by cataloging and processing the photographs for use by the institution's clients. They should be represented in the main catalog with the designator "picture." While written descriptions are valuable, the catalog should not take the place of access to the photographs by clients. Dating information is important when cataloging photographs, as is the type of processing. Collation data should include the number and type of picture, color or black and white, and the size of the picture. Additional notes could include information regarding the amount of time between the taking of the photograph and its being printed. Subject headings and classification schemes may vary widely for fine-art photography. A system based on an established collection, such as the Metropolitan Museum's, may prove more usable to the institution's clients. Providing valuable assistance would be any sort of union listing of area institutional collections. While one does not currently exist on the national level, such a project could be locally compiled.

Photographs, properly protected, should circulate as do other materials in the institution, using existing circulation systems. Policies relating to the use of photographs should duplicate those of other materials. Protective bags might be provided to further lessen the possibilities of damage. The issue may arise of providing copy prints of photographs in the collection. The institution may want to provide this as a service, following proper copyright guidelines.

Photographs should be treated as other materials, intershelved and interstored with print materials wherever possible. Since mounted photographs are better displayed, a permanent display area should be considered. Rotating photographs from storage to display can prolong the life of the photograph. Proper storage conditions should be maintained wherever possible to ensure the collection's longevity. The scope of the institution's collection will help to determine the needs for correct storage procedures. Photographs can be treated as ephemeral or archival material. This decision will have major impact on the storage conditions provided for the photograph collection.

ADDITIONAL RESOURCES
Books

Adams, Ansel. *The Print*. Boston: Little, Brown, 1983.

Bayer, Jonathan, and others. *Reading Photographs*. New York: Pantheon, 1977.

Bennett, Edna. *Pictures Unlimited: Sources of Pictorial Illustrations*. New York: Photographic Trade News Corp., 1968.

Blodgett, Richard. *Photographs: A Collector's Guide*. New York: Ballantine, 1979.

Brettell, Richard, and others. *Paper and Light: The Calotype in France and Great Britain, 1839–1870*. Boston: David R. Godine, 1984.

Buckland, Gail. *Fox Talbot and the Invention of Photography*. Boston: David R. Godine, 1980.

Coe, Brian, and Mark Haworth-Booth. *A Guide to Early Photographic Processes*. London: Victoria and Albert Museum, 1983.

Crawford, William. *The Keepers of Light: A History and Working Guide to Early Photographic Processes*. Dobbs Ferry, N.Y.: Morgan & Morgan, 1979.

Davies, Thomas L. *Shoots: A Guide to Your Family's Photographic Heritage.* Danbury, N.H.: Addison House, 1977.

Eastman Kodak Co. *Encyclopedia of Practical Photography.* New York: Amphoto, 1979.

Frankenberg, Celestine, ed. *Picture Sources.* New York: Special Libraries Assn., 1964.

Gernsheim, Helmut. *The History of Photography.* London: Oxford Univ. Pr., 1955.

——— and Alison Gernsheim. *The History of Photography from the Camera Obscura to the Beginning of the Modern Era.* New York: McGraw-Hill, 1969.

Goldberg, Vicki. *Photography in Print: Writings from 1816 to the Present.* New York: Simon & Schuster, 1981.

Langford, Michael. *The Master Guide to Photography.* New York: Knopf, 1982.

Lutz, Robert D. *1984 Photographer's Market.* Cincinnati: Writer's Digest Books, 1983.

Morgan, Willard, ed. *The Encyclopedia of Photography.* New York: Greystone Pr., 1967.

Newhall, Beaumont. *The History of Photography.* 4th ed. New York: Museum of Modern Art, 1981.

———. *Photography: Essays and Images.* New York: Museum of Modern Art, 1980.

Rosenbaum, Naomi. *A World History of Photography.* New York: Abbeville, 1985.

Society of American Archivists. *Archives and Manuscripts: Administration of Photographic Collections.* Chicago: Society of American Archivists, 1984.

Sontag, Susan. *On Photography.* New York: Farrar, Straus & Giroux, 1977.

Time-Life Books. *Caring for Photographs.* Alexandria, Va.: Time-Life Books, 1982.

Warner, Glen. *Building a Print Collection.* Toronto: Van Nostrand Reinhold, 1981.

Weinstein, Robert, and Larry Booth. *Collection, Use and Care of Historical Photographs.* Nashville: American Assn. for State and Local History, 1977.

Wilhelm, Henry. *Preservation of Contemporary Photographic Materials.* Grinnell, Ia.: East Street Gallery, 1977.

Witkin, Lee, and Barbara London. *The Photograph Collector's Guide.* Boston: New York Graphic Society, 1979.

Encyclopedia Articles

Encyclopaedia Britannica. 1982, s.v. "photography, art of" and "photography, technology of."

Great Soviet Encyclopedia. 1981, s.v. "photography."

McGraw-Hill Encyclopedia of Science and Technology. 1982, s.v. "photography."
World Book Encyclopedia. 1983, s.v. "photography."

Films

Moving Still. 16mm, 60 min. 1980. Paramus, N.J.: Time/Life Video.
A Moment in Time. 16mm, 53 min. 1975. Morris Plains, N.J.: Lucerne Film & Video.

Journal Articles

Austin, Judith. "The Care and Feeding of Photography Collections." *Idaho Librarian* 27 (1975): 3–7.

Canavor, N. "Anyone for Singles? Ability to Evaluate Photographs." *Popular Photography* 71 (1972): 114–19.

Kach, David. "Photographic Dilemma: Stability and Storage of Color Materials." *Industrial Photography* (Aug. 1978): 28 + .

Kusnerz, Peggy. "Acquisition of Slides and Photographs: Results of a Survey of Colleges, Museums and Libraries." *Picturescope* 20 (1972): 66–77.

Shaw, Renata. "Picture Organization Practices and Procedures." *Special Libraries* 63 (1972): 448–56 and 502–6.

Stephenson, Genevieve. "Some Notes on the Care of Prints and Photographs at the National Portrait Gallery." *Picturescope* 20 (1972): 174–79.

Vanderbilt, Paul. "Filing Your Photographs: Some Basic Procedures." *History News* 21 (1966): 117–24.

Weinstein, Robert. "If You Collect Photographs." *Hawaii Library Association Journal* 29 (1972): 15–17.

Wilhelm, Henry. "Color Print Instability." *Modern Photography* 43 (1979): 92 + .

Other Resources

Bry, Dorothy. "An Approach to the Care of Photographs". Pamphlet available from Sotheby Parke Bernet, New York.

Hill, Joy, and others. *Photo Storage and Retrieval.* Washington, D.C.: American Newspaper Publishers' Assn., 1973. ERIC ED 107 278.

David H. Jonassen

Programmed Materials

THE MEDIUM

Definition

Programmed learning is defined in terms of what learners (hereafter "users") do when working through programmed instructional materials (PIM), that is, from a learning perspective. Generally, users work at their own rate through a highly structured sequence of information, which requires a response of some sort (writing answers, solving problems, selecting optional answers, etc.), for which fairly immediate feedback (confirmation of answer) is provided.

Much, but not all, programmed learning involves the notion of errorless learning. That is, the programmed, instructional sequences are constructed in such a way as to reduce the errors in users' responses to a minimum. The rationale for this is based on reinforcement theory. Simply stated, if information can be acquired and practiced in small enough bites, then users' responses would nearly always be correct. Correct responses lead to success which is reinforcing. Learning behaviors (writing or choosing the correct answer) that are reinforced are more likely to recur, given the same question.

This chapter was written while I was a Visiting Research Fellow in the Department of Psychology, University of Keele, Keele, Staffordshire, U.K. I should like to gratefully acknowledge the support of the department and especially its chairman, James Hartley, a noted authority on programmed learning and educational technology, who kindly provided editorial commentary on the draft of this chapter.

274

The process of programmed learning can be defined as interactive, adaptive learning. It is interactive because the individual user actively responds to—that is, interacts with—the PIM, rather than passively viewing and (hopefully) assimilating information from a noninteractive medium of instruction (e.g., normal text, filmstrips, television, etc.). Programmed learning is adaptive because PIM are often designed to accommodate individual characteristics of users, such as background knowledge or the pace at which they learn.

Programmed instruction (PI), as compared with programmed learning, is concerned only indirectly with what users do. Rather, programmed instruction refers to the practice of writing programmed materials. It is therefore concerned with what program writers do. It represents the teaching side of the teaching/learning distinction. More specifically, programmed instruction refers to the strategies used by program writers to construct PI. These strategies comprise the process of PI, a process which most commonly employs a systematic approach to instruction.

FORMS OF PROGRAMMED INSTRUCTION
Text forms look like books, workbooks, or kits of instructional sheets. This form includes books with an audiovisual medium (e.g., filmstrip, slides).

Information can be recorded on videodisc or videotape, or in combination with other equipment and a variety of media.

Teaching machines can be a page holder or a delivery vehicle—anything from simple page turning to complex interactions.

Brief History

The antecedents to 20th century PI are not well defined. The rhetoricians of democratic Athens in 400 B.C., and later the catechumens of the Middle Ages, approached an early counterpart to the small steps, sequential instruction, and question-and-answer pattern of 20th century programmed instruction. Their teaching procedures included the determination of subsequent instruction as a result of the user's answers to the questions. This tutorial form of instruction, which adapts the teaching to the users, is similar to branching programmed instruction and the embodiment of the Socratic method of instruction.

PI, however, is basically a 20th century phenomenon. In its current forms, its history comprises only 30 years. However, significant contributions were made by Sidney L. Pressey as early as 1915 in his efforts at the Ohio State University to build a simple machine for testing comprehension of material that had been taught.[1] These crude machines presented multiple-choice questions to users while providing immediate knowledge of their results. Only later did Pressey conceive of their usefulness as instructional devices. It is important to note that these early teaching machines represent what Pressey called "adjunct autoinstruction," that is, the use of test questions presented after conventional instruction.[2] This means that the machines were not integrated into the instructional material; rather, they were added to (or adjunct to) traditional instruction (usually text), much the same as adjunct questions. However, the seeds of PI had been sown.

SKINNER'S LINEAR PROGRAMMING

Modern PI is normally associated with B. F. Skinner, the Harvard behavioral psychologist. While there were a number of programmed precursors to Skinner's method of programming (e.g., Pressey, as discussed above), it was his influence which created the PI phenomenon of the 1950s and 1960s. His involvement is usually traced to his famous 1954 professional address, "The Science of Learning and the Art of Learning," in which he decried the traditional classroom instruction as being too aversive, too large, too negative, and improperly sequenced. His solution to these problems was linear programmed instruction.

Unlike Pressey's "adjunct" programming, designed to supplement regular course study, Skinner's linear teaching programs were designed to replace traditional courses of study—that is, to function as an instructor for users with no prior knowledge of a subject. Skinner's PI required the user to construct an answer by filling in a blank with the correct response, rather than to select one of four options as correct, as in Pressey's machine. Filling in a blank is a recall type of learning, because the user has to recall the answer from memory, rather than merely recognizing it (as in multiple choice). After filling in the blank, the user compares his or her answer with the correct one.[3]

The characteristics were designed by Skinner to overcome the classroom limitations stated above. Specifically, users learn without aversive threats; they work one step at a time, from simple to hard;

1. S. L. Pressey, "A Sample Apparatus Which Gives Tests and Scores—and Teaches" in *Teaching Machines and Programmed Learning,* ed. A. A. Lumsdaine and R. Glaser (Washington, D.C.: National Education Assn., 1960).

2. James Hartley and Ivor K. Davies, "Programmed Learning and Educational Technology," in Michael Howe, ed., *Adult Learning* (New York: Wiley & Sons, 1976).

3. James Cabeceiras, *The Multimedia Library: Materials Selection and Use* (New York: Academic Pr., 1978), 188.

they work at their own pace; and they are frequently reinforced for their responses.[4]

Skinner's ideas regarding PI may not have been taken very seriously, had it not been for the acute shortage of teachers in the 1950s. This situation forced many educators to consider using PI as an alternative teaching method.

The use of PI grew until the early 1960s, when low-quality programs flooded the educational market and gave many educators a negative impression of PI that lasted until the early 1970s. The most frequent complaints against the Skinnerian form of linear programming were that it was boring and monotonous, especially for capable users, and that the level of learning being supported was rote and meaningless. Although many programs were challenging and of high quality, the complaints were often justified. It is easier to publish poor programs than properly developed, thoughtful programs, as is evidenced by the bulk of drill-and-practice microcomputer programs being marketed today.

CROWDER'S INTRINSIC PROGRAM

Norman Crowder, a contemporary of Skinner, was working independently for the armed services on programmed instruction. He felt that a program was a form of communication between a programmer and a user. Like any communication, the program must be directed to the individual. Unlike Skinner, Crowder was not working from a psychological perspective, but from a communications point of view.

In an intrinsic or branching program, each frame presents more text than the average linear frame (often a paragraph or two). After reading, the user responds to an adjunct question, usually in a multiple-option format. Unlike Pressey's autoinstructional approach, which provides only confirmation of the correctness or incorrectness of that response, branching-style optional choices lead users to optional forms of feedback, most of which is corrective. If the user makes a correct response, the program asserts the reason(s) why she or he was correct and moves on to new material. If an incorrect response is made, the program, at the very least, informs the user that an error was made and then branches the user back to the previous frame for another try. The primary purpose of feedback "is to determine whether the communication was successful, in order that corrective steps be taken."[5]

4. Hartley and Davies, "Programmed Learning."
5. Norman Crowder, "Automatic Tutoring by Intrinsic Programming," in Lumsdaine and Glaser, eds., *Teaching Machines and Programmed Learning,* 288.

Depending upon the complexity of the error committed, the program may initiate a remedial sequence of instruction, a practice designed to eliminate the learning deficiency. Branching instruction adapts the sequence of the program, to a limited degree, to fit the prior learning and processing capabilities of the user. The term *intrinsic* refers to the fact that all program options are intrinsic to the program and, therefore, not dependent on any external programming device. This approach is especially adapted to machine presentation, which provides for greater levels of adaptability. Branching texts tend to be large and confusing, especially when users try to access them in a manual way.

The primary difference between Skinner's conception of programming and Crowder's is in the function of the response. To Skinner, learning results from making the correct response. Contrary to this response orientation, Crowder believed that learning results from the realignment of the user's knowledge structure, and that the response is simply a means for controlling the program or machine. The larger chunks of information need to be assimilated and integrated with what the user already knows. The response, he believed, tests the level of integration. This type of programming benefits the higher-ability user, who is more capable of higher-level integration of ideas, more than it does the lower-ability user.

SHIFTING CONCERNS

As indicated earlier, the emphasis in programmed learning began to change during the sixties, from concern with what users do to concern for the process of constructing PI.[6] The early enthusiasm for the potential of PI was waning. With PI no longer perceived as a panacea and, therefore, the automatic medium of choice when one is faced with learning problems, proponents were forced to justify its use based upon an analysis of learning needs and the nature of the content. They began to rely more on instructional systems development processes, including statements of objectives, task analysis, evaluation, and revision.[7] The process of creating programs was being applied to alternative media, such as slides, filmstrips, and instructional television. The design questions were more sophisticated. Various methods for sequencing PI were being investigated. PI was just turning into a true technology as it began to fade from prominence.

6. James Hartley, "Programmed Instruction 1954–1974: A Review," *Programmed Learning and Educational Technology* 11, 6 (1974): 278–91.
7. Hartley and Davies, "Programmed Learning."

THE DECLINING YEARS

The popularity of PI reached its zenith in the mid-1960s, but declined steadily through the 1970s. This decline in popularity is attributable to a variety of recognizable and other somewhat vague reasons. Three primary reasons were the nature of the material and processes, the higher publishing costs, and the attitudes of teachers.[8] Programmed materials were perceived as boring, often because of the way in which they were used. Also, their success was largely predicated on users' adequate reading ability, which notably declined during the same period. On the economic side, programmed materials were more expensive to produce, because of their nonstandard typography. Because of lower sales, the development costs could not be spread out, forcing up the unit cost of programs, which further depressed their sales. It wasn't until the latter sixties, when a corpus of research became available which indicated that PI was most effective as a supplement to normal instruction, that fear began to abate, but by then it was too late to arrest the trend.

Teachers were not the only group opposed to PI. Humanists decried its highly structured, centralized methodology and its use of behavioral psychological principles. Programmed learning, they averred, sought to control not only the learning behavior of users, but also their thoughts, minds, and wills. Rejoinders, touting the efficiency and predictability of learning from PI, only seemed to galvanize the humanistic position of a number of important educationalists.

PI surely represents one of the greatest bandwagons in the history of education. By the mid-sixties, instructional programs were available on virtually every topic taught in schools, as well as home-based study. Hundreds of articles per year were written, which either examined or extolled the virtues of PI. Professional journals, devoted to PI, were started in several countries. More than 5,000 articles on PI appeared between 1960 and 1978,[9] most of them written in the mid-sixties. PI held more exciting promise than any past or current educational innovation. But, like all bandwagons, it began to grind to an inexorable halt, because bandwagon processes tend, like most natural occurrences, to be cyclical. PI in the late sixties was clearly on the downslope of its development cycle.

Concurrent to PI's decline, the newest bandwagon in education, computer-assisted instruction, was gathering steam. This new tech-

8. Michael S. Hanna and James W. Gibson, "Programmed Instruction in Communication Education: An Idea behind Its Time," *Communication Education* 32, 1 (1983): 1–7.

9. James A. Kulik, Peter A. Cohen, and Barbara J. Ebeling, "Effectiveness of Programmed Instruction in Higher Education: A Meta-Analysis of Findings," *Educational Evaluation and Policy Analysis* 2, 6 (1980): 51–64.

nological focus only accelerated the apparent demise of programmed instruction. Yet PI never really disappeared. Rather, it was transformed into new issues and technologies that dominated attention in the seventies and eighties.

PRESENT AND FUTURE

Programmed learning is nowhere near extinction. Its dinosaurs consist of the linear programmed texts and teaching machines that occupied classrooms and school libraries in the sixties. Gone also are the scrambled books. However, many programmed texts and teaching materials are still consistently used in the military, in industrial and management training situations, and in distance (correspondence) education projects. While not as universally popular today as in the sixties, programmed materials remain a viable instructional medium. More importantly, the principles of programmed learning continue to contribute to educational technology in a variety of forms.

First, instructional design and text design continue to be greatly influenced by PI. Much of the instructional research conducted under the rubric of the mathemagenic hypothesis embodies principles of PI. Mathemagenic activities are those which (from the Greek) "give birth to learning."[10] This birth of learning, based upon intended, objectively stated outcomes, results from the identification of the combination of information-seeking processes that will most efficiently lead to the acquisition of a skill or knowledge. Chief among the teaching aids that give rise to mathemagenic activities are adjunct questions, which may be added before or after or inserted in a unit of text. These are meant to check comprehension and call attention to important material.

In addition to the insertion of questions, modern text materials make frequent use of typographic and layout effects similar to traditional programmed instruction in the form of chunking and blocking of material into frames (e.g., information mapping).[11] Many other programming techniques, such as learner verification and revision, are still commonly practiced in designing textual and media materials.

The second example of the continued usefulness of principles of PI is self-teaching guides. While most educators believe that PI died in the sixties, the need for self-instructional teaching materials

10. Ernst Z. Rothkopf, "The Concept of Mathemagenic Learning Activities," *Review of Educational Research* 40 (1970): 325–36.

11. See Robert Horn, *How to Write Information Mapping* (Lexington, Mass.: Information Resources, 1976), and David H. Jonassen, "Information Mapping: A Description, Rationale, and Comparison with Programmed Instruction," *Visible Language* 15, 1 (1981): 55–66.

remains.[12] If you look at current publishers' booklists, you will still find self-study guides. The self-instructional market, in fact, is burgeoning because of increased leisure time and the diverse interests of the public. So the demand for self-teaching guides, such as those published by Wiley, is expanding.

Programmed instruction represents a model of how instruction should occur. Nowhere is this model more consistently applied than in computer-assisted instruction (CAI). Even though PI and CAI were developing independently in the sixties, the instructional sequences and techniques of the former were borrowed by the latter. While PI (in its traditionally identifiable form) has declined in popularity, CAI has yet to crest. Its continued development has been fueled by the "explosion" of microcomputers in the eighties. Approximately 70 percent of the educational programs for microcomputers comprises a class known as *drill-and-practice*. Even a casual examination clearly indicates that such programs are linear PI, delivered by the computer onto a video screen. In fact, most drill-and-practice programs are devoid of the subtlety and intricacy of even a decent linear program. The visual and auditory embellishments afforded by the graphics and sound capabilities of microcomputers make the reinforcement initially more desirable, and the programs are able to keep records on users' performance, but the fundamental instructional model is that of PI.

Another popular form of microcomputer courseware is the *tutorial* mode, which replicates on the screen branching programmed instruction. The computer's program presents some information, followed by questions on the screen, and, based upon the response, branches the user to alternative parts of the program. These programs, like intrinsic PI, may confirm the correct response, remediate an incorrect one, or move the user forward or backward in the program stream. A number of authoring systems are available to help would-be computer courseware authors circumvent the need for computer-language proficiency.

It is only when you find simulation or problem-solving types of courseware (still a small, but growing minority of programs) that CAI escapes the conceptual boundaries of PI. So, computer-based learning systems represent the latest reincarnation of PI. The difference between most CAI and PI is in the form of instructional delivery—the former electronic and the latter print. They can be used interchangeably with equivalent results.[13] As the capabilities of computers are further ex-

12. Judy Wilson, "A Look at Programmed Instruction from within the Publishing Industry," *Performance and Instruction* 21, 9 (1982): 19–21.

13. John S. Edwards and Murray Tillman, "Computer Assisted Instruction (CAI): A Partner for PI?" *Performance and Instruction* 21, 9 (1982): 19–21.

ploited, CAI and PI are destined to diverge. However, for the present, we see evidence of programmed learning principles in numerous educational endeavors. It is obvious: "Programmed Instruction Lives. But Under Other Names."[14]

Unique Characteristics

PI is a method for structuring, and presenting, information.

The development of programs usually employs a systematic approach, including

Statement of terminal objectives

Task analysis to determine the type of mental/physical activity required by the objective

Evaluation of learning referenced to the objectives

Most programs are also characterized by a structure that includes

Some sequence which implies a progressive development of ideas which successively approximates the behavior stated in the objective

Some form of active response to some form of question appearing after each unit of information

Feedback, or confirmation of the correctness or incorrectness of the response

Participative, interactive learning in which the user is actively involved with the material while reading or viewing.

Another general characteristic of programs is evaluation, or learner verification and revision: a tenet of programming which requires the programmer to try out the program with a group of users, similar to those for whom the program is intended, and then to revise the program, based upon the feedback, until it reaches a predictable level of effectiveness. (Traditionally, the accepted success criteria have been a 90% level of performance with 90% of the users 90% of the time.)

Advantages and Disadvantages

The advantages and disadvantages are specific to the situation, expected outcomes or learning requirements, users, the type of program, and the way it is utilized; and do not necessarily apply to each use of PI or to each program.

14. Wilson, "A Look at Programmed Instruction," 19.

ADVANTAGES

Programs are normally validated as part of the development process to ensure reliable, replicable learning results; that is, they are "automatic and guaranteed."[15]

They are developed to meet specific needs, since the process usually begins with a needs assessment.

Programming provides for adaptation of instruction to the characteristics and capabilities of individual users.

Users can usually proceed at their own rate of learning. This avoids unfair comparisons with other users.

Users are required to be active participants in the program, engaging in learning activities rather than passively receiving information.

Programs can be sequenced to match the information processing requirements of the task to the structure of the content.

Different sequences or delivery strategies can be used to meet the same objectives, allowing for further adaptation.

The reinforcement resulting from the completion of a set of frames leaves the user with a sense of accomplishment or success, which in turn increases the motivation to learn. This may be especially important for low-ability or handicapped users who are otherwise seldom successful in their learning endeavors. The small step size reduces the information processing requirements, thereby compensating for some deficiencies.

All or parts of the program can be repeated or restudied as required.

Learning may be accomplished at any convenient time or place, in many formats. PIM may be used for primary or (more effectively) for supplemental instruction for whole or partial courses.

The difficulty and conceptual level can be adapted to the user.

Programs can be used without supervision. Self-teaching guides are common and effective.

Knowledge is usually gained more quickly than with traditional instruction. This is the most consistent research finding.

A wide variety of media or display devices can be employed to deliver the programs.

PI materials provide flexibility in arranging the user's work load; they are logistically easy to administer.

PI materials are well suited to many kinds of learning tasks and learning models.

The feedback is continuous throughout the learning process. Users always know "where they are" and "how they are doing."

15. Donald Bullock, *Programmed Instruction* (Englewood Cliffs, N.J.: Educational Technology Pub., 1978).

Slow learners do not become lost and discouraged as the material becomes more complex and detailed.

Spelling generally improves, due to constant repetition.

The highly structured nature can help users move well beyond their normal level of progress.

One of the major advantages frequently stated for PI is cost effectiveness. Based upon extensive use of PIM in public service agencies, Corcoran and Lenaerts report the following cost effective advantages of PI (especially for training workers in high turnover situations):

Reduces need for large instructional staff

Reduces need for travel

Does not require special facilities or equipment

Content can be easily tailored to specific jobs or locational needs.

The results of using PIM, they report, are:

Reduction in turnover

Improved worker morale

Cost reductions in training

Improved service to clients

Reduced fraud and error rates

Improved worker performance[16]

It should be obvious that all of the above factors contribute to the overall effectiveness of the operation, not just to the specific task of training employees. These are the reasons that PI is still used frequently in business and industry.

DISADVANTAGES

In linear programming, all users follow the same path. This uniformity prevents adaptation of content to users' needs.

Pushing a button or filling in a blank does not necessarily represent active participation. Many poorer programs require only copying tasks, which actually can inhibit learning.

Programmed materials tend to depend too extensively on verbalization to convey content, thereby placing heavy reliance on the reading ability of the user. This is not necessary, and is often changed by the programming of other media, such as video, slides, and filmstrips.

PIM, especially linear materials, are often said to be boring. In a way, this is true. Many are tedious, especially if you diligently work through hundreds or even thousands of linear frames. However, this

16. George J. Corcoran and John Lenaerts, "If . . . You Manage a Public Sector Human Services Program Then . . . You Need to Look Closely at Programmed Instruction," *Performance and Instruction* 21, 9 (1982): 22–24.

claim is based on the common misconception that learning is necessarily fun.[17]

Writing and validating PIM is time consuming and may be more expensive to produce than other print materials. It usually consumes more paper.

It is difficult to use programmed materials for reference. They are not well structured for access.[18]

Branching texts can be awkward to use, especially if you lose your place in the sequence.

Linear texts can be frustrating for users who already know much of the material. Good programs provide a diagnostic option for moving such users ahead.

The highly structured organization of the material can discourage independent inquiry and creative thought.

Machine-based programs are usually unique to one machine; they cannot be displayed on another type of teaching machine. Efforts to standardize on a common format have failed.

Program questions usually emphasize only content knowledge, and do not accommodate emotions or feelings. (This may or may not be a disadvantage.)

Good programs are difficult to prepare on a local basis.

Many programs overemphasize short-answer questions that do not require understanding of the information.

Little interaction among users usually occurs while working on PIM, because of the self-pacing characteristic. However, PIM can be used successfully in small groups.

There is not as wide a selection of high-quality programmed materials available today as in the sixties.

Cheating is possible with virtually all programs, especially linear ones.

SELECTION

Special Criteria

The Joint Committee of Programmed Instruction and Teaching Machines in 1963 recommended distinguishing between internal characteristics of the program (which can be judged by an inspection of

---

17. Donald Bullock, "Programs for Self-Instruction: One Aging Guru's Point of View," *Performance and Instruction* 21, 9 (1982): 4–8.

18. David H. Jonassen, "Information Mapping: A Description, Rationale, and Comparison with Programmed Instruction," *Visible Language* 15, 1 (1981): 55–66.

the program) and external characteristics (features which are only revealed by the performance of users after the completion of the program, or by objective features).[19]

INTERNAL CRITERIA

Is the subject matter appropriate for, or needed by, the intended audience?

Are the objectives of the program, if stated, appropriate for or needed by the intended audience? Are they relevant to some real-world need or prerequisite to further study?

Is the sequence of frames consistent with the structure of the subject-matter content?

Is the sequence of frames appropriate for the type of users in the intended audience?

Is the step size appropriate for the ability of the users?

Are the response opportunities frequent enough for the type of users or the structure of the content?

When a response is required, does feedback follow at some appropriate point, not too delayed from the response?

Are there any provisions for individualizing the sequence or content of the program (e.g., branching, diagnostic tests) or is every user required to proceed through each step?

Is an instructor's guide available which contains recommendations for administration, placement, or integration with other study materials?

Is a post-test available which measures attainment of the objectives?

EXTERNAL CRITERIA

Is there evidence of any testing or user tryout of the program prior to distribution?

Was the group used to field-test the program (if stated), similar to the group for which you are selecting a program, in terms of age, ability, experience, and prior knowledge?

Did the program, as tested in the tryout, produce a sufficient level of learning?

The National Education Association cautioned that an internal inspection alone can be deceptive. External data from tests involving users at your institution or a similar group should be included in the

---

19. Gabriel D. Ofiesh, *Programmed Instruction: A Guide for Management* (Washington, D.C.: American Management Assn., 1965), 207.

evaluation process.[20] The users should represent, as closely as possible, the intended population of users.

OTHER CRITERIA

Are the directions on how to use the program clear, adequate, and appropriate for the target users?

Are the technical terms and symbols adequately defined?

Does the content cover the stated objectives without unnecessary redundancy and superfluous information? (Some redundancy for the purpose of practice is a normal part of PI.)

Does the program periodically review what has been taught most recently throughout the program?

Does the achievement test measure the users' comprehension of the content of the program, as opposed to mere recall of facts?

Does the program allow for individual differences in learning other than pacing, such as prior knowledge or background, ability level, and learning styles?

Are active responses required of the user? Do they require comprehension of the material, rather than mere recall or copying of information?

Are the responses an appropriate form for the users and relevant to the objectives? Are there enough responses for each skill or unit of information?

Do the questions require the user to utilize the critical information in the frame, or to recall only trivial facts?

Are the prompts (if present) necessary for making the correct response, or do they replace the thought processes in which you want users to engage? Are there too many prompts?

Are enough questions asked to allow the user to apply the information to a variety of situations? Will the skills taught in the program transfer to a real-world setting?

Is there at least one question requiring users to respond to each important piece of information or skill?

Is the feedback accurate and clear to the user? (It is surprising how often this simple criterion is violated.) Does it immediately follow the response? Can the feedback be seen by the user while responding?

Are alternative answers to questions acceptable and are the acceptable responses indicated?

---

20. National Education Assn., Division of Audiovisual Service, *Selection and Use of Programmed Materials: A Handbook for Teachers* (Washington, D.C.: National Education Assn., 1964), 65.

Are helpful, remedial comments provided when wrong or alternative answers are anticipated?

Do the instructions allow the user to skip unnecessary repetition or to return to material when necessary?

If a nonprint medium is used, is it an appropriate format for the content of the program? Could the program be more effectively delivered in another format?

Is the delivery mode (machine/text) or control of pacing (self-paced, programmed, or group-paced) appropriate for the maturity level and ability of the intended users?

Are there a sufficient number of review questions and feedback to keep all parts of the program curent and active in memory?

Evaluative Review Sources

PERIODICALS

Booklist
Choice
Library Journal

Programmed Learning and Educational Technology (formerly *Programmed Learning*)
School Library Journal

BOOKS

Taggert, Dorothy T. *A Guide to Sources in Educational Media and Technology*. Metuchen, N.J.: Scarecrow, 1975.

Wasserman, Paul, ed. *Learning Independently: A Directory of Self-Instruction Resources*. Detroit: Gale, 1979.

Wynar, Christine Gehrt. *Guide to Reference Books for School Media Centers*. 2nd ed. Littleton, Colo.: Libraries Unlimited, 1981. (Evaluates relevant reference works, not PI materials)

Nonevaluative Sources

PERIODICALS

Datamation
Educational Technology (New Products–New Services)
Instructional Innovator
International Index to Multi-Media Information
Audiovisual Materials
Performance and Instruction

BOOKS

Cabeceiras, James. *Multimedia Library: Material Selection and Use*. 2d ed. San Diego: Academic Pr., 1982.

Educational Media Yearbook. Littleton, Colo.: Libraries Unlimited, 1973– . Annual.

Hendershot, Carl. *Programmed Learning and Individually Paced Instruction.* 5th ed. Bay City, Mich.: Carl Hendershot, 1973. Supplements 1–6.

International Directory of Programmed Instruction. Repertoire International d'Enseignement Programme. Paris: Unesco, 1973.

International Yearbook of Educational and Instructional Technology: 1982/1983. London: Kogan Page, for APLET, 1983.

National Information Center for Educational Media. *NICEM Media Indexes.* Los Angeles: NICEM, Univ. of Southern California.

Rufsvold, Margaret I. *Guides to Educational Media: Films, Filmstrips, Multimedia Kits, Programmed Instruction Materials, Recordings on Discs and Tapes, Slides, Transparencies, Videotapes.* 4th ed. Chicago: American Library Assn., 1977.

Sive, Mary. *Selecting Instructional Media.* 2d ed. Littleton, Colo.: Libraries Unlimited, 1978.

MAINTENANCE AND MANAGEMENT

Storage and Care

Linear, text programs should be maintained in the following manner:

1. Make certain the disclosure mask, if there is one, is kept with the text.

2. Shelving and other storage and maintenance procedures are the same as those for other texts or workbooks.

Programmed teaching machines should be maintained in the following manner:

1. For nonelectronic teaching machines, make sure that there is an adequate supply of replacement response paper (frequently comes in rolls) and that it is properly fitted to the machine.

2. Return the program to the beginning after each use, unless it is being used by only one user, in which case it should remain at the place the user left off.

3. For electronic teaching machines, be certain that the film on which the programs are encoded is protected, especially along the edges which contain the advance signals. (They should be returned to their containers immediately after use.)

These machines are often unpredictable. Refer electronic problems to a qualified technician, if you can find one. These machines are not in common use today.

Management Problems and Solutions

PI is normally thought of as instructional material, to be placed in classrooms or libraries of educational institutions. However, its potential use extends beyond those limited applications, as evidenced by the newer forms of PI now appearing. The diversity of subjects treated by programs will continue to attract users to them. For instance, self-teaching guides are still popular among self-motivated people who desire enrichment or improvement of a skill. Programmed materials cover a range of topics, from repair of a leaky faucet to advanced programming techniques for microcomputers.

"Special libraries with demands in particular subjects and skills can also use programmed materials to satisfy individual instructional needs. With the increasing diversity of subjects programmed and the development of the computer and microfilm technology it will be entirely possible for all libraries to accommodate many more individual differences in learning."[21]

Currently, PI is most widely used in business and industry, where employees must learn procedures for running a particular machine or selling a particular product in as little time as possible. In fact, General Motors recently invested millions of dollars to equip each dealership with hardware to display programmed videotapes or videodiscs. Programmed teaching guides remain popular for enrichment or remediation at all levels of schooling. Many students who are unable to learn by using their textbooks and traditional classroom methods frequently turn to programmed self-teaching guides to remediate their understanding.

USING PI

The ways for using PI are as varied as its characteristics:

Enrichment	By handicapped and mentally retarded
Review	
Remedial instruction	Alternative instruction for absentees and transfers
Independent study	
Self-instruction	In association with audiovisual materials
Home-bound instruction	
Initial learning	

---

21. Warren B. Hicks and Alma M. Tillen, *Developing Multi-Media Libraries* (New York: Bowker, 1970), 26.

Other Concerns

TYPES OF PROGRAMS

Two major types of programs have dominated the field since 1960, but there has been a great deal of variability in these programs. Likewise, PI has been produced in many different forms. In this section, the different types of programs will be discussed.

Linear (Extrinsic, Unisequential)

Linear programs were the earliest and most prominent form of programming. Linear PIM usually consists of the following characteristics:

Presentation of written material (normally), enclosed in frames, introduces or reviews small increments of information per frame.

The information contained in a series of frames is normally graduated from easy to difficult, simple to complex, concrete to abstract (i.e., generally a simple inductive sequence).

Users make an active response in each and every frame presented in the same sequence to every user, requiring them to recall information contained in the frame or review and practice information presented in a recent frame. The nature of these responses varies. The important point is that some response is made. Therefore, linear PI is referred to as *response-centered programming*.

The program provides immediate confirmation of the correctness of the user's responses, which serves to reinforce the particular responding behavior.

Following feedback, each and every learner proceeds to the next frame in the sequence, regardless of the result of the previous one.

Learners proceed through the programmed sequence of frames at their own pace.

No effort is usually made to check one's understanding of the material—only to reinforce a particular response set; that is, to make a particular form of behavior more predictable.

As the practice of programming evolved, exceptions to these basic characteristics began to appear. These modifications made linear programs appear more like branching programs.

Modified Linear

The programmer continually varies the context of the review materials. Often, if a user answers a review question correctly, she or he will be directed to skip a sequence of questions. An incorrect response to some review questions will send the user back to repeat a sequence of frames.

Linear with Sublinears

These programs include additional material, so that rapid learners, who may become bored with straight linear programming, have an opportunity to learn supplemental information. This supplemental information is contained in linear subprograms which branch out from the main program.

Linear with Criterion Frames

Criterion frames are used to determine if a user should complete a given sequence within a program. They may also be used to assign users to individual linear tracks within a program.

Branching (Intrinsic) Programs

The entire conceptual orientation of branching programming is different from that of linear programming. Essentially, branching programs test whether communication has succeeded.

Branching programs generally possess the following features:

Branching programs are larger, with more coherent segments of text that require users to read and comprehend the information presented. Branching PI is therefore said to be *stimulus centered*.

Responses are less overt and more intrinsic to the program, and are meant to confirm comprehension of the material or completion of a skill. Users are required to think through the frame and understand where the program is going.

User responses are not intended always to be correct. Incorrect responses indicate inadequate comprehension of the material or completion of a skill. The role of feedback is informative or corrective, not reinforcing as in linear programs.

The sequence of frames or text units that learners complete varies with the user's comprehension of the material. The emphasis is on adapting the sequence to accommodate differences in prior learning or learning ability.

The emphasis is on relating the material in the program to prior learning, which facilitates comprehension of the material.

Branching programs are better adapted to machine (rather than text) presentation. They are not well suited to book format.

TRANSITIONS

PI has now been in the educational mainstream for thirty years—time enough to complete a full development cycle. The initial fervor led to critical analysis, which precipitated skepticism, which resulted in its cyclical decline from prominence. The bandwagon began to rust in the seventies. But rather than corroding into extinction, PI now has renewed impetus, albeit in different forms than in its first cycle. Principles and processes of PI appear in generic instructional development models, self-teaching texts, interactive videotape/videodisc projects, and most notably in computer-assisted instruction. The new cycle of PI has gained momentum, though there is no reason to believe that its amplitude or duration will be as great as in the first cycle. In fact, as greater understanding of the processes of human learning produces more effective instructional designs, the PI model will be comparatively less effective. The more sophisticated technologies of computers and videodiscs have stretched the PI model to its limits.

These and other technologies, now evolving, are clearly more powerful than the model can accommodate; so in order to more fully utilize such technologies, educational technologists will be forced to increasingly abandon the PI model in favor of more flexible and powerful design models, no doubt based on principles of artificial intelligence. Exactly how long that transition will require is at best speculative. Until then—and even after, to a lesser extent—programmed learning will continue to function as a reasonably effective and very utilitarian approach to training and instruction.

ADDITIONAL RESOURCES

Becker, J. L. *A Programmed Guide to Writing Auto-Instructional Programs.* Camden, N.J.: Radio Corp. of America, 1963.

Boucher, Brian G, Merril J. Gottlieb, and Martin L. Morganlander. *Handbook and Catalog for Instructional Media Selection.* Englewood Cliffs, N.J.: Educational Technology Pub., 1973.

Brethower, D. *Programmed Instruction: A Manual of Programming Techniques.* Chicago: Educational Methods, 1963.

Bullock, Donald. *Programmed Instruction.* Instructional Design Library, No. 14. Englewood Cliffs, N.J.: Educational Technology Pub., 1978.

Callendar, Patricia. *Programmed Learning: Its Development and Structure.* New York: Longmans, Green, 1969.

Calvin, Allen D. *Programmed Instruction: Bold New Venture.* Bloomington: Indiana Univ. Pr., 1969.

Coulson, John E. *Programmed Learning and Computer-Based Instruction.* New York: Wiley & Sons, 1962.

Cram, David. *Explaining Teaching Machines and Programming.* San Francisco: Fearon, 1961.

Cronbach, Lee J., and Richard E. Snow. *Aptitudes and Instructional Methods.* New York: Irvington Pr., 1977. (Chapter on programmed instruction)

Crowder, Norman. "Automatic Tutoring by Intrinsic Programming." In A. A. Lumsdaine and Robert Glaser, eds., *Teaching Machines and Programmed Learning.* Washington, D.C.: National Education Assn., 1960.

Davies, Ruth A. *The School Library Media Program: Instructional Force for Excellence*. 3rd ed. New York: Bowker, 1979.

Duane, James E., comp. *Individualized Instruction—Programs and Materials: Selected Readings and Bibliography*. Englewood Cliffs, N.J.: Educational Technology Pub., 1973.

Espich, J. E., and B. Williams. *Developing Programmed Instructional Materials: A Handbook for Program Writers*. Belmont, Calif.: Fearon, 1967.

Friesen, Paul. *An Introduction to Instructional Programming*. Ottawa: Friese, Kay, 1970.

Fry, Edward B. *Teaching Machines and Programmed Instruction: An Introduction*. New York: McGraw-Hill, 1968.

Gagne, Robert M. *Teaching Machines and Programmed Learning, II*. Washington, D.C.: National Education Assn., 1965.

Gerlach, Vernon, and Donald P. Ely. *Teaching Media: A Systematic Approach*. 2nd ed. Englewood Cliffs, N.J.: Prentice-Hall, 1982.

Gilbert, Thomas. "Mathetics—The Technology of Education." In M. D. Merrill, ed., *Instructional Design: Readings*. Englewood Cliffs, N.J.: Educational Technology Pub., 1971.

Gilman, David A. "The Origins and Development of Intrinsic and Adaptive Programming." *AV Communication Review* 20 (Spring 1972): 64–76.

Glaser, Robert. "Some Research Problems in Automated Instruction." In John E. Coulson, ed., *Programmed Learning and Computer-Based Instruction*. New York: Wiley & Sons, 1962.

———, J. I. Taber, and H. Shaifer. *Using Programmed Instructional Technology*. Englewood Cliffs, N.J.: Educational Technology Pub., 1971.

Hartley, James. "Programmed Instruction 1954–1974: A Review." *Programmed Learning and Educational Technology* 11, 6 (1974): 278–91.

———, ed. *Strategies for Programmed Instruction: An Educational Technology*. London: Butterworths, 1972.

——— and Ivor K. Davies. "Programmed Learning and Educational Technology." In Michael Howe, ed., *Adult Learning*. New York: Wiley & Sons, 1976.

Hendershot, Carl H. *Programmed Learning and Individually Paced Instruction: Bibliography*. 5th ed. Bay City, Mich.: Hendershot (4114 Ridgewood Dr.), 1975.

Hughes, J. L. *Programmed Learning: A Critical Evaluation*. Chicago: Educational Methods, 1968.

International Directory of Programmed Instruction. Paris: Unesco, 1972.

Jacobs, Paul I., Milton H. Maier, and Lawrence M. Stolurow. *A Guide to Evaluating Self-Instructional Programs*. 2nd ed. New York: Holt, Rinehart & Winston, 1966.

Komoski, P. Kenneth. *Programmed Instruction Materials, 1964–65: A Guide to Programmed Instructional Materials Available for Use in Elementary and Secondary Schools as of April, 1965*. New York: Center for Programmed Instruction of the Institute of Educational Technology, Teachers College, Columbia Univ., 1965.

Lange, Philip C. *Programmed Learning: A Critical Analysis*. Chicago: Educational Methods, 1968.

_____. "What's the Score on Programmed Instruction?" *Today's Education* 61 (Feb. 1972): 59.

Lawson, Dene R. "Who Thought of It First? A Review of Historical References to Programmed Instruction." *Educational Technology* 9, 10 (1969): 93–96.

Leith, George O. *A Handbook of Programmed Learning*. Birmingham, UK: University of Birmingham.

Mager, Robert F. "On the Sequencing of Instructional Content." In Ivor K. Davies and James Hartley, eds., *Contributions to an Educational Technology*. London: Butterworths, 1961.

Markle, Susan. *Good Frames and Bad: A Grammar of Frame Writing*. 2nd ed. New York: Wiley & Sons, 1969.

National Education Assn. Division of Audiovisual Service. *Selection and Use of Programmed Materials: A Handbook for Teachers*. Washington, D.C.: National Education Assn., 1964.

New Media and College Teaching. Washington, D.C.: National Education Assn., 1968.

Oates, Stanton C. *Instructional Materials Handbook*. Dubuque: Kendall/Hunt, 1971.

O'Day, Edward F. *Programmed Instruction: Techniques and Trends*. Englewood Cliffs, N.J.: Prentice-Hall, 1971.

Ofiesh, Gabriel D. *Programmed Instruction: A Guide for Management*. Washington, D.C.: American Management Assn., 1965.

_____ and Wesley C. Meierhenry. *Trends in Programmed Instruction*. Washington, D.C.: National Education Assn., 1964.

Pipe, Peter. *Practical Programming*. New York: Holt, Rinehart & Winston, 1965.

Pocztar, Jerry. *The Theory and Practice of Programmed Instruction*. Paris: Unesco, 1972.

Roucek, Joseph S. *Programmed Teaching*. London: Peter Owen, 1965.

Rowntree, Derek. *Basically Branching*. London: Macdonald, 1966.

Schramm, Wilbur. *Programmed Instruction: Today and Tomorrow*. New York: Fund for the Advancement of Education, 1962.

_____. *The Research on Programmed Instruction: An Annotated Bibliography*. Washington, D.C.: U.S. Dept. of Health, Education, and Welfare, 1964.

Silberman, H. F. "Characteristics of Some More Recent Studies of Instructional Methods." In John E. Coulson, ed., *Programmed Learning and Computer-Based Instruction*. New York: Wiley and Sons, 1962.

Skinner, Bhurrus F. "The Science of Learning and the Art of Teaching." In Arthur A. Lumsdaine and Robert Glaser, eds., *Teaching Machines and Programmed Learning*. Washington, D.C.: National Education Assn., 1954.

Stolurow, Lawrence M. *Teaching by Machine*. Washington D.C.: U.S. Dept. of Health, Education, and Welfare, 1961.

Taylor, Albert J. "Those Magnificent Men and Their Teaching Machines."
    Educational Forum 36 (Jan. 1972): 239–46.
Wohl, Seth F. "Pointers on the Purchase and Use of Programmed Instruction."
    Educational Product Report 2 (Oct. 1968): 14–17.

Esther Green Bierbaum

Realia

THE MEDIUM

Definition

In this chapter, *realia* will be defined as "tangible, three-dimensional physical objects of, or from, the real world." The term implies what advertising copywriters like to call "the real thing," and the definition is derived from the meaning of *real*, which *Webster's Third New International Unabridged Dictionary* (1968) defines as "not artificial or counterfeit; actually existing, occurring, or present in fact."

Brief History

The history of realia is the history of human existence. Burial-site evidence indicates that objects were used not only for sustenance and survival in early, preliterate history but were also valued for themselves, for communication, comfort, or pleasure. Often they were symbols not of mere possession, but also of personal or tribal qualities: the totem of the Northwest Indians, the Ebenezer of the ancient Hebrews, and the conch shell of the Pacific islanders were real objects, invested with symbolic and communication values beyond the thing itself.[1]

---

1. For a discussion of the relationship of objects and cultures, see James Deetz, "The Link from Object to Person to Concept," in Zipporah W. Collins, ed., *Museums, Adults, and the Humanities* (Washington, D.C.: American Assn. of Museums [AAM], 1981), 24–34.

The collecting of objects was not an activity indulged in solely by our ancestors! Teachers and parents are well acquainted with childhood collections, while auctioneers, antique shop proprietors, hobby magazine publishers, and other entrepreneurs depend on the proclivity of grown-up children to continue collecting realia. Nor is a fascination with objects confined to the human species; it is also seen in some animals, a phenomenon giving rise to such colorful expressions as "pack rat" and "magpie's nest."

While archaeological evidence suggests very early beginnings for object collections, it was not until literate times that organized collections of both objects and writings appeared.[2] Formal libraries and museums had to wait for some members of the society to achieve the wealth and the leisure to take advantage of collections of writings and realia. Often the two institutions existed as one: the famous library at Alexandria, established in the 3rd century B.C., was a collegium of scholars and researchers as well as a repository of written records and of objects from the natural world. Records and objects were designed to serve scholarship and research.[3] The temple collections of Greece and Rome gave way to medieval reliquaries and collections of artifacts symbolizing the lives of saints and sinners. Growing royal wealth, the wonders brought back from the Crusades, and the increase of trade and commerce all led to the popularity of "cabinets," or collections of curios which were often intended by their wealthy and powerful owners to strike wonder and envy in the hearts of beholders. The 17th and 18th centuries saw the creation of a number of "public" museums—"public" largely in the sense that the collections were removed from the owner's residence and made available to a carefully selected group of persons on a carefully limited schedule. Still, museums such as the Basel and Ashmolean fulfilled the basic museum function of bringing realia together for pleasure and enlightenment.[4]

The rapid rise in scientific endeavor meant that there was no end of collectors in the next hundred or so years and, therefore, no end of donors. Consequently, museums and their collections grew apace. In the latter years of the 19th century, and particularly in America, philanthropy sought to justify itself by teaming efforts with the educational movement, a development chronicled by Daniel M. Fox.[5] For several decades after the turn-of-century work of John Cotton Dana

---

2. G. Ellis Burcaw, *Introduction to Museum Work* (Nashville: American Assn. for State and Local History [AASLH], 1975), 15–17.
3. Edward P. Alexander, *Museums in Motion* (Nashville: AASLH, 1979), 6–7.
4. Ibid., 7–8.
5. Daniel M. Fox, *Engines of Culture* (Madison: State Historical Society of Wisconsin for Dept. of History, Univ. of Wisconsin, 1963).

and his colleagues in the "new museum" movement, American museums were agencies of collections or of public education.[6] In the last quarter-century, however, there has been a general perception that objects may be collected and admired and beheld and, at the same time, be media of communication and information, and enhancements to learning. Rare is the museum which does not offer educational programs based upon the realia in its collection.

The use of realia for teaching and instruction also goes back to our very beginnings; for by their nature, objects are the essence of the real world and the optimal means of teaching about it. In preliterate times, which are the major span of human history, oral tradition and the artifacts made or secured by the group were the carriers of both the group's history and instructions from members regarding the future.

Using objects to teach about the world and to develop skills for dealing with it has always been a preschool technique, and the use of objects in the classroom setting has increased with the growing awareness of the value of direct experience in reinforcing concepts.[7] During the years when education consisted of reading, writing, and ciphering, there was little need for classroom objects: the students dealt directly with the real world, side by side with their parents, in field or shop, and even the urban environment provided opportunities for collecting, manipulating, and experiencing real things. Missionaries, travelers, and importers brought objects from foreign regions to the attention of adults and children alike; but until the notions of "visual education" penetrated into the classroom, an "antiseptic" attitude was maintained toward real things from the real world.[8] This attitude persists in the literature as well as in practice. For example, neither the *NICEM Index to Producers and Distributors* nor the most recent edition of the *Educational Media Yearbook* includes realia or models in the indexes;[9] the tactile, spatial, and manipulative dimensions of the media and learning are overlooked.

Much of the research investigating the communicative values of

6. John Cotton Dana, *The New Museum* (Woodstock, Vt.: Elm Tree Pr., 1917).
7. S. Dillon Ripley, "From the Castle," *Smithsonian* 6 (May 1975). See also Ira J. Gordon, *Baby Learning through Baby Play* (New York: St. Martin's, 1970), for a popular treatment of the role of realia in early childhood education, and J. Steven Soulier, *Real Objects and Models* (Englewood Cliffs, N.J.: Educational Technology Pub., 1981), 5–6, for the viewpoint of instructional use of realia.
8. John Cotton Dana, *Aids in High School Teaching: Pictures and Objects,* Part XIX of Vol. II, *Modern American Library Economy as Illustrated by the Newark N.J. Free Public Library* (Woodstock, Vt.: Elm Tree Pr., 1916), 141–11, 183–53–55.
9. *NICEM Index to Producers and Distributors* (Los Angeles: National Information Center for Educational Media [NICEM]); *Educational Media Yearbook, 1978* (New York: Bowker, 1978).

realia has been undertaken in the museum field,[10] and it has not been confined to work with child populations. As Greg Mertz points out: "People of all ages and capacities learn through a sensory approach. . . . The process is an easy and lifelong one [but] by the time most people become adults, they tend to ignore or distrust new information provided through intermediary symbols."[11] He sums up the unique force of realia: "Museum education succeeds in teaching about objects, concepts and, in a broader sense, the world, because it focuses the learner's attention on one object or collection of objects at a time."[12]

As Dana's work suggested, museums and classroom teachers may deal directly with one another.[13] Indeed, there are now some model programs of library and museum resource sharing.[14] Before school libraries became widely developed as media centers, there was also some interest in offering "museum services," from the school library to the classroom teacher.[15] Such instances of dealing with realia as part of classroom instruction helped pave the way for their acceptance in the school and school media center as viable means of communicating what print and paper could not. Realia's mixed history in the schools has, however, produced budgetary anomalies and issues of "ownership" which have sometimes impeded effective management (see "Management Problems" section).

Realia have lagged well behind print and conventional audiovisual materials in achieving acceptance in public library collections. The work of the Toys, Games and Realia Committee of ALA's Children's Services Division provided a rationale for realia in libraries.[16] (It also fueled discussion in the literature!)

10. The following are a few representative studies: Minda Borun, *Measuring the Immeasurable: A Pilot Study of Museum Effectiveness* (Washington, D.C.: Assn. of Science-Technology Centers [ASTC], 1979); Duncan F. Cameron, "A Viewpoint: The Museum as a Communications System and Implications for Museum Education," *Curator* 11 (Jan. 1968): 33–40; Mary B. Hyman, "Science Museums and Gifted Students," *Museum News* 59 (July/Aug. 1981): 33–38; Barbara Reque, "From Object to Idea," *Museum News* 56 (Jan./Feb. 1978): 45–47; Thomas A. Rhodes, "The Museum as a Learning Environment . . . ," D.Ed. diss. (Memphis State Univ., 1978); and Herbert D. Thier and Marcia C. Linn, "The Value of Interactive Learning Experiences," *Curator* 19 (Sept. 1976): 233–45.

11. Greg Mertz, *An Object in the Hand . . . : Museum Educational Outreach for the Elderly, Incarcerated & Disabled* (Washington, D.C.: Smithsonian Institution Collaborative Educational Outreach Program, 1982), 8.

12. Ibid., 9.

13. See note 8 above.

14. Hilda L. Jay and M. Ellen Jay, *Developing Library-Museum Partnerships to Serve Young People* (Hamden, Conn.: Library Professional Publications, 1984).

15. Sara Frances Seaman, "Museum Services in School Libraries" (thesis, Columbia Univ., 1944), and Brown, Lewis, and Harcleroad, *A-V Instruction . . . ,* 293.

16. Children's Services Division, "Realia in the Library," *Booklist* 73 (Jan. 1, 1977): 671–74.

Unique Characteristics

The characteristic which sets apart realia, or "things," from all other types of nonprint media is the tangible connection to the real world; these objects are indeed what they seem to be: *real.*

The other characteristics of realia are further aspects of their essential, unique quality:

They are related to the real world.

They are usually more portable and accessible than the whole environment they represent.

They can be touched, manipulated, and observed.

They are often inexpensive and readily obtainable.

They are almost infinitely various.

They are versatile, and may fill several learning objectives or educational and recreational needs.

They are often meaningful, without language.

They are accessible to the visually handicapped, deaf, and physically handicapped.

They transcend age barriers.

They combine elements of instruction and recreation and appeal to the cognitive and affective domains.

They excite interest about the unknown environment they represent, and encourage exploration.

They may lead from the general to the particular, or the reverse.

The range and variety of realia is virtually unlimited, except for considerations of space, portability, and safety.

Advantages and Disadvantages

The advantages of realia are inherent in their nature: they are not a representation of the world, but part of the world itself. As Mertz observes, "Learning directly from objects can help make the learner a first class citizen of the real world."[17]

The disadvantages of realia are also found in their nature: even though they are part of the world, the world cannot be fully brought to the learning situation along with the object. Thus realia are often presented out of context, so that their inherent advantage is lessened. Then they become abstractions of the very reality we try to convey!

As Thomas and Swartout suggest, a demonstration and explanation of the object will help dispel the sense of abstraction we get from viewing, or even handling, realia in isolation and away from the

17. Mertz, *An Object in the Hand . . . ,* 4.

environment which gave it meaning.[18] Another way to invest the object with meaning is to involve the user or learner in locating and interpreting it; herein is the unique value of outdoor education.[19]

Russel B. Nye suggested four disadvantages of realia in the museum setting:

> First, . . . the artifact is out of its context, divorced from its purpose. . . . Second, museums can exhibit only those things that survive. . . . Third, certain artifacts are valued for qualities other than those for which they were intended. A Greek coin on an illuminated pedestal . . . has qualities ascribed to it that the maker and user certainly never intended. . . . Fourth, our examination of the past can never be complete, because no museum can exhibit sound.[20]

Some advantages of realia are:

They are a part of the real world, and do not simply represent it: a terrarium with its various life forms, an item of clothing made without buttons, or a dinosaur femur as tall as a child all convey a sense of the part of the world from which they came.

They are more portable and, therefore, more accessible than in their original environment: the terrarium brings part of the forest floor with it.

They may often be obtained readily, and for little or no cost.

They offer a range of sensory stimulation in addition to sight: the feel of the fabric, or the snake's skin, or the odor of the salt-water aquarium convey more than simply seeing the costume, the snake, or the fish.

They furnish readily comprehensible comparisons of size, mass, and color which even pictures cannot convey. Scale is a difficult abstraction to gain from pictures, while the relative sizes of different species of shells are apparent when they are actually accessible.

They transcend language but help to develop language: the physical activity of using tools reinforces the words describing the activity, while the beauty of rocks, shells, or flowers does not need language to convey it.

18. R. Murray Thomas and Sherwin G. Swartout, *Integrated Teaching Materials,* rev. and enl. (New York: David McKay, 1963), 16–18.

19. Donald R. Hammerman and William M. Hammerman, *Teaching in the Outdoors,* 2nd ed. (Minneapolis: Burgess, 1973), 1–6.

20. Russel B. Nye, "The Humanities and the Museum: Definitions and Connections," in Zipporah W. Collins, ed., *Museums, Adults and the Humanities: A Guide for Educational Programming,* 10–11.

They help develop concepts: size, color, spatial relations, and more sophisticated concepts, such as ecological relationships, are enhanced through the observation and handling of real things.

They transcend age: adults and children alike learn from and enjoy objects.

They enhance the affective as well as cognitive domains: a scarred wooden bowl tells us much about the poverty of its owner who could afford only that one utensil.

They enhance the learning experience and excite the interest of the verbally unskilled: a demonstration of a process such as weaving does not require words to express the origin of the end product, the length of fabric.

They encourage the perception of likeness and difference and the basis for classification and collection.

They enhance other media, as the popularity of kits attests.

They enrich the learning experiences of the visually and physically handicapped, and the deaf: other senses can be used to interact with realia.

They are versatile and not subject linked: the costumes which are used in the social studies setting may also be used in the study of languages, or the appreciation of form and color.

Some disadvantages of realia are:

They are separated from their original environment, so that the connection is not always apparent: verbal explanations or demonstrations may be needed to connect the terrarium to the forest. (The connection is more than apparent to the learners who have also done the collecting!)

They may be rare or important, and thus costly and even irreplaceable, or may require security measures. Costs, then, may become a constraint upon the use of some realia, such as gold or silver artifacts or hybrid orchids.

They may require instruction in observation and attention before their use is effective.

They may have inherently unsafe features which limit use: tools with cutting edges, weapons, and venomous animals are not appropriate for manipulating.

They may require special storage or care: climate control for live animals and plants, large boxes and requisite shelving for bulky items may be arguments against some kinds of realia.

Because they often are readily available, they may be used inappropriately or indiscriminately: good full-color prints are better guides to plant identification than sheaves of dried, faded plant specimens on botanical paper. (Which is not to deny the value in the original act of collecting!)

They may have (for some institutions) problems of description, labeling, and general control which discourage acquisition and use.

They may have special care problems (such as live animals) during vacations and weekends.

They may be fragile or valuable, and so should only be observed and not handled. The advantages of the touch-and-feel encounter are lost to such items as ancient silk komonos.

Realia may (for some institutions) present budgetary and location problems which limit their accessibility.

SELECTION

Special Criteria

The proposed use to which the object is to be put is the basic selection criterion. To some extent, the object itself is its own criterion, for when the object is unique, there are no alternative editions, recordings, or printings. Once the appropriateness of the realia is established, other criteria are important. Durability, safety, versatility, and skill level should be considered in evaluating toys and games.[21] The first two criteria, durability and safety, are of primary importance, after appropriateness, in selecting any realia which will be handled or manipulated.

In 1977 the Toys, Games, and Realia Committee of ALA's Children's Services Division developed extensive sets of selection criteria, which were published in *Booklist*.[22] The criteria, however, are almost entirely directed at toy selection, except for the items of "natural elements," "musical instruments," and games listed under "dramatic play" and "strategy skills." Among criteria suggested for toys, which may also be applied more broadly to realia, are durability, nonflammability (related to safety), and selection according to the Consumer Products Safety Commission's list of banned toys.

The *Booklist* criteria also address questions of collection development, such as quantity, variety, range, and affective values; but these are questions which must be answered in relation to the instructional and behavioral objectives which suggest three-dimensional media in the first place.

21. Joy K. Moll and Patricia Hermann, "Evaluation and Selection of Toys, Games, and Puzzles: Manipulative Materials in Library Collections." *Top of the News* 31 (Nov. 1974): 87–88.

22. See note 15 above.

The nature and state of the object will make some uses appropriate and others impossible, so that considerations of durability may be tempered by the proposed use. If, for example, the object is intended for display, then the fragile, delicate, and intricate object may be suitable. On the other hand, if the intent is to engage the learner with the object, provision must be made for the safety of the object and the person handling it. Many objects are inherently sturdy enough or well enough constructed to be resistant to vigorous handling and manipulation: rock specimens, tools and utensils, and fossilized bones of large animals come to mind as examples of use-resistant realia. Costumes which are constructed of washable material and with closely sewn seams are also amenable to considerable usage. Thus, while its authenticity, its condition, or state of health may make one specimen a better choice than another, the *kind* of realia is predetermined by the needs and objectives of the setting or educational situation.

Fragility may be overcome, so that the needs of the situation and the care of the object may both be achieved. Many objects which are inherently delicate may be preserved or packaged so that handling becomes possible. Encapsulation or preservation in Lucite is a technique often used to protect biological specimens while making them accessible to close observation. Plant specimens may be presented in clear plastic containers, and insects may be displayed in plastic boxes. Very small biological realia may be presented on slides with inexpensive, fixed-stage microscopes which protect the slide from damage.

Careful instructions in handling and care can make firsthand encounters safe for vulnerable realia. Such precautions are particularly necessary in the case of live specimens, whether plant or animal. (Tetanus inoculations for the human side of the encounter are a recommended precautionary measure!) Then there are the objects for which no artificial safety measures can be devised. Fragile, breakable, historic relics, live plants, and some fossil materials are examples of realia which must either be encased to permit limited handling or must be restricted to observation. Inherently dangerous yet important objects, such as weapons, glassware, and edged instruments, are also candidates for safety measures (such as display and demonstration, rather than direct handling).

Evaluative Review Sources

As argued in the "Special Criteria" section, realia are, by their very nature, selected for their intrinsic value and application to the particular situation rather than according to the criteria customarily associated with "media selection." The selector, then, must have firmly established the behavioral objectives or other reasons for deciding on the use of realia, and will then decide whether a particular object or set of objects will further those objectives or fulfill the instructional or recreational purposes.

There are few guides for selection; for example, *Children's Media Market Place* (New York: Neal-Schuman, 1982) does not list a selection tool for realia. There are, however, some sources of general guidance. One may find, for example, reviews of exhibits in local or regional newspapers, newsmagazines, and the museum journal literature such as *Museum News* and *Museum*. Such reviews are valuable sources of professional assessment and judgment regarding the display of objects or groups of objects, and the remarks of the reviewer may often be applied to similar types of objects.

It is also wise to turn to experts in a particular field who will be able to judge the condition, value, or authenticity of an item of realia, and who will also be able to furnish more information about it. *Parents* (New York: Parents Magazine Enterprises) and other home-and-family magazines often report on toy recalls, and publish evaluations of particular toys. Product review and evaluation magazines are also sources of assessment and information about toys and games.

While there are no systematic and regular sources of reviews and evaluation of realia, in addition to the journal and magazine suggested above, the following titles from time to time offer helpful comments, if not formal evaluations:

Booklist. From time to time describes kits which may contain realia.
Curriculum Review. Also describes kits.
Media Review Digest
Museum
Museum News
Science and Children. Suggestions for use of realia, especially naturally occurring specimens.
Science Teacher.

Nonevaluative Sources

Separate finding lists for realia and listings in general for audiovisual sources are not readily available. The selector must depend upon local sources and expertise and upon suppliers of specimens and objects. ("On approval" purchase is the wise course until one has confidence in a supplier.)

LOCAL SOURCES

The following are suggested as sources of realia, information about them, and instructions for care and storage:

Collectors', naturalists', and hobbyists' groups. The knowledgeable amateur is a ready source of realia and information. Local archaeological societies, "rock hound" clubs, coin and stamp clubs, and historical associations will usually be able to supply not only the object, but the benefit of study about it.

Local collectors. Since private collectors seldom advertise, discovering them comes by word of mouth. They may be members of the groups suggested above; often they are expanding an interest acquired from other areas of activity. Returned missionaries, retired military and diplomatic personnel, and persons working for international firms will have collected realia and have had the personal experience as well.

Museums. Many museums today have loan collections, often in kit form, with information about the objects and their relation to the learner. Often such kits and services are geared to instructional units.

College and university libraries. The special collections in college and university libraries often include realia.

Public libraries. Public libraries, particularly in communities with strong genealogical and historical interests, will collect realia associated with the history of the community.

College and university academic departments. Biology, history, archaeology, and geology departments are sources of expertise and often of objects.

State and/or district education, historical, and archaeological departments. These agencies often have realia available, as well as the necessary expertise. State museums may also have loan collections.

Local businesses and industries. Samples of products and manufactures may often be obtained from local businesses and industries, along with information about the realia, the steps in its production, and the materials used in making it.

Language societies and ethnic groups. Local ethnic heritage groups are sources of costumes, utensils, crafts, musical instruments, and information.

COMMERCIAL SOURCES

Two generally available sources of information about manufacturers, producers, and suppliers are:

Thomas Register of American Manufacturers. New York: Thomas. Annual.

Children's Media Market Place. New York: Neal-Schuman, 1982, 120.

The following list of commercial sources of realia and of supplies associated with their storage and care is not complete since it includes only those firms which replied to a letter of inquiry and whose catalogs indicated an appropriate range of products and specimens.

MANUFACTURERS, PRODUCERS, SUPPLIERS, AND SOURCES

ABC School Supply
6500 Peachtree Industrial Blvd.
P.O. Box 4750
Norcross, GA 30071

Audio-Visual Enterprises
911 Laguna Rd.
Pasadena, CA 91105

Bi-Folkal Productions
Route 1 Rainbow Farm
Blue Mounds, WI 53517

Burt Harrison & Co.
(Formerly SEE)
P.O. Box 732
Weston, MA 02193-0732

Carolina Biological Supply
2700 York Rd.
Burlington, NC 27215

Central Scientific Co.
2600 S. Kostner Ave.
Chicago, IL 60623

Childcraft Education Corp.
20 Kilmer Rd.
Edison, NJ 08818

Children's Museum
The Resource Center
Jamaicaway
Boston, MA 02130

Community Playthings
Rifton, NY 12471

Creative Teaching Associates
5629 Westover
P.O. Box 7766
Fresno, CA 93747

Curriculum Production Co.
Dept. 4
Box 457
Churchville, PA 18966

Denoyer-Geppert Co.
5235 Ravenswood Ave.
Chicago, IL 60640

Educational Teaching Aids
159 W. Kinzie St.
Chicago, IL 60610

F. A. O. Schwarz
Fifth Ave. and 58th St.
New York, NY 10151

GAMCO
(Formerly Math-Master)
P.O. Box 1911
Big Spring, TX 79720-0022

Gessler
900 Broadway
New York, NY 10003

Hubbard Scientific Co.
P.O. Box 105
Northbrook, IL 60062

Lab-Aids, Inc.
130 Wilbur Pl.
Bohemia, NY 11716

Math-Master (see GAMCO)

Milton Bradley
74 Park St.
Springfield, MA 01105

NASCO
901 Janesville Ave.
Fort Atkinson, WI 53538

Nienhuis Montessori USA
320 Pioneer Way
Mountain View, CA 94041

Pacific Bio-Marine Labs
P.O. Box 536
Venice, CA 90291

Page Museum Shop
5801 Wilshire Blvd.
Los Angeles, CA 90036

Replogle Globes
1901 Narragansett Ave.
Chicago, IL 60639

Schoolmasters Teaching Aids
745 State Circle
P.O. Box 1941
Ann Arbor, MI 48106

Ward's Natural Science
    Establishment
5100 W. Henrietta Rd.
P.O. Box 92912
Rochester, NY 14692-9012

SUPPLIERS BY TYPE OF REALIA OR SUBJECT

Toys, Games, and Musical Instruments
ABC School Supply
Audio-Visual Enterprises
Childcraft Education Corp.
Community Playthings
Creative Teaching Associates
Educational Teaching Aids
F. A. O. Schwarz
GAMCO
Milton Bradley

Cultural Materials
Burt Harrison & Co. ("Family of Man" kits contain both realia and models)
Gessler (flags, games, realia for language and social studies)
Nienhuis Montessori USA (flags)

Live Biological Specimens
Carolina Biological Supply
Central Scientific Co.
Lab-Aids
Pacific Bio-Marine Labs
NASCO
Schoolmasters Teaching Aids
Ward's Natural Science Establishment

Live Animal Supplies and Housing
Carolina Biological Supply
Central Scientific Co.
Hubbard
Lab-Aids
Ward's Natural Science Establishment

Preserved Biological Specimens
Carolina Biological Supply
Central Scientific Co.
Denoyer-Geppert
NASCO
Schoolmasters Teaching Aids
Ward's Natural Science Establishment

Rock, Mineral, and Fossil Specimens
ABC School Supply
Carolina Biological Supply
Central Scientific Co.
Curriculum Productions Co.
Hubbard
NASCO
Page Museum Shop
Schoolmasters Teaching Aids
Ward's Natural Science Establishment

Miscellaneous
Replogle (sundial)
Bi-Folkal Productions (kits include realia and olfactory items)
Children's Museum, The Resource Center (material and activities for teachers
     and children; MATCH Program; kits for various subjects)

MAINTENANCE AND MANAGEMENT
Storage and Care

The storage and care of an active realia collection will involve more
than providing a resting place between uses, and can present difficulties, particularly in a print- or audiovisually oriented environment.
Storage needs will vary according to use and sites. Moreover, the range
of shapes, sizes, bulk, and weight, as well as the greatly varied use to
which the objects will be put, means that standard storage in the sense
of book shelving and audiovisual storage is difficult and sometimes
seemingly impossible.

Storage solutions, however, may often be found in the local hardware, office supply, or variety store, as well as in the pages of library and office supply catalogs. Bins, particularly the "milk crate" storage units, are especially useful for many kinds of objects. So are other forms of modular storage and carrying units. Criteria for storage should include accessibility, carrying capacity, durability, safety, and labeling space. Color coding, particularly in the modular items, may also be a useful feature. The three Cs—cases, cabinets, kits—must also be provided for loans.

Particular attention must be paid to items with parts, for it is a law of nature that separate parts will go separate ways. Zip-top, see-through plastic bags will keep pieces and parts together. Information about the object, its care, and (when appropriate) precautions regarding its use should accompany each loan. Many useful suggestions for nonbook storage will be found in Jean Weihs' book, *Accessible Storage of Nonbook Materials*.[23]

Preservation is an important aspect of the upkeep of a realia collection; so also may be repair and restoration. An inventory (basically a check against an inventory list accompanying the item) should be taken before accepting the object back from circulation. If any repairs or replacements are needed, the object should not be stored or circulated until they have been taken care of.

Adequate housing, food, and care instructions must be provided for live specimens. The American Humane Association and the American Society for Prevention of Cruelty to Animals (ASPCA) have materials on animal care. The local veterinary society or pet store will also be able to supply information, including pamphlets on the care of particular species. Suppliers of animal care equipment, such as Carolina Biological Supplies, also furnish food and housing information.

Caring for a creature who is dependent upon humans for food, shelter, and affection can have many positive benefits for children and adults alike. (A number of studies have shown that elderly persons who own pets tend to have more satisfactory life situations than those who do not.) On the other hand, neglect and mistreatment of live specimens of whatever phylogenetic placement offer a negative lesson which is to be avoided!

In the case of animals likely to inflict injury, extreme caution must be taken in handling and housing. Those who handle animals should have received recent tetanus inoculations and should (in most cases) wear handlers' gloves. Gloves are particularly helpful with reptiles and with animals who are nervous in new surroundings. Weekend care of

23. Jean Weihs, *Accessible Storage of Nonbook Materials* (Phoenix: Oryx, 1984).

animals is often a problem when heating and cooling systems are cut back. If specimens are sent home over the weekend and for holidays, *written* acceptance must be received in advance. Persons who care for animals temporarily or who borrow them from a collection should have all the necessary information, equipment, and food on hand in advance of receiving their charge.

For animal care information, contact

American Humane Assn.   American Society for the
5351 S. Roslyn St.   Prevention of Cruelty to
Englewood, CO 80111   Animals (ASPCA)
                                  441 E. 92nd St.
                                  New York, NY 10028

Management Problems and Solutions

The management of object collections offers both problems and opportunities not found in the management of other media. Acquisition and collection development, especially, are not as straightforward as selecting, acquiring, and planning collections of print and audiovisual media. There is little guidance in evaluation, partly, of course, because many items of realia are simply collected in the old-fashioned, informal sense of picking up, gathering, or receiving as gifts. Moreover, the form and format of realia are so various that overall management considerations will vary from institution to institution. The use to which the item will be put, storage facilities, and retrieval systems are all considerations which will have an effect upon management.

COLLECTION MANAGEMENT AND DEVELOPMENT

Because there are few evaluative sources for realia, the institution must develop appropriate criteria for objects and apply those criteria to acquisitions. In most instances, common sense, reinforced by experience and information about the instructional or other objectives, will serve well in evaluating objects.

Frequently, one attraction of realia is a modest cost of acquisition. Since realia are also often acquired as gifts, it is necessary to remember that *free* is not necessarily equated with *good*. Items which are too valuable for the institution to store securely, items which are too fragile for the proposed use and handling, and items which are in such a poor state of preservation as to obscure their meaning should not be acquired, even though the cost may be attractive. There are several schools of thought regarding gifts, but all agree that loans, conditional and temporary gifts, and gifts with stipulations are all better refused.

On the other hand, truly offered gifts may be accepted, even though they are not just what is wanted at the moment, in the hope that other gifts may come later which will be suitable. Whether such gifts are stored or exchanged is subject to storage facilities and the imminence of further donations.

Because realia may come so readily to a collection, maintaining a balance among them and within the collection may become a management problem. To help forestall such problems, there should be from the beginning firm collection policies, guidelines based on stated objectives both for realia and for the collection as a whole, and a multimedia philosophy which recognizes that different users respond to and learn from different media. "Pickup" collecting is another source of realia, and is often the primary source of gifts as well.

A well-ordered collection will have a value in terms of communication which is greater than the sum of its parts. Similarly, a single, perfect, and unique specimen will have its singular greater value. Much of the educational value of realia, from the collector's viewpoint, is in the gathering and ordering of the collection, and must be weighed in any consideration of realia as instructional or recreational media.

The extent to which users are involved in the selection of realia will depend upon the institution, the user population, selection policies for other media, and the kinds of realia acquired. Teachers in a school will, for example, have an interest in the realia collection different from that of the parents at the children's department of the public library. Again, community interest and involvement in local history will shape the local history museum's collection. Demand and interest will also dictate the answers to such collection questions as multiple sets of items, length of loan periods, and deposits and fees.

ORGANIZATION, STORAGE, AND RETRIEVAL

Because of the conditions under which realia are stored (see preceding section), the collection is not amenable to browsing. Thus it is extremely important that the collected realia be described in a finding device which is incorporated with a system of retrieval. Depending upon the nature and extent of the collection and the sponsoring institution, realia may be described and listed in one of several ways: in a book format, in a file system, as a separate section of a card or other catalog, or integrated into an omnicatalog, whether card or online.

For many institutions, the last solution is the best, since the omnicatalog allows all formats and manifestations of an intellectual content to be located together. Thus real fossils will be found in the catalog along with books, filmstrips, and posters about fossils.

Museum registration—which is to say accessioning and cataloging objects—exhibits little uniformity of practice from institution to institution. The result, however, is uniform in outcome: a complete record about the object, including its date of accession, a unique number, details of its source and cost, a complete description, a record of the location in the institution, and documents concerning authentication, provenance, history, care, and so on. The record is changed when the object is moved within or outside the museum; and whenever information is received about the object, it is added to the file.[24]

Some aspects of museum methods may be usefully adopted by other institutions, particularly the information files associated with each object. Other cataloging methods and practice will be more appropriate for some institutions. *Standards for Cataloging Nonprint Materials*, 4th ed. (*AECT4*), and Chapter 10 of the *Anglo-American Cataloguing Rules*, 2nd ed. (*AACR2*), which was based in part upon it, are the primary contenders in the nonprint cataloging area. Frost suggests that *AACR2* Chapter 10 is gaining increasing acceptance.[25] The general adaptability of *AACR2* Chapter 10 recommends its use in multimedia collections;[26] and with the widely recognized value of realia in the communication process, there is no reason other than print-and-word tradition to segregate their cataloging records in the institution's finding files.

DISSEMINATION, LOAN, AND DISPLAY

The use for which the realia is intended and its physical condition and value will determine loan policies and similar management considerations. Three stages of circulation may be considered. First of all, toys, games, boxed collections of specimens, encapsulated items, and large and sturdy individual objects such as utensils, tools, and naturally occurring specimens will present few problems and may be handled in the same manner and under the same policies as the institution's audiovisual collection. Written care and use information should be part of each transaction.

24. Daniel B. Reibel, *Registration Methods for the Small Museum* (Nashville: AASLH, 1978). Such institutions as the Detroit Institute of Arts have developed computerized registration software (Detroit Art Registration and Information System [DARMIS]). For further information about online museum registration, see Robert G. Chenhall, *Museum Cataloging in the Computer Age* (Nashville: AASLH, 1975), and entire issues of *Museum News* 63 (Aug. 1985) and *Curator* 28 (June 1985).

25. Carolyn O. Frost, *Cataloging Nonbook Materials,* ed. Arlene Taylor Dowell (Littleton, Colo.: Libraries Unlimited, 1983), 28.

26. Jean Weihs, Shirley Lewis, and Janet Macdonald, *Nonbook Materials: The Organization of Integrated Collections,* 2nd ed. (Ottawa: Canadian Library Assn., 1979).

Secondly, there will probably be items of realia for which more restrictive circulation is appropriate: the rare, the fragile, the large and bulky, and the complex. Conditions of restriction should be noted on the catalog record (e.g., "One week loan to high schools"). The realia should be made available for in-house examination so that the circulation restrictions apply only to removal from the premises.

In the third instance, there will be unique realia—too fragile, too valuable, or too dangerous—for which circulation or even handling is not appropriate. The records in such cases should be marked "Display" and the objects should be available for visual inspection, most appropriately in relation to the print media on the same subject. Thus a Japanese tea set may be displayed near works on travel in Japan, while a set of Victorian doll dishes may be located near other kinds of media pertaining to the period.

BUDGET AND FISCAL MATTERS

Historically, realia have been budgeted to different areas of departments and stored in decentralized locations: the biology department will have its specimens; social studies, its costumes; and preschool, its toys. If the collection is integrated as far as budget and records are concerned, it is possible to administer realia centrally, while dispersing them throughout the institution. In the same way, budgets may be decentralized, yet the overall media holdings will be recorded in one place. It is economically feasible and realistic to handle realia in a centralized manner. Just as print media are not limited in application, realia should be available to users as their needs dictate.

Whether it is politically or physically feasible to centralize the storage of realia is a question best answered by the situation and facilities of the individual institutions. Ease of access and retrieval is the key consideration in managing realia collections.

Insurance is a cost item often overlooked in the management of realia. Valuable items may need to be insured separately in a policy rider, or the overall collection may need to be insured. Liability and in-transit insurance, and extraordinary hazard coverage should all be investigated. Since local conditions vary greatly, the best advice is to seek advice—in this case, from the institution's agency or liability experts.

STAFF

A last area of management concern is that of staff and staff allocation to realia. Where particular expertise is required—the authentication of historical or archaeological artifacts, for example—it is best to go to experts, and in some cases even to pay the professional's fee for authentication, counsel on storage and preservation, or guidance in procuring particular objects.

Whether special training in realia management should be provided for some staff members, or whether all staff should be directly involved in that aspect of the overall collection, are, again, matters for local decision. Certainly, all staff should feel at ease with the concepts of omnimedia collections, and value the role of realia in communication and information.

Since in so many instances the outlay for realia is relatively minimal, the institution can afford to invest in staff training, time, and effort, and in effective storage, cataloging, and loan systems to provide the users with a useful and meaningful collection of realia.

All media convey messages. The acceptance of realia as a medium has had a spotty history in an environment directed toward visual and auditory symbols and messages. With growing awareness of different cognitive and learning styles, the value of the direct experience with an object rather than with its abstraction or representation has been recognized. As a result, realia have been increasingly given a place in media collections.

It is useful to keep in mind that the management of realia is the management of information.

ADDITIONAL CONSIDERATIONS

There are several considerations remaining for the staff of an institution undertaking a realia collection, thinking about incorporating realia into a media collection, or organizing realia into a working collection:

1. Purposes and objectives. It cannot be emphasized enough that the purposes for which the realia are to be collected and the ultimate users of the collection are the primary consideration. When the goals and objectives of the collection are clear, much else falls into place.

2. Background information and research. The literature concerning realia is sparse and often treats a particular type or kind of object rather than the medium as a class. Much of the research appears in the museum literature, and discusses realia as elements in exhibits and displays.

    Research which appears in the literature of psychology and education, particularly regarding multisensory learning and learning reinforcement, may be usefully cited in support of the educational value of realia in media collections. Many of these issues and the rationale for realia were addressed in the library literature in connection with the "Toys to Go" controversy.

3. Relations with users. Connections with the public and the users of realia collections are important to the vitality of collections. There are many ways to bring the collection to the attention of its users, both actual and potential:

Displays, publicity, and hand-out information have been successfully used to awaken interest in the realia collection and to encourage its use. The local press is usually interested in a truly different aspect of a local agency.

Ease of access and streamlining of loan procedures lead to a more pleasant experience and encourage repetition.

Soliciting suggestions from users and acting upon them fosters a sense of involvement and engenders good will.

The development of a community resource file is another connection to the public. The file may either augment the realia collection or, in some cases, stand in lieu of such a collection. The resource file lists persons, agencies, and other sources of information about realia. Thus (with their permission!) local collectors and experts will be listed under their areas of interest and expertise. Collections which are available for viewing or borrowing are also included, together with the persons or agencies responsible for them. Local and national sources of objects and supplies, as well as books, journals, and vertical file materials, should also be included. While such a resource file cannot be considered a realia collection, it is both a reasonable and positive first step toward one, and remains a useful supplement to an active collection of objects and things.

A final word about realia. Realia can be a challenging and exciting medium of communication. Whether they are a major aspect of an institution's information offerings or a supplement to verbal and visual media, the third dimension adds an extra dimension of meaning, understanding, and pleasure.

Other Concerns

It is frustrating to try to retrieve information on realia. The term is a relatively recent entrant into the thesauri and indexes, with the result that earlier materials must be searched under "audiovisual" headings. Confusion in terminology is also reflected in more recent indexes and in many of the definitions in the literature: locating information about realia is a sort of *caveat* researcher situation. The following are suggested as search terms in library catalogs, thesauri, book indexes, and other finding tools: audiovisual education; audiovisuals—realia; cultural materials; manipulative items/materials/objects; models and specimens; museum objects/specimens; ceremonial/natural/physical objects; realia; specimens (and also biological, fossil, preserved, and zoological specimens); three-dimensional objects; and toys and games.

There is considerable confusion of terminology in the literature, with *realia, models, specimens,* and *objects* used interchangeably, and *realia* often used not at all. Harrod, for example, defines realia as: "Three-dimensional objects such as museum materials, dioramas, models and samples which may be borrowed or purchased by a school library and used in connection with class lessons."[27] Illustrating the tendency in the literature to lump together various kinds of three-dimensional items, the *ALA World Encyclopedia of Library and Information Services* offers the following definition of *realia*: "Toys, games, sculpture, models, three-dimensional art, and a range of other tangible objects that are designed to be handled, used, and studied rather than being exhibited in display cases come under the heading of realia, which in some extreme instances has come to include such library-circulated items as jigsaw puzzles, automotive repair tools, and live pets."[28] Sive uses *manipulative materials* as an umbrella term to cover "models, realia, specimens, games, toys, mock-ups, etc."[29]

The origin, size, and functions of an item are useful in making distinctions between realia and other three-dimensional objects. Two questions may be asked: Did the item originate in the living or nonliving *natural* world? If it did not (and is, therefore, of human devising), is it in the original size and functional condition? An affirmative answer to any one of these questions indicates an item of realia.

Object is another term encountered in the literature. In museum studies, the discipline which has traditionally been most concerned with the acquisition, care, and use of realia, the word *objects* is used generically to signify the "things" contained in the collection. *Objects* was used synonymously with *realia* in this chapter. The term *replica* also needs to be distinguished from *model, object,* or *realia.* A replica is an *exact* reproduction or copy, and is used to stand for the original object. A replica is useful when the original is rare or fragile. Profes-

27. Leonard Montague Harrod, *The Librarians' Glossary and Reference Book of Terms Used in Librarianship, Documentation and the Book Crafts,* 4th ed. (Boulder, Colo.: Westview, 1977), 687.

28. *ALA World Encyclopedia of Library and Information Services* (Chicago: American Library Assn., 1980), 60.

29. Mary Robinson Sive, *Selecting Instructional Media: A Guide to Audiovisual and Other Instructional Media Lists,* 3rd ed. (Littleton, Colo.: Libraries Unlimited, 1983), 286.

sionals in the museum disciplines, however, always identify an object as a replica, copy, or reproduction. Whether the original was of natural or created origin, the replica is human made and is, of course, an item of realia.

Toys and *games* are another area of blurred interpretation. Hektoen and Rinehart's useful and often cited booklet, *Toys to Go*, treats toys and games as realia, rather than as a *type* of realia.[30] Unless the underlying purpose of a toy or game is to function as a model or as a device for modeling reality and behavior, toys and games should be included in realia.

A final distinction is between *objects* (or *realia*) and *models*. Brown et al. distinguish between "unmodified" and "modified" real things (i.e., realia and models),[31] while Haney and Ullmer group realia under "natural objects" and "manufactured objects," and deal with models as "representational objects."[32] More explicitly, Wittich and Schuller state: "An object is the real thing, whereas a model is a recognizable three-dimensional representation of the real thing." Wittich and Schuller also make a useful distinction between *objects* and *specimens*, the latter being "representative of a group or class of similar objects."[33] In this chapter, *specimen* has been used to connote an object, or an item of realia, particularly when the specimen is a member of a larger set.

There will remain, inevitably, some gray areas and questions of interpretation in distinguishing between models and realia. For example, is the old-fashioned, hand-cranked telephone which still "works" an item of realia or a working model? In the end, the communicative value of the object, whether realia or model, is more important, and the final definition will become operational.

ADDITIONAL RESOURCES

The sources in this bibliography have been categorized subjectively, according to their probable usefulness. The entries are not repeated from classification to classification. Older editions may contain useful material omitted from more recent editions.

30. Faith H. Hektoen and Jeanne R. Rinehart, *Toys to Go* (Chicago: American Library Assn., 1976).

31. James W. Brown, Richard B. Lewis, and Fred F. Harcleroad, *A-V Instruction: Materials and Methods,* 6th ed. (New York: McGraw-Hill, 1977), 292–93. The distinctions appear in the 5th ed. (1977), pp. 269–70.

32. John B. Haney and Eldon J. Ullmer, *Educational Communication and Technology: An Introduction,* 3rd ed. (Dubuque: Wm. C. Brown, 1980), 147.

33. Walter A. Wittich and Charles F. Schuller, *Instructional Technology: Its Nature and Use,* 5th ed. (New York: Harper & Row, 1973), 162.

DEFINITION, EVALUATION, ACQUISITION

Anderson, Ronald H. *Selecting and Developing Media for Instruction.* 2nd ed. New York: Van Nostrand, 1983.

Pages 123–29 provide guidance for selection and use (though mockups [i.e., models] and realia are confused).

Borun, Minda. *Measuring the Immeasureable: A Pilot Study of Museum Effectiveness.* Washington, D.C.: Assn. of Science-Technology Centers (ASTC), 1979.

Evaluates realia as media.

Brown, James W., Richard B. Lewis, and Fred F. Harcleroad. *A-V Instruction: Materials and Methods.* 6th ed. New York: McGraw-Hill, 1983.

Useful resource, though "Real Things, Models, and Demonstrations" (Chap. 13, pp. 292–95) is sketchy. List of sources (p. 506). Page 293 and "The Community as a Learning Center" (Chap. 3, pp. 40–58) give useful suggestions about museums, field study, resource persons. In the 5th ed. (1977), see pp. 269–75, 465–66, and Chap. 3.

Cabeceiras, James. *The Multimedia Library: Materials Selection and Use.* 2nd ed. New York: Academic, 1982.

Useful definition (p. 21); summary of types of realia (p. 27); criteria for selection, use, and handling (pp. 208–12).

Children's Services Division (ALA), Toys, Games, and Realia Committee. "Realia in the Library." *Booklist* 73 (Jan. 1 1977): 671–74.

The "legitimizing" study of realia; deals principally with toys.

Educational Media Yearbook, 1973– . New York: Bowker, 1973– .

Part II, "Mediagraphy," occasionally lists realia sources.

Haney, John B., and Eldon J. Ullmer. *Educational Communication and Technology: An Introduction.* 3rd ed. Dubuque: Brown, 1980.

Katz, William A. *Collection Development: The Selection of Materials for Libraries.* New York: Holt, Rinehart, c1980.

Points of view in definition; suggestions for community resource file (pp. 309–10).

Moll, Joy K., and Patricia Hermann. "Evaluation and Selection of Toys, Games, and Puzzles: Manipulative Materials in Library Collections." *Top of the News* 31 (Nov. 1974): 86–89.

Selection criteria for certain types of realia; some sources.

Sive, Mary Robinson. *Selecting Instructional Media: A Guide to Audiovisual and Other Instructional Media Lists.* 3rd ed. Littleton, Colo.: Libraries Unlimited, 1983.

Comprehensive, cross-indexed lists and sources; "Manipulative Materials" are indexed on p. 314 and defined on p. 286.

Wittich, Walter A., and Charles F. Schuller. *Instructional Technology: Its Nature and Use.* 5th ed. New York: Harper and Row, 1973.

Still a good resource; see Chap. 4. 6th ed. (1979) has information on pp. 73–75, 78–82. Both editions have suggestions for using museums as resources.

Woodbury, Marda. *Selecting Materials for Instruction.* Littleton, Colo.: Libraries Unlimited, 1980.

Good resource, though emphasis is on toys (pp. 164–76).

REALIA IN COMMUNICATION, INSTRUCTION, AND RECREATION

Alexander, Edward P. *Museums in Motion: An Introduction to the History and Functions of Museums*. Nashville: American Assn. for State and Local History (AASLH), 1979. See Chap. 1.

Burcaw, G. Ellis. *Introduction to Museum Work*. Nashville: AASLH, 1975. Good general presentation of role of realia in a particular type of institution.

Cabeceiras, James. "The Application of Media in Various Forms to Assist Teachers in Specific Learning Objectives." *Catholic Library World* 50 (Apr. 1979): 389–92.

Cameron, Duncan F. "A Viewpoint: The Museum as a Communications System and Implications for Museum Education." *Curator* 11 (Jan. 1968): 33–40. Seminal article on communication values of realia.

Collins, Zipporah W., ed. *Museums, Adults and the Humanities: A Guide for Educational Programming*. Washington, D.C.: American Assn. of Museums (AAM), 1981. Using realia with adults; intergenerational learning and experience.

Dana, John Cotton, and Blanche Gardner. *Aids in High School Teaching: Pictures and Objects*. Vol. II, Part XIX of *Modern American Library Economy as Illustrated by the Newark N.J. Free Public Library*. Woodstock, Vt.: Elm Tree Pr., 1916. Pioneering study of multimedia collections, together with list of sources.

Hammerman, Donald R., and William M. Hammerman. *Teaching in the Outdoors*. 2nd ed. Minneapolis: Burgess, 1973. Guide to use of realia in natural settings.

Hektoen, Faith H., and Jeanne R. Rinehart. *Toys to Go: A Guide to the Use of Realia in Public Libraries*. Chicago: American Library Assn. (ALA), 1975. Excellent for toys; suggestions for other types of realia.

Jay, Hilda L., and M. Ellen Jay. *Developing Library-Museum Partnerships to Serve Young People*. Hamden, Conn.: Library Professional Publications, 1984. Programs using museum and library resources; extensive treatment also of collection organization and administrative considerations.

Latta, Richard. "Guppies and Grasshoppers." *Teacher* 90 (Feb. 1973): 102–4. Care and use of *small* live animals in the classroom.

Mertz, Greg. *An Object in the Hand . . . : Museum Educational Outreach for the Elderly, Incarcerated & Disabled*. Washington, D.C.: Smithsonian Institution Collaborative Educational Outreach Program, 1982. Using realia with special groups.

Muckelroy, Duncan G. "America's Ranching Heritage." *Parks and Recreation* 8 (July 1973): 16–19. Example of realia studied in context of original environment.

Rinehart, Jeanne. "Heritage & Concept Boxes." *School Library Journal* 26 (Mar. 1980): 108. Multimedia kits include realia (such as "try-on" costumes); with bibliography and books. Project of Urban Five Libraries (Conn.).

Schurk, William L. "Popular Culture and Libraries: A Practical Perspective."
  Drexel Library Quarterly 16 (July 1980): 43–52.
  Using objects in association with other media.
Seaman, Sara Frances. "Museum Services in School Libraries." Thesis, Columbia
  Univ. (N.Y.), 1944.
  Early research in classroom use of realia.
Smith, M. A. "Culture Kits." *Iowa Regional Library System Newsletter* 1 (Jan.
  1984): 9.
  Sets of cultural and ethnic realia available on loan from libraries; spon-
  sored by International Resource Center, Iowa State Univ., Ames.
Smith, Marlene Gates. "A Museumlike Setting . . ." *Teacher* 90 (Feb. 1973):
  98–101.
  Creating a classroom setting for realia.
Soulier, J. Steven. *Real Objects and Models.* Englewood Cliffs, N.J.: Educa-
  tional Technology Publications, 1981. (Instructional Media Library, vol.
  12.)
  Brief history (Chap. 1, pp. 3–6); instructional use and techniques (Chap.
  7, pp. 63–66).
Zevin, Jack. "Visual Economics: Inquiry through Art and Artifacts." *Peabody
  Journal of Education* 57 (Apr. 1980): 183–90.
  Study of use of realia in specific subject area.

ADMINISTRATION AND MANAGEMENT

Anglo-American Cataloguing Rules. 2nd ed. Prepared by American Library
  Assn., British Library, Canadian Committee on Cataloging, Library Assn.,
  Library of Congress. Ed. Michael Gorman and Paul Winkler. Chicago: ALA;
  Ottawa: Canadian Library Assn., 1978.
Bloomberg, Marty, and G. Edward Evans. *Introduction to Technical Services
  for Library Technicians.* 4th ed. Littleton, Colo.: Libraries Unlimited,
  1981.
  Models for *AACR2* cataloging of realia (pp. 208–10).
Frost, Carolyn O. *Cataloging Nonbook Materials: Problems in Theory and
  Practice.* Ed. Arlene Taylor Dowell. Littleton, Colo.: Libraries Unlimited,
  1983. See Chap. 8.
Hicks, Warren B., and Alma M. Tillin. *Developing Multi-media Libraries.* New
  York: Bowker, 1970.
  Organization and storage (Chaps. 5 & 7).
Reibel, Daniel B. *Registration Methods for the Small Museum.* Nashville:
  AASLH, 1978.
  Useful, brief compendium of museum practice.
Tillin, Alma M., and William J. Quinly. *Standards for Cataloging Nonprint
  Materials: Interpretation and Practical Application.* 4th ed. Washington,
  D.C.: Assn. for Educational Communications and Technology (AECT),
  1976.
  "AECT4" (pp. 178–82).

Weihs, Jean. *Accessible Storage of Nonbook Materials*. Phoenix: Oryx, 1984.
     Chap. 9 (pp. 64–70) offers many useful and inexpensive storage solutions.
_____, Shirley Lewis, and Janet Macdonald. *Nonbook Materials: The Orga-
     nization of Integrated Collections*. 2nd ed. Ottawa: Canadian Library
     Assn., 1979.
     Set of standards and procedures for organizing and describing nonprint
     media, including realia.

John W. Ellison
and Patricia Ann Coty

Ch. 19

Simulation Materials

THE MEDIUM

Definition

Simulation is a learning process which involves participants in role abstractions, simplifications, or presentations representing real-life social, physical, or biological situations, processes, or environments. A simulation permits a person to become a working member of a system, setting goals and objectives, processing and analyzing information, and developing policies for further activity. A simulation is a substitute, model system which presents certain features of the real world in learning activities.

Brief History

Theoretically, the history of simulations predates written history. Various ancient games were attempts to simulate real-life activities, most notably war. In the Middle Ages, the development of chess was a crude attempt to simulate battle between two nations. Prussia pioneered modern war-gaming with "Neue Kriegsspiel" at the beginning of the 19th century. The chess board was replaced by maps and terrain models, and pieces representing infantry, artillery, and cavalry units were used to simulate combat. The value of this technique for training military personnel was appreciated by a number of European countries, which soon adopted it.

In the 20th century, the U.S. military began to seriously develop military simulations as training exercises. World War I was preceded by extensive war-gaming simulations by all participating nations, and the Japanese and Germans used them heavily during World War II. Development of the computer after World War II allowed war gaming to be greatly refined; it was in America in 1954 that such computerized simulations of military operations were first exhibited.[1]

In addition to war gaming, other complex simulations were developed around this time. Royal Air Force pilots were training on the Link Trainer, a full-scale, full-size working model of an airplane cockpit. Once inside, the student pilot simulated the flying of an airplane, and his performance was recorded for subsequent evaluation with trainers. The simulator allowed the pilot to experience a model of the actual flight situation, without the inherent dangers of flight.[2]

Modern use of the term *simulation* originated with the work of John von Neumann and Stanislaw Ulam in the late 1940s, when they created "Monte Carlo analysis," allowing them to approximate solutions to problems which were either too expensive for experimental solution or too complicated for analytical treatment.[3] The technique greatly enhanced researchers' abilities to create models which approximated real-world validity, and to predict the outcomes of various situations.

In the 1950s, the use of simulations began to interest political scientists, sociologists, and psychologists. The RAND Corporation developed simulations, known as *crisis games*, which attempted to portray possible international crises. Makers of foreign policy, involved in these simulations, could formulate policy alternatives to be used in the event of similar crises. The Massachusetts Institute of Technology was also active in the creation of political and social simulations during this time. The U.S. Army Management School, established in 1954 at Fort Belvoir, Virginia, was an early user of simulations for instruction in management science.[4]

The American Management Association adopted simulation as an

1. Alfred H. Hausrath, *Venture Simulation in War, Business, and Politics* (New York: McGraw-Hill, 1971), 68.

2. John L. Taylor and Rex Walford, *Simulation in the Classroom* (Baltimore: Penguin, 1972), 13–14.

3. Thomas H. Naylor et al., *Computer Simulation Techniques* (New York: Wiley & Sons, 1966), 1.

4. Hausrath, *Venture Simulation,* 193.

educational tool for management trainees with its creation of the AMA Top Management Decision Simulation in 1957. Using an IBM computer for calculations, the program involved teams of participants representing officers of companies, making business decisions, and receiving feedback regarding those decisions. The program was a great success with business executives and educators, although inclusion of the computer somewhat limited its adoption. Within three years of the AMA program's debut, nearly 100 similar simulations, most not requiring computer support, had been noted in the professional literature.[5] By 1971 it was reported that business games and management simulations were in use in Canada, the United Kingdom, France, Germany, Italy, Spain, Belgium, the Netherlands, Switzerland, Denmark, Sweden, Finland, Australia, Japan, Argentina, Brazil, Mexico, and several other countries in Latin America.[6] Business simulations continue to be widely accepted, with hundreds available on the market today.

Four researchers who have influenced the modern growth of simulation as an educational method are Harold Guetzkow, Clark C. Abt, James Coleman, and Jerome Bruner. Guetzkow's Inter-Nation Simulation (INS), developed from 1957 on at Northwestern University, was an early application of simulation for research and training in international relations, and has been refined and developed by various researchers through the years. INS is still one of the most popular simulations for the teaching of international relations.[7]

Abt, a systems engineer who was initially involved with the design of computer simulations of air battles and other military problems, began applying war-gaming techniques to the social sciences. In 1965 he founded Abt Associates, which became a major source of educational and training simulations.

Coleman, the educational sociologist, led the Academic Games Program at Johns Hopkins University during the late 1960s and early 1970s, where a number of innovative games and simulations (i.e., the Life Career Game) were developed. He also conducted research which confirmed the advantages of these activities. Coleman's summary of the purpose of one of the programs he developed can be applied to most educational simulations: "It allows [the participant] to act through situations before he faces them in real life, to see the indirect and long-

5. Robert Heinich, Michael Molenda, and James D. Russell, *Instructional Media and the New Technologies of Instruction* (New York: Wiley & Sons, 1982), 298.

6. Hausrath, *Venture Simulation,* 202.

7. Robert E. Horn and Anne Cleaves, *The Guide to Simulations/Games for Education and Training,* 4th ed. (Beverly Hills, Calif.: Sage, 1980), 453.

range consequences of choices he may make, before it is too late, and he must face the consequences in real life."[8]

Bruner, advocating the importance of active student involvement in learning, was a leader in two projects which yielded several well-known simulations: the American High School Geography Project, supported by the federal government, and the Social Studies Curriculum Program, "Man: A Course of Study," supported by the Ford Foundation. Bruner, an eminent instructional theorist, has advanced the academic applications of simulations with his research.

The 1960s and 1970s witnessed a great increase in the adoption of simulations for multiple uses. The recent widespread availability of microcomputers has caused a new surge of interest in simulations. By 1980, Chambers and Bork estimated that about half of schools with microcomputers use them for instructional games and simulations at least part of the time.[9] The National Technical Institute for the Deaf, in Rochester, New York, created one of the first interactive videotape-microcomputer simulations, to assist students in practicing speech reading and job interviewing. A stressful and challenging interpersonal situation is provided by this branching program, which uses a videotaped interviewer.[10]

In 1983 the U.S. Army War College opened a $1.5 million war-gaming center, and the Naval War College has, since the mid-seventies, been developing the complex computer simulator called the Warfare Analysis and Research System (WARS). In November 1983, the Army initiated use of STAR (Strategic and Tactical Assessment Record), an interactive, video war game designed to measure the effects of stress on participants' efficiency, speed, memory, information processing, risk taking, and decision-making.[11]

Another development in November 1983 was ABC-TV's national broadcast, on its *Nightline* program, of a "crisis game" to explore alternatives in a possible Soviet-American nuclear confrontation.[12] All of America was given the opportunity to participate in a simulation.

8. J. S. Coleman, "The Social System of the High School and the Game of Adolescence" (paper presented at Conference on Simulated Environments, Yorktown Heights, N.Y., June 28–29, 1962), 4.

9. J. A. Chambers and A. Bork, *Computer Assisted Learning in U.S. Secondary/Elementary Schools* (Fresno: California State Univ. Center for Information Processing, 1980).

10. Diane Gayeski and David Williams, "Simulation," in *Interactive Media* (Englewood Cliffs, N.J.: Prentice-Hall, 1985), 174–75.

11. Robert Mandel, "Professional-Level War Gaming: A Critical Assessment," in *Theories, Models, and Simulations in International Relations: Essays in Honor of Harold Guetzkow* (Boulder, Colo.: Westview Pr., 1985), 483.

12. Mandel, "Professional-Level War Gaming," 484.

Airlines today commonly employ simulated jets for pilot training, and simulations are widely used in medical training. Simulations are also important in driver education, labor negotiations, international relations, and counselor training. Advances in computers, videographic systems, and electronic game technology have contributed greatly to the ability to design more realistic simulations, at an ever more afford-able cost.

Evidence of the strides made in recent years includes the popularity of the Flight Simulator II program, available from SubLogic Corpora-tion for use on personal computers. Realistic displays in high-resolution color graphics simulate the flight of a small plane, which the user pilots. Similar inexpensive programs are becoming increasingly popular for educational, recreational, and vocational use.

Unique Characteristics

Simulation is not defined by media; it is a style of presentation or com-munication. While incorporating the characteristics of the various media in which they are presented, simulations are unique as a learn-ing process. Following are some of the unique characteristics of simulations:

Simulations provide practice in representative aspects of real situations.
Simulations provide a method for rehearsing what to do in stressful
    situations.
Simulations can provide a way for analyzing problems before taking
    action.
Simulations provide discovery through immediate and direct feedback,
    with the consequences of decisions seen by participants.
Simulations allow participants to reproduce a chain of events that could
    not be repeatedly observed in a natural setting.
Simulations are dynamic; they allow opportunities for change and
    development during all sequences of the activity.
Simulation group activities require interaction among participants.
Simulations require a critique or debriefing period.
Simulations allow a practical alternative when the real experience is
    too dangerous, too expensive, too slow, too rapid, or simply im-
    possible to experience.

Advantages

Because simulations encompass so many different forms and applica-tions, they do not all share the same characteristics. However, simula-tions can generally be said to have the following advantages:

Simulations are based on experiential learning.

Simulations provide results of the participants' decisions shortly after they are made, giving the participants near-immediate feedback regarding their actions.

Time can be greatly compressed or expanded in simulations, so that situations that might otherwise be impractical can be experienced.

Simulations allow the study of processes that cannot be examined in their natural occurrence, because they are too rare, too dangerous, or inaccessible.

Simulations require participants to solve real-world problems by themselves, rather than read about or look at the way others have solved them.

Simulations provide the learner with the opportunity to be more than a passive recipient of information.

Learners can develop their own goals and sources for motivation from simulation experiences.

Intuitions are encouraged, rewarded, and judged according to pragmatic standards in simulations.

Dangerous situations can be tested in a nonthreatening environment, using simulations.

Participants can repeat simulations, trying different strategies or solutions.

Training costs can be reduced by use of simulations, which allow for unlimited repetition.

Experiences which are available only rarely or not at all in the real world can be explored in simulations.

Simulations have a high rate of transfer to real-life situations.

Generally, simulations increase learner motivation.[13]

Participants in simulations commonly experience emotions, and often experience attitudinal changes.[14]

Simulations require virtually 100 percent involvement by participants.

Simulations are often fun.

Simulations help participants gain intellectual control and discipline over their behavior.

Simulations often provide intensive practice in verbal and written communication.

Simulations help sharpen learner decision-making skills, allowing participants to observe the consequences of alternative decisions.

13. James W. Brown, Richard B. Lewis, and Fred F. Harcleroad, *AV Instruction: Technology, Media and Methods,* 6th ed. (New York: McGraw-Hill, 1983), 319; William Ray Heitzmann, *Educational Games and Simulations,* rev. ed. (Washington, D.C.: National Education Assn., 1983), 17–18.
14. Heitzmann, *Educational Games and Simulations,* 19–20.

Since there is usually no single "right" outcome or any "one" best
strategy in a simulation, a flexible approach to problem solving
is encouraged.

Simulations involving groups encourage interaction and communication, and enable participants to learn from each other.

Simulations encourage groups to learn collaboratively.

Simulations can be designed to provide for different levels of learning.

Simulations can be used as an economical research technique, for purposes of experimentation or prediction, when the model being
used in the simulation reflects reality.

Disadvantages

While there are many advantages to the use of simulations as a learning method, certain cautions should be kept in mind. Following are
some of the characteristics which may be seen as impeding the adoption of simulations in certain circumstances.

Simulations may be more time consuming than alternative learning
activities.

The time spent on preparing participants for the simulation (organizing people in groups, explaining directions, distributing materials)
may rule out the use of the activity.

Participants in simulations may become wrapped up in the activity and
lose sight of the objectives.

Group simulation activities may create a fairly high noise level.

Participants in a group activity will have varying experiences, and may
fail to see or understand the experiences of others in the group.

Success of the simulation may depend heavily on the group leader's
managerial techniques, especially in regard to spontaneous problems.

It is possible that negative biases may exist in the design of the simulation, and undesirable attitude changes may be produced.

Financial support may be difficult to obtain for simulations, since those
unfamiliar with these materials often equate them with games and
entertainment.

Published research on simulations is sketchy and in many cases incon-
clusive.

No widely accepted criteria have been established for decisive evaluation of simulations.

SELECTION
Special Criteria

In addition to the considerations involved in selecting any learning media, there are special criteria which need to be addressed when simulations are selected:

The simulation should be a realistic model.

The most relevant features of the object system must be simulated.

Participants in the simulation should be practicing meaningful skills. Strategies available to participants should correspond to real life.

The simulation should have a sufficient amount of realism to convey the essential truths of the process.

Activities in the simulation should present a consistent sequence of behavior as the result of meaningful and deliberate decisions.

The simulation should be tested by an actual run-through to determine how it "flows" and what it teaches. Examination of the material, no matter how thorough, cannot reveal the flow of interactions that may occur during actual use.

All rules and directions should be clear, both for the activity leader and the participants. Guidelines should provide consistent limits on the options available to participants, but should not distort strategies or outcomes.

The experience and capabilities needed by the participants should match those of the group for whom the simulation is meant.

The simulation should not be so complex or elaborate that it will confuse participants or be unmanageable by the leader.

The motives and the resources available to each participant should be defined.

Advance leader preparation time needed for the simulation should be reasonable.

Special arrangements necessary to use the simulation, such as those involving time, equipment, and facilities, must be attainable.

The group to use the simulation should match the intended group size of the material.

Adequate time for debriefing must be available, over and above the time needed for the activity itself.

Debriefing guidelines should be included, and should offer adequate application to the objectives of the simulation.

Supplemental activities should be included or suggested.

Consumable or lost parts should be replaceable, at a reasonable cost. Be cautious if a continuous supply of commercially purchased consumable items will be needed each time the simulation is used.

Evaluative Review Sources

PERIODICALS

Simgames
Simulation and Games: An International Journal of Theory, Design and Research
Simulation/Games for Learning: The Journal of SAGSET

Occasional reviews of simulations may be found in various journals in applied fields, such as *Creative Computing; Instructor; Man, Society & Technology; Training and Development Journal; Journal of Nursing Education;* and *Electronic Learning.*

Not all good simulations need be purchased; often, simulations appear in the professional literature, such as *Man, Society & Technology.* These simulations can be used freely by readers.

BOOKS

Dukes, Richard L., and Constance J. Seider. *Learning with Simulations and Games.* Beverly Hills, Calif.: Sage, 1978.
Gibbs, G. I., ed. *Handbook of Games and Simulation Exercises.* Beverly Hills, Calif.: Sage, 1974.
Horn, Robert E., and Anne Cleaves, eds. *The Guide to Simulations/Games for Education and Training.* 4th ed. Beverly Hills, Calif.: Sage, 1980.
MicroSIFT: Clearinghouse for Instructional Software. Northwest Regional Educational Laboratory, 300 SW 6th Ave., Portland, OR 97204.
Stadsklev, Ronald. *Handbook of Simulation Gaming in Social Education, Volume 2: Directory—Noncomputer Materials.* 2nd ed. Tuscaloosa: Univ. of Alabama, 1979.
_____ and Cheryl L. Charles, eds. *Learning with Games: An Analysis of Social Studies Educational Games and Simulations.* Boulder, Colo.: Social Science Education Consortium, 1982.

Nonevaluative Sources

There is currently no publication which offers comprehensive listings of simulations, with the exception of those listed as evaluative sources. As the abundance of microcomputer programs grows, it is likely that new publications will emerge which will offer updates on computer simulations.

For college-level computer simulations, CONDUIT, a nonprofit organization affiliated with the University of Iowa, publishes a newsletter, *Pipeline*, which announces innovative instructional software.[15] At

15. Additional information can be obtained from CONDUIT, Box 388, Iowa City, IA 52244.

the precollege level, an important source is the Minnesota Educational Computing Consortium.[16]

MAINTENANCE AND MANAGEMENT
Storage and Care

Storage and care of simulations can range from simple to complex, since simulations come in a variety of sizes, shapes, and formats. It is usually wise to use the producer's container to store these materials. No particular temperature control or protective container is needed, unless the simulation includes nonbook formats such as film or tape. In that case, consult the appropriate chapter in this book for recommendations for storage and care of the particular media.

Loss of pieces is the most common problem with many simulations. Three solutions are offered to control this problem: (1) caution the user before lending the material; (2) check the simulation carefully upon return for missing parts; and (3) order replacement parts immediately upon discovery of loss. Computer simulations should be duplicated if the copyright holder permits production of a backup copy.

Mechanical simulators may necessitate the availability of a trained technician for maintenance and repair. They may also require specialized housing. Requirements of this type should be specified by the vendor.

Management Problems and Solutions

The term *simulation* covers many different types of materials: Link flight simulators, military war games, business management simulations, electrical analog devices, videodisc/microcomputer simulations, and the computer-assisted Resusci-Anni mannequin of the American Heart Association. Some simulations require no supporting media; they may consist solely of paper instructions with which a leader can organize a simulation activity.

Simulations vary greatly in their complexity as well as the purpose of their use. They can be used in exploring the implications of theories, in research, in testing hypotheses and theories, as predictive tools, and as educational activities.

When simulations are used, it is the process or method that is crucial, not the content or results. The decision-making process is of

16. Additional information can be obtained from MECC, 2520 Broadway Dr., St. Paul, MN 55113.

critical importance in simulation activities. It may often be necessary for the simulation leader to remind the participants of this notion. Evaluation in education has so long focused on correct answers as the measure of success that the task of focusing on the method and process may not come easy for the leader or participants.

It should be kept in mind that fact- and task-oriented people may find the use of simulations very frustrating. They may find it difficult to focus on a process where clear answers are not available. An experienced simulation leader can do much to help this type of learner reap optimal benefits from simulation activities.

Simulations teach or communicate by letting participants explore different solutions to a given problem or task. Some simulation activities are purposely open ended, or unpredictable. Behavioral, human relations, and political simulations are prime examples. Like experiences in the real world, simulations often offer many possible solutions for attaining a goal. Instructors, acting as group leaders in simulations, are removed from their traditional authority role and placed in the role of referee or facilitator. The experience—rather than the teacher—becomes the source of learning. Inherent is a potential loss of control for instructors, which may be threatening to some.

Depending on the philosophy of the staff, simulations may present departures from the norm. They often require movement and involve a certain amount of noise, especially group simulations. They may require the alteration of schedules, to allow sufficient time for lengthy programs. They may require the expenditure of funds not normally spent on such activities, especially where equipment is necessitated.

To the untrained eye, a room of participants engaged in various activities during a simulation may appear as chaos. Administrators and parents alike may be unaware of the learning potential of simulations, believing that learning cannot be taking place in such apparent disorganization. It is extremely important that the user of simulation activities be prepared to justify use of these materials if called upon to do so.

The most important role in a group simulation is that of the group leader. The interaction of the participants should be directed as little as possible by the leader, whose function is to define acceptable guidelines for the participants and to facilitate briefing and debriefing. The group leader should not intervene in the decisions of the participants, no matter how tempting the prospect might be. The interaction of the group can easily be influenced by the perception of positive or negative signals from this person, especially if the group leader is normally an authority figure in the group.

Because simulations may involve human behavior on the part of participants that is self-disclosing, often beyond their conscious awareness (especially when they involve children), it is necessary for the group leader to maintain ethical standards for protecting participants from experiences that could damage their self-confidence or place them in situations that they cannot handle, either emotionally or intellectually. The participants should never be criticized or ridiculed for decisions made during simulation activities.

Expenditure of sufficient preparation time by the group leader is necessary for the simulation to be a success. The leader must become very familiar with the rules, the materials, and the anticipated flow of action. In individualized simulations, it is likewise critical that instructions for users be thorough and well designed.

The debriefing process is particularly important in the effectiveness of simulations, particularly those that involve groups. Debriefing also allows participants to learn from the experience of the simulation. The group leader, during debriefing, assists the participants in refining their interpretations of the previous activity. Rather than interpreting or evaluating the behaviors of the participants as individuals, the group leader provides questions which help the participants to articulate their own interpretations. The leader also assists participants in drawing connections between their behaviors in the simulation and their behaviors in the real world.

Other Concerns

One of the primary problems with managing simulation materials and activities is the false notion that all simulations are games. Although the two formats may appear quite alike to the untrained observer, they are very much different in practice. Both simulations and games often come in packages with multiple parts, and the users may appear to have similar behavioral patterns during use of these formats; however, there are distinct differences between them. Following are some comparisions of simulations and games.

Simulations	Games
Study issues, methods, and processes	Emphasize content or results
Usually no "winner"	Inherent element of competition.
Use role-playing; are often "open" models	Use structured model, simple to complex, with strict rules
Involve dynamic interaction	Involve competition
Modeled on reality	Diverge from reality; involve chance

Ken Jones discusses this problem in his *Simulations: A Handbook for Teachers*:

> Some see the two words as interchangeable. . . . Others think that a simulation is a type of game, while Tansey and Unwin . . . define a game as being a type of simulation. The double-barrelled "simulation-game" is frequently used, sometimes as an all-embracing category. On the other hand, Bloomer . . . makes a useful distinction by defining games and simulations as being two distinct concepts and uses the phrase "simulation/game" only to cover those which have the properties of both. As Bloomer remarks, "There can be few areas in which semantic clarity is a more pressing need."[17]

In addition to the confusion between simulations and games, there may also be confusion regarding different types of simulations. J. Barton Cunningham succinctly divides simulations into four categories: experimental simulations (where an investigator deliberately creates a setting for scientifically testing a hypothesis, which may or not approximate real behavior); predictive simulations (which attempt to predict *what* may happen, rather than explaining *why* it happened; evaluative simulations (for assessing decision makers' capability to respond to situations that might occur in reality); and educational simulations (directed at changing behavior by introducing and implementing knowledge).[18]

Depending on a practitioner's background, the term *simulation* may have different connotations. The economist and mathematician will likely be more familiar with predictive simulations, while sociologists and experimental psychologists will tend to use simulations as experimental tools.

ADDITIONAL RESOURCES

Abt, Clark C. *Serious Games*. New York: Viking, 1970.

Anderson, Ronald E. "Innovative Microcomputer Games and Simulations." *Simulation and Games* 14, 1 (Mar. 1983): 3–9.

Basinger, A. M. "A Bibliography of *Simulation and Games* Game Reviews." *Simulation and Games* 15, 4 (Dec. 1984): 500–504.

Berg, Roger. "Analytical Criteria for Microcomputer-Based Simulation/Games." Washington, D.C.: ERIC Clearinghouse on Teacher Education (June 1983), ED 231 741.

17. Ken Jones, *Simulations: A Handbook for Teachers* (New York: Kogan Page, 1980), 9.

18. J. Barton Cunningham, "Assumptions Underlying the Use of Different Types of Simulations," *Simulation and Games* 15, 2 (June 1984): 215.

Cloud, Lewis E. "Using Simulation Materials in Social Studies Instruction." *High School Journal* 54, 7 (Apr. 1974): 273–77.

Cruickshank, Donald R., and Ross A. Telfer. "Simulations and Games: An ERIC Bibliography." Washington, D.C.: ERIC Clearinghouse on Teacher Education (Sept. 1979), ED 177 149.

Dekkers, John, and Stephen Donatti. "The Integration of Research Studies on the Use of Simulation as an Instructional Strategy." *Journal of Educational Research* 74, 6 (July/Aug. 1981): 424–27.

Elder, Charles D. "Problems in the Structure and Use of Educational Simulation." *Sociology of Education* 46 (Summer 1973): 335–54.

Gayeski, Diane, and David Williams. "Simulation." In *Interactive Media*, by Diane Gayeski and David Williams. Englewood Cliffs, N.J.: Prentice-Hall, 1985 (pp. 151–83).

Gibbs, G. Ian. *Dictionary of Gaming, Modeling and Simulations.* Beverly Hills, Calif.: Sage, 1978.

Gilliom, M. Eugene. "Trends in Simulation." *High School Journal* 57, 7 (Apr. 1974): 265–72.

Heitzmann, William Ray. *Educational Games and Simulations.* Rev. ed. Washington, D.C.: National Education Assn., 1983.

Horn, Robert E., and Anne Cleaves, eds. *The Guide to Simulations/Games for Education and Training.* 4th ed. Beverly Hills, Calif.: Sage, 1980.

Jones, Ken. *Simulations: A Handbook for Teachers.* New York: Kogan Page, 1980.

Keating, Barry. "Simulations: Put the Real World in Your Computer." *Creative Computing* 11, 11 (Nov. 1985): 56–64.

Lederman, Linda Costigan. "Debriefing: A Critical Reexamination of the Postexperience Analytical Process with Implications for Its Effective Use." *Simulation and Games* 15, 4 (Dec. 1984): 415–31.

Nebenzahl, Israel D. "Motivations, Criteria, and Attributes of Business Games." *Simulation and Games* 15, 4 (Dec. 1984): 445–66.

Raser, John R. *Simulation and Society: An Exploration of Scientific Gaming.* Boston: Allyn and Bacon, 1969.

Romiszowski, A. J. "Simulators and Games." In *The Selection and Use of Instructional Media.* New York: Wiley & Sons, 1974. 289–329.

Stadsklev, Ronald. *Handbook of Simulation Gaming in Social Education (Part I: Textbook).* Tuscaloosa: Univ. of Alabama Pr., 1974.

Tansey, P. J., ed. *Educational Aspects of Simulation.* New York: McGraw-Hill, 1971.

————, P. J., and D. Unwin. "Simulation and Academic Gaming: Highly Motivational Teaching Techniques." In *Aspects of Educational Technology II*, ed. W. R. Dunn and C. Holroyd. London: Methuen, 1968.

Taylor, John L., and Rex Walford. *Simulation in the Classroom.* Baltimore: Penguin, 1972.

Leslie J. Walker

ch. 20

Slides

THE MEDIUM

Definition

A slide is an image, photographed, drawn, or otherwise reproduced on film or on a transparent material, and mounted in a rigid 3¼ × 4, 2¼ × 2¼, or 2 × 2-inch frame for use in a slide projector which transmits the image onto a screen or similar surface for viewing.

Brief History

Early slide use depended solely on the lantern slide. Dating from the 17th century, lantern slides were first hand painted and later printed on a 3¼ × 4-inch glass plate.[1] Viewed in a "magic lantern" (the modern slide projector's prototype), lantern slides were relatively expensive to produce, fragile, and heavy, compared to the standard 2 × 2-inch slides used today. Lantern slides were produced commercially by the Langenheim Brothers of Philadelphia as early as 1860.[2]

In 1884, George Eastman patented the roll film system, the now familiar strip of film wound on a spool. The development of roll film greatly facilitated the cost and ease of producing slides. Initially, the proliferation of a variety of film sizes produced different-size slides,

    1. Betty Irvine, *Slide Libraries: A Guide for Academic Institutions, Museums, and Special Collections* (Littleton, Colo.: Libraries Unlimited, 1979), 25.
    2. Nancy Carlson Schrock and Christine L. Sundt, "Slides," in *Conservation in the Library* (Westport, Conn.: Greenwood Pr., 1983), 103.

including the 2¼ × 2¼ –inch slide. In the 1880s the 2 × 2–inch slide was also developed, and has since become the standard of the industry.

Concomitant with the development of the 2 × 2–inch slide came the appearance of the first noted slide collections in the United States. The American Museum of Natural History of New York City, the Buffalo Society of Natural Sciences, Cornell University, Massachusetts Institute of Technology, the Metropolitan Museum of Art, and Wellesley College are a few institutions which exemplify the wide range of subjects represented in early slide collections. Although slide collections established before 1940 still may have relatively large quantities of lantern slides, most institutions began to convert or duplicate lantern slides into 2 × 2–inch slides.[3]

In the 1930s the development of the three-color film process did much to increase the popularity of 2 × 2–inch slides. The added benefit of color, as well as a growing interest in the humanities, particularly in art-history studies, contributed to the slide collections' period of largest growth, between 1930 and 1960.[4]

Management systems for slide collections have developed as the size of collections has increased. More sophisticated cataloging systems have been devised to accommodate the increased depth of special collections. Computer progams are increasingly utilized to handle the growing number of slides processed and circulated. In addition, most large collections now require one or more full-time professional curators to supervise collection maintenance and development.

Today, the slide format's wide acceptance may be evidenced in collections spanning a broad range of topics used in multifarious ways, ranging from art instruction and architectural rendering to scientific documentation and historical preservation. The medium's simplicity, efficiency, and cost effectiveness have made it a very accessible and workable communication tool, whether the user be an elementary school child or engineer.

Technological developments in slide equipment have also increased the versatility of the slide. Sound-slide units, remote systems, computer-control interface programs, and random access projectors are a few innovations which have increased its utility.

Unique Characteristics

Slides consist of individual still images which must utilize a lens and light source to be viewed.

3. Irvine, *Slide Libraries,* 146.
4. Ibid., 25.

Slides are static and two dimensional, and can only convey animation or a three-dimensional effect when specially treated.

The use of photographic film provides an image with as much resolution as its source and technical equipment make possible.

Slides offer greater flexibility of organization than other projected media, with flexible sequencing and flexible pacing.

Slides are housed in discrete, rigid frames.

Simple, inexpensive production makes slides uniquely adaptable for in-house production of materials.

Advantages

Like many other media, the advantages of the slide stem from a combination of its unique characteristics. This combination has resulted in the slide's primary asset: its acceptance as a communication tool. Versatility, cost, and ease of use have contributed to the slide's widespread use in educational institutions, businesses, and homes. As a consequence, many individuals have been familiarized with the format at an early age. Any discussion of the relative effectiveness of a particular medium must include the user's receptivity to its unique characteristics. The slide format has received a sufficient degree of exposure to enjoy such receptivity while providing the user with the following additional advantages:

Flexible sequencing and pacing make the slide useful for individual as well as group screening.

Multiscreen projection, or the use of two or more projectors, allows the user to study a panoramic or multi-angled still view of a subject or subjects with relative ease of operation and simple equipment.

Slides are compatible with a variety of other media, such as sound recordings. Multimedia sets, which include slides in combination with other media, can be purchased or produced with a minimal amount of equipment.

The slide's small size encourages handling by children. Viewing can be particularly easy when a hand-held viewer is used. Small size also reduces the space needed for storing, and contributes to the medium's portability.

When used with a rear-screen projection system, slides can be viewed in a lighted room, permitting other activities in conjunction with their use.

Slides are low cost per unit in relation to other projected media. Startup costs in building a collection generally make slides a favorable medium in terms of affordability.

Special effects can be produced with specially treated slides to create the appearance of animation or a three-dimensional effect.

Slides can project images of microscopic material, excluding the need for individual microscopes when viewed by a group.

Slides can be easily produced by amateurs.

Many factors contribute to the slide's ease of maintenance. Compared to other media (e.g., film, holography, the model or art reproduction) which perform a similar function, (i.e., reproduce an image), the slide costs a fraction to reproduce or replace. Due to the proliferation of suppliers and distributors, the development of more stable film, increased standardization within the industry, and simplicity of viewing equipment, the slide has become an effective, low-maintenance medium.

Disadvantages

The disadvantages of using slides also stem from their unique characteristics. Their small size allows for easy loss or theft. Individual slides in a set can easily become disarranged, especially when they are not housed in a projection tray. Sets of slides are bulky, compared to filmstrips.

Various slide-mounting materials may present problems. Paper mounts are not very durable, and become dogeared with use. Glass mounts may be too thick to fit the aperture chamber in some equipment.

With the exception of rear-screen projection and hand-held viewers, slides require a darkened room for screening. The necessary use of mechanical equipment for viewing as well as processing slides also incurs concomitant purchases, upkeep, time delays, maintenance, and repairs.

Since slides are rarely captioned, guides or other methods of interpreting the visuals must be available. Cataloging and processing single slides are very time consuming, and usually cannot be justified.

SELECTION

Special Criteria

The Visual Resources Committee of the Art Libraries Society of North America and the College Art Association issued the following joint statement on slide quality standards:

COLOR: The color should be as true as possible to the original work of art, neither over- nor under-exposed, nor off-color due to the lighting or the film-type.

FILM: The film should have fine-grained resolution and color should be stable with a minimum shelf-life of ten years. Duplicate slides should be newly printed as far as possible to maximize their shelf-life. High contrast in duplicate slides should be controlled. The film should be clean with no dirt or scratches on the surface nor duplicated into the film from the master transparency or negative. The size 24 × 36 mm is preferable: the supplier should indicate other sizes if used.

PHOTOGRAPHY: The slides must be in a focus and full-frame as far as possible without being cropped. Lighting should be adequate and even throughout, and without glare or reflections. In photographing paintings and buildings, distortion should be avoided.

INFORMATION: Accurate and complete information is necessary: artist's full name, nationality and dates, title of the work, medium, date and dimensions if known, and location. Cropped slides should be identified as such, and details should be described. An indication of the orientation is important, especially on details and abstract works of art. It should be clear which is the front of the slide.

It is important to indicate whether the slide will be an original or a duplicate: specific information on the source of the slide, film type and processing would be appreciated. Return and replacement policies should be spelled out.

PRICE: The price of the slide should fairly reflect the costs of production and distribution.[5]

Other selection considerations include the mounting material, continuity of sequence in slide sets, and compositional integrity of slide images.

Evaluative Review Sources

PERIODICALS

Arts and Activities
Booklist
Choice
International Bulletin for
   Photographic Documentation
   of the Visual Arts

Library Journal
Media Review
Media Review Digest
School Library Journal
TechTrends
Visual Education

5. Nancy DeLaurier, ed., *Slide Buyers' Guide* (Kansas City, Mo.: Mid-America Art College Assn., 1980), 9.

BOOKS
Cashman, Norine, ed. *Slide Buyers' Guide*. 5th ed. Littleton, Colo.: Libraries
    Unlimited, 1985. Updates printed in *International Bulletin for
    Photographic Documentation of the Visual Arts*.

Nonevaluative Sources

PERIODICALS
Art Documentation
Educational Technology

BOOKS
Audio Video Market Place. New York: Bowker, 1969– . Annual. Formerly
    Audiovisual Marketplace.
Bowker AV Guide: A Subject Guide to Audio-Visual Educational Material.
    New York: Bowker, 1975.
Catalog of U.S. Government Produced Audiovisual Materials. Washington,
    D.C.: General Services Administration, 1974– .
NICEM Index to Educational Slides. 4th ed. Los Angeles: National Informa-
    tion Center for Educational Media (NICEM), 1980.

Many public and private institutions offer slides for direct purchase.
Lists of slides and slide sets may also be obtained from a seemingly
inexhaustible supply of commercial vendors. Professional associations
and societies are good sources of information on commercial vendors
who offer material related to particular fields of study.

MAINTENANCE AND MANAGEMENT

Storage and Care

The primary concerns of anyone who must store and care for slides
are light, humidity, and heat. These three environmental factors contribute most to the life and quality of a slide. According to Kodak, the
leading manufacturer of photographic films, the following standards
should be met:
    Light. Slides should never be stored in direct sunlight. Prolonged
projection (over 1 minute) with high-wattage lamps or arc lamps should
also be avoided, since this will accelerate fading and shorten the life
of slide transparencies.
    Humidity. The optimum relative humidity for slide storage is be-
tween 15 and 40%. Low relative humidity (under 15%) may cause brittleness. High relative humidity (over 60%) may cause fungus growth.

Heat. Slides should never be stored near sources of heat. A range of 60° to 70° F is tolerable, with 70° F the preferred optimum.[6]

Ideally, slides should be stored in a facility that provides adequate ventilation, air circulation and filtration, controlled humidity, and a constant temperature. Since light accelerates fading, especially of color images, slides should be stored in darkness when possible. Silica gel or calcium chloride may be placed in storage cabinets to absorb moisture if excessive moisture is a problem. However, air conditioning or mechanical dehumidifiers are preferred, since silica gel can produce abrasive or reactive dust.

Because of the special characteristics of slides, it may not be possible to integrate the shelving of slides with other formats unless climate control is available throughout the facility. After environmental conditions are taken into account, care must be taken in selecting storage facilities.

There are four basic types of slide storage available. Plastic-sleeve storage will generally accommodate 20 slides per sleeve, and they can be arranged in loose-leaf binders and easily shelved. Sleeves work best with cardboard-mounted slides. They allow for immediate visual access and easy browsing by potential users, especially if a light table is available nearby.

Although many slide sets can be purchased in sleeves, they are not recommended for rapidly expanding and/or heavily used collections. Sleeves do not allow for guide or backup cards for frequent removal and refiling of slides. Sleeves should be made of inert, nondestructive plastic or acrylic. Polyvinyl chloride (PVC) sleeves can damage slides by releasing harmful gases. Additionally, moisture can collect in the sleeve pockets and damage film.

Trays or magazine storage can also be shelved on standard library shelves. Like plastic sleeves, trays are portable and hold a discrete number of slides. Carousel trays are particularly convenient for storing medium to large sets of related slides because the slides can be loaded directly into the projector without additional handling. Slides that are stored in plastic sleeves will need to be removed from the sleeves, mounted in a tray, and then returned to the sleeves after each use. Trays, however, pose the same problems as sleeves with regard to accommodating an expanding collection, without providing the benefit of easy visual access.

Visual rack cabinets, available commercially, consist of units with several racks that can be pulled out individually and illuminated by

---

6. Eastman Kodak Co., *Storage and Care of Kodak Color Films* (Rochester: Eastman Kodak Co., Pamphlet E-30), 4.

back lighting. Each rack can hold 100 or more slides for easy browsing. Integration of new material, however, can be tedious unless slides
are filed by accession number and indexed elsewhere.

Filing-drawer cabinets (also available commercially) are the preferred storage unit for large or heavily used collections. Cardboard or
plastic inserts fit inside cabinet drawers to accommodate slides and
backup cards, and guide cards can be added to facilitate browsing and
refiling. Cabinets are available in metal or wood and in various sizes
to accommodate the available space and the projected growth of a particular collection.

For any collection whose slides are used or lent as individual pieces,
boxes or trays will be needed for circulating and transporting slides.
The extra handling of slides will mean increased damage and wear,
and cleaning will be required more often. Although slides can sometimes be purchased uncut and therefore unmounted, most commercial slides are produced in cardboard or plastic mounts.

Slides which will be handled extensively should be mounted or
remounted between glass in plastic or metal mounts, a process known
as *slide binding*. Glass protects the slide film from dust, abrasion, and
the heat of the projector lamp. Fingerprints and dust can be easily
cleaned from the glass surface without damaging the slide. Specially
treated (or anti-Newton) glass is available which counteracts the
"Newton rings" which sometimes appear during projection of glass-
covered slides. Care should be taken to perform slide binding in an
area that has low humidity, to prevent moisture from getting trapped
between the glass layers during the binding process.

It is very helpful for users of the collection if "thumbspots" are
placed on all slides. Thumbspots are small stickers or, preferably, ink
marks on the lower left-hand corner of the nonemulsion side of the
slide, so that when the slide is in the proper position for placement
into the projector (i.e., with the image upside down), the user's right-
hand thumb will be on the thumbspot. This helps users load the slide
into the projector so that the image will not be backward or upside
down when projected.

Management Problems and Solutions

Staff requirements for slide collections have received increasing attention with the development of professional status for the curator. The
steady growth of slide collections since 1940 has contributed to a demand for a more systematic, professional training path for those interested in managing slide collections. The desirability of past work
experience in a slide collection, as well as postgraduate degrees in

library science and/or a special subject area, continue to be debated. The Art Libraries Society of North America has published helpful guidelines in its *Standards for Art Libraries and Fine Art Collections* (1983), which delineates professional versus nonprofessional staff needs in various types of institutions. Formulae for calculating staffing needs are also provided.

The still elusive choice of which classification system to use for a given collection is an indication of the proliferation of collection-specific cataloging schemes in use by slide curators. This has been due primarily to the lack of systematic training and communication within the field. This has improved dramatically in the past ten years through the efforts of professional organizations. Within the field of art and art history, the College Art Association (CAA), the Mid-America College Art Association (MACAA), and the Art Libraries Society of North America (ARLIS/NA) have addressed specific cataloging problems through their respective publications and meetings. Taking into account a collection's use patterns, adopting a classification system used by one of the major academic slide collections is recommended (such as Columbia, Yale, Harvard, or the Metropolitan Museum of Art). Those collections considering automated or computerized indexing systems should refer to the *Introduction to Visual Resource Library Automation*, edited by Zelda Richardson and Sheila Hannan (MACAA/VR, 1980). On-site investigations or interviews should also be conducted with institutions that use the systems under consideration.

The organization and management of a slide collection includes a multitude of problems, ranging from circulation procedures to ensuring adequate work space. As with most logistical problems, an experienced practitioner is the best solution. Establishing and maintaining communication with other slide curators, particuarly those with common interests and/or similar settings, can prove to be an invaluable and often expeditious means to discovering practical solutions to problems. Failing firsthand experience, a search in recent periodical literature may yield many possible answers for specific problems. Professional publications contain useful information for the practitioner. There are relatively few monographs which deal specifically with slide collections. Betty Irvine's *Slide Libraries: A Guide for Academic Institutions, Museums, and Special Collections* continues to be the most widely cited text, though journal articles and monographs continue to appear as professional communication channels improve.

Other Concerns

In view of the increased innovation and complexity in reprographic technology, slide users need to be aware of copyright laws and how they may affect slide duplication and service. Minimum standards of fair use under Section 107 of Public Law 94–553 have received various interpretations by publishers, from allowing only one illustration per source used to several illustrations per source.[7] The most recent professional guideline concerning copyright was published by the Visual Resource Association in the *International Bulletin for Photographic Documentation of the Visual Arts* article "Copyright Update" (vol. 12, no. 2, 1985), and includes a 10 percent maximum for copy photography from a single source. A priori conclusions regarding publishers' policies are not recommended. The safest procedure is to write for permission from the publisher and/or illustrators or photographers whenever the propriety of a request is questionable.

Information regarding slide production methods is an additional concern often overlooked by those involved with slide purchase or duplication. Knowledge of photographic processes and methods is necessary to effectively evaluate and maintain the quality of slides. Nancy DeLaurier, the originator of the *Slide Buyers' Guide*, contributed considerable effort to procure such information from slide suppliers. A compilation of this, as well as other useful information regarding slides, can be found in DeLaurier's *Guide*.

Other developments in the field point to increased networking and computerization. An *Art and Architecture Thesaurus* project, funded by the J. Paul Getty Foundation and directed by Toni Peterson, is currently under development and will greatly facilitate automation. Computerized classification systems and software with subject-search capability are becoming easier to obtain. As the demands for more visual resource programs become articulated, it will be the responsibility of slide library managers to ferret out those that meet their needs most effectively and affordably.

ADDITIONAL RESOURCES

ARLIS/NA. *Standards for Art Libraries and Fine Arts Slide Collections*. Occasional Papers No. 2. Tucson: Art Libraries Society of North America, 1983.

Arntzen, Ella, and Robert Rainwater. *Guide to the Literature of Art History*. Chicago: American Library Assn., 1980.

7. David Walch, "Slide Duplication and the New Law: A Survey of Publishers," *Audiovisual Instruction* (Mar. 1979): 64–65.

Bunting, Christine, ed. *Reference Tools for Fine Arts Visual Resources Collections*. Tucson: Art Libraries Society of North America, 1984.

DeBardeleben, Marian, and Carol Lunsford. "35mm Slides: Storage and Retrieval for the Novice." *Special Libraries* 73 (Apr. 1982): 135–41.

Eastman Kodak Co. *Planning and Producing Slide Programs*. 3rd ed. Rochester: Eastman Kodak Co., 1981.

_____. *Storage and Care of Kodak Color Films*. Rochester: Eastman Kodak Co., Pamphlet E-30.

Green, Stanford. *The Classification and Cataloging of Pictures and Slides*. Denver: Little Books, 1981.

Hess, Stanley, ed. *An Annotated Bibliography of Slide Library Literature*. Syracuse: Syracuse Univ. Pr., 1978.

Hoffberg, Judith, and Stanley Hess, eds. *Directory of Art Libraries and Visual Resource Collections*. Oxford: Clio Pr., 1979.

Irvine, Betty. *Slide Libraries: A Guide for Academic Institutions, Museums, and Special Collections*. 2nd ed. Littleton, Colo.: Libraries Unlimited, 1979.

Kuehn, Rosemary, and Zelda Richardson. *Guide to Copy Photography for Visual Resource Collections*. Albuquerque: Mid-America College Art Assn., 1979.

Richardson, Zelda, and Sheila Hannah, eds. *Introduction to Visual Resource Library Automation*. Albuquerque: Mid-America College Art Assn., 1981.

Schrock, Nancy Carlson, and Christine Sundt. "Slides." *Conservation in the Library*, ed. Susan Swartzburg. Westport, Conn.: Greenwood Pr., 1983.

Schuller, Nancy, ed. *Guide to Management of Visual Resources Collections*. Albuquerque: Mid-America College Art Assn. and Univ. of New Mexico, 1979.

Scott, Gillian, ed. *Guide to Equipment for Slide Maintenance and Viewing*. Albuquerque: Mid-America College Art Assn., 1978.

Simons, Wendell, and Luraine Tansey. *A Universal Slide Classification System with Automatic Indexing* (preliminary ed.). Santa Cruz: Univ. of California, 1969.

Univ. of Michigan. *Classification for Slides and Photographs*. Ann Arbor: Dept. of Art History, Univ. of Michigan, 1973.

Vance, David. "Computer and Fine Arts in the United States." Inventaire informatise des oeuvres d'Art = Computerized Inventory Standards for Works of Art. Conference Proceedings, Nov. 1–3, 1979, Ottawa, Canada, 89–97. Montreal: Fides, 1981.

Daniel R. Schabert

ch. 21

Videodiscs

THE MEDIUM

Definition

A videodisc is a shiny, platter-shaped silver disc, commonly made of polyvinyl chloride, usually 12 inches in diameter, without grooves, but with information printed on tracks that are imperceptible to the naked eye. A laser is required to "read" the image, which can be "played" over an ordinary television. Discs may contain digital, motion, audio, or still images, and combinations of all four. Even though discs with each variation have many similarities, they are very different in the way they are produced and played.

The laser videodisc has three layers. A transparent core is stamped in similar fashion as a phonorecord. Then a reflective aluminum layer is applied, followed by a protective acrylic layer (1.1mm). It is the protective layer that gives the videodisc its remarkable durability and a finish that looks like a mirror with a rainbow sheen.

Brief History

EARLY DEVELOPMENTS

John Logie Baird is considered the first person to develop a videodisc system, called Phonovision. In 1927 Baird, a Scotsman, used a waxed phonorecord as his medium to store the video signal. At the time, Baird was transmitting television as a series of tones via AM radio stations.

349

Baird could transmit the signal within the narrow AM bandwidth because the television pictures were 30 scanning lines at 12.5 frames per second. The phonodisc was produced by recording the audio-like television signals on a disc. By 1935, Baird was marketing his prerecorded disc in London, under the Major Radiovision label.[1] However, it was unsuccessful in gaining consumer acceptance.

It was not until 1965 that the next major advancement occurred, when ABC-TV Sports used a magnetic disc, provided by Ampex, to record and playback stop-action and instant replays. Limited by the expense ($150,000), the complexity of the equipment, and a 2-minute record time, it was only used in commercial television. Machines today have been improved by the addition of color and slow motion.

In Europe, Telefunken of Germany and Decca Records of Great Britain joined together to form TelDec, which formally introduced the TelDec videodisc system in 1974. TelDec was significant for many reasons. It was the first commercial videodisc system marketed for the consumer since 1935. In order to accommodate today's broader bandwith, frequency modulation (FM) was chosen for encoding the video and audio signals. During the FM coding process, the television signal is converted to a series of bumps and pits on the surface of the videodisc. The resulting playback signal can then be viewed on a television monitor. This process of FM encoding was the basis for virtually every videodisc system.[2] The grooves were placed tightly together, approximately 280 grooves per millimeter, and the disc revolutions require 1,500 rpm in Europe and 1,800 rpm in the USA.

TelDec also had its disadvantages. The playing time for a 9-inch-diameter disc was about 5 minutes. To compensate for the short playing time, TelDec introduced a 12-disc changer to give up to 2 hours of play (there was a 4-second wait between discs). Since there was contact between the disc and the stylus, the discs, like phonorecords, were also affected by scratches, finger oils, and dirt. A protective sleeve or caddie was needed. Finally, the "mastering" process was difficult. Programming had to be transferred to film, and then the disc was mastered from the film.

TelDec obviously had drawbacks and was not successful; it is no longer available.

RECENT DEVELOPMENTS

Until recently, there were two basic types of videodisc systems: capacitance or CED (no longer produced), which had stylus contact with

---

1. Efrem Sigel, Mark Schubin, and Paul F. Merrill, *Video Discs: The Technology, the Applications and the Future* (White Plains, N.Y.: Knowledge Industry, 1980), 2.
2. Ibid., 16.

the disc, and optical, which has no physical contact with the disc. The capacitance system will not be discussed further, since the equipment is no longer being produced.

The optical system uses a neonhelium laser beam to modulate the signal that cuts billions of micropits in a smooth disc surface. On playback, a low-powered laser is focused on, and reflected from, the disc surface into a light sensor. In this manner, light variations received by the sensor form an electrical signal which is translated into the video signal. The main advantage of this method is that discs are easy to duplicate inexpensively, and the disc players are also produced at a reasonable cost.

In 1972, MCA Incorporated in the United States and Philips in Holland demonstrated virtually identical systems. Since Philips had extensive manufacturing and marketing capabilities and MCA, the owner of Universal Studios, had a large collection of films, the two companies chose to work jointly on an optical system.

In 1976 both organizations, in conjunction with others investigating optical disc systems, issued the first videodisc standard, calling for a particular FM coding system featuring two sound channels and provision for either 12- or 8-inch-diameter discs. Both sizes can be played on the same machine without adjustments, because discs are played from the inner track to the outer track. In 1978 both players and discs were marketed in the United States.

Producing the videodisc involves several steps. Once the disc's transparent core is stamped, a reflective, iridescent, silver-colored coating is applied, followed by the transparent acrylic protective layer. Since the light from the laser focuses below the surface of the protective coating, surface dirt, fingerprints, and small scratches will not affect the signal quality.

While Magnavox, a U.S. subsidiary of Philips, was marketing a consumer version of the optical disc, Universal-Pioneer, a joint operation of MCA and Pioneer Corporation of Japan, began production of an institutional system. General Motors ordered about 10,000 units for dealers. By 1979 International Business Machines (IBM) entered an agreement with MCA, forming Disco-Vision Associates. Disco-Vision was to replicate and distribute discs, with the production of players left as an option for a later date. Pioneer introduced a player for the consumer market in 1980. Both the Magnavox and Pioneer systems are compatible. Finally, Quixote Corporation has been working on a system that permits local production and rapid reproduction turn-around time, and uses commercially available optical videodisc players.

Unique Characteristics

The characteristic that separates the videodisc from other nonprint media is the ability to store more than one medium. That is, videodisc can be produced to store a linear television program, stills, audio, or digital information. No other medium has such a diverse range of storage capabilities.

The linear television program can run the entire length of the videodisc or show a series of short segments. Just as in videotape, a computer can interface with the videodisc to determine which short segment to run, forming an interactive system.

The videodisc can store up to 108,000 unique frames (54,000 per side) of graphic or textual information. Information is arranged in circular tracks, each track constituting a separate frame for continuous or individual display. Each frame is "addressed" through the use of a keypad. Since there is no direct physical contact with the videodisc, a still image can be played for an indefinite length of time without damage to the videodisc or the player.

Two-track audio is available on the videodisc. The audio signal can be analog, which has quality approaching the high fidelity of videocassette recorders. A more recent development allows for a digital signal that is the same format as compact discs (audio).

The most recent development in the use of videodisc is information retrieval. The videodisc can be used for data storage, such as Information Access Company's InfoTrac data base system for literature searches. Many indexes and abstracts are integrated onto one videodisc. Information can be stored on one videodisc that would normally fill 5,000 floppy discs. These systems are used for automated information retrieval. Instead of using an online data base, the videodisc system allows the user to do research locally without incurring telecommunication costs associated with dial access.

The videodisc is truly a multimedia medium. No other medium can be used in the variety of ways as can the videodisc. The characteristics discussed above are common to some other media formats, but only the videodisc is capable of all of them.

Advantages

Picture and sound quality. Both the picture and sound quality surpass that of a videocassette recorder (VCR). The videodisc picture has more than 300 lines of resolution while a VCR has only 250 lines. While the standard VCR sound is surpassed by the laser disc, the sound of the digital signal, similar to the compact disc, surpasses even the sound quality of a hi-fi VCR. The resulting combination of sound and picture is the finest that is available for the consumer.

Durability. The videodisc is very durable. The protective layer makes playback of the signal unaffected by dirt, fingerprints, or even scratches. Since there is no contact with the disc by the playback equipment, there is no wear on the disc.

Play only. Since there is no record feature currently available, the programming on the videodisc cannot be accidentally erased or recorded over. It appears that record units are not far in the future—maybe even before you read this statement.

Random access. Random access allows the user to find a segment on the videodisc in seconds. In comparison, both film and videotape must be played through or fast forwarded until the desired segment is located.

Production costs. In mass production, the cost per program is much lower than other formats such as film or videotape. The reduced costs make videodisc attractive for buying special programming and feature-length entertainment.

Fading. Colors and images on videodisc do not fade, as they do on some film and slides.

Equipment costs. The videodisc player is simpler to produce than a videocassette recorder, and the cost of the equipment will probably continue to fall.

Repairs. The modular construction of the player makes it easily repairable.

Interactive. The videodisc can be interfaced with a microcomputer. The combined technology is far more powerful than the sum of the two components.

Disadvantages

Playback only. While a "play only" disc can be an advantage, it can also be a disadvantage, since no local recording is possible. Available programming is mostly limited to commercial production. To produce a videodisc, a master videotape must be sent to a videodisc producer. Many times there is a long wait for the disc to be stamped. There are, however, recent improvements in shortening the turnaround time.

Update. Once a disc is stamped, the information is there to stay. There is no way to update the videodisc, without creating a new disc.

Availability. There are many more ½-inch videotapes available in the marketplace than videodiscs, and rental of ½-inch videocassettes is much more prevalent than rental of videodiscs. The readily available videotapes and low cost of players make the ½-inch videotape more attractive for home use.

SELECTION
Special Criteria

Currently, there is only one format available in the United States, the optical laser disc. Therefore, if a new collection is established, it must be optical. The selection of videodiscs is the same as for film and video formats, except when the content is mainly dependent on the capabilities of the equipment that is being used.

If the collection is of feature films, the equipment does not need to be more than a standard player offering forward, reverse, and still frame.

If the collection is of the art collections of various museums or of any series of individual frames, a player must have the capability to call up any frame randomly.

If the collection is of instructional videodiscs, the player must be integrated with a microcomputer to form an interactive video system.

If the collection is of digital information, the equipment must be capable of accessing or reacting to the data.

Evaluative and Nonevaluative Sources

With the exception of those videodiscs being produced for industry, the titles are the same as those produced on film and video for the general public. Therefore, film and video evaluative sources should be used when videodiscs are selected.

The videodisc is running a distant second to videotape in the consumer market. In 1984, 200,000 videodisc players were purchased by Americans, as opposed to 7.6 million videocassette recorders. The commercial industrial market is growing, leading one to believe that the uses may be specific and that the discs will continue to be developed for that market.

MAINTENANCE AND MANAGEMENT
Storage and Care

The optical disc is very durable; in fact, it is practically indestructable with normal use. The lack of grooves and the protective acrylic layer, which coats the disc, makes the disc impervious to dust, heat, surface dirt, fingerprints, and scratches. The discs are packaged in the familiar phonograph record jacket. They can be cleaned with plain water or with commercial disc cleaner kits, though they usually need not be cleaned at all. Discs should be stored vertically away from direct sunlight and heat. A temperature of 65–75 °F is suitable for videodiscs. Even though the videodisc is not susceptible to damage, care should be taken not to touch the disc surface.

Manufacturing imperfections have been reported in approximately 30 percent of the discs purchased by libraries. Therefore, every title should be carefully inspected and played in its entirety before being added to the collection. Spot checking, as often done with the film and videotape, is not an acceptable quality control measure for videodiscs.

Management Problems and Solutions

Prior to RCA's withdrawal of the capacitance (CED) from the videodisc market, a major consideration for the videodisc manager was which format to purchase. To some extent that is still true today. Those who own CED players are in a bind: Should they continue to collect the CED discs or should the system be abandoned? For two reasons, the latter is the better path to take. First, the equipment is no longer manufactured; and second, since it is not, it is only a matter of time before RCA will discontinue, or greatly reduce, the manufacture of discs.

As mentioned earlier, the intended use of the videodisc is dependent on the features that are available on the equipment. In an entertainment collection, there are advantages to using discs. They are extremely durable, and inexpensive when mass produced. Two disadvantages, though, are that currently there are many more titles available in ½-inch videotape, and videotapes can be recorded by the user while videodiscs cannot. These factors may outweigh the advantages. The manager may then opt for a videotape collection.

The instructional uses of videodiscs are exciting. Even though there are few titles available commercially, this medium is well suited for instruction, with a capability for random access, still frame, slow motion, and interactive use with a computer. Now that disc producers will accept ¾-inch videotape to master a disc, producing a videodisc with specialized programming is more readily available to many institutions. There is also a cost factor to consider. The cost is high for a single disc to be pressed, but if multiple pressings are needed, the per item cost is dramatically lower. Another way to reduce costs is for more than one institution to join together, each paying for its portion of the disc. This way, the total cost will be shared by several institutions.

Instructional videodisc is probably best used in small groups or for individualized learning. This may be costly, but in the long run the overall benefit for the institution and the user may far exceed the cost. Instruction can be standardized. Major corporations, such as Ford, American Telephone and Telegraph, International Business Machines, and Digital Equipment, are using intelligent videodisc systems to train employees in sales and marketing, and at the consumers' point of sale.

When one thinks of instructional videodisc, interactive video immediately comes to mind. As stated earlier, interactive video is the marriage of two mediums, video and computer-assisted instruction. Each medium is capable of instructing in its own right. But, when joined together, the resulting medium is much more powerful. The computer controls which video segments will be shown, depending upon the user's response to various questions or "menus." An excellent example of this is the cardiopulmonary resuscitation (CPR) videodisc program, developed and used by the American Heart Association, which simulates cardiac first-aid response. This CPR training system is completely computerized. Mannequins are used that have sensors at critical points, and these sensors input to the computer, which in turn controls the videodisc. The image on the screen represents the care the mannequin receives. This system has saved countless hours in training sessions. The program also includes an exam mode for testing the students. This is highly effective because of the very fast response time in finding particular segments on the disc and the ability to adjust playing speed to coincide with the student's response time.

The sophisticated technology makes new demands on the video manager. A videodisc for interactive video must be designed differently than a videotape. It must account for the intricate branching that is needed in the program. This means that the program segments do not follow each other in a linear fashion, as if the disc were played from start to finish.

Using the videodisc to store individual frames of information is another application. The ability to view a single frame repeatedly, without damaging the disc or the player, makes this medium excellent for single-frame storage. The Library of Congress recently transferred rare glass photographic plates to videodisc. This not only makes these resources available to many more people and institutions; it also preserves the images from the plates, without any further deterioration of the image.

As with any medium, the selection of a videodisc should follow the mission of the institution and should be previewed by both subject and media specialists. By having both subject and media specialists view the videodisc, strengths and weaknesses of the discs can be evaluated objectively. The subject specialist assesses the content while the media specialist evaluates the technical quality of the disc.

Other Concerns

The optical laser disc can be broken down into two subgroups:

1. Reflective—the system reads laser light reflected off the surface of the disc.

2. Transmissive—the system reads laser light transmitted through the disc. It is not necessary to turn the disc over to play the other side; the laser beam is simply refocused. The French firm Thomson-CSF is currently the only producer of the transmissive laser videodisc system.

SPECIAL FUNCTIONS

Visual search "scanning" enables linear high-speed scanning of the disc in either the forward or reverse modes; sound is muted.

Random access enables searching for particular frames in any order. Each frame has an identifying number, or "electronic address," which aids in its retrieval. The frame number can be displayed on the screen, along with the actual frame picture. The user accesses the frame by entering its number on a keypad. The sound is muted during this function. This is standard on optical videodisc systems.

Rapid access enables scanning of the disc at more than 15 times normal speed, in either the forward or reverse modes, to find a certain time segment (as opposed to locating a particular frame). Both sound and picture are muted. Slow-motion access is also possible, except on extended-play discs where there are two frames per track.

Pause control allows stoppage of the program at any point and restart at the same point, in the event that an interruption should be necessary.

Freeze frame allows separate viewing of an individual frame or picture indefinitely, without harm to the disc. This is accomplished when the beam or stylus repeats scanning of a particular track. This cannot be done on extended play because more than one frame/picture is encoded on a single track.

Chapter index is similar to frame-by-frame access. It allows accession of a particular segment or "chapter" (instead of only a single frame).

Constant-speed turntable means that special circuitry ensures constant disc speed. Variations in power voltage do not affect the player; therefore, the proper turntable speed is maintained. This feature assures optimum video stability.

Interactive discs allow the viewer to participate in the program being viewed, utilizing all special effects (standard scan, forward, reverse, slow-motion play, dual audio, reject control, and freeze frame).

Video responder is Sony's device to allow two-way interaction between the user and the video program. At present, it is intended for the educational/industrial market.

PLAY MODES
Standard play is 1 frame per track, or 54,000 frames per side. One revolution of the disc plays 1 frame. The system can still frame, search frame by frame, and operate in slow motion.

Extended play increases storage capacity to 2 frames per track or 108,000 frames per side. This means that 1 revolution of the disc displays 2 frames. In this mode, two features are lost, slow motion and still framing, since each track contains 2 frames.

DISC PRODUCTION TECHNIQUES
The production of videodiscs is essentially the same as for regular phonorecordings:

Mastering: the process of creating an original video disc.

Optical disc manufacturing process (DiscoVision Associates): pressing heated material and then cooling it. This produces a hard disc.

Photopolymerization process (Philips): cold-stamping process, utilizing ultraviolet light to harden the material, avoids dimensional changes that occur when cooling is involved. This produces a hard disc.

Laser process (Sony): uses clear, flexible polyvinyl chloride (PVC) material which is covered with clear vinyl. This produces a flexible disc.

Recording on a disc is done by using a chemical coating on the glass master disc, which is then radiated by laser beams.

COMPARISON OF PLAYERS AND MANUFACTURERS
The following titles represent publications since 1981, comparing players and manufacturers:

Apar, Bruce, and Henry B. Cohen. *The Home Video Book.* New York: AM Photo Books, 1982. 129–32.

Bensinger, Charles. *The Home Video Handbook.* 3rd ed. Indianapolis: Howard W. Sams, 1982. 293–301, 304, 305.

Blumenthal, Howard J. *The Media Room*. New York: Penguin, 1983. 47–59, 85–90.

"Buyer's Guide to Videodisc Players." *VIDEOPLAY Magazine* IV, 5 (Winter 83/84): 48–51.

Cheshire, David. *The Video Manual*. New York: Van Nostrand Reinhold, 1982.

Dean, Richard. *Home Video*. London: Butterworth, 1982. 77–87.

Grosswirth, Marvin. *Home Video*. Garden City, N.Y.: Dolphin Books, Doubleday, 1981 69–75.

"Tape and Disc Previews." *Video Review* IV, 8 (Nov. 1983).

Utz, Peter. *The Complete Home Video Book*. Vol. II. Englewood Cliffs, N.J.: Prentice-Hall, 1983. 419–29, 524–26.

"Videodisc Players." *Consumer Guide Video Equipment Buying Guide* 395 (Dec. 1985): 98–105.

ADDITIONAL RESOURCES

Bahr, Alice Harrison. *Video in Libraries: A Status Report, 1979–1980*. 2nd ed. White Plains, N.Y.: Knowledge Industry, 1980.

"The Battle Starts at Last, Videodiscs." *Economist* 275 (Apr. 19, 1980): 70.

Bensinger, Charles. *The Video Guide*. 3rd ed. Santa Fe: Video-Information Pub., 1982.

Berger, Ivan. "Life with Video Disc." *Popular Electronics* 19 (Mar. 19, 1981).

Blumenthal, Howard J. *The Media Room*. New York: Penguin, 1983. 85–90.

Boyle, Diedre. "A Librarian's Guide to Consumer Video Magazines." *Library Journal* 106 (Sept. 1981): 1700–3.

_____. "Video Fever." *Library Journal* 106 (Apr. 15, 1981): 849–52.

Butler, David. "Five Caveats for Videodisc Training." *Instructional Innovation* 26 (Feb. 1981): 16–18.

Cherry, Susan S. "Videodisc Proves Popular in Pioneering Libraries." *American Libraries* 11 (Sept. 1980): 509–11.

Clement, Frank. "Oh Dad, Poor Dad, Mom's Bought the Wrong Videodisc and I'm Feeling So Sad." *Instructional Innovator* 26 (Feb. 1981): 12–15.

Cohen, Henry B. *The Home Video Survival Guide*. New York: AM Photo Books, 1983.

Delson, Donn, and Edwin Michalove. *Delson's Dictionary of Cable, Video, and Satellite Terms*. Thousand Oaks, Calif.: Brandon Pr., 1983.

Dranov, Paula, Louise Moore, and Adrienne Hickey. *Video in the 80's: Emerging Uses for Television in Business, Education, Medicine, and Government*. White Plains, N.Y.: Knowledge Industry, 1980.

Dunn, Donald H. "How to Screen VideoDisc Players." *Business Week*, Mar. 9, 1981.

Eckhardt, N. "Disc or Tape?" *Media & Methods* 16 (Oct. 1979): 22.

Emmens, Carol A. "The Videodisc Competition." *School Library Journal* 27 (May 1981): 41.

Hawkins, W. J. "Videodisc Player—Instant Movies with Push-Button Options." *Popular Science* 218 (Jan. 1981): 22.

"His Master's Text." *Economist* 269 (Nov. 11, 1978): 99–100.

The Home Video Yearbook, 1981–82. White Plains, N.Y.: Knowledge Industry, 1981. 151–72.

Hon, David. "Interactive Video: Welcoming the New Colossus." *Video User* (Jan. 1984): 15.

Kaplan, Michael, ed. *Consumer Guide: Video Equipment Buying Guide.* Skokie, Ill.: Publications International, 1985. 99.

Kybett, Harry, and Peter L. Dexnis. *Complete Handbook of Home Video Systems.* Reston, Va.: Reston Pub., 1982.

Love, J. "Videodisc: Television's New Horn of Plenty." *Media & Methods* 16 (Oct. 1979): 16–18.

Marcus, Leonard, ed. "Video Discs Decoded: How They Work and Differ." *High Fidelity* 30 (Dec. 1980).

National Assn. of Educational Broadcasters. *Television Cartridge and Disc Systems: What Are They Good For?* Washington, D.C.: NAEB, 1971.

Nugent, Gwen. "Video Disc & Industrial Television: The Possible vs. the Practical." *E&ITV* 11 (Aug. 1979): 54–56.

Patrick, Lucy. "Is There a Video Disc in the House?" *Georgia Librarian* 16 (Aug. 1979): 6.

"The Philips-Magnavox/MCA Magnavision/Discovision System." *E&ITV* 11 (Jan. 1979): 35, 78.

Prentiss, Stan. "P.M.'s Complete Guide to the New Videodiscs and Cassettes." *Popular Mechanics* 152 (Sept. 1979): 118–21 + .

Pipes, Lana. "What's New in Video." *Instructional Innovator* 26 (Feb. 1981): 8–11.

"RCA's Biggest Gamble Ever." *Business Week* Mar. 9, 1981, 79–84.

Sigel, Efrem. *Videodiscs: The Technology, Application and the Future.* White Plains, N.Y.: Knowledge Industry, 1981.

"Sources and Resources: Products for the Home and Programs for the Products." *Home Entertainment* II, 1 (Sept.–Oct. 1983): 27.

Stock, Gary. "Finally: A Videodisc Hits the Market." *Stereo Review* 42 (Mar. 1979): 30, 32.

"Tomorrow Things: A Million Chances to Get It Right." *Home Entertainment* II, 1 (Sept.–Oct. 1983): 118.

Unwin, Derick, and Ray McAleese. *Encyclopedia of Educational Media Communications and Technology.* Westport, Conn.: Greenwood Pr., 1978.

Utz, Peter. *Video User's Handbook.* 2nd ed. Englewood Cliffs, N.J.: Prentice-Hall, 1982. 368–72.

"Viva Videodisks" *Forbes* 135, 5 (Mar. 11, 1985): 13.

"Video Discs: Another Option for TV Viewers." *Consumer Reports* 44 (Oct. 1979): 568.

"Video Discs: Where the Action Is." *High Fidelity* 31 (Apr. 1981): A6, A10.

White, Gordon. *Video Recording.* London: Newnes-Butterworths, 1972.

"Who If Anyone Will Win? Videodiscs." *Economist* 274 (1980): 86–87.

Winslow, Ken. "Videodisc Software: What's the Holdup?" *Stereo Review* 46 (Jan. 1981): 50.

Daniel R. Schabert

ch. 22

Videotapes

THE MEDIUM

Definition

Videotape is a flexible, ribbonlike strip of polyester upon which magnetic signals are arranged and thus stored. The signals may be recorded, by rearranging magnetic particles that are on the tape, or played back, by reading signals from the arranged particles of the tape.

There are many types of devices that are capable of processing video and audio information in such a way that it may be stored or recorded in a code on a medium. The stored signals may at a later time be read off this medium by playback devices capable of reading the exact specifications of the recording device. The most widely used medium for this storage function today is videotape.

Brief History

Television dates back to the 1920s. It was the period from the late 1920s to the postwar 1940s that saw many changes and improvements in broadcast television. The "film chain," a mechanical-optical device, was used to telecast films on television, but there was no equipment to record a televised image. "Once a program was telecast it was lost forever."[1] Throughout this period of development it became

---

1. Christopher Sterling and John M. Kittross, *Stay Tuned: A Concise History of American Broadcasting* (Belmont, Calif.: Wadsworth, 1978), 252.

clear that there was a need to record the programming being broadcast.

During the period 1947–1948, a special film camera was developed to record off a television tube or kinescope. "Film or kinescope recordings of television programs were less clear, less defined, had less contrast than the original television picture, and were far poorer than an original film. Thus, making kines was an art . . . some programs were recorded this way for archival purposes, but the networks used kinescope recordings only to supply programs to affiliate stations not yet connected by wire or microwave relay for simultaneous transmission."[2] The unacceptable qualities of the kinescope encouraged many firms to continue researching alternative mediums to record television programming.

Bing Crosby Enterprises conducted one of the first demonstrations of magnetic videotape recording in late 1951. The speed at which the tape advanced (100 inches per second) made this system commercially impractical. However, the advantages of videotapes were readily apparent; the broadcast videotape quality was about equal to live programming; no processing was needed for playback; tapes could be reused; it was cheaper than kinescope; and it was electronic.[3]

It was not until 1956, however, that Ampex unveiled the first practical videotape recorder, at the National Association of Broadcasters convention. The quadruplex recorder used four record heads that were mounted on a spinning drum. The speed of the tape was reduced to 15 inches per second. The recorder had "a tape to head contact speed (writing speed) far in excess of anything previously dreamed of: roughly 1560 inches per second. This was achieved by spinning the heads transversely across the width of the two inch tape."[4] Over the course of the convention, Ampex wrote $4.1 million worth of orders.[5]

While the quadruplex videotape recorder (VTR) was becoming the standard for broadcast recording, there was a desire to develop a VTR that was more affordable and used less videotape. In 1967 the helical scan (or "slant" scan) VTR was introduced.[6] The tape followed a helical path around the drum that housed two spinning heads. The heads formed diagonal or slanted video tracks on the tape, rather than the

---

2. Ibid.
3. Ibid.
4. Efrem Sigel, Mark Schubin, and Paul F. Merrill, *Video Discs: The Technology, the Applications and the Future* (White Plains, N.Y.: Knowledge Industry, 1980), 11, 12.
5. Sterling and Kittross, *Stay Tuned,* 321.
6. Paula Dranov, Louise Moore, and Adrienne Hickey, *Video in the 80's: Emerging Uses for Television in Business, Education, Medicine and Government* (White Plains, N.Y.: Knowledge Industry, 1980), 3.

perpendicular tracks of the quadruplex format. Tape sizes included 1 inch and ½ inch. The tape speed was reduced from the 15 inches per second down to 10 inches per second, and sometimes slower. These systems did not rival the quality of quadruplex, which remained the broadcast standard. It would be another ten years before a broadcast-quality 1-inch VTR would be produced.

Sony had the foresight to see the consumer potential for marketing a VTR. In 1967 the consumer video (CV) series was introduced. The CV used ½-inch tape that traveled at 7.5 inches per second. The CV failed in the marketplace, partly because the cost still exceeded that of a color television set. Even though the CV was not commercially successful, this system "spawned many successors who banded together to introduce the first helical recorder standard, under the Electronics Industry Association of Japan (EIAJ)."[7]

In 1969 Sony introduced the ¾-inch U-Matic format. Up to this point, all videotape was on open reels that had to be threaded manually. U-Matic tape was in a plastic case, called a *cassette*; once inserted into the videocassette recorder (VCR), the tape would be threaded by the machine. "Once the U-Matic cassette player went on sale in 1972, it was quickly adopted by business and government organizations attracted by its simplicity, compactness, good picture quality and reasonable price."[8] In addition, this format had one other advantage: any tape recorded on a U-Matic VCR could be played back on any other U-Matic VCR, regardless of the manufacturer.

The mid-1970s saw a resurgence in interest to market a home video system. By 1975 a number of manufacturers were marketing ½-inch home videocassette recorders. The unfortunate fact about ½-inch VCRs is that there are two formats, Beta and VHS, which are incompatible with each other. By 1984, over 7 million VCRs were being produced each year.[9] It is clear that the video industry is finally successful in the consumer marketplace, and VHS has won highest acceptance. Beta may no longer be marketed by the time you read this sentence.

The Type C 1-inch broadcast-quality format was introduced in 1977.[10] Sony and Ampex petitioned the Society of Motion Picture and Television Engineers (SMPTE) to standardize the new format. This format is the one being utilized by schools, industry, cable stations, and

7. Sigel et al., *Video Discs,* 13.

8. Dranov et al., *Video in the 80's,* 3–4.

9. U.S. Bureau of the Census, *Statistical Abstracts of the United States, 106 Edition* (Washington, D.C., 1985), 770.

10. John A. Bunyan, James C. Crimmins, and N. Kyri Watson, *Practical Video: The Manager's Guide to Applications* (White Plains, N.Y.: Knowledge Industry, 1978), 7.

small television stations seeking broadcast quality. Its reduced cost and portability give it a significant advantage over the 2-inch quadruplex format.

The most recent development is the 8mm video format. Learning from the experience of the incompatible Beta and VHS formats, video manufacturers formed a committee in 1982 to formulate a set of standards for the 8mm format.[11] This was before a single unit was introduced. In April 1984, 127 electronics manufacturers signed the 8mm Standard Agreement,[12] which made provisions for future improvements and applications. Kodak and General Electric were the first to introduce the 8mm video recorder, late in 1984. Since then, many manufacturers have introduced 8mm recorders.

Unique Characteristics

Videotape electronically reproduces visual images with synchronized sound.

Videotapes can be viewed immediately after recording. No developing or processing is required.

Type of videotape does not determine color. Color is the function of the camera, recorder, and receiver/monitor. Any videotape can record in either color or black and white.

Advantages

Videotape can present color, motion, and sound to the user.

No time or money is expended for processing. You can play the videotape immediately after recording it.

When the videotape content is no longer useful, the tape can be erased and reused.

Special lighting is not usually necessary for producing or viewing videotapes. However, extremes in lighting (one way or the other) can hinder a good image.

Video equipment is relatively easy to operate.

Videotape that is encased in a cassette is protected by the cassette. The tape is never touched by the user's hands, and only comes out of the case while the cassette is engaged in the VCR. This extends the life of the tape.

---

11. Art Pushkin and Brad Alves, "Is 8mm the New World Format?" *Intelligent Decisions* 3 (May/June 1986): 24.
    12. Ibid.

The cost of producing a videotape is much less than that for a comparable-length film.

Editing videotape is easy with an electronic system. The edits are made by copying segments from the original tape. Segment frames that are to be added or deleted are logged into a controller and are inserted automatically on a new tape, without changing the original tape.

Distribution of video programming to multiple locations is possible. A number of remote locations can access the programming via a closed-circuit television system (CCTV).

Many of the newest generation of ½-inch and ¾-inch VCRs have the capability of interfacing with a microcomputer, forming an interactive video system. In interactive video, the VCR is controlled by the computer. Video segments are played for original information or reinforcing an idea, depending on the response to questions by the user. This is a powerful tool for independent, individualized learning.

The growing popularity of home video systems makes videotape a good medium for circulation to users for home use, and for at-home education of special audiences such as the handicapped and aged.

Disadvantages

Without the necessary precautions, videotape is easily erased. Once it is erased, it is gone forever.

The cost of production equipment is high. The initial investment ranges from about $1,200 for a consumer-grade camera and portable recorder to well over $100,000 for a production studio that uses ½- or ¾-inch formats. Type C and quadruplex studios run even more.

The numerous formats that are available make it difficult to choose which to purchase. This lack of standardization also makes it difficult to exchange tapes.

The equipment is somewhat fragile. Extremes in temperature, moisture, and shock can damage the VCR. Cameras are easily damaged by pointing the lens at excessively bright light sources.

The institution may need additional and technically trained staff to aid in using video equipment. Personnel with the necessary technical skills are needed for production, preventive maintenance, and repair of equipment.

The legality of copying and distributing copyrighted material must be considered. With the proliferation of videocassette recorders, guidelines have been established for home use, but there are still gray areas for institutions. In most cases, if a program is taped off the air it cannot be shown without permission of the copyright holder or designate.

Animation is not easy. Each taped segment must be edited frame by frame. This is very time consuming and labor intensive. Animation done on film is more economical.

Storing videotape in poor environmental conditions can damage the tape. For instance, if the humidity is high, the tape will stretch, causing poor playback.

Because videotape is an electronic medium, there are many problems that can cause poor recording or playback, disrupting the program. For example, a "short" in the audio cable will cause a loud buzzing.

SELECTION

Special Criteria

As with any medium, a potential user should answer the basic question, Which medium is best suited to deliver the message? Criteria unique to the selection of videotape are:

When purchasing or renting a videotape, it is important to view the tape to ensure that portions of the programming have not been edited. This is especially true for motion pictures which have been dubbed to tape format.

Check the speed at which the tape was recorded. The Beta and VHS formats are capable of recording at different tape speeds. The slower the tape speed during recording, the grainier the television picture during playback.

Check the quality of the tape. As with audiotape, there are different grades of tape. The higher the grade, the less "dropout" or "noise" (degradation of the television image). Low-quality tape also has a tendency break or stretch at the beginning, where much stress is placed on it.

For videocassettes, check the casing to ensure that it does not show signs of wear or breakage, which can be caused by abuse or poor construction. If the cassette case breaks while the tape is played, the tape player could be damaged.

Consider the type of audio on the tape. VCRs have been recently introduced that are capable of playing the audio in stereo, for better sound quality. These recorders are more expensive than standard recorders, and unless you have a stereo system to play through or a new television capable of playing sound in stereo, this feature does not change the audio quality; the audio is still played in monaural if your television is monaural.

Evaluative Review Sources

PERIODICALS

American Film Magazine
American Libraries
Ampersand
Art and Cinema
Audio-Visual Communications
AV Video
Back Stage
Billboard
Booklist
The Business Magazine of the
    Motion Picture Industry
Business Marketing
Choice
Classic Images
The Communication Industry
    Report
Development Communication
    Report
E & ITV
Educational Technology
Educator's Curriculum Product
    Review
EFLA Evaluations
EPIEgram Materials
ETV Newsletter
Film Comment
Film Culture
Films in Review
First Take
GPNewsletter
High Fidelity Magazine
Home Video Publisher
Hope Reports Briefing
Instant Replay
Instructor

International Television
Journal of Broadcasting and
    Electronic Media
Journal of Film and Video
Journal of Information and
    Image Management
Jump Cut: A Review of
    Contemporary Media
Library Journal
Literature/Film Quarterly
Media and Methods
Media Profiles: The Career
    Development Edition
Media Profiles: The Health
    Science Edition
Media Review
Media Review Digest
Millimeter
Photographic Trade News
Photomethods
Quorum Quotes
School Product News
Science Books and Films
Sightlines
Stereo Review
Technical Photography
Telezine
Variety
Video Business
Video Manager
Video Marketing Newsletter
Videography
The Videoplay Report
VideoPro
Videotape and Optical Disk

Nonevaluative Sources

PERIODICALS

Access
Advanced Technology Libraries
AV Business Communications
Audiovideo International

BOOKS

Audio Video Market Place, 1985–86. New York: Bowker, 1985.

Boyle, Deirdre. *Video Classics: A Guide to Video Art and Documentary Tapes.* Phoenix: Oryx Pr., 1986.

Brooks, Tim, and Earle Marsh. *Complete Directory of Prime Time Network Television Shows, 1946 to the Present.* New York: Ballantine, 1981.

Chicorel, Marietta, ed. *Chicorel Index to Video Tapes and Cassettes.* Vol. 27. New York: American Library Publishing Co., 1978.

Dorset, Gerald. *Video Tapes.* New York: New England Pr., 1978.

Eidelberg, Lawrence, ed. *Videolog: Programs for General Interest and Entertainment.* Guilford, Conn.: Video-Forum, 1979.

———. *Videolog: Programs for the Health Sciences.* Guilford, Conn.: Video-Forum, 1979.

Limbacher, James L. *Feature Films Available for Rental, Sale and Lease: A Directory of Feature Films on 16mm and Video Tape.* 8th ed. New York: Bowker, 1985.

Martin, Mick, and Marsha Potter. *Video Movie Guide 1986.* New York: Ballantine, 1986.

National Information Center for Educational Media. *Index to Educational Video Tapes.* 6th ed. Los Angeles: Univ. of Southern California, National Information Center for Educational Media, 1985.

National Video Clearing House. *Video Source Book.* 6th ed. Syosset, N.Y.: National Video Clearing House, 1984.

Schorn, J. L. *Video Magazine's Guide to What's on Tape.* New York: McGraw-Hill, 1985.

Video Blue Book, 1985. Durango, Colo.: Orion Research, 1985.

MAINTENANCE AND MANAGEMENT
Storage and Care

Videotape needs special storage and care in order to preserve its playback quality. For the best results, store videotapes in an environment with 55–75° F temperature and a relative humidity of 50%, plus or minus 5%. If tape is stored in an environment beyond these limits, it should be allowed to "normalize" to within the limits for at least 24 hours before being played. High humidity increases abrasiveness, which can damage both the tape and the video player.

Store videotapes away from any magnetic field which can be created by electric motors, demagnetizers, or bulk erasers. The magnetic field can damage both the video and audio signals and the control track.

Store videotapes in their protective boxes in a dust-free atmosphere. Dust particles (including cigarette smoke) can cause "dropouts" (white specks on the monitor screen) and damage the tape recorder heads.

Do not touch the oxide side of videotape. With the advent of videocassettes, the only time the tape should be outside the cassette is when it is in the VCR.

Splicing the videotape should be avoided. For a reel tape, cut off any creased or damaged tape at the beginning or end of the program. Do not play creased or damaged tape, since it can cause head wear or, worse, permanently damage the head.

Store the tape on edge on a shelf, in a properly fitting container. For a reel tape, make sure there is support for the hub of the reel.

Always handle reel tape by the hub, and never squeeze the tape.

Management Problems and Solutions

The management of videotape is complex and far ranging. There are many decisions to be made in regard to format, recording facilities, and users.

VIDEO USAGE

The first issue that should be investigated is how the videotape collection will be used. This will help resolve many future decisions. Most important, the function of the collection will determine the format of the collection. The most commonly collected formats are ½-inch VHS and Beta, and ¾-inch U-Matic.

The ½-inch formats are often utilized in circulating collections of feature-length motion pictures, educational programming, and general-entertainment videotapes. One advantage of ½-inch tape is that the play length can be as long as 8 hours on one cassette. The relatively low cost of ½-inch equipment makes the in-house production of training or educational tapes a possibility. Recently, the quality of ½-inch studio production equipment has been approaching that of ¾-inch. At the high end of the ½-inch formats is broadcast-quality equipment. In fact, the newest generation of broadcast ½-inch VHSs from Panasonic is to be used by the National Broadcasting Corporation (NBC) for coverage of the 1988 Olympics in Korea.

The ¾-inch U-Matic has been used most successfully in educational and training situations. U-Matic ¾-inch tape has been the standard for education since it was first marketed in the 1970s, and the majority of available ¾-inch programming is educational in nature. Many film rental firms offer the choice of ¾-inch or 16mm film when renting or purchasing educational titles. A big drawback with the U-Matic format is the 1-hour maximum play length. It does, however, have a better quality than the ½-inch tape; it can be used to "master" videodiscs; and it can serve as a master for multiple copies. The ¾-inch tape is often used in production studios. Broadcast-quality equipment is available in the U-Matic format. Many news departments use U-Matic for videotaping on remotes and playing back during news broadcasts.

One-inch Type C and 2-inch quadruplex are used in high-end production and broadcast studios. They make excellent masters for videodiscs and videotape copies.

In most cases, the choice of videotape for a collection will be limited to the ½- and ¾-inch formats. The media manager must decide how many formats should be acquired. The ½-inch formats have an advantage of pricing over the ¾-inch format: the equipment and tapes are less expensive. Three-quarter-inch has been around for a long time and there is a wide selection of tapes available commercially. Half-inch not only replicates most programming available in ¾-inch; it also provides for additional titles. In the final analysis, many video managers currently have both formats. A lending collection is apt to be just ½-inch VHS because the vast majority of home VCRs on the market today are VHS. An institutional collection that does only in-house production may have just ¾-inch. Any collection that serves a variety of users will need the versatility of having two formats.

Promoting the videotape collection is a very important function of the media manager, who must walk a fine line between being overly aggressive and too low key. Two methods of promoting videotape use are suggested. First, single out an individual and work extensively with him or her. (The individual should be pleasantly outspoken and respected by colleagues.) Once that person is pleased with and successfully working with videotape, he or she will be an informal advocate of videotape.

Second, identify a problem area and develop a videotape program with either in-house-produced material or tapes on loan, and propose the program as a possible solution.

There are many other ways to promote videotape, so the manager should experiment and try methods that best suit the situation.

ACQUISITION POLICIES
Policies for acquiring videotapes should be set and followed to ensure a quality collection. The staff, in conjunction with the media manager and subject specialists, should make up a selection committee, which should preview tapes to assure that they meet the minimum criteria for purchase. Since the production and content quality vary greatly, previewing the tapes should be emphasized. The criteria should follow the mission of the institution and represent a meaningful collection-development policy. The quality of production should also be considered. Even though the content may be correct, distraction may be

caused by a poor production that may preclude conveying the information. If the videotape has been produced in-house, it should be previewed by the selection committee to ensure that the production objectives are met.

A quality collection is wasted if it is not used. Involving users as subject specialists during the selection process will help expand the user population. For those who are not asked to be involved, there should be notices of new titles so that all potential users are aware of what is available. Screenings promoting new titles, coupled with effective workshops of videotape use, will help those unfamiliar with the medium feel more comfortable.

BUDGETING AND PROGRAMMING

Along with a philosophical commitment to video, a financial commitment is very important. The cost of maintaining a video collection and the necessary equipment is high. The rationale for justifying such an expenditure must be well thought out and buttressed by sound reasoning. The main thrust of the argument should stress the positive uses in areas such as training, communications, orientation, and entertainment. One must "sell" the idea of using video to increase the flow of information and level of learning.

Beyond the philosophical argument, proposals for practical video application by the institution should be included. Proposals should detail who the prospective users are and what objectives will be achieved by using video.

Even with sound reasoning and a persuasive argument, the funding may not be there to support all or part of the proposal. The alternative is to pursue outside funding through grants. Grants are usually offered in specific areas of study or research. To pursue a grant, an outline of the video project must be written to conform to the requirement set by the funding organization. Many times, grants are not available for individual video projects, but video projects can be funded as an integral part of a larger project. All needs, such as equipment, supplies, and release time, should be included. It takes imagination and thorough research to find a funding source and make the project fit the requirements of the grant. Many states offer grants through their education departments.

COLLECTION AND LOAN POLICIES

An immediate question, when a video collection is discussed, is whether to rent, purchase, or produce. When a videotape program can be purchased for $400 or rented for $50, it may be wiser to rent for the $50 if the program will only be used once or twice a year. If the subject is one that is constantly updated, purchasing a tape that will be outdated within a couple of years may be unwise, unless the tape has a current high demand. The video manager must weigh the pros and cons of purchasing versus renting and make a decision based on the cost of buying or borrowing, the timeliness of the subject material, the nature of the anticipated use, and the expected frequency of use.

Having an in-house production facility does not exclude the acquisition of commercially produced tapes. It costs money to produce a program, and if a comparable videotape can be obtained commercially for less than it costs to produce, it would be best to buy or rent it.

The media manager must consider designing policies for the use of materials outside of the institution. In the interest of cooperation, many institutions engage in resource sharing. This allows each institution to focus on purchase or production in specific subjects while other institutions are concentrating on other subjects. Each of the participating members has access to the others' collections. The media manager must set a policy within the mission of his or her respective institution.

While each institution may have different circulation criteria for users, some suggested guidelines are:

Lend videotapes *only*, not equipment. Whether or not a fee is assessed is an institutional matter.

Have borrowers sign a form detailing their responsibilities.

If the original tape is valuable and there is no copyright infringement, a duplicate or copy can be substituted for the original.

If there are shipping costs, you may wish to charge the borrower for those costs.

If a user from within the institution requests a videotape that is not in the collection, it should be the responsibility of the media staff to obtain the tape from an outside source. If there are charges involved, a decision needs to be made concerning who will absorb the costs.

Once a collection is established, not only are tapes added, but they should be weeded as well. An appropriate committee should be established to recommend the removal of tapes that no longer meet the mission of the institution and/or are outdated. This can be the same group of people who constitute the selection committee.

STORAGE

Establishing a videotape collection is one thing, but housing it is another. Two obvious places to house the collection are the institutional library or the media department (if separate). If housed in the library, the videotapes can be intershelved with other materials, offering the user all print and nonprint formats in an integrated collection. This can make it convenient for a user to locate all information on a given topic. A VCR should be made easily available to users to maximize the use of video.

If it is decided to maintain a separate videotape collection, a logical location for it is in the media department (if one exists). This might be especially desirable if the media department offers equipment delivery or a distribution system within the institution.

Regardless of the location of the videotapes, catalog card information should be interfiled with the library's public catalog (if the institution has a library). Otherwise, some type of index to the items available in the video collection must be prepared. This can take the form of catalog cards, print or microform descriptions and indexes, or an online data base.

NEW ON THE VIDEO SCENE

Sony has a tab marker which leaves a "pip" (electronic mark) on the tape whenever it is switched into record mode. This makes it easier to rewind to the spot where recording last began.

The Grundig Company (in Germany) has a unit which measures how long the tape is and how much space is left to be recorded. If you set the machine to make a timer-controlled recording longer than the time remaining on the tape, it will automatically tell you that not enough room is left.

The Olufsen 8002 videocassette recorder permits electronically marked spots on tapes, so that a tape can be advanced directly to the marked spot.

Long play is now achieved by a reversible, dual-track cassette that flips over. The two tracks, on standard ½-inch tape, give 4 hours of playing time in both directions. This was developed by Philips in the Netherlands, to be marketed by Magnavox in the United States.

There have been several unsuccessful ¼-inch systems, also known as 8mm, but since Kodak introduced KodaVision, many other manufacturers have followed suit. The cassettes are about the size of a deck of playing cards. Of course, the 8mm is mechanically incompatible with Beta and VHS, but they are electronically compatible with an adapter, which means that it is possible to dub an 8mm cassette to another format.

The 8mm will not replace Beta or VHS. The purpose of the new format is portability for home moviemaking. The entire unit weighs just 5 pounds, and puts the video camera and the VCR into one piece. The *camcorder*, as it is called, is not unique to 8mm, but it is designed to be more compact and lighter than ½-inch camcorders, to make it much easier for the home videographer to use.

Following are some forthcoming developments:

Miniaturization. The tiny, charged couple device (CCD) is a solid-state substitute for a camera tube. The CCD is much more sensitive than a video tube in low-light situations, yet it is not susceptible to "burning" if the lens is pointed at a bright light source.

LVR. The longitudinal video recorder (LVR) uses a fixed video head to scan small, multiple-track tape. Such a system requires fewer moving parts; it is small, portable, and easy to use.

Cassette stacking. This will permit up to 15 hours of playing time.

The video industry is marketing new products at a faster and faster rate. What is state-of-the-art today will not remain so for any length of time. The video manager must weigh all possibilities and then make a decision, based on the information at hand—and not only on what may be available in the future.

ADDITIONAL RESOURCES

Bahr, Alice J. *Video in Libraries: A Status Report.* 2nd ed. White Plains, N.Y.: Knowledge Industry, 1980.

Barwick, John H., and Stewart Dranz. *The Complete Video-Cassette Users' Guide: Principles and Practice of Programming.* White Plains, N.Y.: Knowledge Industry, 1973.

———. *Why Video? A Study (of 100 Video Users) for Reference Purposes Documenting Cost/Effectiveness of Video Medium.* New York: Sony, 1975.

Bensinger, Charles, et al. *Petersen's Guide to Video Tape Recording.* Los Angeles: Petersen Pub., 1973.

Berger, Ivan, and Lancelot Braithwaite. "Video Tests by Berger-Braithwaite Labs." *Video* (Jan. 1979): 24–31.

Boyle, Deirdre. "Getting it Together: Video Information and Librarians." *American Library* 9 (June 1978): 393–94.

———. "A Librarian's Guide to Consumer Video Magazines." *Library Journal* 106 (Sept. 15, 1981): 1700–3.

———. "The Library, TV, and the Unconscious Mind." *Wilson Library Bulletin* 52 (May 1978): 696–702.

———. "VHS (Video Home System) at SFPL." *Wilson Library Bulletin* 53 (June 1979): 682.

Bunyan, John A., and James C. Crimmins. *Television and Management: The Manager's Guide to Video.* White Plains, N.Y.: Knowledge Industry, 1977.

———, and N. Kyri Watson. *Practical Video: Manager's Guide to Applications.* White Plains, N.Y.: Knowledge Industry, 1978.

"Clearing Up the Confusion over Video Recorders." *Business Week,* June 25, 1979, 124–26.

Covert, N. "Video vs. Film or Video and Film." *Sightlines* 11 (Winter 1977/78): 2.

Dorn, Manfred. "A Guide to Selecting 1-Inch VTRs." *Video Systems* (Oct. 1980): 22–29.

Dranov, Paula, Louise Moore, and Adrienne Hickey. *Video in the 80's: Emerging Uses for Television in Business, Education, Medicine and Government*. White Plains, N.Y.: Knowledge Industry, 1980.

Drolet, Leon L. "Reference Readiness for AV Questions." *American Libraries* 12 (Mar. 1981): 154–55.

———. "Software: The Key to a Successful Video Program." *American Libraries* 10 (Dec. 1979): 668–70.

Ellison, John W. "Taking Care of Tape." *Videography* 5 (May 1980): 37.

Emmens, C. A. "Video Use Today." *Sightlines* (Winter 1977/78): 5–7.

Feldman, S. "Programming Video: The Hardware, the Software, and Some Directions." *Film Library Quarterly*, no. 3–4 (1974): 91–102.

"Film Copying Barred in NY Court Ruling." *Library Journal* 103 (Apr. 15, 1978): 800.

"Film Producers Charge NY BOCES with Infringement of Copyrights." *School Library Journal* 24 (Dec. 1977): 9.

Genova, B. K. L. "Video, Cable TV and Public Libraries." *Catholic Library World* (Mar. 1978): 324–29.

Harrison, Helen. "Video in Libraries." *Audiovisual Librarian* 5 (Feb. 1980): 47–53.

Harvey, J. "Video: Visual Stories in the Children's Library." *Ontario Library Record* 62 (Sept. 1978): 189–94.

Kybett, Harry, and Peter L. Dexnis. *Complete Handbook of Home Video Systems*. Reston, Va.: Reston Pub. Co., 1982.

LaComb, Denis J. "Video Technology: Its Future in Libraries." *Library Journal* 101 (Oct. 1, 1976): 2003–9.

Markuson, Carolyn. "Video Technology—Past and Present." *Catholic Library World* (Oct. 1981): 112–15.

Miller, J. K. "Licenses to Videotape Films." *Library Trends* 23 (Summer 1978): 101–5.

Penland, Patrick R. *Media Resources and Audiovisual Bibliography*. Pittsburgh: Univ. of Pittsburgh Communication Media Research Center, 1978.

———. "One-half-inch Videocassctte Equipment for Library Use." *Library Technology Reports* 14 (Sept. 1978).

Powell, Jon T. "Buying Video Equipment: A Guide for the Thrifty." *Media and Methods* 14 (Oct. 1977): 42 + .

Primer for Media Resources Librarians. U.S. Dept. of Health, Education, and Welfare. Public Health Service–National Institutes of Health, National Library of Medicine. Washington, D.C., Feb. 1975.

"Public Libraries Engaged in Video/Cable Activities." *Journal of Library Automation* 11 (June 1978): 164–65.

"Public TV Library Report Identifies Videocassettes Users." *School Library Journal* 24 (Jan. 1978): 8.

Pushkin, Art, and Brad Alves. "Is 8mm the New World Format?" *Intelligent Decisions* 3 (May/June 1986): 22–24.

Robinson, J. F. *Videotape Recordings: Theory and Practice.* 3rd ed. London and Boston: Focal Pr., 1981.

———, and P. H. Beards. *Using Videotape.* New York: Hastings House, 1976.

Robinson, Richard. *The Video Primer.* New York: Links, 1974.

———. *The Video Primer.* New York: Quick Fox, 1978.

Schmid, William T. *Media Center Management.* New York: Hastings House, 1980.

Sigel, Efrem, Mark Schubin, and Paul F. Merrill. *Video Discs: The Technology, the Applications and the Future.* White Plains, N.Y.: Knowledge Industry, 1980.

Sirkin, A. F. "A Guide to Video Resources." *Journal of Library Automation* 12 (Sept. 1979): 233.

Sterling, Christopher H., and John M. Kittross. *Stay Tuned: A Concise History of American Broadcasting.* Belmont, Calif.: Wadsworth, 1978.

Thomassen, Cora E., ed. *CATV and Its Implications for Libraries.* Urbana-Champaign: Univ. of Illinois Graduate School of Library Science, 1974.

Troost, F. William. "Off-Air Videotaping: An Issue of Growing Importance." *Audiovisual Instruction* 21 (June/July 1976): 60–63.

Upton, Graham. "A Video Unit in School—Is It Worthwhile?" *Special Education: Forward Trends* 8 (Mar. 1977): 23–25.

Utz, Peter. *Video User's Handbook.* 2nd ed. Englewood Cliffs, N.J.: Prentice-Hall, 1982.

White, Gordon. *Video Recording: Record and Replay Systems.* London: Butterworth, 1972.

Whiting, R. "Potential of the 1/2″ VCR: Video Cassette Recorders for Home, School, Libraries." *Wisconsin Library Bulletin* 74 (July 1978): 171–72.

Winslow, Ken. "Off-Air Videotaping—When Is It Legal?" *Educational and Instructional Television* 81 (June 1976): 21–23.

———. "Video Programming—Where It Is, Where It's Going." *Educational and Industrial TV* 11 (Nov. 1979): 31–33.

Wright, Gwendolyn. "Trends in Video." *Instructional Innovator* 26 (Feb. 1981): 11.

Bibliography of Evaluative and Nonevaluative Periodicals Cited

Absolute Sound. Sea Cliff, N.Y.: Absolute Sound, 1973– . Quarterly.

Access. Washington, D.C.: Telecommunication Research and Action Center, 1975– . Monthly.

Access: Microcomputers in Libraries. San Diego: Access: Microcomputers in Libraries, 1975– . Monthly.

Advanced Technology Libraries. White Plains, N.Y.: Knowledge Industry, 1971– . Monthly.

American Artist. New York: Billboard, 1937– . Monthly.

American Cartographer. Washington, D.C.: American Congress on Surveying and Mapping, 1974– . Semiannual.

American Film Magazine. Washington, D.C.: American Film Institute, 1975– . 10 issues/year.

American Libraries. Chicago: American Library Assn., 1907– . Monthly, exc. bimonthly July/Aug.

American Music. Champaign: Sonneck Society and Univ. of Illinois Pr., 1983– . Quarterly.

American Photographer. New York: CBS Magazine, 1978– . Monthly.

American Record Guide. Washington, D.C.: Heldref, 1935– . Twice monthly.

Ampersand. Burbank: Alan Weston Communications, 1977– . Bimonthly.

Annals of Assn. of American Geographers. Washington, D.C.: Assn. of American Geographers, 1911– . Quarterly.

Art and Cinema. Imperial Beach, Calif.: VRI, 1971– . 3 issues/year.

Art in America. New York: Brant Art, 1913– . Monthly.

Art Documentation. Tucson: Art Libraries Society of North America, 1982– . 5/year. (Supersedes *ARLIS/NA Newsletter*).

Artnews. New York: ARTnews Associates, 1902– . Monthly.

Arts and Activities. Skokie, Ill.: Jones Publishing Co., 1937– . Monthly. (Previously called *Junior Arts and Activities*).

Arts and Humanities Citation Index. Philadelphia: Institute for Scientific Information, 1977– . Triquarterly. (Also available online).

Arts Magazine. New York: Art Digest, 1926– . Monthly.

Audio. New York: CBS Pub., 1947– . Monthly.

Audiovideo International. New York: Dempa, 1973– . Monthly.

Audiovisual. Croydon, England: Current Affairs, 1972– . Monthly.
Audio-Visual Communications. New York: Media Horizons, 1966– . Monthly.
Audio Visual Journal. Minneapolis: Univ. of Minnesota Audio-Visual Library
    Service, 1966– . 3/year.
Audiovisual Librarian. London: Audiovisuals Group of the Library Assn.,
    1973– . Quarterly.
Audiovisual Materials. Washington, D.C.: Library of Congress, Cataloging
    Distribution Service, 1953– . Quarterly with annual and 5-year
    cumulations.
Australian Geographer. Sydney: Geographical Society of New South Wales,
    1928– . Semiannual.
AV Business Communications. Toronto: Maclean Hunter, 1978– . Quarterly.
    (Formerly AV Canada/Business Communications).
AV Guide Newsletter. Des Plaines, Ill.: Educational Screen, 1922– . Monthly.
AV Video. Torrance, Calif.: Montage, 1978– . Monthly.
Back Stage. New York: Back Stage Pub., 1960– . Weekly.
Bibliography and Index of Geology. Falls Church, Va.: American Geologic
    Institute, 1969– . Monthly, with annual cumulations.
Billboard. Los Angeles: Billboard Pub., 1894– . Weekly.
Black Music and Jazz Review. Sutton, England: IPC Specialist and Professional
    Pr., 1974– . Monthly. (Formerly *Black Music*).
Bluegrass Unlimited. Broad Run, Va.: Bluegrass Unlimited, 1966– . Monthly.
Blues Link. Barnet, England: Blues Link, 1973– . Quarterly.
Blues Unlimited. London: BU Pub., 1963– . Bimonthly.
Booklist. Chicago: American Library Assn., 1905– . Twice/month, exc. once
    in July and Aug.
British Catalogue of Music. London: British Library Bibliographic Services Divi-
    sion, 1957– . Quarterly, with annual cumulation.
Bulletin of the American Congress on Surveying and Mapping. Falls Church,
    Va.: American Congress on Surveying and Mapping, 1950– . Every 2
    months (Ceased in 1981).
Bulletin/Special Libraries Association, Geography and Map Division. Beth-
    esda, Md.: The Division, 1947– . Quarterly.
Business Magazine of the Motion Picture Industry. Hollywood, Calif.: RLD
    Communications, 1920– . Monthly.
Business Marketing. Chicago: Crain Communications, 1916– . Monthly.
Byte. Petersborough, N.H.: Byte Pub., 1975– . Monthly.
Cadence: The American Review of Blues and Jazz. Bozeman: Montana Music
    Educators' Assn., 1942– . 3 issues/year.
Canadian Cartographer. Canadian Assn. of Geographers, 1964– . Semiannual.
Canadian Composer/Compositeur Canadien. Toronto: Published for Com-
    posers', Authors', and Publishers' Assn. of Canada by Creative Arts Co.,
    1965– . Monthly.
Cartactual. Budapest: Institute of Surveying, 1965– . Bimonthly.
Cartographic Journal. Aberystwyth, Wales: British Cartographic Society,
    1964– . Semiannual.

Cartographica. Toronto: International Publications on Cartography, 1971– . Quarterly.

Cartography. Canberra: Australian Institute of Cartographers, 1954– . Semiannual.

Cash Box. New York: Cash Box Pub., 1942– . Weekly.

Catechist. Dayton: Peter Li, 1967– . 8/year.

Changing Times: The Kiplinger Magazine. Washington, D.C.: Kiplinger Washington Editors, 1947– . Monthly.

Choice. Chicago: Assn. of College and Research Libraries, ALA, 1964– . Monthly, exc. bimonthly July/Aug.

Cineaste. New York: Cineaste Pub., 1967– . Quarterly.

Cinema/Canada. Ottawa: Cinema/Canada, 1971– . 10/year.

CIPS Review. Toronto: Canadian Information Processing Society, 1979– . Every 2 weeks.

Circus Magazine. New York: Circus Enterprises, 1966– . Monthly.

Classic Images. Davenport, Ia.: Classic Images, 1962– . Monthly.

Clavier. Northfield, Ill.: Instrumentalist, 1962– . 10/year.

CM: Canadian Materials for Schools & Libraries. Ottawa: Canadian Library Assn., 1971– . Bimonthly.

Coda. Toronto: Coda Pub., 1958– . Bimonthly.

Communication Industry Report. Fairfax, Va.: International Communications Industries Assn., 1946– . Monthly.

Compute! Greensboro, N.C.: Compute! Pub., 1979– . Monthly.

Computer Age. Software Industry Report. Annandale, Va.: EDP News Services, 1984– . Semimonthly. (Formerly *Software Digest* and *Computer Age: Software Digest*).

Computing Reviews. New York: Assn. of Computing Machinery, 1960– . Monthly.

Consumer Information Catalog: A Catalog of Selected Federal Publications of Consumer Interest. Washington, D.C.: U.S. Government Printing Office, 1970– . Quarterly.

Creative Computing. New York: Ziff-Davis, 1974– . Monthly.

Creem. Birmingham, Mich.: Creem, 1969– . Monthly.

Curator. New York: American Museum of Natural History; Meckler, 1958– . Quarterly.

Current Geographical Publications. New York: American Geographical Society, 1938– . Monthly.

Curriculum Review. Chicago: Curriculum Advisory Service, 1960– . 5/year.

Data Base Alert. White Plains, N.Y.: Knowledge Industry, 1983– . Monthly.

Database. Weston, Conn.: Online, 1978– . Quarterly.

Datamation. New York: Dun & Bradstreet, 1957– . Monthly.

Datapro Directory of Software. Delran, N.J.: Datapro Research Corp., 1976– . Monthly (since 1985).

Datapro Reports on Office Systems. Delran, N.J.: Datapro Research Corp., 1975– . Monthly updates.

Data Sources: The Comprehensive Guide to the Information Processing Industry. New York: Ziff-Davis, 1981– . Quarterly.

Development Communication Report. Washington, D.C.: Clearinghouse on Development Communication, 1972– . Quarterly.

Down Beat. Chicago: Maher Pub., 1934– . Monthly.

E&ITV. Danbury, Conn.: C. S. Tepfer, 1968– . Monthly.

Ear for Children. Roslyn Heights, N.Y.: Sound Advice Enterprises, 1983– . Quarterly.

Early Music. London: Oxford Univ. Pr., 1973– . Quarterly.

Educational Technology. Englewood Cliffs, N.J.: Educational Technology Pub., 1961– . Monthly.

Educator's Curriculum Product Review. New Canaan, Conn.: Educat Pub., 1980– . 9/year.

EFLA Evaluations. New York: Educational Film Library Assn., 1946– . Quarterly.

Electronic Library. Marlton, N.J.: Learned Information, 1983– . Quarterly.

English Dance and Song. London: English Folk Dance and Song Society, 1936– . 3/year.

English Journal. Urbana, Ill.: National Council of Teachers of English, 1912– . 8/year.

EPIEgram Materials. Watermill, N.Y.: Educational Products Information Exchange, 1977– . 9/year. (Formerly *EPIEgram*).

Ethnomusicology. Ann Arbor: Society for Ethnomusicology, 1955– . 3/year.

ETV Newsletter. Danbury, Conn.: C. S. Tepfer, 1966– . Biweekly.

Exceptional Children. Reston, Va.: Council for Exceptional Children, 1922– . Every 2 months.

Fanfare. Tenafly, N.J.: Fanfare, 1977– . Bimonthly.

Film & History. Newark, N.J.: Historians' Film Committee, New Jersey Institute of Technology, 1972– . Quarterly.

Film Comment. New York: Film Society of Lincoln Center, 1962– . Bimonthly.

Film Culture. New York: Film Culture Non-Profit, 1955– . Quarterly.

Film Library Quarterly (FLQ). New York: William Sloan, 1967– 84. Quarterly. (Absorbed by *Sightlines*).

Film Quarterly. Berkeley: Univ. of California Pr., 1945– . Quarterly.

Film Video News. Peru, Ill.: Gorez Goe, 1979– . 4/year.

Films & Filming. South Croydon, England: Brevet, 1954– . Monthly.

Films in Review. New York: National Board of Review of Motion Pictures, 1950– . 10/year.

First Take. Skokie, Ill., 1979– . Monthly.

Folk Music Journal. London: English Folk Dance and Song Society, 1965– .

Folk Review. Nantwich, England: Folk Review Ltd., 1971– . Monthly.

Forecast for Home Economics. New York: Scholastic, 1906– . 8/year.

Geo Abstracts. Norwich, England: Univ. of East Anglia, 1966– . Bimonthly.

The Geographical Journal. London: Royal Geographical Society, 1893– . 3/year.

Geographical Magazine. London: IPC Magazines, 1935– . Monthly.

Geographical Review. New York: American Geographical Society, 1916– . Quarterly.

Geography. Sheffield, England: Geographical Assn., 1901– . Quarterly.

Good Housekeeping. New York: Hearst, 1885– . Monthly.

GPNewsletter. Lincoln, Neb.: Great Plains National Instructional Television, 1962– . Quarterly.

Gramophone. Harrow, England: General Gramophone, 1923– . Monthly.

Guitar Player. Cupertino, Calif.: GPI Pubs., 1967– . Monthly.

Guitar Review. New York: Society of the Classic Guitar, 1946– . Quarterly.

Hi-Fi News and Record Review. Croydon, England: Link House Magazines, 1956– . Monthly.

High Fidelity. New York: ABC Leisure Magazine, 1951– . Monthly.

Holosphere. Orlando, Fla.: ILS, 1972– . Monthly.

Home Video Publisher. White Plains, N.Y.: Knowledge Industry, 1984– . Weekly.

Hope Reports Briefing. Rochester, N.Y.: Hope Reports, 1985– . Quarterly.

Information Bulletin of the Western Association of Map Libraries. Santa Cruz: Western Association of Map Libraries, 1969– . 3/year.

Information Processing and Management. Elmsford, N.Y.: Pergamon Pr., 1963– . Bimonthly.

Information Today. Medford, N.J.: Learned Info, 1983– . Monthly.

Infosystems. Wheaton, Ill.: Hitchcock, 1958– . Monthly.

Instant Replay. Coconut Grove, Fla.: Instant Replay, 1977– . Quarterly.

Instructional Innovator. Washington, D.C.: Assn. for Educational Communications and Technology, 1956– . Monthly. (Formerly *Audiovisual Instruction*).

Instructor and Teacher. New York: Instructor Pub., 1981– . 9/year. (Formerly *Instructor*).

Instrumentalist. Northfield, Ill.: Instrumentalist Co., 1946– . Monthly.

Interface Age. Cerritos, Calif.: McPheters, Wolfe & Jones, 1975– . Monthly.

International Bulletin for Photographic Documentation of the Visual Arts. Kansas City, Mo.: MACAA Visual Resources, 1980– . Quarterly. (Formerly *Mid-American College Art Association Slides and Photographs Newsletter*).

International Index to Multi-media Information. Pasadena: Audio-Visual Associates (distributed by Bowker), 1973– . Quarterly. (Continues *Film Review Index*).

International Journal of Micrographics and Video Technology. Elmsford, N.Y.: Pergamon Pr., 1982– . Quarterly. (Incorporated *Microdot* and *Micropublishing of Current Periodicals*).

International Television. New York: Lakewood Pub., 1983– . Monthly.

Irish Geography. Dublin: Geographical Society of Ireland, 1944– . Annual.

Jazz Journal International. London: Pitman Periodicals, 1948– . Monthly. (Formerly *Jazz Journal*, incorporating *Jazz & Blues*).

JEMF Quarterly. Los Angeles: John Edwards Memorial Foundation at the Folklore & Mythology Center, Univ. of California, 1965– . Quarterly.

Journal of American Folklore. Washington, D.C.: American Folklore Society, 1888– . Quarterly.

Journal of Broadcasting and Electronic Media. Kent, O.: Kent State Univ., Broadcast Education Assn., 1956– . Quarterly. (Formerly *Journal of Broadcasting*).

Journal of Film and Video. River Forest, Ill.: Rosary College Dept. of Communication, 1947– . Quarterly.

Journal of Geography. Chicago: National Council for Geographic Education, 1902– . Bimonthly.

Journal of Information and Image Management. Silver Spring, Md.: Assn. for Information and Image Management, 1967– . Monthly.

Jump Cut: A Review of Contemporary Media. Berkeley: Jump Cut Associates Media, 1974– . Irregular (Formerly *Jump Cut: A Review of Contemporary Cinema*).

Keyboard. Cupertino, Calif.: GPI Pubs., 1975– . Monthly.

Landers Film Reviews. Escondido, Calif.: Landers Associates, 1956– . Quarterly.

Library High Tech. Ann Arbor: Pierian Pr., 1983– . Quarterly.

Library Journal. New York: Bowker, 1876– . Semimonthly, exc. monthly in July and Aug.

Library Software Review. Westport, Conn.: Meckler, 1982– . Quarterly.

Library Technology Reports. Chicago: American Library Assn., 1965– . 6/year.

List-O-Tapes. San Diego: Phonolog, 1944– . Weekly.

Listening Post. City of Industry, Calif.: Bro-Dart, 1970– . Monthly.

Literature/Film Quarterly. Salisbury, Md.: Salisbury State College, 1973– . Quarterly.

Media and Methods. Philadelphia: American Society of Educators, 1964– . 5/year.

Media Digest. Finksburg, Md.: National Film & Video Center, 1971– . Bimonthly.

Media in Education & Development. Hitchin, England: British Council/Peter Peregrinus, 1967– . Quarterly.

Media Profiles: The Career Development Edition. Hoboken: Olympic Media Information, 1983– . Bimonthly. (Formerly *Training Film Profiles*).

Media Profiles: The Health Science Edition. Hoboken: Olympic Media Information, 1983– . Bimonthly (Formerly *Hospital Health Care Training Media Profiles*).

Media Review. Pleasantville, N.Y.: Media Review, 1979– . Monthly. (Formerly *Media Index*).

Media Review Digest. Ann Arbor: Pierian Pr., 1974– . Annual, with quarterly supplements. (Formerly *Multi Media Reviews Index*).

Melody Maker. London: IPC Specialist and Professional Pr., 1926– . Weekly.

Microform Review. Westport, Conn.: Meckler, 1972– . Quarterly.

Millimeter. New York: Millimeter Magazine, 1973– . Monthly.

MLA International Bibliography. New York: Modern Language Assn. of America, 1921– . Annual. (Also available online).

Monthly Catalog of United States Government Publications. Washington, D.C.: U.S. Government Printing Office, 1895– . Monthly.

Monthly Checklist of State Publications. Washington, D.C.: U.S. Government Printing Office, 1910– . Monthly.

Museum. Paris: Unesco, 1948– . Quarterly.

Museum News. Washington, D.C.: American Assn. of Museums, 1924– . Bimonthly.

Music and Letters. Oxford, England: Oxford Univ. Pr., 1920– . Quarterly.

Music and Musicians. London: Brevet, 1981– . Monthly. (Formerly *Records & Recording*).

Music Journal. New York: Hampton International Comm., 1942– . Monthly.

Music Review. Cambridge, England: W. Heffer, 1940– .

Musical Times. London: Novello, 1844– . Monthly.

Musician. Gloucester, Mass.: Amordian Pr., 1976– . 8/year.

National Preservation Report. Washington, D.C.: U.S. Library of Congress, 1979– . 3/year. (Formerly *Newspaper and Gazette Report*).

New Geographical Literature and Maps. London: Royal Geographical Society, 1918– . Semiannual.

New Records. Philadelphia: H. Royer Smith, 1933– . Monthly.

New York Times Film Reviews. New York: New York Times Co., 1913– . Weekly.

New Zealand Journal of Geography. Christchurch: New Zealand Geographical Society, 1946– . Semiannual.

Notes. Philadelphia: Music Library Assn., 1942– . Quarterly.

Ohio Media Spectrum. Columbus: Ohio Educational Library/Media Assn., 1955– . Quarterly.

Online. Weston, Conn.: Online Inc., 1976– . Bimonthly.

Online Review. Marlton, N.J.: Learned Information, 1977– . Bimonthly.

Opera Journal. New York: National Opera Assn., 1968– . Quarterly.

Opera News. New York: Metropolitan Opera Guild, 1936– . 17/year.

Opera Quarterly. Chapel Hill: Univ. of North Carolina Pr., 1983– . Quarterly.

Ovation. New York: Ovation Magazine Assn., 1980– . Monthly.

Parents. New York: Parents Magazine Enterprises, 1926– . Monthly.

Performance and Instruction. Washington, D.C.: National Society for Performance and Instruction, 1980– . 10/year. (Formerly *NSPI Journal, NSPI Newsletter*).

Personal Computing. Hasbrouck Heights, N.J.: Hayden, 1976– . Monthly.

Phonolog Reporter. San Diego: Trade Service Pub., 1948– . Weekly.

Photograph Collector. New York: Photograph Collectors' Newsletter, 1980– . Monthly.

Photographic Trade News. Woodbury, N.Y.: PTN Pub., 1937– . Semimonthly.

Photographics: A Collector's Newsletter. New York: Photographics, 1981– . Bimonthly.

Photomethods. New York: Lakewood Pub., 1958– . Monthly.

Piano Quarterly. Wilmington, Vt.: Piano Quarterly, 1952– . Quarterly.

Popular Computing. Peterborough, N.H.: McGraw-Hill, 1979– . Monthly.

Popular Photography. New York: CBS Pub., 1937– . Monthly.

Print Collector's Newsletter. New York: PCN Inc., 1970– . Bimonthly.

Professional Geographer. Washington, D.C.: Assn. of American Geographers, 1949– . Quarterly.

Programmed Learning and Educational Technology. London: Kogan Page Ltd. for the Assn. of Educational and Training Technology, 1964– . Quarterly. (Formerly *Programmed Learning*).

Public Affairs Information Service Bulletin. New York: Public Affairs Information Service, 1915– . Semimonthly and quarterly.

Publications of the Geological Survey. Reston, Va.: U.S. Geological Survey, 1879/1961– . Monthly list and cumulated annual supplements.

Quorum Quotes. Oakton, Va.: International Quorum of Film and Video Producers, 1968– . Quarterly.

Reading Teacher. Newark, Del.: International Reading Assn., 1948– . 9/year.

Record. New York: Straight Arrow, 1981– . Monthly.

Record Collector. Ipswich, England: Pamela Dennis, 1948– . Bimonthly.

Record Review. Los Angeles: Ashley Communications, 1976– . Bimonthly.

Review of the Arts: Film and Television. New Canaan, Conn.: NewsBank, 1975– . Monthly. (Also available online).

Rockingchair. Philadelphia: Cupola Productions, 1977– . Monthly.

Rolling Stone. New York: Straight Arrow, 1967– . Biweekly.

Saturday Evening Post. Indianapolis: Saturday Evening Post Society, 1821– . 9/year.

School Library Journal. New York: Bowker, 1954– . 10/year.

School Library Media Quarterly. Chicago: American Library Assn., 1981– . Quarterly, (Formerly *School Library Quarterly*).

School Product News. Cleveland: Penton/IPC, 1962– . Monthly.

Schwann-1 Record and Tape Guide. Boston: W. Schwann, 1949– . Monthly.

Schwann-2 Supplementary Record and Tape Guide. Boston: W. Schwann, 1949– . Semiannually.

Science and Children. Washington, D.C.: National Science Teachers' Assn., 1963– . 8/year.

Science Books and Films. Washington, D.C.: American Assn. for the Advancement of Science, 1975– . 5/year. (Formerly *AAAS Science Books*).

The Science Teacher. Washington, D.C.: National Science Teachers' Assn., 1950– . 9/year.

Scottish Geographical Magazine. Edinburgh: Royal Scottish Geographical Society, 1885– . 3/year.

Serials Review. Ann Arbor: Pierian Pr., 1975– . Quarterly.

Siecus Report. New York: Human Sciences Pr., Sex Information & Education Council of the U.S., 1972– . Bimonthly. (Formerly *SIECUS Newsletters*).

Sight and Sound. London: British Film Institute, 1932– . Quarterly.

Sightlines. New York: Educational Film Library Assn., 1967– . Quarterly. (Incorporated *Filmlist, Film Review Digest*, and *EFLA Bulletin*).

Simages. New Wilmington, Pa.: North American Simulation and Gaming Assn., 1979– . Quarterly.

Simgames: The Canadian Journal of Simulation and Gaming. Lennoxville, Quebec: Champlain Regional College, 1973– . Quarterly.

Simulation and Games: An International Journal of Theory, Design, and Research. Beverly Hills, Calif.: Sage, 1970– . Quarterly.

Simulation/Games for Learning: The Journal of SAGSET. London: Kogan Page, 1970(?)– . Quarterly. (Formerly *SAGSET Journal*).

Sing Out! Folk Song Magazine. Easton, Pa.: Sing Out! Magazine, 1950– . Bimonthly.

Spin: The Folksong Magazine. Wallasey, England: Spin Pub., 1961– . Quarterly.

Softside. Amherst, N.H.: Softside/Software, 1978– . Monthly.

Software Reviews on File. New York: Facts on File, 1985– . Monthly. (Looseleaf).

Sources, a Guide to Print and Nonprint Materials Available from Organizations, Industry, Government Agencies, and Specialized Publishers. Syracuse: Gaylord Brothers, 1977– . 3/year.

Stereo Review. New York: Ziff-Davis, 1958– . Monthly.

SUC Bulletin: Bulletin of the Society of University Cartographers. Liverpool, England: The Society, 1966– . Semiannually.

Technical Photography. Woodbury, N.Y.: PTN Pub., 1969– . Monthly.

TechTrends. Washington, D.C.: Assn. for Educational Communications and Technology, 1985– . Bimonthly. (Formerly *Instructional Innovator* and *Audiovisual Instruction with Instructional Resources*).

Telezine. Philadelphia: Media Concepts Pr., 1981– . Bimonthly.

T.H.E. Journal. Santa Ana, Calif.: Information Synergy, 1973– . Monthly.

Top of the News. Chicago: ALA/Assn. of Library Services to Children and Young Adult Services Division, 1942– . Quarterly.

U*N*A*B*A*S*H*E*D* Librarian. New York: U*N*A*B*A*S*H*E*D* Librarian, 1971– . Quarterly.

U.P.A. Journal. New Orleans: University Photographers Assn. of America, 1962– . Quarterly.

Variety. New York: Variety, 1905– . Weekly.

Vertical File Index. New York: H. W. Wilson, 1932– . Monthly.

Video Business. New York: CES Pub., 1981– . Monthly.

Video Manager. White Plains, N.Y.: Knowledge Industry, 1978– . Monthly, exc. July/Aug. (Formerly *Video User*).

Video Marketing Newsletter. Hollywood, Calif.: Video Marketing, 1980– . Bimonthly.

Videodisc and Optical Disk. Westport, Conn.: Meckler, 1981–85. Bimonthly. (Changed to *Optical Information Systems*, 1986–).

Videography. New York: Media Horizons, 1976– . Monthly.

The Videoplay Report. Washington, D.C.: Winslow Information, 1971– . Biweekly.

VideoPro. New York: VideoPro Pub., 1982– . Monthly.

Visual Education. London: National Committee for Audio-Visual Aids in Education, 1950– . Monthly.

Visual Resources. Redding Ridge, Conn.: Iconographic Publishers, 1980– . Triquarterly.

VOYA: Voice of Youth Advocates. University, Ala.: Voice of Youth Advocates, 1978– . Bimonthly.

Wilson Library Bulletin. New York: H. W. Wilson, 1914– . 10/year.

Woodwind-World Brass and Percussion. Deposit, N.Y.: Evans, 1970– . 8/year.

Worldwide Art Catalogue Bulletin. Brighton, Mass.: Worldwide Books, 1963– . Quarterly.

Young Children. Washington, D.C.: National Assn. for the Education of Young Children, 1944– . Bimonthly.

Editors and Contributors

Gerald R. Barkholz *Audiotapes*
Associate Professor, College of Education, University of South Florida, Tampa, Florida 33617

Esther Green Bierbaum *Realia*
Assistant Professor, School of Library and Information Science, University of Iowa, Iowa City, Iowa 52242

Marie Bruce Bruni *Pamphlets*
Director, Huntington Memorial Library, Oneonta, New York 13820

J. Gordon Coleman, Jr. *Flat Pictures, Posters, Charts, and Study Prints*
Assistant Professor, Graduate School of Library Service, University of Alabama, Tuscaloosa, Alabama 35486

Patricia Ann Coty *Overhead Transparencies, Simulation Materials*
National Center for Earthquake Engineering, Research Information Services, State University of New York at Buffalo, Buffalo, New York 14260

Clara DiFelice *Holographs*
Media/Outreach Section Coordinator, Palm Springs Public Library, Palm Springs, California 92262

John W. Ellison *Simulation Materials, Photographs*
Associate Professor, School of Information and Library Studies, State University of New York at Buffalo, Buffalo, New York 14260

Donald L. Foster *Original Art*
Associate Professor of Librarianship, Zimmerman Library, University of New Mexico, Albuquerque, New Mexico 87131

Billie Grace Herring *Art Reproductions*
Associate Dean, Graduate School of Library and Information Science, University of Texas, Austin, Texas 78712

Lee David Jaffe   *Phonograph Records*
Reference Librarian, University Library, University of California, Santa Cruz, California 95064

David H. Jonassen   *Programmed Materials*
Professor and Director of Instructional Technology Program, School of Education, University of Colorado at Denver, Denver, Colorado 80202

Mildred Knight Laughlin   *Overhead Transparencies*
Professor, School of Library Science, University of Oklahoma, Norman, Oklahoma 73019

Nancy Bren Nuzzo   *Music Scores*
Associate Librarian, Music Library, State University of New York at Buffalo, Buffalo, New York 14260

Daniel R. Schabert   *Videodiscs, Videotapes*
Director of Media Services, State University of New York College of Technology, Utica, New York 13504

Marilyn L. Shontz   *Microfilms*
Assistant Professor, Library Science, Shippensburg University, Shippensburg, Pennsylvania 17257

Diana L. Spirt   *Filmstrips*
Professor, Palmer School of Library and Information Science, C. W. Post Campus/Long Island University, Greenvale, New York 11548

Kathleen M. Tessmer   *Models*
Assistant Professor, School of Library and Information Science, and Division of Psychological and Quantitative Foundations, University of Iowa, Iowa City, Iowa 52242

Leslie J. Walker   *Slides*
Curator, Art History Department, State University of New York at Buffalo, Buffalo, New York 14260

Paul B. Wiener   *Films*
Film and Video Librarian, Main Library, State University of New York at Stony Brook, Stony Brook, New York 11794

Ernest L. Woodson   *Maps*
Maps and Geology Librarian, Science and Engineering Library, State University of New York at Buffalo, Buffalo, New York 14260

A. Neil Yerkey   *Machine-Readable Data Files*
Associate Professor, School of Information and Library Studies, State University of New York at Buffalo, Buffalo, New York 14260